Natasha Distiller

Natasha Distiller

DESIRE IN THE RENAISSANCE

DESIRE IN THE RENAISSANCE

PSYCHOANALYSIS AND
LITERATURE

EDITED BY
VALERIA FINUCCI AND
REGINA SCHWARTZ

PRINCETON UNIVERSITY PRESS

PRINCETON, NEW JERSEY

Copyright © 1994 by Princeton University Press
Published by Princeton University Press, 41 William Street,
Princeton, New Jersey 08540
In the United Kingdom: Princeton University Press,
Chichester, West Sussex
All Rights Reserved

Library of Congress Cataloging-in-Publication Data

Desire in the Renaissance : psychoanalysis and literature /
edited by Valeria Finucci and Regina Schwartz.
p. cm.
Includes index.
ISBN 0-691-03403-6 (CL) — ISBN 0-691-00100-6 (PA)
1. English literature—Early modern, 1500–1700—History and
criticism. 2. Psychoanalysis and literature. 3. Desire in
literature. 4. Renaissance—England. I. Finucci, Valeria.
II. Schwartz, Regina M.
PR428.P75D47 1994
820.9'353—dc20 94-14499

This book has been composed in Adobe Sabon

Princeton University Press books are printed
on acid-free paper and meet the guidelines for
permanence and durability of the Committee on
Production Guidelines for Book Longevity
of the Council on Library Resources

Printed in the United States of America

10 9 8 7 6 5 4 3 2 1
10 9 8 7 6 5 4 3 2 1
(Pbk.)

To Our Students

CONTENTS

DESIRE IN THE RENAISSANCE

INTRODUCTION

WORLDS WITHIN AND WITHOUT

Regina Schwartz with
Valeria Finucci

T HE LITERATURE of psychoanalysis is preoccupied with the literature of the Renaissance. Exploring homosexuality, Freud turned
to Leonardo da Vinci; inquiring into identification and art, he
went to Michelangelo; studying the creative process, he cited Ariosto;
ruminating on the compulsion to repeat, he examined Tasso; focusing on
mourning and melancholia, he went to Shakespeare's *Hamlet*; and inves-
tigating gender relations, he turned to the stories of daughters and fathers
in *The Merchant of Venice* and *King Lear*. Conversely, the writers of
Renaissance literature were preoccupied with their versions of the inner
life, concerns that would come to constitute the purview of psychoanalysis. Surely, the dynamics of sexual identity, gender definition, doubling,
identification, voyeurism, memory, melancholy, the uncanny, even the
unconscious, were concerns that arose, not in the context of nineteenth-
century Vienna, but were already evident in the social, political, and religious upheavals of the early modern period (as they were in the classical
world). Literary history attests to the peregrinations of the Ovidian and
Virgilian traditions throughout the Renaissance, traditions that include
cross-dressing, twinning, sibling rivalry, sexual conquest, rape, and mistaken identity. This volume will explicitly bring these discourses—clearly
already akin—together.[1] For all of their differences—Shakespeare did not
read Freud (if Freud did Shakespeare)—Renaissance literature and psychoanalysis are both obsessed with the "inner life" and the ways in which
it interacts with the more external spheres. But both the literature of psychoanalysis and Renaissance literature are testimony to how specious
that distinction between inner and outer worlds is, embracing, as they do,
a continuum between the psychological, social, economic, scientific, and
physical realms. Freud maintained that the workings of civilization itself
are propelled by our drives, and in the Renaissance, it was generally believed that even nature is animated by our loves and hates.

Taken as a whole, then, these essays do not privilege any single psychoanalytic narrative; instead, they explore the dynamics between that
psychoanalytic discourse known as "Renaissance literature" and that

psychoanalytic discourse more commonly (and erroneously, we would add) believed to have begun in the nineteenth century. They are also persistently grounded in history, economics, and nonliterary cultural formations of the period, as imagined identities necessarily are. We have also joined discussions of the literatures of England and Italy, for to isolate works according to nationality is to create stronger boundaries than existed in the early modern period; to isolate Spenser from Ariosto, Milton from Tasso, the English sonnet from Petrarch does not do justice to the cultural texture that so deeply intertwined them. The desire we trace in this volume, then, not only crosses the borders of England and Italy, and the discourses of Renaissance literature and psychoanalysis, it also bursts through the disciplinary borders that have isolated psychoanalysis from our other cultural codes.

When we begin to historicize, to distinguish the forces that shaped the thought on the inner life in the early modern period from the forces propelling nineteenth-century psychoanalytic preoccupations, we confront that inextricable interweaving of economic, demographic, and environmental factors. The differing household structures, child-rearing practices, educational conventions, the impact of capitalism, of industrialization, and of urbanization—let alone the vast epistemological gulf between early modern England and Italy and fin de siècle Vienna with their differing religious, philosophical, and scientific assumptions—all are vital parts of this vast puzzle. To raise the specter of just a few of these factors: What effect did the gross inflation of dowries in Italy during the early modern period, endlessly regulated but never successfully curbed, have on rivalry between men and on relations between husbands and wives? Did the new emphasis on childhood as a distinct stage of development change household arrangements and thereby affect household relations? How did the common practice of routinely beating children to discipline them disfigure their psychic development? Among aristocrats and the nouveaux riches of the early modern period, the common experience of bonding with a wet nurse for the first years of life, then abruptly losing her and acquiring a mother, must surely reconfigure any facile application of nineteenth-century oedipal drive theory. Changing demographics are no small factor in imagining a Renaissance psychology: husbands were typically twice the age of their wives; fathers in early modern Italy were the age of men who were grandfathers in nineteenth-century Vienna. Was such a father less a sexual role model than a bequeather of property? And how did he influence the sexuality of his developing daughters? Broadly speaking, how did the generalized shift from the extended to the nuclear family affect intergenerational relationships? Inheritance laws have everything to do with how sibling rivalry is configured. In England, where the rule of primogeniture held fast, second sons and illegitimate sons were not even competitors for inheritance—unless, that is, the eldest suffered an untimely death, one of Shakespeare's favorite plots. In Italy, inheritance was bequeathed "in fraterna," divided between the sons, a practice that soon issued in "restricted marriage" wherein only one of the sons could marry; dowried daughters were rushed to the altar while their sisters typically found the roads to the convent or prostitution the only ones they could travel. In the early modern period the rise of capitalism—and with it the shift of the workplace from the shop upstairs to a location away from home—shaped new gender roles, but it wasn't until the nineteenth century that the construct we know as "the angel of the house" developed. Clearly, there is no obvious delimitable area of the inner life that is not impinged upon by the external world.[2]

And vice versa: to the extent that social and economic "necessities" are expressions of inner impulses, conflicts, desires, and expectations, the external landscape changes in response to the internal one. Early modern assumptions about the inner life shaped their outer landscape as thoroughly as our beliefs about human psychology shape our social structures. The fear that excessive grief could be disruptive of the social order gave rise to laws regulating public lamentation.[3] Anxiety over sexual behavior led to an outpouring of sodomy laws.[4] Assumptions about male sexual desire in tandem with the social norm of late marriage not only kept courts occupied with trials of *stuprum* and *defloratio* but also led to the institutionalization and elaborate regulation of prostitution. In turn, prostitution institutionalized misogyny: prostitutes were typically the victims of gang rape or were sold into the profession by their parents.[5] Epistemological notions of vision underwrote the raging iconoclastic controversies of the Reformation, and a magical understanding of the power of anger—the fear that anger against the deity could provoke his wrath—gave rise to blasphemy laws.[6] Marriages were economic arrangements, love something else altogether (and that something was potentially disruptive to the social order until Reformers saw fit to advocate joining love to marriage). The theory of humors looked at character according to the dominance of four bodily fluids: blood, yellow bile, black bile, and phlegm; the preponderance of one had social as well as physical and psychological implications. Melancholic women, showing an excess of black bile, were regarded as afflicted with erotomania; sedentary women, guilty of developing phlegm, were believed to be infested with vermin.[7] Dietary recommendations had as much to do with worries about bodily temperature and temperament as with economic conditions and religious requirements; a low-fat diet of white meat was deemed good to the soul and one of fish bad to the balance of humors. The desire to restore psychic health can perhaps best explain the early modern period's fad for dishes "reminiscent of anatomical structures,"[8] for the heroic purges, vomitings, fastings, bleedings, and enemas to which the ascetic and the rich alike submitted themselves, for the stoic acceptance of noxious fumigations, for decoctions used interchangeably orally and anally, and for excreta put to use in the most formidable combinations.

The fluid boundaries between the inner and the outer, the body and the law, have also been studied by looking at the sexual and gender instability of the early modern period, manifest in the recurring, almost obsessive interest in the figures of the hermaphrodite, the transvestite, the freak, the monster, the eunuch, the androgyne, and the amazon.[9] Gender fluidity has been attributed to such epistemological factors as a highly (self)conscious and deliberate sense of fashioning a self and to such economic forces as the change in gender roles that emerged from changes in labor division. Deep anxiety about gender definitions gave rise to a spate of sumptuary laws[10] and to the ubiquitous appearance of conduct books prescribing proper behavior for men, women, courtiers, princes, servants, knights, and horses alike.[11] If gender was unstable, subject to contingent historical and cultural factors, understandings of sexuality rested on shaky ground as well. There was no clear-cut grasp of the sexual differences between men and women in the period. Doctors and anatomists persisted in relying heavily on Aristotelian and Galenic theories of sexual homology in which males and females have identical sexual organs that protrude or remain inside according to a caloric economy. That belief left the frightening specter of a person's sex changing with changes in bodily heat and humidity. There were documented cases of women turning into men (since nature tends toward perfection), raising the unwelcome possibility, for such a male-centered culture, that men could turn into women.[12] Confusion about sexual difference contrasted with the generative "certainty," which found its illustrators in Paracelsus and Della Porta, that living beings could come from nowhere, be born of putrefaction and fermentation, and once dead, still procreate with their decomposing bodies.[13] It was not until the end of the sixteenth century that the philosophical understanding of sexual differences between men and women finally caught up with advances in anatomy and put a stop to the proliferation of generative theories. But even then physical distinctness served ideological purposes: the observation that women had larger pelvises than men led naturally to the conclusion that they were all mothers-to-be; the shape of their cranial suture (*sutura sagittalis*) meant that they were more subject to perturbations and passions than men; and the presence of the uterus, the only organ that had no correspondence in the other sex, provided the necessary link to identify womanhood with femininity and motherhood. By Freud's time, sex and gender differences were fixed so deeply that even his halting efforts to unfix and reexamine the social construction of gender were revolutionary.

Vision

The nineteenth-century focus on visual power centered on sexuality: in "Instincts and Their Vicissitudes" Freud joined discussions of sadism and masochism to voyeurism and exhibitionism, thereby setting the stage, nuanced with Lacanian discourse, for subsequent debates on "the male gaze" in contemporary film criticism. If today looking is implicated in domination and in fixing (or unfixing) gender, in the early modern period the power of vision was regarded as no less formidable and it was no less socially contested—not in film but in church. The fear that visual images had the power to corrupt the soul and to lead the faithful astray from devotion to God erupted in iconoclastic controversies that raged throughout the period, debates that were carried on not only by theologians but by a populace who mutilated sculpture, smashed stained-glass windows, and defaced canvases—or objected virulently to such destruction. When thirty commissioners entrusted with zealously removing images throughout England ordered the removal of the Rood from Saint Paul's on November 17, 1547, the work was carried on at night to avoid public outcry. The Rood fell from the loft, killing two workmen; needless to say, the accident served as grist for the mill of the clergy who believed this was a sacrilege.[14] When the workmen who oversaw the dissolution of the priory of Saint Nicholas at Exeter attempted to take down the Rood-screen and loft with its images of saints so important in popular devotion, the local women formed a mob.[15] Renaissance visual theory differed markedly from our own: before Kepler, light was not central to the process; rather, objects were visible by their own agency. Visual power lay not in the eye of the observer, but in the object seen, for it generated infinite images of itself through space until it reached the receptive human eye.[16] Images were active, the eye was passive; therefore, to control what the eye saw required the destruction of the objects that offended. Zwingli claimed that because his eyesight was poor, "the images injure me little."[17] Nonetheless he asserted that the sensible world was seductive to others, so much so that it, instead of God, becomes the object of veneration. During the Reformation, images were destroyed because it was feared they were venerated; in contemporary psychoanalytic discourse, gazing upon an object does not venerate but degrades it, for in the context of voyeurism, veneration itself is degrading.[18]

When Freud wrote that "there are many more means of creating uncanny effects in fiction than there are in real life,"[19] he was thinking of literature in general, but to illustrate his thoughts he went back once more to the Renaissance, to the "supernatural apparitions" in Shakespeare's *Hamlet*, *Macbeth*, and *Julius Caesar*.[20] These stories, he wrote, may be gloomy, but they exert no uncanny influence because readers adjust their responses to the reality that the writer constructs. But when he read Tancredi's wounding of the tree in Tasso's *Gerusalemme liberata* as a rewounding of his beloved Clorinda, he had no doubt that this was a wonderful instance of the return of the repressed.[21] Why was the early modern period so preoccupied with the frightening, the unreal, the dreadful, and the horrific? Was this not, after all, the period of the humanists' "unbridled subjectivity," as Jakob Burckhardt put it, of man's pompously declared narcissistic omnipotence over his psychic nature and his highly publicized claim to successfully fashion a self (as in Pico della Mirandola's "Thou mayest fashion thyself in whatever shape thou shalt prefer")?[22] Here again some tantalizing questions come to the fore: Could the presence of the uncanny in the Renaissance have been the dark underside of the bright portrait of man's rational, controlling, and cognitive nature? If, as Kerrigan and Braden have argued, the epoch was "yearning for a positive version of the Narcissus complex,"[23] are ego overvaluation and omnipotence of thought not fertile grounds for the appearance of the *unheimlich*? Now, wasn't the nineteenth century also marked by its own narcissistic overvaluation of the (male) mind? And wasn't it the time when the Enlightenment's confidence in the power of rationality was put to the test? A typical uncanny occurrence tied to primary narcissism is undoubtedly the motif of the split self, the recognized/misrecognized identity (as in the notorious case of Martin Guerre). The appearance of "that strange thing" was also usually expressed, as Freud would have it, through a compulsion to repeat (Milton's Satan can only repeat his Fall in mankind).[24] Clearly, as there is no obvious delimitable area of the inner life that is not impinged upon by social structures and strictures, so historically there are psychosexual fears, displacements, and repressions that are bound to return, and return, again, and again.

In this collection, the issues of the fluidity of gender, the economics of sexual and sibling rivalry, the power of the visual, and the return of the repressed are given center stage. By concentrating on them we certainly do not claim to exhaust the range of possible foci; rather, we offer only a taste of what we discern to be a recent revitalized interest in psychoanalysis in conjunction with Renaissance literature, one we hope this volume will nourish. Marjorie Garber describes how women can turn the commodification of their social body in marriage to their own advantage by commodifying sex. Rather than disempowering women, faking orgasm can allow them to control their personal relationships and enjoy the effect of their faking on others. Natasha Korda documents the anxieties accompanying the construction of identities in a system of patronage. The impersonation of "natural" gentility and the plagiarizing of elite manners do not save Castiglione's courtiers from becoming the punchline of courtly jokes: no amount of "sprezzatura" can fill the lack around which the profession of courtiership ("cortegiania") is structured. Focusing on the uses and misuses of clothes in Ludovico Ariosto's *Orlando Furioso*, Valeria Finucci shows that the masquerade of femininity through apparel used for narcissistic, or even masochistic, purposes can be culturally condoned as long as women appear feminine and young. Conversely, the casting aside of specific gender identities and the inappropriate desire to be desired when there is no femininity left for men to desire call for authorial intervention and ridicule. Along the way, these authors also engage psychoanalytic discourses on virginity, jokes, and fantasy.

The essays by Berger, Enterline, and Schwartz all center on the power of the gaze. Concentrating on sexual warfare and generational conflict, Harry Berger, Jr., examines how Spenser critiques the ideology informing male dominant and female submissive roles in literary history. Through his allusions, Spenser creates a Venus who is both erotic and matriarchal, thus recasting normative gender positions and gynephobic discourses. Lynn Enterline follows the metamorphoses of the poetic subject caught in the seesaw of seeing and punishment, error and exile, self-affirmation and self-alienation. By analyzing how Petrarch read Ovid, and how rhetoric informed sexuality through the emblematic figure of Actaeon, Enterline argues for a reading of (Petrarchan) subjectivity as in a continuous state of (Ovidian) change. The resulting existential moments of anguish, crisis, and alienation are used to shape a new history of the self. Challenging the assumption that the object of vision is necessarily an object of degradation, Regina Schwartz explores the empowering of Eve in *Paradise Lost* despite a world of divine and poetic voyeurs. Gender fixity is questioned, as Milton, nicknamed the Lady of Christ, becomes not only the voyeur, but also the exhibit; the poet and narrator's obsession with sight and blindness issues in a refiguration of the dynamics of power.

Issues of rivalry, competition, and commodification play a large role in Schiesari's and Kerrigan's essays. Juliana Schiesari examines the economic forces shaping configurations of gender and class in her study of Machiavelli's letter about a prostitute. Here the role of woman as commodity is tied to man's fear of a symbolic order capriciously run by Fortuna. A recast male dread of woman is also central to William Kerrigan's essay on sibling rivalry in Shakespeare's *As You Like It*. Here, the economics of scarcity informing male aggression are answered by the balance of female friendship.

Bellamy and Miller turn to the Renaissance version of the *unheimlich*. Elizabeth Bellamy reads the uncanny occurrences of the motif of the bleeding branch from Homer, Virgil, and Dante to Ariosto and Tasso. Given the frequency of the return of the repressed in literary history, and specifically the way the transformations of this topos in the epic world seem to escape conscious authorial control, she argues that literature serves not simply as the unconscious of psychoanalysis but also to repress the repetition compulsion itself. David Lee Miller, for his part, retraces in Jonson, Freud, and Lacan a similar return to the *unheimlich* in the figure of the specular son's untimely death. Bellamy and Miller examine narratives of repetitions that have no origin other than in the author's compulsion to repeat their losses. As the trees of the epic world call for their dismemberment, so the sons of fathers are lost because they represent the sacrifices that they are asked to make in the Name of the Law, to bear the burden of their elders' resistance to death, and to allow for the reinscription of their masculine identities.

language

In all of these essays, language is foregrounded as the medium of desire, of oppression, or of transgression. Psychoanalysis never offered a cure, but it did speak of a "talking cure" with the emphasis on talking, and it soon became a kind of science of representation, devoted to exploring the representation of wishes, needs, and fears in dreams, in slips of the tongue, and in the representations of analysis. Language is our mode of desire and of conflict; it structures our unconscious and our conscious lives. Garber writes that dissembling is theater, Korda understands masquerade as linguistic, and Schwartz describes the narrator and poet as voyeurs. Bellamy's interest in the linguistic transformations of an epic topos is echoed by Enterline, who argues that the Petrarchan subject is tormented as much by language as by desire. Kerrigan stresses the importance of verbal wit in love-games, while Finucci turns to the power of language's seduction. Berger argues that Spenser uses conspicuous allusion to rectify the dominant discourses he inherits, and Miller insists on the complementary and resisting nature of dreams that need to be told and written down. The alliance of the literatures of the Renaissance and psychoanalysis deepens and assumes greater specificity over this mutual preoccupation with language.

In a classic essay on literature and psychoanalysis, "To Open the Question," Shoshana Felman argues for a real dialogue between the disciplines, not between one body of language (literature) and one body of knowledge (psychoanalysis) but "between two different bodies of knowledge and two different bodies of language."[25] Our volume calls attention to these dual spheres: Renaissance drama, lyric, and epic are not "merely" poetry (as if there were such a thing); they are also spheres of knowledge about the psyche. Psychoanalysis has never imagined itself as a body of knowledge apart from language—Freud's case histories are works of fiction, and Lacan and Kristeva have moved language to the center of their discussions of the psyche. Lacan claimed that the unconscious is structured like a language. We would add that the unconscious of the Renaissance *is* language and that it is given best expression in its literature.

NOTES

1. Studies that have already treated Renaissance literature in the context of psychoanalysis include: Janet Adelman, *Suffocating Mothers: Fantasies of Maternal Origin in Shakespeare's Plays* (New York: Routledge, 1992); Elizabeth Bellamy, *Translations of Power: Narcissism and the Unconscious in Epic History* (Ithaca: Cornell University Press, 1992); Harry Berger, Jr., *Revisionary Play: Studies in the Spenserian Dynamics* (Berkeley: University of California Press, 1988); Jonathan Dollimore, *Sexual Dissidence: Augustine to Wilde, Freud to Foucault* (Oxford: Clarendon Press, 1991); Margaret Ferguson, *Trials of Desire: Renaissance Defenses of Poetry* (New Haven: Yale University Press, 1983); Joel Fineman, *Shakespeare's Perjured Eye: The Invention of Poetic Subjectivity in the Sonnets* (Berkeley: University of California Press, 1986); Valeria Finucci, *The Lady Vanishes: Subjectivity and Representation in Castiglione and Ariosto* (Stanford: Stanford University Press, 1992); Barbara Freedman, *Staging the Gaze: Postmodernism, Psychoanalysis, and Shakespearean Comedy* (Ithaca: Cornell University Press, 1991); Marjorie Garber, *Shakespeare's Ghost Writers: Literature as Uncanny Causality* (New York: Methuen, 1987); Jonathan Goldberg, *Sodomitries: Renaissance Texts, Modern Sexualities* (Stanford: Stanford University Press, 1992); Stephen Greenblatt, "Psychoanalysis and Renaissance Culture," in *Literary Theory/Renaissance Texts*, ed. Patricia Parker and David Quint (Baltimore: Johns Hopkins University Press, 1986); Linda Gregorson, *The Reformation of the Subject: Spenser, Milton, and the English Protestant Epic* (Cambridge: Cambridge University Press, 1994); William Kerrigan, *The Sacred Complex: On the Psychogenesis of Paradise Lost* (Cambridge: Harvard University Press, 1983); Theresa Krier, *Gazing on Secret Sights: Spenser, Classical Imitation, and the Decorums of Vision* (Ithaca: Cornell University Press, 1990); David Lee Miller, *The Poem's Two Bodies: The Poetics of the 1590 Faerie Queene* (Princeton: Princeton University Press, 1988); Christopher Pye, *The Regal Phantasm: Shakespeare and the Politics of Spectacle* (London: Routledge, 1990); Juliana Schiesari, *The Gendering of Melancholia: Feminism, Psychoanalysis, and the Symbolics of Loss in Renaissance Literature* (Ithaca: Cornell University Press, 1992); Murray Schwartz and Coppelia Kahn, eds., *Representing Shakespeare: New Psychoanalytic Essays* (Baltimore: Johns Hopkins University Press, 1980); Regina Schwartz, *Remembering and Repeating: On Milton's Theology and Poetics* (Cambridge: Cambridge University Press, 1988; rpt., Chicago: University of Chicago Press, 1993); Valerie Traub, *Desire and Anxiety: Circulations of Sexuality in Shakespearean Drama* (New York: Routlege, 1992); Susan Zimmerman, ed., *Erotic Politics: Desire on the Renaissance Stage* (New York: Routledge, 1992).

2. Work on these topics is extensive. See especially Jacob Burckhardt, *The Civilisation of the Renaissance in Italy*, trans. S. G. C. Middlemore (New York: Harper and Row, 1958); Lawrence Stone, *The Family, Sex and Marriage in England, 1500–1800* (New York: Harper and Row, 1977); Philippe Ariès, *Centuries of Childhood: A Social History of Family Life*, trans. Robert Boldick (New York:

Knopf, 1962); Natalie Zemon Davis, *Society and Culture in Early Modern France* (Stanford: Stanford University Press, 1975); Norbert Elias, *The Civilizing Process*, vol. 1, *The History of Manners*, trans. Edmund Jephcott (New York: Pantheon Books, 1978); Margaret Ferguson, Maureen Quilligan, and Nancy Vickers, eds., *Rewriting the Renaissance: The Discourses of Sexual Difference in Early Modern Europe* (Chicago: University of Chicago Press, 1986); Michel Foucault, *The History of Sexuality*, vol. 1, *An Introduction*, trans. Robert Hurley (New York: Random House, 1978); David Kerzner and Richard Saller, eds., *The Family in Italy from Antiquity to the Present* (New Haven: Yale University Press, 1991); Christiane Klapish-Zuber, *Women, Family and Ritual in Renaissance Italy*, trans. Lydia Cochrane (Chicago: University of Chicago Press, 1985); James Casey, *The History of the Family* (Oxford: Blackwell, 1989); Christopher Durston, *The Family in the English Revolution* (Oxford: Blackwell, 1989); Stanley Chojnacki, "Dowries and Kinsmen in Early Renaissance Venice," *Journal of Interdisciplinary History* 4 (1975): 571–600; Diane Owen Hughes, "From Prideprice to Dowry in Medieval Europe," *Journal of Family History* 3 (1978): 262–96; and Julius Kirshner and Anthony Molho, "The Dowry Fund and the Marriage Market in Early Quattrocento Florence," *Journal of Modern History* 50 (1978): 403–38.

3. See Sharon Strocchia, "Funerals and the Politics of Gender in Early Renaissance Florence," in *Refiguring Woman: Perspectives on Gender and the Italian Renaissance*, ed. Marilyn Migiel and Juliana Schiesari (Ithaca: Cornell University Press, 1991), 155–68; and Moshe Barash, *Gestures of Despair in Medieval and Renaissance Art* (New York: New York University Press, 1976).

4. On sodomy laws, see Michael J. Rocke, "Il controllo dell'omosessualità a Firenze nel XV secolo: gli 'Ufficiali di Notte,'" *Quaderni storici* 66 (1987): 701–23; Kent Gerard and Gert Hekma, eds., *The Pursuit of Sodomy: Male Homosexuality in Renaissance and Enlightenment Europe* (New York: Haworth Press, 1989); Patricia Labalme, "Sodomy and Venetian Justice in the Renaissance," *Revue d'histoire du droit* 52 (1984): 217–54; Alan Bray, *Homosexuality in Renaissance England* (London: Gay Men's Press, 1982); Guido Ruggiero, *The Boundaries of Eros: Sex Crime and Sexuality in Renaissance Venice* (New York: Oxford University Press, 1985); and Jonathan Goldberg, *Sodometries: Renaissance Texts, Modern Sexualities* (Stanford: Stanford University Press, 1992).

5. See Ruggiero, *Boundaries of Eros*; James Brundage, *Law, Sex, and Christian Society in Medieval Europe* (Chicago: University of Chicago Press, 1987); Carlo Cipolla, *Before the Industrial Revolution: European Society and Economy, 1000–1700* (New York: Norton, 1976); Edward Muir and Guido Ruggiero, eds., *Sex and Gender in Historical Perspective: Selections from Quaderni Storici* (Baltimore: Johns Hopkins University Press, 1990); and Carol Weiner, "Sex Roles and Crime in Late Elizabethan Hertfordshire," *Journal of Social History* 8 (1975): 38–60.

6. See Ernest Gilman, *Iconoclasm and Poetry in the English Reformation* (Chicago: University of Chicago Press, 1986); and Renzo Derosas, "Moralità e giustizia a Venezia nel '500–'600, gli esecutori contro la bestemmia," in *Stato,*

società e giustizia nella Repubblica Veneta (sec. 15–18), ed. Gaetano Cozzi (Rome: Jouvence, 1980), 431–528.

7. See Wayne Shumaker, *Natural Magic and Modern Science: Four Treatises, 1590–1657* (Binghamton, NY: Center for Medieval and Renaissance Studies, 1989); Piero Camporesi, *The Incorruptible Flesh: Bodily Mutation and Mortification in Religion and Folklore* (Cambridge: Cambridge University Press, 1988); Ian Maclean, *The Renaissance Notion of Woman: A Study in the Fortunes of Scholasticism and Medical Science in European Intellectual Life* (Cambridge: Cambridge University Press, 1980); and Daneille Jacquart and Claude Thomasset, *Sexuality and Medicine in the Middle Ages*, trans. Matthew Adamson (Princeton: Princeton University Press, 1985).

8. Camporesi, *The Incorruptible Flesh*, 67. See also *I balsami di Venere* (Milan: Garzanti, 1989).

9. See, for example, Marjorie Garber, *Vested Interests: Cross-dressing and Cultural Anxiety* (New York: Routledge, 1992); Jonathan Dollimore, "Subjectivity, Sexuality and Transgression: The Jacobean Connection," *Renaissance Drama* n.s. 17 (1986): 53–81; Vern Bullough and Bonnie Bullough, *Cross Dressing, Sex, and Gender* (Philadelphia: University of Pennsylvania Press, 1993); Stephen Orgel, "Nobody's Perfect: Or Why Did the English Stage Take Boys for Women?" *South Atlantic Quarterly* 88 (1989): 7–29; Goldberg, *Sodometries*; Valerie Traub, *Desire and Anxiety: Circulations of Sexuality in Shakespearean Drama* (New York: Routledge, 1992); Mary Beth Rose, *The Expense of Spirit: Love and Sexuality in English Renaissance Drama* (Ithaca: Cornell University Press, 1988); Susan Zimmerman, ed., *Erotic Politics: Desire on the Renaissance Stage* (New York: Routledge, 1992); Jean Howard, "Crossdressing, the Theatre, and Gender Struggle in Early Modern England," *Shakespeare Quarterly* 39 (1988): 418–40; Ann Rosalind Jones and Peter Stallybrass, "Fetishizing Gender: Constructing the Hermaphrodite in Renaissance Europe," in *Body Guards: The Cultural Politics of Gender Ambiguity*, ed. Julia Epstein and Kristina Straub (New York: Routledge, 1991), 80–111; Lauren Silberman, "Mythographic Transformations of Ovid's Hermaphrodite," *The Sixteenth Century Journal* 19 (1988): 643–52; and Julia Epstein, "Either/Or—Neither/Both: Sexual Ambiguity and the Ideology of Gender," *Genders* 7 (1990): 99–142.

10. On sumptuary laws, see Diane Hughes, "Sumptuary Laws and Social Relations in Renaissance Italy," in *Disputes and Settlements: Law and Human Relations in the West*, ed. John Bossy (Cambridge: Cambridge University Press, 1983), 66–99; James Brundage, "Sumptuary Laws and Prostitution in Late Medieval Italy," *Journal of Medieval History* 13 (1987): 343–55; Elizabeth Baldwin, *Sumptuary Legislation and Personal Regulation in England* (Baltimore: Johns Hopkins University Press, 1926); and Cumberland Clark, *Shakespeare and Costume* (London: Folcroft Library, 1977).

11. On conduct books, see Constance Jordan, *Renaissance Feminism: Literary Texts and Political Models* (Ithaca: Cornell University Press, 1990); Frank Whigham, *Ambition and Privilege: The Social Tropes of Elizabethan Courtly Theory* (Berkeley: University of California Press, 1984); Marina Zancan, ed., *Nel cerchio della luna: figure di donna in alcuni testi del XVI secolo* (Venice: Marsilio,

1983); Linda Woodbridge, *Women and the English Renaissance: Literature and the Nature of Womankind, 1540–1620* (Urbana: University of Illinois Press, 1984); Adriano Prosperi, ed., *La corte e il cortegiano*, vol. 2 (Rome: Bulzoni, 1980); and Maclean, *Renaissance Notion of Woman*.

12. See Thomas Laqueur, *Making Sex: Body and Gender from the Greeks to Freud* (Cambridge: Harvard University Press, 1990); Nancy Tuana, "The Weaker Seed: The Sexist Bias of Reproductive Theory," *Hypatia* 3.1 (1988): 35–59; Stephen Greenblatt, "Fiction and Friction," in *Shakespearean Negotiation: The Circulation of Social Energy in Renaissance England* (Berkeley: University of California Press, 1988), 66–93; Douglas Radcliff-Umstead, ed., *Human Sexuality in the Middle Ages and the Renaissance* (Pittsburgh: University of Pittsburgh Publications of the Middle Ages and the Renaissance, 1978); Londa Schiebinger, *The Mind Has No Sex? Women in the Origins of Modern Science* (Cambridge: Harvard University Press, 1989); Jacquart and Thomasset, *Sexuality and Medicine*; and Maclean, *Renaissance Notion of Woman*.

13. See Carlo Ginzburg, *The Cheese and the Worms: The Cosmos of a Sixteenth-Century Miller* (Baltimore: Johns Hopkins University Press, 1980); Walter Pagel, *Paracelsus: An Introduction to Philosophical Medicine in the Era of the Renaissance* (Basel: Karger, 1992); Peter Stallybrass and Allon White, *The Politics and Poetics of Transgression* (Ithaca: Cornell University Press, 1986); and Camporesi, *The Incorruptible Flesh*.

14. Eamon Duffy, *The Stripping of the Altars* (New Haven: Yale University Press, 1992), 454.

15. Ibid., 403.

16. See Lee Palmer Wandel, "The Reform of the Images: New Visualizations of the Christian Community in Zurich," *Archive for Reformation History* 80 (1989): 105–24, 108–9. See also Gilman, *Iconoclasm and Poetry*.

17. In Wandel, "Reform of the Images," 116.

18. Work on vision and voyeurism is extensive. See, for example, Laura Mulvey, *Visual and Other Pleasures* (Bloomington: Indiana University Press, 1989); Jacqueline Rose, *Sexuality in the Field of Vision* (London: Verso, 1986); Nancy Vickers, "Diana Described: Scattered Woman and Scattered Rhyme," in *Writing and Sexual Difference*, ed. Elizabeth Abel (Chicago: University of Chicago Press, 1982), 95–109; Teresa De Lauretis, *Alice Doesn't: Feminism, Semiotics, Cinema* (Bloomington: Indiana University Press, 1983); Norman Bryson, *Vision and Painting: The Logic of the Gaze* (New Haven: Yale University Press, 1983); and Barbara Freedman, *Staging the Gaze: Postmodernism, Psychoanalysis, and Shakespearean Comedy* (Ithaca: Cornell University Press, 1991).

19. Sigmund Freud, "The Uncanny," in *The Standard Edition of the Complete Psychological Works of Sigmund Freud*, 24 vols., ed. and trans. James Strachey (London: Hogarth Press, 1953–74), 17 (1955): 219–52, 249, 250.

20. On the connections between narrative and the uncanny, see, for example, Hélène Cixous, "Fiction and Its Phantoms: A Reading of Freud's *Das Unheimliche*," *New Literary History* 7.3 (1976): 525–48; Samuel Weber, "The Sideshow, or: Remarks on a Canny Moment," *Modern Language Notes* 88.6 (1973): 1102–33; and Marjorie Garber, *Shakespeare's Ghost Writers: Literature as Uncanny Causality* (New York: Methuen, 1987).

21. Freud, *Beyond the Pleasure Principle*, in *SE* 18:22.

22. Giovanni Pico della Mirandola, *De dignitate hominis* (Oration on the dignity of man), in *The Renaissance Philosophy of Man*, ed. Ernst Cassirer et al. (Chicago: University of Chicago Press, 1948), 225. On self-fashioning, see especially Stephen Greenblatt, *Renaissance Self-Fashioning: From More to Shakespeare* (Chicago: University of Chicago Press, 1980). For the historical and social impossibility for women to achieve a comparable status of selves, constructed or not, see Catherine Belsey, *The Subject of Tragedy: Identity and Difference in Renaissance Drama* (New York: Methuen, 1985), 149; and Valeria Finucci, *The Lady Vanishes: Subjectivity and Representation in Castiglione and Ariosto* (Stanford: Stanford University Press, 1992).

23. William Kerrigan and Gordon Braden, *The Idea of the Renaissance* (Baltimore: Johns Hopkins University Press, 1989), 147.

24. Regina Schwartz, *Remembering and Repeating: On Milton's Theology and Poetics* (Cambridge: Cambridge University Press, 1988; rpt. Chicago: University of Chicago Press, 1992).

25. Shoshana Felman, "To Open the Question," in *Literature and Psychoanalysis: The Question of Reading, Otherwise*, ed. Shoshana Felman (Baltimore: Johns Hopkins University Press, 1982), 6.

FAKING IT

SEX, CLASS, AND GENDER MOBILITY

THE INSINCERITY OF WOMEN

Marjorie Garber

> Reflect on the whole history of women: do they not *have* to be
> first of all and above all else actresses? Listen to physicians who
> have hypnotized women; finally, love them—let yourself be
> "hypnotized by them"! What is always the end result? That
> they "put on something" even when they take off everything.[1]
> Woman is so artistic.
> (Nietzsche, *The Gay Science*)

IMAGINE the scene.

Beatrice-Joanna, rummaging in her new husband's closet, is desperate about the impending wedding night, since she has yielded her virginity, under duress, to the aptly named DeFlores. Now she fears discovery and disgrace.

DeFlores, at her bidding, has secretly murdered Alonzo de Piraquo, her father's choice, the man to whom she was first engaged, so that she is now free to marry Alsemero. To confirm the deed, DeFlores has cut off his victim's finger with its ring and brandishes it before her in triumph. Welcome to the "other scene." *The Changeling* is not a play that will hide castration under a bushel.

Thinking to buy him off with gold, Beatrice-Joanna is dumbfounded to learn that DeFlores expects instead a sexual reward. "Y'are the deed's creature," he tells her (3.4.137). The "deed" here is, prospectively, both sex and murder. He is implacable in his demand: "Can you weep fate from its determin'd purpose? / So soon may you weep me" (161–62). And he is coolly knowing. He anticipates, in fact, that she will enjoy herself, despite her demurrals. "'Las, how the turtle pants," he grins at her, "Thou'lt love anon / What thou so fear'st and faint'st to venture on" (169–70).

So here is Beatrice-Joanna, on the night of the wedding, convinced that her husband will detect her deflowered condition and denounce her. What remedy? Luckily for her, Alsemero has gone for a walk in the park, leaving the key in the closet door. It is only a moment's work to open it. And what does she see? Alsemero's pharmacy, "A right physician's closet," as she describes it, "set round with vials" (4.1.20–21), and a book of experiments called "Secrets in Nature" open upon the table. Her worst fears are confirmed by the table of contents.

> "How to know whether a woman be with child or no."
> I hope I am not yet; if he should try though!
> Let me see: "folio forty-five." Here 'tis;
> The leaf tuck'd down upon't, the place suspicious.
> "If you would know whether a woman be with child or
> not, give her two spoonfuls of the white water in glass
> C—"
> Where's that glass C? O, yonder, I see't now—
> "and if she be with child, she sleeps full twelve hours
> after, if not, not."
> None of that water comes into my belly:
> I'll know you from a hundred.
>
> (26–36)

This pregnancy test, as the Revels editor N. W. Bawcutt notes, bears some resemblance to a test contained in Thomas Lupton's *A Thousand Notable Things of Sundry Sorts* (1579): "If you would know whether a Woman be conceived with Child or not, give her two spoonfuls of Water and one spoonful of Clarified Honey, mingled together, to drink when she goes to sleep; and if she feels Gripings and Pains in the Belly in the night, she is with child; if she feel none, she is not."[2]

But for Beatrice-Joanna, the worst is yet to come—"ten times worse," as she declares. For the next experiment offers advice on "How to know whether a woman be a maid or not."

> If that should be applied, what would become of me?
> Belike he has a strong faith in my purity,
> That never yet made proof; but this he calls
> "A merry sleight, but true experiment, the author
> Antonius Mizaldus. Give the party you suspect the
> quantity of a spoonful of the water in the glass M,
> which upon her that is a maid makes three several
> effects: 'twill make her incontinently gape, then fall
> into a sudden sneezing, last into a violent laughing;
> else dull, heavy, and lumpish."
>
> (40–49)

Bawcutt's note informs the reader that, although Alsemero is apparently consulting Mizaldus's *De Arcanis Naturae*, "there are no passages in it resembling those quoted by Beatrice." Such tests are, however, very common in the scientific literature of the period, he observes, ultimately deriving perhaps from Pliny's *Natural History*[3]; and in another collection by Mizaldus, a sixteenth-century French scholar and compiler of scientific knowledge, virginity and pregnancy tests are given, two of which involve the ingestion of liquids by the woman being tested, "though," as Bawcutt reports, "in none of them are her reactions those described" in Middleton and Rowley's play. "The fantastic nature of the virginity test," he concludes, in language that is worth our noting, "makes it seem very probable that Middleton devised it himself and then fathered it upon Mizaldus."

"Fathered it upon Mizaldus." The editor's note here makes explicit the implicit link between glass M and glass C. For what would be the economic and political usefulness of "scientific" tests for virginity and pregnancy? Manifestly, to ensure the legitimacy of offspring. A wise father—and the bridegroom Alsemero is described by Beatrice-Joanna, despairingly, as a "wise man" who will detect her secret—will want to know his own child. Thus a materialist reading of the contents and effect of glass M in *The Changeling* will take the agency of the letter—M for maid—at its word. The test is a test for virginity, the commodification of the well-born bride and her expected children, part of a nobleman's marriage bargain. In the next moments Beatrice-Joanna—and the audience—will witness a graphic demonstration of the efficacy of that test, as in desperation she hits upon a plan to employ a changeling, sending her waiting-woman Diaphanta in her place to Alsemero's bed.

First, however, she must be sure that Diaphanta is herself a "maid"—an identification the waiting-woman puts in doubt by volunteering with alacrity to take her mistress's place. "Y'are too quick, I fear, to be a maid" (93), observes Beatrice-Joanna pointedly, and she proposes an "easy trial." Both of them will drink from glass M. The results are just what she fears—and hopes. She herself feels no effect, but Diaphanta produces all the appropriate symptoms, and in the prescribed sequence. She gapes ("there's the first symptom. And what haste it makes / To fall into the second" [107–8]), then sneezes, then laughs ("Ha, ha, ha! I am so—so light / At heart! Ha, ha, ha!—so pleasurable! / But one swig more, sweet madam" [112–14]), and finally grows "sad again" (115). "Just in all things and in order," observes Beatrice-Joanna ruefully, "As if 'twere circumscribed; one accident / Gives way unto another" (110–12). The bargain between them is struck: Diaphanta, convinced that her mistress is afraid of sex and wants someone else to describe it to her before she tries it, is to have "the bride's place, / And . . . a thousand ducats" (125–26), while Beatrice-Joanna prepares to slip into the bed at midnight, after the supposed defloration has occurred.

Glass M, then, would seem to be as aptly and transparently named as the deflowerer DeFlores. If we ask Malvolio's question from *Twelfth Night* "What should that alphabetical position portend?" as he ponders a similarly enigmatic letter "M," we may if we like rest content with a version of Malvolio's answer—"why this is evident to any formal capacity. There is no obstruction in this" (*TN* 2.5.117—20). M stands for "maid" and "maidenhead." Drinking glass M's contents reveals, to the skilled scientific eye, the unmistakable symptoms of virginity.

But does it? Alsemero clearly thinks so, but then Alsemero, while no Malvolio, is a somewhat hapless and inattentive observer, for all of his vaunted experience and knowledge. He is an investigator with an answer already in mind as he conducts his experiment, and, like many such investigators, he finds his desired result.

We may recall that the Revels editor, who found precedents in the scientific literature for the pregnancy test of glass C, regarded the "virginity test" of glass M as "fantastic" in nature, and noted that "in none of the tests" in Mizaldus's works—including tests "Mulierem corruptam ab incorruptam discernere" and "Noscendi ratio an mulier sit virgo integra & intacta an non"—"are her reactions those described in 11.48–50": that is, first gaping, then sneezing, then laughing, then falling into a fit of melancholy.

What if we were to ask, then, not "what is the agency of the letter M" but, rather, of what are these things symptoms? Or, even, of what are they *supposed to be* symptoms? In other words, what is being tested here? And what is being displayed?

Let us consult some putative experts, some latter-day Mizalduses. "I maintained years ago that the dyspnoea and palpitations that occur in hysteria and anxiety neurosis are only detached fragments of the act of copulation." This is Freud, describing the patient known as Dora, one of whose chief symptoms was "dyspnoea," or shortness of breath. He notes "[Dora's] concern whether *she* might not have over-exerted herself in masturbating—an act which, like [her father's copulation with her mother], led to a sexual orgasm accompanied by slight dyspnoea—and finally came a return of the dyspnoea in an intensified form as a symptom."[4] Dyspnoea; shortness of breath. Not always, perhaps, with open mouth—but to "gape" is also to gasp, with pain or pleasure. " 'Twill make her *incontinently* gape" says the symptom book describing the effects of glass M. This is stage one.

And now to stage two, the telltale sneeze.

Sneezing has been associated with omens and the supernatural at least since Aristotle.[5] In the early seventeenth century the physician William Harvey took special note of the sneeze reflex as an involuntary reflex *in women* and compared it to labor pains: "the throes of childbirth, just as sneezing, proceed from the motion and agitation of the whole body."

Harvey tells the story of a young woman patient who fell into a coma during labor and could not be roused. "Finding that injections and other ordinary remedies has been employed in vain" to rouse her, he "dipped a feather in a powerful sternutatory"—that is, a substance, like pepper, that induces sneezing—"and passed it up the nostrils. Although the stupor was so profound that she could not sneeze, or be roused in any way, the effect was to excite convulsions throughout the body, beginning at the shoulders, and gradually descending to the lower extremities."[6] The impulse to sneeze is deflected or displaced physiologically into convulsions, which here facilitate a healthy completion of labor. In Harvey's description these convulsions, "roused" by the sternutatory, appear to mimic the involuntary spasms of sexual orgasm. Notice, however, that the woman feels nothing, neither pain nor pleasure. It is the (male) doctor who produces these effects, without her conscious participation, or even her knowledge.[7]

In the early days of psychoanalysis, with its emphasis upon hysteria and the body that unconsciously speaks its symptoms, the sneeze again figured memorably as a sign. Here is Freud's collaborator Josef Breuer: "Sexuality at puberty appears," he writes, "as a vague, indeterminate, purposeless heightening of excitation. As development proceeds, this endogenous heightening of excitation, determined by the functioning of the sex-glands, becomes firmly linked (in the normal course of things) with the perception or idea of the other sex."[8]

To explain the ways in which repressed sexual feelings are acted out in "hysterical" symptoms, Breuer instances a particular physiological event: "I will select an extremely trivial example—the sneezing reflex. If a stimulus of the mucous membrane of the nose fails for any reason to release this preformed reflex, a feeling of excitation and tension arises, as we all know. . . . This everyday example gives us the pattern of what happens when a psychical reflex, even the most complicated one, fails to occur" (*SE* 2:206–7).

But for Freud sneezing and sexual energy are not merely analogous. Freud had, he said, "begun to suspect" his patient Dora of masturbating when he heard her complain of gastric pains, since, according to his friend Wilhelm Fliess, "it is precisely gastralgias of this character which can be interrupted by an application of cocaine to the 'gastric spot' discovered by him in the nose" ("Fragment," *SE* 7:78). The famous "gastric spot"—we could call it a G spot—was, Fliess thought, a seat of sexual passion, and he and Freud corresponded avidly about "the therapy of the neurasthenic nasal neurosis." Freud referred to Fliess for surgery patients, both male and female, who evidenced "a suspicious shape to [the] nose" or other symptoms indicative of masturbation.[9] So sex, desire, is seated in the nose. (The recurrent popularity of both cocaine and snuff as pleasurable stimulants attests to the enduring autoerotic *jouissance* of the sneeze.)

Furthermore, it is worth noting that at about the same time that Freud and Breuer were regarding the sneeze as suspiciously sexual, sexy sneezes were also occurring in literature and film. *Studies on Hysteria* was published in 1893. In 1891 Thomas Hardy described, in *Tess of the D'Urber-villes*, the effect of Tess's beauty on Angel Clare: "Clare had studied the curves of those lips so many times that he could reproduce them mentally with ease; and now, as they again confronted him, clothed with colour and life, they sent an *aura* over his flesh, a breeze through his nerves, which wellnigh produced a qualm; and actually produced, by some mysterious physiological process, a prosaic sneeze."[10] The juxtaposition here of the lips, the "*aura*," and the sneeze, however the latter is dismissed as "prosaic," tells its own story. The body—here the body of the neurasthenic male Angel—speaks.

Meanwhile, the pioneers of film technology were recording the sneeze as a visual document of involuntary pleasure. *Fred Ott's Sneeze* was one of the earliest test films made by the Edison Laboratory, in 1893–94. The short film record (eighty-one frames) of a man in the act of sneezing has been celebrated by film historians as Edison's first film, the first film to use an actor, and the first cinematic close-up.

But in fact the initial impetus to film a sneeze specified a *female* subject. The idea for the film came from a journalist for *Harper's Weekly*; bored with the dull topics of previous experiments in film, he wrote to Edison suggesting the possibility of a "nice looking young person to perform a sneeze," explicitly a woman "in the act of sneezing."[11] Ott, a young laboratory technician with a flowing mustache, was chosen by Edison as a substitute, for reasons of convenience.

The original idea of a "pretty young woman who would have lent prurient interest to the involuntary comic action of a sneeze," as Linda Williams notes, indicates the way in which "technicians of pleasure," "from Charcot to Muybridge, from Freud to Edison," solicit for their science "further confessions of the hidden secrets of female pleasure."[12]

"The animating male fantasy of hard-core cinema," maintains Williams, might be described as "the (impossible) attempt to capture visually this frenzy of the visible in a female body whose orgasmic excitement can never be objectively measured . . . the woman's sexual pleasure is elicited involuntarily, often against her will" (Williams, 50). When *Fred Ott's Sneeze* appeared as a series of photographs in *Harper's Weekly*, it was accompanied by a text that analyzed in detail the ten stages of "this curious gamut of grimace," a sequence that seems cognate in some ways to Alsemero's—or Mizaldus's—four-stage sequence of female involuntary pleasure.

Freud's and Breuer's observations about panting and sneezing are taken from some of their earliest work. Interestingly, however, it was to very similar questions about sexual pleasure and displaced physiological response that Freud recurred in his last years, and, indeed, in his journal jottings just before his death.

"The ultimate ground of all intellectual inhibitions and all inhibitions of work," he wrote on August 3, 1938, "seems to be the inhibition of masturbation in childhood."

> But perhaps it goes deeper; perhaps it is not its inhibition by external influences but its unsatisfying nature in itself. There is always something lacking for complete discharge and satisfaction—en attendant toujours quelquechose qui ne venait point—and this missing part, the reaction of orgasm, manifests itself in equivalents in other spheres, in *absences*, outbreaks of laughing and weeping . . . , and perhaps other ways. Once again infantile sexuality has fixed a model in this.[13]

Gaping, sneezing, laughing—and finally melancholy sadness. For this last symptom, perhaps, we do not need the testimony of psychoanalysts to augment that of the poets: Post coitum omni animal triste est. But in fact the relationship between orgasm and sadness, hypnosis, and sleep is repeatedly noted in the psychoanalytic literature. Thus Breuer insists that "the sexual orgasm itself, with its wealth of affect and its restriction of consciousness, is closely akin to hypnoid states"; "in orgasm thought is almost completely extinguished."[14]

In a letter to Fliess, Freud finds "Instructive!" (the ejaculatory punctuation is his own) the story of a young woman who—according to her wealthy lover—had "from four to six orgasms during one coitus. But—at the very first approach she is seized with a tremor and immediately afterwards falls into a pathological sleep; while she is in this she talks as though she was in hypnosis, carries out post-hypnotic suggestions and has complete amnesia for the whole condition."[15] Later Freud would write in his "Three Essays on Sexuality" that in infants "sensual sucking involves a complete absorption of the attention and leads either to sleep or even to a motor reaction in the nature of an orgasm."[16]

Of what, then, might this sequence of diagnostic symptoms in *The Changeling* be indicative? A list of symptoms, detailed from Mizaldus's "The Book of Experiments, Call'd Secrets in Nature," that Bawcutt found "fantastic," and that seem, indeed, to have more than a little to do with fantasy? They are not, in fact, the telltale signs of virginity, but rather of *orgasm*. Not the commodification and ownership of women, as virgins, as mothers, but rather the intangibility of desire.

Here again is Sigmund Freud, writing to Fliess in the early days of psychoanalysis about the case of one "Frau P.J.," aged twenty-seven, who was suffering from feelings of oppression, anxiety, and abdominal discomfort. The tone in this letter, as in many of Freud's communications with Fliess, is man-to-man, self-congratulatory, much—to strain the comparison a little—like Alsemero's confident assertions to his friend Jasperino. "What I expected to find was this. She had had a longing for her husband—that is, for sexual relations with him; she had thus come upon an idea which had excited sexual affect and afterwards defence against the idea; she had then taken fright and made a false connection or substitution."[17] And from the same account:

> I then asserted that before the attack there had been thoughts present to her which she might not remember. In fact she remembered nothing, but pressure [on her forehead] produced "husband" and "longing." The latter was further specified, on my insistence, as longing for sexual caresses. . . ." . . . There was certainly something besides this: a feeling in the lower part of the body, a convulsive desire to urinate."—She now confirmed this. The insincerity of women starts from their omitting the characteristic sexual symptoms in describing their states. So it had really been an *orgasm*." (emphasis in original)

Notice the astonishing scientific "detachment" of this last pair of assertions. "The insincerity of women starts from their omitting the characteristic sexual symptoms in describing their states. So it had really been an *orgasm*."

The male doctor here detects—and shares with his male friend—the woman's secret, and thus her power. "Insincerity" seems a harsh word for the concealment of symptoms; Freud's response in fact appears overdetermined, both by his own agency in producing this result (the pressure of his hands on her forehead, an early aspect of the treatment of his neurotic patients, later discontinued) and by his desire to *know* what he cannot know except through her confession and confirmation. "So it had really been an *orgasm*."

Freud and Alsemero, in fact, are fellow physicians in this quest for certainty and power over the stories told by women's symptoms. One curious paradox of Alsemero's glass M is the fact that it produces, or is expected to produce, orgasmic effects in *virgins*, and not in women of sexual experience. Should we not expect the opposite to be the case? Furthermore, contemporary physiology held that female orgasm was necessary for conception.[18] Why then are the orgasmic symptoms in Middleton and Rowley's play not elicited by glass C (for "child") rather than by glass M? The answer to both questions, I think, is that glass M—the detection of a virgin—represents the fruits of a male fantasy, the fantasy of the male doctor/lover as at once the inventor and the scientific investigator of female pleasure. Glass M, like the whole pharmacopoeia so carefully locked away by Alsemero for his private use, is in fact a fantasy projection of the lover's power. He will elicit signs of sexual pleasure in their most manifest form from a woman who knows sexuality, and physical love, only through him. Just as Freud knows better than Dora (or even the married Frau P.J.) what pleasures her body betrays, so Alsemero's drugs test his power, not, or not only, Beatrice-Joanna's response.

Let us now consider what happens in *The Changeling* once Beatrice-Joanna learns, by precept (Mizaldus's book) and example (Diaphanta's display of "symptoms"), how to respond to the contents of glass M.

The plot has reached a crucial juncture. It is still the night of the wedding when Alsemero is advised first of Piraquo's murder and then of a private conversation between Beatrice-Joanna and DeFlores. "The very sight of him is poison to her," Alsemero protests (4.2.98), but once again the border between "poison" and "remedy" appears to have been breached. Beatrice-Joanna has pleaded her "fears" as a "timorous virgin" (117–18) and has asked to come to her husband's bed modestly in the dark. Can she be lying? Has she betrayed him with DeFlores? Discovery, exposure, and denunciation lie apparently just around the corner. Is De-Flores a *pharmakeus* (magician, sorcerer) or a *pharmakos* (scapegoat)?

Good empiricist that he is, determined to find the truth, Alsemero sends immediately to his closet for "A glass inscrib'd there with the letter M" (114) and offers it to his bride. Her response, aside, has all the horror of classic melodrama: "The glass, upon my life! I see the letter" (130); "I am suspected" (131). Yet, forced to drink, she produces all the appropriate symptoms, in the right order—gaping, sneezing, laughing, melancholy. As she confides to the audience, "th'effects I know, / If I can now but feign 'em handsomely" (137–38). Alsemero is completely won over, convinced that she is "Chaste as the breath of heaven, or morning's womb" (149–50). His faith in her is tied to his faith in science, and, indeed, to his own sexual expertise—for, as he notes confidently to a male friend, glass M "ne'er missed, sir, / Upon a virgin."

What Beatrice-Joanna learns in Alsemero's pharmacy, and turns immediately to her own use, is "what every woman knows": how to fake it. She produces the symptoms, the simulacra of orgasmic response, that delight her husband and confirm his apparent mastery of her. When she does so, Alsemero clasps her to him; "thus my love encloses thee" (150).

The Changeling is a play about the pleasure and danger of woman's desire. In the complex dynamics of its heterosexual power relations, the power to withhold becomes the power to control. Beatrice-Joanna romanticizes her feelings about the dashing Alsemero ("This was the man meant me!" [1.1.84]), but she finds in DeFlores the frisson of involuntary response: "I never see this fellow but I think / Of some harm towards me; danger's in my mind still, / I scarce leave trembling of an hour after" (2.1.89–91). Her ruse to employ him to dispatch her inconvenient fiancé ("men of art make much of poison. Keep one to expel another. Where was my art?" [2.2.46–47]; "Why, put case I loathed him. . . . / Must I needs show it? Cannot I keep the secret / And serve the turn upon him?" [2.2.66–69]) leads inexorably to a relationship in which loathing and desire are intertwined and finally beyond her control. "I have kissed poison" for your love, she tells Alsemero (5.3.66), but it is never finally clear whether for Beatrice-Joanna there is any real difference between danger, trembling, loathing, and desire.

With Alsemero, however—the idealized lover, the longed-for husband, the handsome romantic lead, Ashley Wilkes to DeFlores's sinister Rhett Butler—she is, paradoxically, in control, once she learns, from his own pharmacy, how to simulate the throes of passion.

Here, then, is our question: Is there any difference between centering a play on woman's desire and centering it on woman's ability to fake it? Which is more threatening?

Recall once more Freud's apparently unfeeling judgment on Frau P.J. (her name itself, to a modern reader, so evocative of bedtime): "The insincerity of women starts from their omitting the characteristic sexual symptoms in describing their states. So it had really been an *orgasm*."

Hollywood mogul Sam Goldwyn gave this famous advice to aspiring actresses: "The most important thing about acting is sincerity. If you can fake that you've got it made." From the analyst's couch to the casting couch, from the "insincerity" of concealing sexual responsiveness to the "sincerity" of faking it, the fear, and the excitement, is of a woman's sexual pleasure. Woman's orgasm is Freud's "dark continent," as well as Mizaldus's "secret of nature." Female pleasure is the unknown and unknowable, the other, less masterable and controllable answer to the question Freud poses over and over again, in different forms, throughout his work: "What does a woman want?"

It is hardly a new question.

Ovid's well-known story about Tiresias, who was asked whether men or women had greater pleasure in sex, is part of the same obsessive inquiry. How could a man ever know? Tiresias was drawn into the dispute between Juno and Jove because he had been both woman and man. Once, having seen snakes coupling, he struck them apart and was instantly turned into a woman. Seven years later he saw them again, struck them again, and was changed back into a man. His answer, that women had more pleasure than men, pleased Jove and displeased Juno, who struck him blind; Jove then, since he could not undo this curse, gave to Tiresias second sight, power to know the future. Thomas Laqueur points out that "Ovid's account would become a regular anecdote in the professorial repertory, told to generations of medieval and Renaissance students to spice up medical lectures," and comments trenchantly that "One might translate the question more specifically as 'which sex had the better orgasm.'"[19]

Was Tiresias himself a changeling? No one more so. In fact he makes a cameo appearance in Middleton and Rowley's play, in the voice and person of the feigned madman Franciscus, who has entered Alibius's madhouse in order to seduce Alibius's wife. The scene is constructed, with some pertinence, as another "pharmacy," with Lollio, Alibius's assistant, cast for a madman's moment in the role of the *pharmakon*, who offers both "poison" and "remedy."

Franciscus. Come hither, Aesculapius. Hide the poison.
Lollio. Well, 'tis hid.
Franciscus. Didst thou never hear of one Tiresias,
  A famous poet?
Lollio. Yes, that kept tame wild-geese.
Franciscus. That's he; I am the man.
Lollio. No!
Franciscus. Yes; but make no words on't, I was a man
  Seven years ago—
Lollio. A stripling I think you might—
Franciscus. Now I'm a woman, all feminine.
Lollio. I would I might see that.
Franciscus. Juno struck me blind.
Lollio. I'll ne'er believe that; for a woman, they say,
  has an eye more than a man.
Franciscus. I say she struck me blind.

(3.3.62–77)

Why did Tiresias's answer anger Juno? Because female pleasure is shameful? Or because a woman's pleasure is her secret—and her power? Can she fake it? And thereby deny her partner the pleasure of her pleasure? How can her partner ever know? For orgasm, *jouissance*, is—as Jacqueline Rose deftly describes it—"what escapes in sexuality."[20] Thus Lacan recurred to Freud's unanswered question "What does a woman want?" by evoking Bernini's Saint Theresa as a model for *jouissance*. "What is her *jouissance*, her *coming* from?" he asks.[21] Thus, too, in discussing Mallarmé's *Mimique* Derrida identifies the "supreme spasm," the orgasm of Columbine as mimed by her husband, Pierrot, as a double miming. "I'm going to tickle my wife to death," Pierrot declares, and for Derrida the "spasm" is also the "hymen," that word that paradoxically incorporates virginity and marriage.[22] Gayatri Spivak saw clearly that this was for Derrida a scene of faked orgasm, in which the male actor appropriates the language of a woman's desire. "The faked orgasm now takes center stage. The Pierrot of the pantomime 'acts' as the woman 'is' ('Pierrot is [plays] Columbine') by faking a faked orgasm which is also a faked crime."[23] Is it worth noting that the boy actor playing Beatrice-Joanna likewise is "faking a faked orgasm" from the ambivalent double position of transvestite theater, a man playing a woman playing a trick on a man? So perhaps we are dealing not—or not only—with the "insincerity of women," but also with the intrinsic and instrumental insincerity of theater, with the mimesis of mimesis itself.

Female orgasm as mimesis, as an act or an acting out, poses a special problem. How can a lover tell the difference between origin and imitation, between the "fake" and the "real"? And, once again, which is more threatening?

Aristotle as a scientist was not interested in female pleasure, or in female orgasm; it did not fit into his theories.[24] Debates about the role, if any, of the clitoris and about the necessity of pleasure for procreation appear from time to time in the writings of medieval and Renaissance physicians.[25] Aphrodisiacs for women were seldom mentioned in the herbals, and then they were recommended for use by unsatisfied husbands with recalcitrant wives.[26] Laqueur suggests that, in the eighteenth century and after, "the routine orgasmic culmination of intercourse became a major topic of debate."

> The assertion that women were passionless, or alternatively the proposition that, as biologically defined beings, they possessed to an extraordinary degree, far more than men, the capacity to control the bestial, irrational, and potentially destructive fury of sexual pleasure; and indeed the novel inquiry into the nature and quality of female pleasure and sexual allurement—all were part of a grand effort to discover the anatomical and physiological characteristics that distinguished men from women. Orgasm became a player in the game of new sexual differences. (Laqueur, 150)

The histories of medicine and sexual sociology appear to offer an either/or choice, between the fantasy of women possessing no desire and the fantasy of women as eros embodied. But more disconcerting remains a third possibility: that women are somehow in control of the sexual rhetoric of desire. Women may lack desire—and therefore stand aloof and untouched by the circuit of courtship, blandishment, arousal, and possession that is the economy of sexual mastery. Or they may act in pursuit of their own desire. Or they can fake it. With no one the wiser but themselves.

Here, for example, is the sage counsel of a nineteenth-century French physician, Auguste Debay, whose manual on the physiology of marriage went through an astonishing 153 editions from its original publication in 1849 to 1880. "O wives! Follow this advice. Submit to the demands of your husband in order to attach him to you all the more. Despite the momentary aversion for the pleasures he seeks, force yourself to satisfy him, put on an act and simulate the spasm of pleasure: this innocent trickery is permitted when it is a question of keeping a husband."[27] If the Victorian Englishwoman had been exhorted to close her eyes and think of England, her Gallic counterpart, with the future of her marriage rather than the Empire in mind, was to keep her eyes open for theatrical opportunity, for simulation and innocent trickery. All this ostensibly in the service of "keeping a husband," preserving the basis of her own social legitimation and economic dependency. Marital truth here depends upon theatrical falsehood, "permitted"—once again—by an authorizing doctor. In Debay's formulation the satisfaction is imagined as entirely the husband's. The woman's pleasure is in her status, not in her bed.

Twentieth-century sex manuals, especially those from the "free to be me" seventies and eighties, stress the usefulness of rehearsal. Here, for example, with theatrical coaching and stage directions included, is a passage from an American self-help book entitled *Becoming Orgasmic: A Sexual and Personal Growth Program for Women*, first published in 1976.

> We call this exercise Role-Playing Orgasm. What we'd like you to do is to fantasize about a wild orgasm and act it out.
>
> Set aside thirty minutes to one hour. Begin one of your self-pleasuring sessions in the usual way. The first time, begin role-playing orgasm after you've pleasured yourself for a while but *before* you become extremely aroused. Move around, tense your muscles, lie very rigid, do some pelvic rocking, make noises—do whatever seems really extreme to you. Moan, scratch, pummel the bed, cry—the more exaggerated the better. Stop pleasuring yourself if you want, or continue while you have your "orgasm." You will probably feel awkward doing this the first few times, but it will become easier with practice. Remember the way you act is not really the way you would or should act. For this exercise, pretend to be the star in your own orgasmic fantasy![28]

In a chapter called "Orgasm—Yours, Not His" "J," the author of *The Sensuous Woman*, notes that she's "never met a woman yet who didn't occasionally fake it" and stresses the theatricality of faked orgasm, which she calls the Sarah Bernhardt maneuver. "J" also emphasizes the importance of rehearsal: "To become a fabulous fake, study again every contortion, muscle spasm, and body response that lead to and make up the orgasm and rehearse the process privately until you can duplicate it." "Women have been faking since time began," she informs us, cautioning against "ham[ming] it up too much" ("then he really will suspect you're acting") and, above all, against telling the truth.

> You must *never, never* reveal to him that you have acted sometimes in bed.
> You will betray a trust shared by every other female in the world if you do.[29]

In this case the presumed homosocial compact among women enforces the "success" of heterosexual relations.

Dr. Ruth Westheimer, "author, psychologist, and media personality," has a different concern about "The Perils of Faking It," since to pretend to be satisfied is to forego real satisfaction. Yet she too sees the congruence between theater and sexual fakery. In a "typical case" of a "lady [who] had never experienced orgasm" although she had been impressed by women thrashing about on the movie screen in the throes of ecstasy, Dr. Ruth's client was manifestly "a good actress," because her husband "never had an inkling that she was faking it." In this case the cure, facilitated through the intervention of a sex therapist, was the one proposed by the authors of *Becoming Orgasmic*, a variant of Beatrice-Joanna's observation and imitation of Diaphanta. The woman learned to masturbate, thus discovering for herself the sensations of pleasure, which she could then reproduce by guiding her husband's hand over her body.[30]

The desire to control a woman's orgasm, and to know when it occurs, has mobilized the agency of the letter. Beyond Middleton's (or Alsemero's) glass M and glass C lie, for example, the elusive G spot, or Grafenberg spot, as well as the erotic advice of "J," the author of *The Sensuous Woman*, and "M," the author of *The Sensuous Man*. Sexologists from Kinsey to Masters and Johnson to Ladas, Perry, and Whipple have sought to describe, delimit, and pin down the female orgasm. Was it clitoral? Vaginal? "Blended"? How could you tell when a woman had one? Consider the case of sex researcher John D. Perry, who attempted to replicate the research of Masters and Johnson on women's muscle contractions. Perry asked a number of male college students who the sexiest women on campus were, and then invited them—without explaining how he got their names—to become research subjects. One agreed.

She passed with flying colors a written test of sexual interest and demonstrated good control over her sexual musculature. They then put her to the test in the lab. "At first, during masturbation, her PC [urinary] muscle showed normal, expected increases in tension. But as she became more aroused, suddenly PC muscle activity ceased. The laboratory technicians assumed that their research subject was taking a break—until the remote signal light flashed that the woman was having an orgasm."[31] This unexpected datum, together with "subjective reports from many women" who claimed that they had experienced more than one kind of orgasm, "our own laboratory evidence that some women achieved what they claimed were satisfying orgasms *without* the characteristic contractions of the orgasmic platform," and "the undeniable fact of female ejaculation, especially in response to G spot stimulation" (147), led the sex researchers to revise completely their understanding of female sexuality. Notice here the conjunction of "subjective reports," women's "claims," and "undeniable fact." Despite all the data, it was upon claims and reports that these scientific findings had, necessarily, to be based.

Is this experiment another example of the "insincerity" of women? How much pleasure does a woman get, and how?

"While the mechanics of an orgasm may be known, it is still a sensation, and like all sensations it's subjective," writes the author of an article called "Evolution of the Big O," in the popular-science journal *Discover*. "As a result, its existence can't be demonstrated or disproved by empirical measures. That unhappy truth becomes especially clear when evolutionary biologists turn their attention to the female orgasm—which they do with unseemly fascination. Even human lovers have to take their lady's word for it. How much more ineffable, then, must be the coital consciousness of Madame Marmoset."[32]

The Big O. When something hits the Renaissance G spot, what is often told is a story of "O." Thus in the final discovery scene of *The Changeling* an incensed Alsemero dispatches DeFlores after the woman he labels, in fury, a "crying crocodile."

> —Get you into her, sir.
> I'll be your pander now; rehearse again
> Your scene of lust, that you may be perfect.
>
> (5.3.113–15)

From the "closet," behind the stage, there now issue ambiguous cries.

> *Beatrice (within).* O! O! O!
> *Alsemero.*   Hark! 'Tis coming to you.
> *DeFlores (within).* Nay, I'll along for company.
> *Beatrice (within).*   O, O!
> *Vermandero [Beatrice-Joanna's father].* What horrid
>   sounds are these?
>
> (5.3.139–41)

The nonplussed father, Vermandero, hearing his daughter's cries, finds them mysterious, unrecognizable. "What horrid sounds are these?" "O, O, O!" Are these the sounds of enforced sexuality, of rape and injury? Or the voice of the woman moved beyond control? The omnipresent Renaissance "die" pun, the simultaneity of sex and death, is in this episode more than usually literal and vivid, not an implication but an enactment, a passionate outcry. Remember Alsemero's scathing epithet "crocodile," his brusque instruction to "rehearse" the "scene" of sexual passion. Even here it is not possible to tell what Beatrice-Joanna feigns, and what she feels.

We might usefully compare this final moment, embedded in a Jacobean tragedy, with what is perhaps the locus classicus of histrionic "faking it" for the 1980s: Rob Reiner's 1989 film *When Harry Met Sally . . .* , with a witty, streetwise screenplay by Nora Ephron. In the climactic scene, set in a New York deli, Sally (Meg Ryan) takes Harry (Billy Crystal) to task for his casual ways with women.

Harry. I don't hear anyone complaining. I think they have an okay time.

Sally. Because they . . . (rotating hand gesture signifying orgasm)

Harry (truculently). Yes, because they . . . (rotating hand gesture signifying orgasm)

Sally. How do you know they really . . . (rotating hand gesture)

Harry. (indignantly). What are you saying, that they fake orgasm?

Sally. Most women at one time or another have faked it.

Harry. Well they haven't faked it with me.

Sally. How do you know?

Harry. Because I know.

Sally. I forgot, you're a man. All men are sure it hasn't happened to them and most women at one time or another have done it, so you do the math.

Harry. You don't think I could tell the difference?

Sally (faking orgasm, as all heads in the restaurant turn). Mmmmm . . . Yes . . . right there . . . Yes, yes yes yes YES!!!

A pause. She lifts one corner of her mouth and grins at him, then casually picks up her fork and resumes stabbing at her salad. Harry looks at her steadily, while everyone around them draws a deep breath. Everyone, that is, except a middle-aged woman—played by Rob Reiner's mother, Estelle—seated a few tables away, who beckons to the waiter and tells him, deadpan: "I'll have what she's having."

"I'll have what she's having." But what she's having is a fake orgasm.

In Middleton and Rowley's play the father, who has attempted to control his daughter's marriage and thus her desires, finds the sounds of a woman's passion indecipherable and "horrid." In Reiner's film the mother—and we might note that practically everyone who has seen the film has somehow learned the "real" identity of the customer in the deli—listens, recognizes, and desires the woman's "passion," even (or especially?) if that passion is only a pretense. "I'll have what she's having." But what if she's having us on?

The potions and philters in Alsemero's pharmacy, like the book of recipes he follows, are designed to decipher, and thus to control, women's bodies and women's pleasure. By learning to fake the responses of pleasure, Beatrice-Joanna, like Sally Albright in the film, retakes control of the relationship, and of the scene. Yet, as all the self-help manuals suggest, to fake pleasure may be the first step in attaining it. Or—and this is more to the point—it may become a pleasure in itself.

When Beatrice-Joanna shifts her mimetic attention from Alsemero's book to Diaphanta's symptoms she shifts from text to theatricalization, from script to stage. In both the written and the acted models she finds, and takes, the cues for passion. And the particular case of orgasm only serves to epitomize the power that actors derive more generally from this "female" capacity to withhold, to dissimulate, to test the boundaries of the real.

Furthermore, these scenes in which instead of faking an orgasm characters fake the faking of an orgasm exhibit something intrinsic to the nature of theater. Isn't the frisson an audience feels both in *The Changeling* and in *When Harry Met Sally . . .* related to this intrinsic paradox of performance, that in acting only the fake is real?

Nor (is it needless to say?) are women the only ones who fake it on or off the stage, when the occasion arises. Martin Sherman's 1979 play *Bent*, with its central scene of two homosexual men in a Nazi prison camp, unable to touch or even to look at each other, brought to simultaneous orgasm by language as they stand facing the audience, is a theatrical tour de force. Compare this onstage fake realness to the commercial phenomenon of telephone sex, its erotic power dynamic linked, fiber-optically, to questions of authenticity, sincerity, and arousal, offering an example of the disparate pleasures of faking it in the real world.

In a rather different performance register, how does the cliché "money shot" of pornographic film, with its evidence of "real" ejaculation by men, put in question protocols of imitation and sincerity? If the ejaculation is "real" and the "passion" is faked, is the actor, male or female, in the position of Beatrice-Joanna?

As we have seen, there is a special theatrical "insincerity" in orgasm enacted on the stage, in precisely the space where grounded scientific knowledge and secure anatomical reference are by the nature of the genre put in question. What is "female orgasm" when mimed by a boy player? "Female," in the context of drama and performance, reveals itself, once again, as a position in a structure rather than as an aspect of anatomical—or even cultural—destiny.

From Dr. Freud to Dr. Ruth the "insincerity of women" has been seen as an ambivalent asset, a poison needed to effect a remedy. It turns out, though, that the poison is its own remedy, the remedy its own poison. The representation of female pleasure is itself a changeling. The existence of the possibility of fakeness protects the privacy and control of pleasure. Perhaps this was the secret that Juno was so angry at Tiresias for disclosing.

NOTES

1. "Dass sie 'sich geben,' selbst noch, wenn sie—sich geben." Literally, "that they 'give themselves' (that is to say, act or play a part) even when they—give themselves." Walter Kaufmann, trans., *The Gay Science* (New York: Vintage, 1974), 317 and n.

2. Thomas Lupton, *A Thousand Notable Things of Sundry Sorts*, The Fifth Book, No. 56 (1579; rpt. 1814), p. 43. *The Changeling*, ed. N. W. Bawcutt (Revels Plays; Cambridge: Harvard University Press, 1958), 69n.

3. Pliny, *Natural History*, xxxvi.19 (translated by Holland, 1601, II, 589). Antonius Mizaldus (1520–78), *Centuriae IX. Memorabiliam* (1566): Centuriae VI, 54, "Experiri an mulier sit grauida" (ed. Frankfurt, 1613, p. 127); Centuriae VII, 12 and 64, "Mulierem corruptam ab incorrupta discernere" (ed. Frankfurt, pp. 141–42, 154); "Appendix Secretorum Experimentorum Antidororumque contra varios morbos," p. 253, "Noscendi ratio an mulier sit virgo integra & intacta an non." Robert Burton, as Bawcutt notes, is dismissive of the entire notion: "To what end are all those Astrological questions, *an sit virgo, an sit casta, an sit mulier?* and such strange absurd trials in *Albertus Magnus, Bap. Porta, Mag. lib. 2, cap.21,* in *Wecker, lib. 5, de secret.,* by stones, perfumes, to make them piss, and confess i know not what in their sleep; some jealous brain was the first founder of them" (*Anatomy of Melancholy*, Pt. 3, Sec. 3, Memb. 2; ed. A. R. Shilleto, 1983, III, 327).

4. "Fragment of an Analysis of a Case of Hysteria," *The Standard Edition of the Complete Psychological Works of Sigmund Freud*, 24 vols. (London: Hogarth Press and the Institute for Psycho-Analysis, 1953–74), 7:80. Subsequent references to these volumes will be indicated by the abbreviation *SE*.

5. "For a man inhales and exhales by this organ [the nose], and sneezing is effected by its means: which last is an outward rush of collected breath, and is the only mode of breath used as an omen and regarded as supernatural." Aristotle, *History of Animals* (*Historia animalium*), trans. D'Arcy Wentworth Thompson. *The Works of Aristotle*, II, ed. W. D. Ross, reprinted in *Great Books of the Western World*, 9, ed. Robert Maynard Hutchins (Chicago: Encyclopaedia Britannica, 1952), 14 (492b, 5).

6. *The Works of William Harvey*, ed. and trans. Robert Willis [*De generatione animalium*] (New York: Johnson Reprint Corp., 1965), 534.

7. Nasal stimulation as a test for fruitfulness was also recommended in the eighteenth century. The author of *Aristotle's Last Legacy* reports that "some make this experiment of a woman's fruitfulness.

"They take myrrh, red florax, and such odoriferous things, and make a perfume of it: which let the woman receive into the neck of the womb, thro' a funnel; if the woman feel the smoak ascend to her nose, then she is fruitful; otherwise barren.

"Others take garlick, and beat it, and let the woman lie on her back upon it, and if she feel the scent thereof to her nose, it is a sign of fruitfulness." *Aristotle's Last Legacy* (London: 1776), 30, rpt. Garland Publishing (New York and London, 1986).

8. Josef Breuer and Sigmund Freud, *Studies on Hysteria*, *SE* 2:200.

9. *The Complete Letters of Sigmund Freud to Wilhelm Fliess, 1887–1904*, trans. and ed. Jeffrey Moussaieff Masson (Cambridge: Harvard University Press, 1985), 45–48. The notorious case of Emma Eckstein, on whom Fliess operated with disastrous results, was the most dramatic of these surgical interventions on the nose. Eager to acquit his friend of culpability in the botched operation, Freud

wrote to him a year after the surgery, "I shall be able to prove to you that you were right, that her episodes of bleeding were hysterical, were occasioned by *longing*, and probably occurred at the sexually relevant times [the woman, out of resistance, has not yet supplied me with the dates]" (183).

10. Thomas Hardy, *Tess of the D'Urbervilles* (New York: Bantam Books, 1981), 148.

11. Gordon Hendricks, *Origins of the American Film* (New York: Arno Press, 1972), 91.

12. Linda Williams, *Hard Core: Power, Pleasure, and the "Frenzy of the Visible"* (Berkeley: University of California Press, 1989), 53.

13. "Findings, Ideas, Problems" (1941 [1938]), *SE* 23. Emphasis in original.

14. Breuer and Freud, *Studies on Hysteria*, *SE* 2:248, 200.

15. Sigmund Freud, Letter 102 (to Fliess), January 16, 1899, *SE* 1:277.

16. "Three Essays," *SE* 7:180.

17. Sigmund Freud, "Extracts from the Fliess Papers," Draft J (1950 [1892–99]), trans. Eric Mosbacher and James Strachey, *SE* 1:217.

18. Thomas Laqueur, *Making Sex: Body and Gender from the Greeks to Freud* (Cambridge: Harvard University Press, 1990), 45–46, 49–52, 66–68.

19. Ibid., 43, 257n. Ovid, *Metamorphoses* 3.323–31.

20. Juliet Mitchell and Jacqueline Rose, eds., *Feminine Sexuality: Jacques Lacan and the Ecole Freudienne* (New York: W. W. Norton, 1982), 52.

21. Jacques Lacan, *Encore: Le seminaire XX. 1972–73* (Paris: Seuil, 1975). Mitchell and Rose, *Feminine Sexuality*, 52.

22. Jacques Derrida, "The Double Session," *Dissemination*, trans. Barbara Johnson (Chicago: University of Chicago Press, 1981), 201.

23. Gayatri Chakravorty Spivak, "Displacement and the Discourse of Woman," in *Displacement: Derrida and After*, ed. Mark Krupnick (Bloomington: Indiana University Press, 1983; 1987), 175.

24. Aristotle, *Generation of Animals*, Loeb Classical Library (Cambridge: Harvard University Press, 1958), 2.4.739a27–3. Laqueur, *Making Sex*, 47–48.

25. Danielle Jacquart and Claude Thomasset, *Sexuality and Medicine in the Middle Ages*, trans. Matthew Adamson (Princeton: Princeton University Press, 1988), 46.

26. Thomas G. Benedek, "Beliefs about Human Sexual Function in the Middle Ages and Renaissance," in *Human Sexuality in the Middle Ages and Renaissance*, ed. Douglas Radcliffe-Umstead (Pittsburgh: University of Pittsburgh Press, 1978), 108.

27. Auguste Debay, *Hygiène et physiologie du mariage*, 153rd ed. (Paris, 1880); see esp. pp. 17–18, 92, 94–95, 105–9. Erna Olafson Hellerstein, Leslie Parker Hume, and Karen M. Offen, eds., *Victorian Women: A Documentary Account of Women's Lives in Nineteenth-Century England, France, and the United States* (Stanford: Stanford University Press, 1981).

28. Julia R. Heilman and Joseph LoPiccolo, *Becoming Orgasmic: A Sexual and Personal Growth Program for Women* (New York: Fireside, Simon and Schuster, 1976, 1987), 91.

29. "J," *The Sensuous Woman* (New York: Dell Books, 1969), 180–81.

30. Ruth Westheimer, *Dr. Ruth's Guide to Good Sex* (New York: Warner Books, 1983), 45–46.

31. Alice Kahn Ladas, Beverly Whipple, and John D. Perry, eds., *The G Spot: And Other Recent Discoveries about Human Sexuality* (New York: Holt, Rinehart, and Winston, 1982), 143.

32. Karen Wright, "Evolution of the Big O," *Discover*, June 1992, 56.

MISTAKEN IDENTITIES

CASTIGLIO(NE)'S PRACTICAL JOKE

NATASHA KORDA

> Two Jews met in a railway carriage at a station in Galicia.
> "Where are you going?" asked one. "To Cracow," was the
> answer. "What a liar you are!" broke out the other. "If you say
> you're going to Cracow, you want me to believe you're going
> to Lemberg. But I know that in fact you *are* going to Cracow.
> So why are you lying to me?"
> (Sigmund Freud, *Jokes and Their Relation to the Unconscious*[1])

T THE END of Book II of Castiglione's *Il Libro del Cortegiano*, Bernardo Bibbiena recounts the tale of a practical joke perpetrated at court, involving a certain cowherd named Castiglio who had been summoned there on business for a gentleman courtier. So "elegantly decked out" was the cowherd for the occasion, we are told, that despite his being accustomed to nothing save tending cattle, anyone making his acquaintance "would have thought him a gallant cavalier" (2:85).[2] A glaring incongruity, however, impedes the verisimilitude of the cowherd's courtly incarnation; an unmistakable Lombard dialect immediately betrays his rustic origins. Recognizing a certain potential for amusement in this situation, several courtiers devise a scheme whereby the cowherd's most vulgar attribute, his rude speech, is itself transformed into the ultimate proof of his gentility. They do so by informing two gullible court ladies that the newly arrived stranger is known to be "the most accomplished courtier in all Spain." So skilled is he in every aspect of courtiership, they report, that he is able to speak all languages fluently, but "especially rustic Lombard." On account of this unusual talent, they caution the women, however, the Spaniard is also held to be a very "great trickster [*gran burlatore*]." Thus prompted, the two court ladies conceive a very "great desire" to meet the stranger and prepare to receive him with appropriately lavish ceremony. Upon hearing with what ease and accuracy their well-dressed visitor "mimics the language" of a Bergamasque cowherd, they are convinced that he must be a very accomplished courtier indeed, and "show him the greatest regard in speaking with him before all the company." The cowherd, we are told, cannot "help giving such proof of his 'gentility,'" for the more he reveals himself to be a doltish peasant, the more noble and ingenious is he taken to be. So long were the two women gulled in this way by their interlocutor's supposed linguistic prowess, Bernardo recounts, "that everyone's sides ached from laughing," until finally they were "persuaded, though with great difficulty," of the cowherd's true identity.

The success of the practical joke hinges on its exploitation of an apparent paradox: the most convincing proof or sign of the stranger's gentility in the eyes of his two charmed interlocutors is his ability to mimic or counterfeit (*contraffare*) the language of a vulgar peasant. The cowherd's uncouth speech is assumed to be an ingenious, courtly lie, elegantly designed to reveal, through the very finesse with which it is concealed, the "truth" of his gentility. This oxymoronic transvaluation of courtly values, far from being reducible to a mere case of comic misrecognition, however, reflects the ambition that informs the text's entire, protracted enumeration of courtly attributes: that of fixing, against the flux of time and place, a "universal rule [*regula universalissima*]" of courtliness, "valid above all the others" (1:26), a quintessential core of *cortegiania* that would obtain in all possible courtly worlds. Admitting from the start "how difficult it is to choose, from among so great a variety of customs as are followed at the courts of Christendom, the most perfect form and, as it were, the flower of courtiership" (1:1), the text nevertheless sets itself the task of defining a constant kernel of courtliness, itself exempt from the diachronic slide of usage or custom, that would serve as a stable, synchronic point of reference, an ultimate guarantee of the "authentic" courtier's identity, beyond the variable cluster of his attributes. The courtier in possession of this minimal unit of courtliness would, like Castiglio, be assured of his elite identity in even the most comically counterfactual of situations. Earlier in Book II, we are told that the ability to impersonate (*travestire*) a "rustic shepherd," or "some such other" peasant, is an effective means of persuading an audience of the "true" gentility concealed behind the courtier's vulgar disguise, and will win him great admiration once his audience realizes that "here there is much more than was promised by the costume" (2:11). By putting on the mask of his vulgar other, the courtier gives proof of his inalienable courtliness, a courtliness that appears to be so natural and proper to him that he may become the very antithesis of gentility without tarnishing it.

The stranger behind the mask in Bernardo's anecdote, however, is not an accomplished courtier in rustic disguise; he is an upstart peasant who presumes to impersonate the "perfect courtier." This far from neutral transposition would seem to reflect a pervasive aristocratic anxiety during the period over the threat of upwardly mobile pretenders to "authentic" elite identity. Courtesy literature began to develop as a genre at a time when aristocratic identity was being encroached upon by a horde of young men not born to it.[3] If it is the proclaimed pastime of the Urbino court "to fashion in speech a perfect courtier," the game of self-shaping by no means constitutes an end in and of itself; the express purpose of this activity, the final object of the game, is to humble, as Sir Thomas Hoby puts it, the "many untowardly Asseheades [*sciocchi*], that through malapertnesse thinke to purchase [*acquistar*] them the name of good courtier" (1:12).[4] This project, which aims at instituting the differentiating traits of elite identity, would seem to account for the necessity that the peasant's imposture be discovered in the end. Read in this way, the anecdote would appear to assuage aristocratic anxiety by casting the impostor as a mere cowherd, who can hardly be said to pose much of a threat. Bernardo is quite clear in stating that the actual perpetrator behind the prank is a savvy group of courtiers and not the obsequious peasant. The joke would thus seem to ridicule the presumption of the "untowardly Asseheade" by relegating the impostor to the status of a mere pawn in a complex courtly game, permitting the cowherd to be mistaken for a courtier in the interest of restoring "true" nobility to its proper place.

Thus construed, the "merry pranks" of the Urbino court would appear to participate in what Thomas Greene calls a strategic "drama of containment" (8) through which the court protects itself from any "imbalances . . . which could threaten the harmony of the group" (3).[5] The success of this strategy, according to Greene, is measured by the resiliency of the court's "saving laughter" (15), which proves that nothing is said that the courtly circle cannot incorporate. Bernardo Bibbiena's discussion of wit in Book II, according to this paradigm, defines a mode of facetious self-fashioning through which the ideal courtier distinguishes himself by gracefully deriding his uncouth other. Bernardo thus counsels the courtier to know how to mock, but not "after the fashion of fools, drunken men, the silly [*sciocchi*], the inept [*inetti*], or buffoons," because "although these kinds of men appear to be in demand at courts . . . they do not deserve to be called courtiers, but each should be called by his own name" (2:46). Such "untowardly Asseheades" are allowed within the circle of the court, it is maintained, in order that they may be *contained* by it. From this perspective, Castiglio's courtly performance would seem to be yet another instance of the court's strategic incorporation of vulgarity.

Within Castiglione criticism, the ideally flexible, expansive circle of the Urbino court has been taken to reflect the courtier's own protean versatility, the capacity of his "enlarged self" (Lanham, 152) to contain any and all attributes, to master all social roles, including that of the base or vulgar.[6] As Rebhorn puts it, the courtier's identity falls "within the realm of art, becomes subject to his creative will; through continual control and conscious direction, he can shape himself to play perfectly those social roles that constitute the essential forms of a humane and elegant civilization" (16). Castiglione's courtiers, he maintains, do not "allow themselves to be tyrannized by the rules: consciously aware of them, they use them and abuse them, manipulating them to suit their own ends" (137). The courtier's "understanding of role playing and his mastery of the myriad forms assumed by human activities," Mazzeo similarly argues, "mocks those un-self-conscious men at the opposite extreme from his ideal, who mechanically perform the parts assigned them . . . enslaved to the tyrant roles they do not understand and cannot manipulate" (14).[7] Monumentalized by Burckhardt as the prototype of the "fully developed individual," the "free personality" or "perfect man of society," Castiglione's "ideal courtier" continues to be read as a figure of the "aestheticized" self, of the self that consciously shapes its image as an artist shapes a work of art (a process that has been variously termed "self-actualization," "enselfment," and, most recently, "self-fashioning").[8] While the compelling fantasy of an autonomous ego within recent scholarship is distinguishable from its nineteenth-century predecessor precisely by its status as fantasy or fiction rather than what Burckhardt calls "psychological fact" (144), in the last instance such accounts seem invariably to return to a belief in the primacy of a self-determining will, in the end "cling[ing] to the human subject and to self-fashioning, even in suggesting the absorption or corruption or loss of the self" (Greenblatt, 256–57).[9] The text's emphasis on seeming rather than being, on surface rather than substance, is seen to reinforce rather than to subvert the informed will or selective agency of a self that is taken to preexist, and even to determine, its own discursive construction. According to this view of the text's construction of courtly identity, the practical joke appears to contrast the "true" courtier's selective self-shaping with the pastiche of the vulgar pretender, the courtier's freedom to enact infinite variations on the social order with the cowherd's rigid adherence to or absorption by convention, his enslavement to the mere trappings of power.

II

> You approach a child with your face covered by a mask: he laughs in a tense, nervous way. You come a little closer, and something happens that is a manifestation of anxiety. You take off the mask: the child laughs. But if, under this mask, you are wearing another, he won't be laughing at all.
> (Jacques Lacan, *The Formations of the Unconscious*[10])

To read the joke's chiastic reversal of elite and vulgar, identity and disguise, courtier and cowherd, solely from the retrospective moment of its final and belated undoing, however, would be to ignore the way in which it positions the text's sacred cow as a kind of straw man, setting up the figure of the "perfect courtier" as an object of protracted ridicule. To read the joke as a "drama of containment" that contrasts the courtier's calculated improvisation of social roles with the cowherd's total abjection would be to ignore the ridicule it levels at his interlocutors, who are humiliated precisely for their stubborn belief in his "calculated" vulgarity, for their tenacious adherence to the notion of an infinitely adaptable and expansive self. If the joke participates in the text's programmatic effort to fashion a "true" courtier by unmasking a vulgar impostor, it also belies this truth by exposing the apparatus through which the "authenticity" of elite identity is reproduced: a courtly code of conduct that dissimulates its own constructedness. If the two court ladies persist in believing the frankly vulgar speech of their guest to be proof of a hidden courtly identity, in spite—or rather, because—of the ever mounting evidence to the contrary, they do so because they *expect* his conduct to be a perfectly constructed, seamless dissimulation.

Courtly conduct, we are told earlier in Book II, is nothing but a form of "circumspect dissimulation [*una certa avvertita dissimulazione*]" (2:40) that is "always careful not to exceed the limits of verisimilitude [*sempre avvertito di non uscir della verisimilitudine*]" (2:41). The courtier who is able to put over the most credible "deceit [*inganno*]," as the text puts it, will win the game of preferment (2:40). So highly do the two court ladies value the verisimilitude of Castiglio's imitation of a Bergamasque cowherd, they do not even consider that he might in fact be the genuine, vulgar (or "artless") article. Like the incredulous Jew in Freud's joke, they assume their interlocutor "is lying when he tells the truth and is telling the truth by means of a lie" (115); they take his straightforward utterance to be evidence of an elaborate deceit, which is in turn taken to be earnest of his "true" identity.[11] The "universal rule" of good courtiership, according to Count Ludovico, is thus "to conceal all art [*nasconda l'arte*] and make whatever is done or said appear to be without effort and almost without any thought about it [*senza fatica e quasi senza pensarvi*] ... facility in such things causes the greatest wonder [*maraviglia*]; whereas, on the other hand, to labor . . . shows an extreme want of grace [*disgrazia*] . . . if it is discovered, this robs a man of all credit [*leva in tutto il credito*] and causes him to be held in slight esteem" (1:26). The slightest appearance of labor or care poses a threat to elite identity insofar as it reveals that identity to be itself nothing more than a web of seamlessly concealed affectations, a facade of dissimulated artifice. It thus becomes the ideological burden of the text to naturalize the traits of the courtier's identity by investing them with an aura of "grace" that must accompany his "actions, his gestures, his habits, in short, his every movement" (1:24). Castiglio's uncouth speech comes to signify a supreme, courtly

sprezzatura

grace insofar as it is apparently performed effortlessly, without any labor or affectation. Within the conceptual economy of the text, "grace" functions as a kind of metaphorical surplus that fixes in place the metonymic slippage of variable courtly attributes; it is "that seasoning without which all the other properties and good qualities would be of little worth" (1:24).

Confronted with the dilemma of teaching that which cannot be taught—"true" grace being a "gift of nature and of the heavens" (1:24)—the text must invent an ersatz grace for the would-be "ideal courtier" (as distinct from the aforementioned "false pretender") who happens to be "less endowed by nature" and who is "capable of acquiring grace" only by putting forth "labor, industry, and care" (1:24). To accomplish this feat of ideological ingenuity, the text is obliged "to pronounce a new word" (1:26): *sprezzatura* is introduced as the most valuable of courtly attributes, the sine qua non of courtliness, insofar as it is able to fabricate the illusion of an authentic, natural grace by dissimulating its own constructedness. Far from being the richest term in the text's vocabulary, as one might expect from a word that aims at condensing the entire range of courtly attributes into a single, quintessential trait, however, *sprezzatura* is found to have no positive consistency; it is defined in purely negative terms, as the "avoidance of affectation," the "concealment of art," the apparent "lack" of effort or care. What from one perspective appears to be a point of absolute saturation of courtly meaning, from another is thus revealed to be the dissimulation of its fundamental lack.

In this sense, *sprezzatura* functions within the text as what Žižek, following Lacan, calls a "quilting point [*point de capiton*]," a point of lack perceived as supreme plenitude, a point of pure difference perceived as identity. Within Žižek's version of ideology critique, the *point de capiton* has a purely structural or performative role in relation to the "floating" signifiers that constitute a given ideological field. Itself devoid of meaning, the *point de capiton* nevertheless functions as if it were a kind of ultimate Signified, conferring meaning retroactively on an entire chain of traits or signifiers, which are thereby transformed into a unified whole or coherent identity.[12] The effect of "quilting" or enchainment takes place, according to Žižek, when a shifting cluster of variable ideological elements or attributes comes to identify itself, to recognize itself as a unified field, in and through the agency of a single signifier. *Sprezzatura* is not merely the supreme courtly attribute; rather, it is that signifier to which the entire field of *cortegiania* must refer in order to recognize itself in its unity. The suspicious sounds that slide from Castiglio's lips are retroactively fixed or "quilted" into their proper place, assigned a courtly meaning or "grace," by his supposed *sprezzatura*. The fantasmatic richness of this surplus factor, this "something" that is in him and yet more than him, functions to produce "wonder [*maraviglia*]" in his interlocutors, the illusion that his courtly identity, rather than being designated retroactively, is immanent, present from the beginning.

In sending the stranger's speech back to him in an inverted form, in taking his "truth" to be a lie, however, the two court ladies are perhaps not entirely mistaken. For in so doing, they raise the more serious question posed by the practical joke, namely: What determines the authenticity of the courtier's "true" identity if that identity is itself nothing more than a cunning dissimulation?[13] Critics who celebrate Castiglione as herald of a self-making, self-mastering self tend to ignore the passage that describes the operation through which the courtier comes by his newfangled identity (a passage that immediately precedes the introduction of the concept of *sprezzatura* in the text), in which we find that the courtier's identity is itself grounded in a constitutive act of impersonation. The would-be "ideal courtier" is instructed to "make every effort to resemble and, if that be possible, to transform himself" into his model or mentor. While the text goes on to counsel the means to secure the appearance of a nonchalant, "natural" grace (by not imitating any one person too closely, but rather, "choosing now this thing from one and that from another") the language it uses to describe this operation belies any illusion of authenticity: "even as in green meadows the bee flits about among the grasses robbing [*carpendo*] the flowers, so our courtier must steal [*rubare*] this grace from those who seem to him to have it, taking from each the part that seems most worthy of praise" (1:26). It is only by plagiarizing the other that the courtier acquires his own, "authentic" self; he literally steals the aura of natural grace that is taken to be his own, proper birthright.[14]

To conceive of elite identity as a mode of imitative action, however, is necessarily to concede that the courtier has no authentic, essential self, that his own identity, like that of the upstart "pretender," is essentially (and "malapertly") taken or "mis"taken. This is perhaps the deeper anxiety inscribed in the joke's paradox: beneath the mask of the "ideal courtier" lies, not an authentic identity, but the mask of a vulgar impostor, beneath which lies the mask of the courtier, who finds himself to be an impostor, and so on. In the very process of assuming his own "ideal" self, the courtier thus comes face to face with, and recognizes himself in, the image of his vulgar other, identifies with him at the precise point that reveals his own lack of a "true" or authentic identity.[15] The joke thus reveals *sprezzatura*, the guarantor of grace, the quilting point that holds together the entire ideological edifice of *cortegiania*, to be the dissimulation of a fundamental lack. Far from distinguishing the "true" courtier from the false "pretender," the prank lays bare their uncanny resemblance.

In order to take the joke's ridicule of the "ideal courtier" seriously, we must ask whether the perceived resemblance between courtier and cowherd extends beyond the latter's lack of authenticity to include his lack of agency, his position as the pawn or plaything of a courtly game that exceeds his own informed will or selective agency. An answer presents itself in Daniel Javitch's assertion that beneath the mask of Castiglione's self-shaping courtier lies that of the abject "prince pleaser" (18) or "beautiful parasite" (26).[16] If the integrity of the courtier's identity is threatened by the horde of eager impostors scrambling up from below, it is equally threatened, Javitch maintains, by the person of the prince looming above. The text counsels the courtier to "devote all his thought and strength of spirit to loving and almost adoring the prince he serves above all else, devoting his every desire and habit and manner to pleasing him," having the "good judgement to perceive what his prince likes, and the wit and prudence to bend himself [*accommodare*] to this, and the considered resolve to like what by nature he may possibly dislike" (2:18). The text reveals a "full awareness," Javitch maintains, of the courtier's utter dependency on the prince's favor for his continued existence, and thus of the absolute exigency to secure or preserve such favor. According to Federico, the ideal courtier should

> . . . so frame his request [for favor], omitting those parts that he knows can cause displeasure, and skillfully make easy [*facilitando con destrezza*] the difficult points, so that his lord will always grant it, or do this in such wise that, should he deny it, he will not think the person whom he has thus not wished to favor goes off offended; for often when lords refuse some favor to someone who requests it so importunately, they judge that the person who asks for the thing with such insistence must desire it greatly, and that, in failing to obtain it, such a one must bear an ill will toward him who denies it; and with this thought they begin to hate the man and can never again look on him with favor. (2:18)

The courtier cannot express his desire too openly, ask too straightforwardly for what he really wants, for he must never appear to be in need. The sovereign's gift must always have the status of a completely gratuitous act of "grace." The patronage relation necessitates a "skillful ease," a studied lack of care—the very definition of *sprezzatura*, which here functions not only as a badge of aristocratic identity, a means of differentiating the elite from the base or vulgar, but as an essential tool for maintaining a felicitous relation with the sovereign, serving at once to procure the prince's favor and to dissimulate, if necessary, the lack of such favor. From this perspective, the courtier's identification with the cowherd's lack of agency, his position as punchline of a courtly joke, would seem to reflect the subordination of his own desire, the "bending" of his own will, to accord with that of the prince.

Sprezzatura at once answers to and finds its limit in the profound un-
predictability of the patronage relation. Even the perfectly fashioned
courtier who follows each and every precept of graceful conduct put forth
in the text, Castiglione warns, is still uncertain of preferment:

> . . . we sometimes see that a gentleman, no matter how good his character may
> be, and though endowed with many graces, will find little favor with the prince,
> and will, as we say, go against the grain [*non gli arà sangue*]; and this for no
> understandable reason [*senza causa alcuna che si possa comprendere*]. So that
> as soon as he comes into the presence of the prince, and before he has been
> recognized by the others, although he may be quick at repartee and may cut a
> good figure by his gestures, manners, words, and all else that is needful, that
> prince will show that he esteems him little, nay, will be the readier to offend
> him in some way [*gli farà qualche scorno*]. And thus it will come about that the
> others will immediately follow the prince's bent [*s'accommodaranno*], and ev-
> eryone will find the man to be of little worth, nor will there be any who prize
> or esteem him, or laugh at his witticisms, or hold him in any respect; nay, all
> will begin to make fun of him [*burlarlo*] and persecute him [*dargli la caccia*].
> Nor will it avail the poor man at all if he makes fair retorts or takes all this as
> if it were in jest [*per gioco*], for the very pages will buzz about him, so that he
> can be the worthiest man in the world [*il più valoroso uomo*] and still be put
> down and derided [*impedito e burlato*]. (2:32)

Sprezzatura, the "universal rule" of *cortegiania*, encounters an insur-
mountable obstacle in that which stands beyond reason or comprehen-
sion, the despotic power of the prince, whose arbitrary judgment has the
power to determine how the courtier will be "recognized" or misrecog-
nized, to disgrace even the most graceful courtly performance. In a scenario that reverses the terms of the practical joke, the "true" courtier here
performs with perfect manners and tells a perfectly urbane joke, and yet
is treated no better than a cowherd—a far from laughing matter. In the
presence of the prince, even the "perfect courtier" may become the punchline of a courtly joke, be demoted from active mocker (*burlatore*) to passive mocked (*burlato*). So too, we are told, may the prince choose to con-
fer favor or grace on the bungling wit of a vulgar impostor: "On the other
hand, if the prince shows a liking for some dullard [*un ignorantissimo*]
who knows neither how to speak nor how to act, this man's manners and
ways (however silly [*sciocchi*] and uncouth [*inetti*] they may be) will often
be praised with exclamations and wonderment [*stupore*] by everyone,
and the whole court will appear to admire [*ammiri*] and respect him, and
everyone will laugh at his clever sayings and at certain rustic [*contadines-
che*] and pointless jests that ought to provoke vomit rather than laughter:
so are men set and obstinate in the opinions that are engendered by
the favor and disfavor of princes" (2:32). From this perspective, the

"wonder" expressed by the two noblewomen in the practical joke would appear to be ridiculed as a kind of "stupor" engendered by their excessive "bending" to received belief; their opinion is wholly determined by the rumor told to them by the scheming courtiers. The joke would thus appear to mock the courtier's subjection to the inscrutable proclivities of the prince; its "misrecognition" reveals the failure of the system of *cortegiania* to achieve closure by unmasking the lack (of any absolute guarantor of "grace") it conceals.

III

> An impoverished individual borrowed twenty-five florins from a prosperous acquaintance, with many asseverations of his necessitous circumstances. The very same day his benefactor met him again in a restaurant with a plate of salmon mayonnaise in front of him. The benefactor reproached him: "What? You borrow money from me and then order yourself salmon mayonnaise? Is *that* what you've used my money for?" "I don't understand you," replied the object of the attack; "if I haven't money I *can't* eat salmon mayonnaise, and if I have some money I *mustn't* eat salmon mayonnaise. Well, then, when *am* I to eat salmon mayonnaise?"
> (Sigmund Freud, *Jokes and Their Relation to the Unconscious*)

If read in the context of the patronage relation, the courtier's wit seems less an exuberant manifestation of his "enlarged self" than a symptom of his "bending" to accommodate the desire of the prince. It may be helpful in light of this context to recall Lacan's definition of *Witz* as essentially a form of dissimulated demand. It is not by chance, Lacan points out, that so many of the jokes Freud recounts in his *Witzbuch* deal with the figure of the parasite or beggar. The primary form of the demand, which derives from the infant-mother dyad, is quite literally an "entrusting" (*de-mandare*) of oneself, a "giving over of one's whole self, of all one's needs," like a beggar, to another; half beggar, half infant, the joker entrusts his pleasure to the goodwill of the other. The joker never presents his demand in its naked state, however, but always disguises or translates it, "bending" or reshaping it to accord with "the system of the signifier as it has been set up, established, in the Other." If the courtier plays the part of an importunate beggar in relation to the prince, as we have seen, he must reframe his request in *motti piacevoli*, reformulate his demand to accord with the prince's humor. The joke nevertheless contains within itself, according to Lacan, a fundamental structural difference that distinguishes it from the demand, a slight transgression of the linguistic code or minimal unit of phonematic difference through which it aims at a "partial regaining of that ideal plenitude" lost when need is reformulated as demand. The joke is properly speaking a "language symptom," in that it attempts to restore enjoyment to the essentially unsatisfied demand through the play of the signifier itself; by transforming its metonymic transgression ("*peu-de-sens*") of the linguistic code into a metaphoric effect of "sense in nonsense" ("*pas-de-sens*"), Lacan maintains, the joke seeks to re-evoke the "dimension through which desire, if it does not recapture [a pre-discursive, ideal plenitude], at least indicates everything that is lost along the way."

The psychoanalytic account of *Witz* would here appear to find its limit, however, insofar as the joke under consideration is a *practical* joke, and as such, according to Freud, is not properly speaking a joke at all. Practical jokes belong, Freud maintains, to the field of the comic (199), which he rigidly distinguishes from the joke at the level both of structure and metapsychology. If the comic is essentially a dual or narcissistic relation, a struggle for prestige that takes place between the subject and the other as object, in the joke proper, he maintains, "something remains over" (143), outside of the dual relation, an excess that seeks to be conveyed in speech to an "interpolated third person." This tertiary Other does not correspond to the comic object but is positioned as a superegoic "agency of criticism," which it is the joke's task to circumvent by inciting laughter (144).[17] Apparently lacking the linguistic sophistication and complex structure proper to *Witz*, comic techniques are given short shrift within psychoanalytic accounts of the risible, and practical jokes, as a subspecies of the comic, are almost completely ignored. Freud mentions them only once in passing (199), and Lacan neglects them entirely.

The psychoanalysis of *Witz* is in this sense, however, quite conventional. Within the "rhetorical joke tradition" (the tradition of joke-theory in classical rhetoric), practical jokes are not deemed worthy of mention.[18] While the exigency of wit in classical rhetoric is maintained in Castiglione's treatise, wit is not so much of concern as the smallest minimal unit of persuasive force; rather, it is considered to be the mode of eloquence proper to courtly converse in particular.[19] Bernardo Bibbiena's rehearsal of classical joke-theory in *The Courtier* is recast in response to a specifically courtly demand for urbane wit. Bernardo explicitly departs from his conventional account of the two types of wit set forth in traditional typologies (the "humorous anecdote" and the "witty retort," respectively) in order to introduce practical jokes as the third type of wit, which, although not included in classical rhetorical treatises, is nevertheless "seen every day" in court circles. In Bernardo's account, far from constituting a disparate order of phenomena from that of verbal wit, practical jokes are conceived to be a hybrid form of humor, in which "both long narratives and short sayings find their place, and sometimes action as well" (2:48). In contrast to the psychoanalytic account, however, Bernardo emphasizes the *symbolic* rather than the imaginary aspect of practical jokes by demonstrating their derivation from the same rhetorical tropes as verbal jokes (2:85).

In Castiglio's encounter with the two noblewomen, imaginary misrecognition is clearly inseparable from its linguistic underpinnings; it is the cowherd's speech, after all, on which the success of the practical joke depends. Nor is the joke's focus on linguistic imitation merely fortuitous, for Castiglio's position within it bears a striking resemblance to Castiglione's own position within the contemporary *questione della lingua* or debate on vernacular imitation, the elaboration of which is a central concern of his text (1:28–40). In his introductory epistle to the *Cortegiano* addressed to Don Michel de Silva, Castiglione takes issue with those who would blame him because he has not imitated the language of Boccaccio and defends the use of his native Lombard dialect: "I do not believe to have erred if I have employed certain of these words in writing, and if I have taken from my own country what is intact and genuine [*l'integro e sincero*], rather than from another's what is corrupted and mutilated [*corrotto e guasto*]. . . . Nor do I believe that it should be imputed to me as an error that I have chosen to make myself known rather as a Lombard speaking Lombard than as a non-Tuscan speaking too much Tuscan—in order not to do as Theophrastus who, because he spoke too much Athenian, was recognized by a simple old woman as non-Athenian" (Intro:2). Castiglione here identifies himself with a linguistic genuineness (and ingenuousness) not unlike that of his Lombard compatriate and namesake in the joke. Like "Castiglio," Castiglione speaks his own native Lombard dialect, and yet is held to be the most accomplished of courtiers.

At this point we must raise the question posed by the "language symptom" of the joke and ask: What *desire* is inscribed within the metaphoric spark of resemblance it ignites between the two minimally different proper names, Castiglio and Castiglione? We have yet to account, that is to say, for Castiglione's *desire* vis-à-vis the figure of "Castiglio." Why does Castiglione, who represents himself as having been absent from the dialogues he recounts (cf. 1:1, 4:38), make a disguised appearance in them; why does he write himself into his text within the apparently trivial context of a practical joke?[20] Why is "Castiglio" the appropriate proper name for an impostor who is *improperly* identified as the most accomplished of courtiers?

IV

> Others say I have thought to take myself as a model, on the
> persuasion that the qualities which I attribute to the courtier
> are all in me . . . but I am not so wanting in judgement and self-
> knowledge as to presume to know all that I could wish to know
> [*che mi presuma saper tutto quello che so desiderare*]. (Intro:3)
> (Baldassare Castiglione, *Il Cortegiano*)

In the early pages of the *Cortegiano*, Castiglione describes Urbino as a pastoral haven, a place "blessed by Heaven with a most fertile and bountiful countryside" and abounding "in all the necessities of life" (1:2). What is abundantly clear, however, from his copious correspondence with his mother during the period, is that the years he spent at the illustrious court were plagued by scarcity and debt.[21] Having chosen to leave the service of the Marquis of Mantua, Francesco Gonzaga, against the marquis's wishes, in order to enter that of Duke Guidobaldo, Castiglione arrived at the Urbino court in 1504 under the sign of an ingrate. This rebuke was leveled at the upstart courtier not only by his resentful former master, but by his mother, Madonna Luigia, as well, who quickly began to realize that her son's chosen path was leading him to financial disaster. Money at the Urbino court was apparently scarce, expenses heavy, and Castiglione's small salary often in arrears. Barely a month after his arrival, he was forced to importune his mother for whatever meager funds she might send from their estate in Mantua. On October 26, 1504, he writes: "The scarcity is great, and we have never received any more pay from the Duke, so our pockets are very light. However, we expect some every day, and are very well, thank God. . . . It is certainly true that I like to hear everything that goes on at home and wish our affairs were more prosperous. However, as long as we can keep out of debt, let Fortune do her worst! You must not take these things too much to heart, but try and remedy what you can, and let the rest go, as I do, with a gay heart" (110). Castiglione would seem to have significantly revised his opinion of debt over the course of his first year at the Urbino court, however, for on September 20 of the following year, he again wrote to Madonna Luigia, imploring her to send him fifty-five ducats to cover a debt incurred in Rome: "I would not lose my credit in Rome," he tells her, "for a thousand reasons, especially as I have managed to keep it till now." Among these reasons was the need to incur still more debt to maintain his courtly identity: "For if I required half a thousand ducats, I need only open my lips to have them; and this is important if I am to effect anything . . . for myself"

(150). In this context, Castiglione's definition of *sprezzatura* as the dissimulation of labor or care—a "care" that, if discovered, would rob "a man of all credit"—takes on a new, more literal signification. Castiglione had clearly come to consider the clever management of debt to be an indispensable tool for advancement at court.

Madonna Luigia soon grew impatient with her son's repeated requests for ever increasing sums of money, however, and rebuked him for his "extravagant" lifestyle, in response to which he replied, on April 28, 1506: " . . . answer to your remark that it is sometimes necessary to use self-restraint, and not to spend more than one has, I must say that I do not think I deserve this reproach. . . . Sometimes, indeed often, I have not known in the morning what I should have for supper at night, but am ready to bear anything gladly rather than lose the small reputation which I have acquired [*quel poco de reputatione che s'è aquistata*]; not that I intend to play the part of a noble lord or fine gentleman, which I neither can nor wish to be [*non già facendo el signore né 'l gran maestro, ch'io non lo so fare, né lo facio*]" (167). Faced with his mother's reproach, Castiglione professes to live under conditions that are little better than those of a peasant. In Madonna Luigia's eyes, however, he more closely resembles "little" Castiglio (the -*ne* suffix being augmentative in Italian), the upstart impostor who lives a life of borrowed extravagance. The mirthful tone Castiglione adopts in many of these letters, the pride he takes in the "part" he is able to play at the Urbino court thanks to his shrewd financial maneuvering, is ridiculed, reduced by his mother's demeaning rebuke to a pathetic, opportunistic joke. Like Theophrastus, Castiglione is castigated by "a simple old woman" who recognizes the imposture behind her son's "ideal" courtly identity. Unlike the credulous noblewomen in the joke, his mother doesn't buy the courtier's witty dissimulation of their mutual "care" or need; refusing to extend him her "credit," she accuses him of being nothing but an "untowardly Asseheade that through malapertnesse thinks to purchase him the name of good courtier."[22]

A profound ingratitude is produced in the subject of the demand by the satisfaction of his needs, according to Lacan, insofar as he is always left wanting more. This "more" or excess is what remains of the initial need once it has "profoundly changed its accent, been subverted, made ambiguous, by its passage through the paths of the signifier." The wit in Freud's beggar, Lacan points out, is precisely that he is not *simply* a subject of need; he is less a mendicant than an ingrate. When given what he asks for, he either misuses it or behaves toward his benefactor "in a particularly insolent way." It is the persistence, beyond the demand, of a desire that is by definition excessive, being needless, that appears as ingratitude in Freud's beggar, as in the case of the impoverished gourmand who indulges his particular penchant for salmon mayonnaise at the expense of a benefactor whose goodwill extends only so far as his professed need. If Castiglione seeks to disavow the dissimulation proper to desire, to deny his wish to "play the part" of a "fine gentleman," by professing "genuine" need, his utterance nevertheless betrays an ironic awareness of the very dissimulation it would negate. Unlike Castiglio, Castiglione's profession of non-knowledge (*non lo so*) or ingenuousness is itself a rhetorical pose, an ingenious courtly lie.

Is the humiliation Castiglione suffers under the mocking gaze of his mother merely turned back against the two noblewomen in the joke, who are ridiculed for not knowing the "true" courtier from the false pretender? The identities of the two court ladies are pointedly left mysterious. Bernardo decorously refuses to name them, claiming that they might take offense, a concern that might appear to be somewhat superficial given that he goes on to recount a joke that is designed to humiliate them. He does so, we must hasten to add, within an enunciative context that is itself presided over by two noblewomen, the Duchess Elisabetta Gonzaga and her "deputy," Emilia Pia. Is the joke therefore legible as a simple "masculine protest" leveled against the Urbino court's "women on top"? Wayne Rebhorn has asserted that the male courtier's pranks permit him "to articulate deep feelings of aggression and status rivalries, sexual antagonisms and fantasies, in a controlled and limiting situation" (192).[23] To ascribe an unproblematic intelligibility to the misogynist aggression underlying the courtier's "antifeminist gibes," however, would be to beg the question of the "fantasies" thus articulated by *assuming* them to be aggressive. Given that Castiglione identifies himself with Castiglio, as the pawn or plaything rather than the perpetrator of the practical joke, we might speculate that his position within its fantasy-scenario is not obviously that of the aggressor.[24]

V

> He [Boccaccio] wrote much better when he let himself be guided solely by his natural genius and instinct [*dall'ingegno ed instinto suo naturale*], without care or concern to polish his writings [*senz'altro studio o cura di limare i scritti suoi*], than when he attempted with diligence and labor to be more refined and correct [*che quando con diligenzia e fatica si sforzò d'esser più castigato*]. (Intro:2)
> (Baldassare Castiglione, *Il Cortegiano*)

At the level of the social, fantasy functions, according to Žižek, as "a means for an ideology to take its own failure into account in advance" (126); at the level of the subject, it likewise serves to fill out "the void, the opening of the desire of the Other," by attempting to give "a definite answer to the question, 'What does the Other want?'"[25] Within the text of the *Cortegiano*, the fantasmatic female Other whose inscrutable desire is held accountable for the failure of the system of *cortegiania* to achieve perfect closure is given the name of Fortune. Ushered in whenever *sprezzatura* fails in its function as guarantor of courtly favor or "grace," Fortune is held to be the final, arbitrary arbiter of success for both courtier and prince alike. Castiglione commences his portrait of the Urbino court with a genealogy of the "excellent lords" who have ruled over it, beginning with the present duke's father, Federico da Montefeltro, renowned for his military prowess. Guidobaldo, Federico's "motherless" son, is initially introduced as the inheritor of all his father's virile virtues, as his greatest accomplishment or "deed." Before he is able to accomplish any full-blown deeds of his own, however, Guidobaldo is literally shriveled by the muscular hand of Fortune:

> But Fortune, envious of so great a worth, set herself against this glorious beginning with all her might, so that, before Duke Guido had reached the age of twenty, he fell sick of the gout, which grew upon him with grievous pain, and in a short time so crippled all his members that he could not stand upon his feet or move. Thus, one of the fairest and ablest bodies in the world was deformed and marred [*deformato e guasto*] at a tender age. And not even content with this, Fortune opposed him so in his every undertaking that he rarely brought to a successful issue anything he tried to do; and, although he was very wise in counsel and undaunted in spirit, it seemed that whatever he undertook always succeeded ill with him whether in arms or in anything, great or small; all of which is attested by his many and diverse calamities, which he always bore with such strength of spirit that his virtue was never overcome by Fortune; nay, despising [*sprezzando*] her storms with stanch heart, he lived in sickness as if in health, and in adversity as if most fortunate, with the greatest dignity and esteemed by all. (1:3)

Sprezzatura, which is etymologically related to the verb *sprezzare* ("to disdain"), would here appear to be invoked in its specifically aggressive dimension in retaliation for Fortune's unjust punishments. We find, however, that the only revenge Guidobaldo is able to mount against her is a project of defensive dissimulation: he lives his life *as if* most fortunate, adopting the same mirthful persona that Castiglione puts on in his letters in response to his own mother's "storms."

In his introductory letter to de Silva, Castiglione attributes his own travails, and his consequent failure to pay a symbolic "debt," to the ill will of Fortune: "I was moved by the memory [of the duke's death in 1508] to write these books of the Courtier: which I did in but a few days, meaning in time to correct [*castigar*] those errors which had resulted from my desire to pay this debt quickly [*dal desiderio di pagar tosto questo debito*]. But Fortune for many years now has kept me ever oppressed by such constant travail that I could never find the leisure to bring these books to a point where my weak judgement was satisfied with them [*il mio debil giudicio ne restasse contento*]" (Intro:1). Castiglione blames Fortune for his "cares" and consequent inability to repay his "debt" to the Urbino court. The form of this payment is conceived as a work of castigation or correction, as the correction, more specifically, of an imagined lack in his text. The decision to publish his text after almost two decades is imputed to yet another malevolent female, Vittoria Colonna, to whom Castiglione had lent his manuscript and who, contrary to her promise, had had it transcribed. "Alarmed at the danger" that his book might be published without his corrections, Castiglione decided "to revise [*riveder*] at once such small part of the book as time would permit, with the intention of publishing it, thinking it better to let it be seen even slightly corrected by my own hand than much mutilated by the hands of others [*poco castigato per mia mano che molto lacerato per man d'altri*]" (Intro:2). What desire is inscribed in the repetition of this tale of male *virtù* crippled at the hands of a demonized, female Other? The term *castigare* as applied to textual editing derives, as Stephanie Jed points out, from the early Florentine humanists' self-described practice of restoring or "castigating" Roman texts to their original state of *integritas*.[26] Jed identifies two conflicting lexical families associated with this project, which represent the two poles of linguistic purity and corruption: on the one hand, "words related to touching or the absence of touching—*tangible, contaminate, contact, integrity, intact*, etc., and on the other hand, words related to cutting—*chastity, castigate, caste*, and Latin *carere* ('to be cut off from, to lack')" (8). In the practical joke, these two poles may be said to converge in the figure of Castiglio, who at once represents an intact and sincere ("*integro e sincero*") linguistic plenitude (he is able to speak all languages fluently, while remaining "true" to his own) and its cunning dissimulation by the linguistically alienated, Theophrastan courtier. Castiglione's fantasy of "castigation" would thus seem to represent both an imagined scene of the mutilation or castration of his courtly ideal, and a wishful attempt to restore or regain, to repair or "correct," that ideal.

If the *Cortegiano* may be called a work of castigation, however, Castiglione's recognition of the impossibility of achieving this lost ideal of *integritas* is perhaps most significantly marked by his failure to "correct" the lack that remains in his own proper name as it appears in the text of his joke. Situated in a space left vacant by the text's failure to achieve ideological closure, its failure to fix a "universal rule" of courtliness that would act as a guarantor of the "true" courtier's identity, Castiglio(ne)'s practical joke seeks to answer to the courtier's passive role as "prince pleaser," to the uncanny resemblance he bears to his vulgar other. Far from representing a straightforward "masculine protest" against a perceived threat of effeminization, however, the joke constructs a frame within which the "bending" desire of the courtier is constituted. By deploying a mutilated form of his own proper name as the joke's punchline, Castiglione names a lack that remains, uncastigated, in his text, a lack that determines the contours of his identity, and around which his desire circulates.

NOTES

1. All references to Freud's joke-book are to Sigmund Freud, *Jokes and Their Relation to the Unconscious*, trans. James Strachey (New York: W. W. Norton and Co., 1960). My thanks to Jonathan Goldberg, Nancy Struever, and Krystian Czerniecki for reading early drafts of this paper. I am grateful to Elizabeth Cropper and Charles Dempsey for their generosity and support during my stay at the Villa Spelman Center for Italian Studies in Florence, where I completed the research for this paper.

2. All references to *The Book of the Courtier* in English are to the Charles S. Singleton translation (New York: Anchor Books, 1959). The parenthetical references following these citations are to book and chapter numbers. I have occasionally emended Singleton's translation where necessary. All references to the Italian text are to *Il cortegiano del Conte Baldesar Castiglione*, ed. Vittorio Cian (Florence: G. C. Sansoni, 1894).

3. Cf. Frank Whigham, *Ambition and Privilege: The Social Tropes of Elizabethan Courtesy Theory* (Berkeley: University of California Press, 1984). Fernand Braudel describes accelerated social mobility and the crisis of the aristocracy in the Italian context and throughout Europe during the sixteenth century, in Chapter 5 of *The Wheels of Commerce* (New York: Harper and Row, 1982), 461–513.

4. Count Baldassare Castiglione, *The Book of the Courtier done into English by Sir Thomas Hoby* (1561) (New York: E. P. Dutton and Co., 1948).

5. Thomas Greene, "*Il Cortegiano* and the Choice of a Game," in *Castiglione: The Ideal and the Real in Renaissance Culture*, ed. Robert W. Hanning and David Rosand (New Haven: Yale University Press, 1983).

6. Richard Lanham, "The Self as Middle Style: Cortegiano," in *The Motives of Eloquence* (New Haven: Yale University Press, 1976). See note 9 below.

7. Joseph A. Mazzeo, "Castiglione's *Courtier:* The Self as a Work of Art," in *Renaissance and Revolution: Backgrounds to Seventeenth-Century Literature* (New York: Random House, 1965).

8. Jacob Burckhardt, *The Civilization of the Renaissance in Italy, Vol. I* (New York: Harper and Row, 1958); Wayne A. Rebhorn, *Courtly Performances: Masking and Festivity in Castiglione's "Book of the Courtier"* (Detroit: Wayne State University, 1978), 18; Richard Lanham, "Middle Style," 152; and Stephen

Greenblatt, *Renaissance Self-Fashioning From More to Shakespeare* (Chicago: University of Chicago Press, 1980), respectively.

9. Thus, Greenblatt's notion of an "improvisational" transforming of fixed symbolic structures depends upon "a moment prior to formal coherence, a moment of experimental, aleatory impulse in which the available, received materials are curved toward a novel shape" (227). The courtier's "calculated mask," Greenblatt maintains, enables him to absorb that which "seems fixed and established" into his own ego, and thereby to "transform given materials into [his] own scenario" (227). While Lanham describes the courtier's identity as "a self built from the outside in," he concludes that Castiglione "wants to reverse the process, recommend purposes which will yield a central self," that he is not a "scorner of the central self, but a chief defender and prophet" (156).

10. Lacan's discussion of Freud's *Witzbuch* takes up the first portion of his unpublished seminar of 1957–58, *Les Formations de L'inconscient*. Translated citations from this seminar are indebted to an excellent, unpublished translation by Cormac Gallagher; my thanks to Paula Mieli for making these texts available to me.

11. In a world in which plain-spoken "truth" is always a sure sign of deception, the courtier must always be on guard to detect a practical joke before it detects him in his folly. Even the theoretician of jokes himself, Bernardo Bibbiena, admits to having been the butt of so many pranks as to be "wary of everything" (2:84). In this sense, the practical joke might be said to tap into a certain paranoia produced by the metadiscursive machinations of the court, by virtue of which any straightforward signifier must be taken as evidence of an elaborate plot, masking itself behind a facade of verisimilitude. "Metadiscursive," in that the paranoid subject, according to Žižek, posits the existence of "an 'Other of the Other': a hidden subject who pulls the strings of the great Other (the symbolic order)," and who manipulates the subject through a network of impostors, speaking through them in obscure, ciphered tongues, and under the guise of apparently spontaneous jokes. See Slavoj Žižek, "The Psychotic Solution: The Other of the Other," in *Looking Awry* (Cambridge: MIT Press, 1991), 18.

12. See Slavoj Žižek, "The Ideological 'Quilt,'" in *The Sublime Object of Ideology* (New York: Verso, 1989), 87–89.

13. See Jacques Lacan, "Analysis and Truth," in *The Four Fundamental Concepts of Psychoanalysis* (New York: W. W. Norton and Co., 1978), particularly 138–42.

14. See Stephen Orgel's account of Renaissance attitudes toward plagiarism in "The Renaissance Artist as Plagiarist," *English Literary History* 48 (1981): 476–95.

15. The joke may in this sense be said to trace a trajectory leading from what Lacan calls imaginary to symbolic identification. The courtier achieves self-identity or "authenticity," constitutes himself as an imaginary totality, by identifying with the image of the other or model at a point of ideal unity, an identification that produces an illusion of the self as an autonomous agent, origin of its acts, present from the beginning. If imaginary identification thus serves as a screen, giving the subject an image to mask its fundamental lack of being or essence,

symbolic identification is, by contrast, constituted around a point of *lack* (failure, weakness, guilt) in the Other. See Žižek's discussion of identification in *The Sublime Object*, 100–110.

16. Daniel Javitch, "*Il Cortegiano* and the Constraints of Despotism," in Hanning and Rosand, *Castiglione.*

17. Lacan reads Freud's theorization of the relation of jokes to the comic as recapitulating, respectively, the relation between the symbolic and the imaginary registers. Whereas the comic, as Lacan formulates it, lures the subject's narcissism with the captivating character of the image, only to destroy the unity of this image by recalling its fragmentary origin, the joke represents what he calls a "language symptom" that seeks, via metonymic approximation, to recover the *jouissance* of the lost object in the form of a demand for meaning addressed to the symbolic Other.

18. The tradition of joke-theory in classical rhetoric begins, at least in its fully developed form, with Cicero's *De Oratore* (2:54–71) and Quintilian's *De Institutione Oratoria* (6:3). Cicero's treatment of jokes is included under the heading of oratory aimed not at instructing an audience, but rather at agitating it by excessive emotion. This form of eloquence, Quintilian concurs, is the "queen of all," because "it is in its power over the emotions that the life and soul of oratory are to be found." Cicero and Quintilian, like Freud, are primarily interested in the technical structure of jokes as a linguistic tool within specific discursive contexts—that of the orator and that of the analyst/analysand, respectively—contexts in which practical jokes are hardly a frequent or welcome occurrence. To the rhetorician, as to the analyst, the practical joke appears to be nothing more than mere buffoonery. To understand why, at a certain moment in its history, joke-theory does open itself up to the discussion of practical jokes, we must look to the discursive context of its enunciation, that of the early modern court. Quintilian, *De Institutione Oratoria*, Loeb Classical Library, trans. H. E. Butler (Cambridge: Harvard University Press, 1985).

19. The courtier must learn "how to sweeten and refresh the minds" of those with whom he is speaking, by moving them "discreetly to gaiety and laughter with amusing witticisms and pleasantries [*con motti piacevoli e facezie discretamente indurgli a festa e riso*], so that, without ever producing tedium or satiety, he may continually give pleasure" (2:42).

20. The ideology of the "author-function," according to Foucault, is not "formed spontaneously through the simple attribution of a discourse to an individual"; rather, it "results from a complex operation whose purpose is to construct the rational entity we call an author" (127). The projection of psychological depth and creative power onto this construction, he maintains, serves the interests of a "unifying" drive or principle that seeks to neutralize any contradictions found in the text. To give a text an author, Barthes similarly maintains, is to "furnish it with a final signified, to close the writing" (147). The notion that one might abandon the author-function completely, however, is equally a mystification, according to Foucault, insofar as it merely transfers the status of transcendency from author to text. "It would be false to consider the function of the author as a pure and simple reconstruction after the fact of a text given as passive material," he maintains, "since a text always bears a number of signs that refer to

the author" (129). The author-function should therefore not be entirely abandoned; rather, "the subject (and its substitutes) must be stripped of its creative
role and analysed as a complex and variable function of discourse" (137). See
Michel Foucault, "What Is an Author?" in *Language, Counter-Memory, Practice*,
ed. Donald F. Bouchard, trans. Donald F. Bouchard and Sherry Simon (Ithaca:
Cornell University Press, 1981); and Roland Barthes, "The Death of the Author,"
in *Image, Music, Text*, trans. Stephen Heath (New York: Noonday Press, 1977).

21. All references to Castiglione's correspondence in English are to Julia Cart-
wright's *Baldassare Castiglione: The Perfect Courtier. His Life and Letters 1478–
1529* (New York: E. P. Dutton and Co., 1908). References in Italian are to Bal-
dassar Castiglione, *Le Lettere: Tomo Primo (1497–Marzo 1521)*, ed. Guido La
Rocca (Verona: Arnoldo Mondadori, 1978).

22. The awkward double life of the courtier became only more burdensome
and unmanageable the following year, when Castiglione's pecuniary embarrass-
ments became so unwieldy that he was forced to take drastic action. Dissatisfied
with the scant funds his mother was able to muster, and with no suitably well-
dowered bride in sight, Castiglione decided to exchange a vast portion of his
family estate for a more lucrative one in Bologna belonging to his friend Sig.
Ercole Bentivoglio. The proposed exchange, he excitedly informed his aghast
mother, would bring him possessions "worth 700 gold ducats a year, and include
payments from tolls and other sources which do not vary in time of plenty or
scarcity" (207); he begged her to show Bentivoglio's servant their Mantuan estate,
but to keep the whole affair a secret. When Bentivoglio died suddenly a few weeks
later, however, the deal fell through, and Castiglione's situation approached desperation. He sold several horses, pledged the family jewels, and was even com-
pelled to pawn the gold collar and pendant given to him by the king of England.
Anxious to redeem this precious gift, however (his trip to the English court being
perhaps the most important mission of his early career), and at his wit's end, he
sent his mother the ornate mantle he had worn for the occasion, asking her to
have all its gold ornaments melted down and sold (210). Still unable to pay off his
debts, he was obliged to relinquish all hope of executing a project that he had long
planned with his mother, that of building a monument to his dead father in the
family chapel at S. Agnese at Mantua. Castiglione vowed to erect an "honorable
memorial . . . if only, please God, the stars change their contrary courses" (211),
a wish that would not be fulfilled, however, until after his own death, when a
monument was finally erected at S. Agnese by Madonna Luigia herself. As he fell
deeper into debt, Castiglione was evidently willing to sacrifice any symbolic capital he could muster to maintain his "ideal" courtly identity.

23. Rebhorn argues that the gender politics of the Urbino court represents a
redoubled humiliation to the courtier's masculinity, in that he must participate in
effeminizing games that limit his "range of emotional . . . and intellectual expression," reducing his statesmanship to mere metaphors, and because he does "not
control the very discussions [he is] nevertheless expected to carry on" (130). Gasparo and "his fellows," Rebhorn maintains, "understandably feel on the defensive" and "bridle at" female rule. If they "tolerate" this "inversion," he maintains, they nevertheless "clearly feel frustration and resentment because of it and
express their feelings in the aggressive attacks they make on women generally . . .

they seek to destroy the thrones from which Emilia Pia and the duchess rule over them with absolute, and even arbitrary, tyrannical authority. . . . Smoldering with frustration, they inevitably and repeatedly blaze up, expressing their antagonism in antifeminist gibes and provocative debates" (128). One might question whether Rebhorn's assumption that misogyny is "understandable" or irreducible serves merely to screen the critic's own frustration with the "effeminacy" of the text's politesse. Does the revelation of a primary "masculine protest" underlying the courtier's "effeminacy" serve merely to ward off the specter of an effeminizing interpretation that might threaten the critic's own "sense of identity" (131)?

24. In his essay "A Child Is Being Beaten," Freud faults Adler's theory of the "masculine protest" precisely for assuming the primacy (in both sexes) of a "struggle toward the masculine line of development, from which gratification can alone be derived" (129). In his analysis of the fantasy/construction "a child is being beaten" as it occurs in boys, Freud maintains that the boy's position in the fantasy is, from beginning to end, *passive*, originating in an "inverted" Oedipus attitude, in which the father is taken as love object. The original fantasy, "I am loved/beaten by my father," is later remodeled into "I am being beaten by my (phallic) mother," in an attempt to evade its homosexual content. In the final form of the fantasy, far from identifying with the active role of the aggressor, the boy thus maintains a passive or "feminine" position. Cf. Sigmund Freud, *Sexuality and the Psychology of Love*, trans. Philip Rieff (New York: Collier Books, 1963).

25. See "'Che Vuoi?'" in Žižek, *The Sublime Object*.

26. "The humanists were self-proclaimed purists who referred to the end product of their philological work . . . as *castigationes*. Made up of two components, *castum agere*, 'to make chaste,' the compound term *castigatio* charged the atmosphere in which philological work was performed with an emotional and moral intensity. The correcting of the ancient texts became somewhat of a moral and political crusade to remove the signs of their depravity, violation, corruption, contamination, etc. and to transmit a faithful, chaste, untouched textual tradition to posterity. . . . The 'integrity' of Florence's political position depended on the philologists' vindication of this integrity in the practice of castigating texts. And the philologists' identification with Brutus' castigating behavior [after the rape of Lucretia] was at the foundation of the Florentines' political claim to be free of the passions and contamination of tyranny. Yet, each castigation produced a further contamination, leaving the traces of the humanists' own hands on the textual legacy of Republican Rome" (32). Stephanie H. Jed, *Chaste Thinking: The Rape of Lucretia and the Birth of Humanism* (Bloomington and Indianapolis: Indiana University Press, 1989).

THE FEMALE MASQUERADE

ARIOSTO AND THE GAME OF DESIRE

VALERIA FINUCCI

> Si vous étiez pris dans le rêve de l'autre, vous étiez foutu.
> Gilles Deleuze

INSTANCES of gender instability and sexual unruliness can be found in most Renaissance works. In *Orlando furioso* (1532), Ludovico Ariosto runs the gamut: he creates cross-dressed characters, makes women opt for ambiguous sexual choices, and has men adapt to same-sex sexual requests. Bradamante, for example, roams the woods dressed as a knight-at-arms, Fiordispina seems to long for other women, Adonio revises his sexual habits for the sake of money, and Ricciardetto coyly plays a woman for the purpose of being taken, literally, for a man. These transgressions titillate, however, rather than scandalize: whether a woman dresses as a man or a man dresses as a woman, whether men are kept as slaves to women in Laiazzo (Canto 20) or women relegated outside the city in Marganorre's reign of men (Canto 37), gender categories seem only temporarily subverted, for the logic of each story moves unflinchingly along heterosexual lines. Therefore, although Ariosto creates characters whose masculinity or femininity is at times unstable, the concept of what constitutes correct sexuality appears quite stable throughout his work.[1]

In this essay, I focus on a previously unstudied aspect of gender fluidity in *Orlando furioso*: the female masquerade. My aim is to show what it means for women to masquerade as women by retracing moments in the Ariostan narrative in which women's masquerade has been psychologically gratifying or physically empowering, regardless of rewards or punishments. I concentrate first on two scenes in which the female characters involved—Dalinda and Gabrina—though dressed according to the codes of their gender, if not of their class, seem not to embody femininity but to masquerade it. What is the purpose of their masquerade without masks? Does it have a defensive or an aggressive reason? Does it further self-knowledge or problematize their female identity? Dalinda's masquerade as a princess appears hardly subversive; her aim is not to pursue sexual license or to confuse gender roles. On the contrary, Dalinda conservatively emphasizes woman's position vis-à-vis man's desire, for she masquerades in order to be desired. And yet, at a closer look, her passive masquerade foregrounds a power game of exhilarating proportions. Unlike Dalinda's, old Gabrina's masquerade as a young woman awakens no desire. Deceptive-looking clothes do not make Gabrina more feminized or masculinized; rather, they show that femininity is a construct and therefore that the female masquerade does not work when there is no femininity to play on, when men, in short, refuse to be caught in the game. Generational gaps cannot ultimately be bridged by clothes, and Gabrina will be the subject of utter ridicule.

But what if the masquerade is not a masochistic act or a cosmetic opportunity for women, but rather a delightful, self-indulging narcissistic choice? Such is the case of Alcina, who plays on femininity so well that men are unable to recognize her posture of femme fatale as a mask. No matter: retribution comes from above when the author cruelly chastens his enchantress for her surreptitious appropriation of men's power. There is, therefore, only one way out of the masquerade of femininity in the *Furioso*, it seems, one that the woman warrior Marfisa, my brief fourth example, seems to understand so well. Marfisa realizes that the female masquerade is just another heterosexual game, a game, moreover, that works only when men allow. In this sense, she behaves more subversively than the enchantress Alcina, for Alcina remains well within her gender when physically enticing her male visitors, while Marfisa transcends it by refusing to play up her femininity for men. The cost of her choice, however, is to be characterized throughout as unfeminine: in the economy of the text, not to play the woman means not to be one; not to enter the circuit of male desire amounts to remaining forever excluded from desire.

The female masquerade involves no cross-dressing: women wear feminine clothes and display outward signs of femininity; they do not blur gender lines by impersonating people of either sex or by playacting; they do not choose to enter the masquerade state as a way of protecting themselves or of putting aside constraints. In fact, as I emphasize in the theoretical history of the masquerade that I retrace in the next section, women are often perceived as masquerading femininity even when they seem to do absolutely nothing. The female masquerade ought to subvert very little therefore; at the most it should challenge class distinctions, when the dress chosen is above or below one's status, but not gender distinctions. A woman overly ornamented could be accused of having too little taste or too much ambition, or of embellishing herself in too original and unruly ways, but her transgression could still be considered inconsequential: after all, she is dressed as a woman.

During the Renaissance (and for a couple of centuries after), sumptuary laws often prescribed sartorial codes appropriate for both gender and

class; in the sixteenth century, for example, more than two hundred
pieces of sumptuary legislation were promulgated. Italian cities were particularly conscientious in the matter of dress and enacted more statutes
than any other European municipality.[2] The laws covered all possible
aspects of female clothing from quality, size, color, and shape of the material to the number and size of buttons, length of trains, width of sleeves,
depth of décolletage, variety of headdress, use of veils, amount of fur or
velvet permitted, rental cost of jewels and brooches, height of heels, and
design of slippers. Rosita Levi Pisetzki cites the example of a Pistoia statute (1332) that painstakingly enumerated the ornaments that women
should not put on their clothes or in their hair, such as gold, silver,
enamel, pearl, precious stone, glass, mother-of-pearl, coral, crystal, and
amber.[3] An Orvieto statute (1581), James Brundage writes, specified
"that the neckline of a woman's dress must not descend more than two
fingers' breadth below the suprasternal notch on the chest, and the same
distance in back."[4] On occasion, Diane Hughes remarks, legislators even
stipulated that fingers had to be placed horizontally rather than vertically
in measuring the correct distance from the collarbone.[5] The fashion for
plunging necklines caused a sumptuary frenzy, often justified on the
grounds that these laws were intended not to muzzle women's freedom
but to curb immoral extravagance. The Church concurred. Occasionally
it even excommunicated the guilty party, although dispensations were
not difficult to obtain.

Sumptuary laws were addressed to all women, no matter their status
("cuiuscumque status et conditionis"), and occasionally even to men.
Their aim was not so much to regulate clothing, however, as to regulate
class behavior. In rich cities like Venice, in which merchants had money
but by law could not break into the ruling oligarchy, transgressions became commonplace since the fines were nominal and men winked at
women's defiance of the law.[6] After all, public display of their female
kin's wardrobe was public display of their own wealth. The cultural historian Pompeo Molmenti even suggests that these paternalistic statutes
were enacted to be transgressed, often by the very lawmakers who passed
them,[7] because what was politically necessary to legislate for the sake of
high moral standards was also socially useless: rich clothes were used by
both women and men to reflect a highly respected current position or a
not-so-hidden aspiration for a better one. One reason for the leniency of
the law was that there were no real advantages for women in overempha-
sizing or in manipulating their womanliness to the point of ridicule. Femininity was thought to come naturally to them; it was not socially empowering and therefore had little strategic use. That there was no danger in
letting women enjoy it was even argued in an astute oration addressed to
Cardinal Bessarion by Nicolosa Sanuti in Bologna. Women, she said, are

now forbidden to enter the priesthood, the law, or the military, although in earlier ages they have proved themselves capable of heroic deeds. Their only area of creativity and expertise has remained clothing. Sumptuary laws have therefore no business legislating this part of their lives: "Ornament and apparel, because they are our insigna of worth, we cannot suffer to be taken from us."[8]

While women who violated restrictions on feminine apparel seldom suffered, those who cross-dressed were harshly punished.[9] A woman dressed as a man was always perceived as dangerous, in part, no doubt, because she was seen as assuming, through a newly invented self, some of the privileges associated with men.[10] As Gasparo Pallavicino earnestly argues in Baldassarre Castiglione's *Il libro del cortegiano* (*The Book of the Courtier*), following Aristotelian explanations of sexual difference, it is common knowledge that all women aspire to be men for the sake of achieving perfection: "Universalmente ogni donna desidera esser omo, per un certo istinto di natura, che le insegna la sua perfezione" ("without exception every woman wants to be a man, by reason of a certain instinct that teaches her to desire her own perfection").[11]

Yet the female masquerade, I claim, even if seemingly a tame form of rebellion, is more dangerous than female transvestism because to dress within one's gender but above one's station in a culture that rests on class differences, or to manipulate at will men's sexual responses, can only be subversive. Unlike transvestism, which abandons or questions a given gender identity, the female masquerade, I argue, casts doubt on something even more fundamental in culture, the concept of femininity itself. Thanks to the masquerade, femininity becomes a mask that can be put on without inverting expectations of biological attributes; this in turn changes, or at least problematizes, the rules of gender. If femininity can no longer be understood as an innate characteristic of women—a view philosophers have loved to reiterate—and is just a cultural given, then what is the basis of masculinity?

Before entering the convolutions of the Ariostan narrative and reading the twists and turns of desire that structure it, I would like to review some critical thinking on the female masquerade. In a case study titled "Womanliness as Masquerade" (1929), later appropriated and revised by Lacan in "The Meaning of the Phallus" (1958), Joan Rivière single-handedly gives the term "female masquerade" a new currency.[12] Rivière describes the case of a powerful woman who on occasion felt ill at ease with her career achievements and feared men's reprobation. To counter these feelings, she decided to emphasize her femininity rather than hide it, since she thought that what was making men uneasy was her "masculine" behavior. Rivière asks who the real woman was—the more feminine or the more masculine one, the coy one or the professional—and concludes that there is no femininity per se, that womanliness itself is a masquerade. Women may put on the mask of femininity, she writes, either to hide an inner masculinity or because the masquerade is part of their inner self, a mode of being. Either choice is the result of social conditioning, although there is a chance that the mask of femininity may also be empowering for women, "a primary mode of enjoyment" (38), as Rivière puts it, because it allows them to keep male-identified desires and compete in a masculine world. The process seems theatrical: femininity is put on, and masculinity can only be stolen. In the final analysis, there is no woman behind the mask and, of course, there never was a man.

The constructedness of femininity is not, of course, a new concept. In "New Introductory Lectures on Psychoanalysis" (1933), Freud insisted that there is no femininity per se, but only one libido, the masculine, and that femininity could be disturbed at any time by the resurgence in women of masculine traits belonging to a previous period of development.[13] Earlier, Nietzsche had postulated even greater female artifice vis-à-vis sexual gratification: women, he wrote, "'give themselves,' even when they—give themselves. The female is so artistic."[14] By emphasizing that women construct a representable self even at the moment of sexual climax, Nietzsche places woman on the stage, always performing femininity.[15]

For Lacan masculine and feminine subjectivities are not fixed but are produced by social negotiations; the subject takes a specific place along the gender division at the moment of the encounter with the Law. The masculine subject constitutes himself by confronting the incest taboo and the paternal law—the Phallus—which installs the primary repression. The process requires that he "mortgage" his penis in order to assure himself access to the symbolic order. The feminine subject is produced through another, more diffuse alignment, this time with lack. Like the boy, the girl accepts castration. Unlike the boy, however, she can obtain only vicarious entrance into phallic power when she associates with the father. In the Lacanian system, woman is the phallus and man has the phallus; that is, woman is the object of desire and man is the subject—a subject, however, who depends on the object to reflect his "I," and thus to endorse it. Being the phallus, Lacan adds, means that woman is associated with the masquerade: "It is in order to be the phallus, that is to say the signifier of the desire of the *Other*, that the woman will reject an essential part of her femininity, notably all its attributes through masquerade. It is for what she is not that she expects to be desired as well as loved."[16] For Lacan, the female masquerade does not mask femininity, because there is no innate femininity; indeed, the mask works to confirm that femininity is a construct. Thus he places it in the symbolic ("Masquerade . . . is precisely to play not at the imaginary, but at the symbolic level").[17] Once again the production of femininity depends on concepts of masculinity. No wonder that Michèle Montrelay concludes that women put on the masquerade of femininity precisely to hide themselves, to cover what they lack. "The objective of the masquerade is to say nothing," she writes, "absolutely *nothing*. And in order to produce this nothing the woman uses her own body as a disguise."[18]

Luce Irigaray understands the female masquerade as something women do for men, something that in turn makes a tabula rasa of their own desire. The masquerade cancels woman's subjectivity: "The woman loses herself, and loses herself by playing on her femininity."[19] But Irigaray also stresses another, more empowering view of the masquerade. Through an overdone, flashy femininity, she writes, woman may call into question the regime of voyeurism and fetishism that structures the look.[20] By assuming an unnatural, flaunted facade, she can disrupt male notions of what she is like and show femininity to be what she knows it to be: a construct. "One must assume the feminine role deliberately," Irigaray emphasizes, "which means already to convert a form of subordination into an affirmation, and thus to begin to thwart it. . . . To play with mimesis is thus, for a woman, to try to recover the place of her exploitation by discourse, without allowing herself to be simply reduced to it. . . . To make 'visible,' by an effect of playful repetition, what was supposed to remain invisible: the cover-up of a possible operation of the feminine in language" (76). Irigaray calls this ostentatious femininity *mimicry*.

In "Film and the Masquerade," Mary Ann Doane sees the female masquerade not as a way of defining femininity (as do Rivière, Lacan, Montrelay, and in a sense Irigaray) but as an act of resistance, the creation of "a lack in the form of a certain distance between oneself and one's image" that works to confound the male-posited structure of the look.[21] In this sense, the female masquerade is an analogue to male fetishism: it too disowns what has been seen and thus permits the objectivity necessary for an ironic second reading. Doane's concept of masquerade allows woman to distance herself from the theorized image of woman as closeness and presence and can be useful in opening up a space, as she points out in a subsequent essay, for "reading femininity differently."[22] Sue-Ellen Case, however, criticizes Doane for offering female viewers only passive roles of identification and for presupposing a heterosexual context for the masquerade. How, she asks, can the taking up of the phallus, which, as we know, requires woman to masquerade as feminine, be played in a same-sex context? In a butch/femme world, the female masquerade is done not to compensate men but to reveal the femme as the active performer, the subject of the representation.[23]

As this excursus makes clear, defining the female masquerade is no simple or single matter. The masquerade has been seen as femininity itself and as a way to act out femininity without destabilizing concepts of masculinity. It has been seen as the representation of a feminine desire that can be illustrated only through the mask and as the denial of the authenticity of this desire in order to align femininity with the law and homosocial privileges. It has been considered a display of femininity for the sake of denying bisexuality and a performance of femininity done to affirm homosexuality. In other words, the female masquerade has been categorized as both utterly dangerous and utterly repressive. I now turn to Ariosto's female characters to see what their masquerade tells us.

.   .   .   .   .

Dalinda is a young and beautiful maid at the court of the Scottish princess Ginevra. She loves Polinesso, Duke of Albany, who sometimes visits her at night in one of Ginevra's bedrooms. Given their different social classes, there can be no marriage between the two; in fact, one day Polinesso even begs Dalinda to help him win Ginevra. He wants to ask the princess's hand in a marriage of convenience and has good reasons to believe that the king would not brush aside his request. He also assures Dalinda that he is in love with her and cares little for the other woman. Dalinda accepts the task, but Ginevra refuses even to hear of Polinesso's suit, for she has already given her heart to a young Italian knight, Ariodante. Soon Polinesso asks Dalinda for a different form of aid: he would like to make love to her while she dresses in Ginevra's clothes and imitates her hairstyle, so as to possess the princess in fantasy and thus rid himself of his obsession with her. The text is ambiguous at this point: Polinesso may be in love with Ginevra, or this request may simply be a plan to ruin her reputation and destroy Ariodante's love for her. No matter: for possession by proxy to be thoroughly empowering, Polinesso has to share it; he therefore boasts to Ariodante that he enjoys Ginevra's sexual favors and can prove it. One night, having arranged for the Italian knight to watch the unfolding of his bravado, he climbs up a rope to Ginevra's balcony, and there Dalinda—dressed in her mistress's clothes, but unaware of the ruse—receives him.

Having seen too much ("perc'ho troppo veduto"; 5, 58), Ariodante decides to drown himself but then changes his mind and swims to safety.[24] Meanwhile his brother Lurcanio defames Ginevra publicly, leaving the king no choice but to apply the cruel law of Scotland ("l'aspra legge di Scozia"; 4, 59): if a maiden is accused of fornication, a knight must come to joust for her reputation within a month or she will be

burned at the stake. Eventually matters are resolved to everybody's satisfaction: the Christian knight Rinaldo claims that the law is unjust for
women, since it does not apply to men, and says that he will defend
Ginevra whether or not she is still a virgin.[25] He thus saves Dalinda from
being murdered by Polinesso's hired men and proceeds to unmask Polinesso's plot. Polinesso is killed in combat, and Ariodante, who himself
is in the process of taking up the challenge of defending the princess's
honor against his own brother, is finally granted his beloved's hand. Wearied by the events, Dalinda retires to a convent in Denmark.[26]

The story of Dalinda has been read as problematic because it seems
utterly masochistic. Attilio Momigliano faults Dalinda's psychological
characterization precisely because her self-negation is too farfetched and
compares it to that of patient Griselda in Boccaccio.[27] Luigi Rajna is no
less scandalized at the ease with which Dalinda seems to agree to her own
victimization and argues that no woman should ever be represented as
having so little sense of self as to consent to the request made by Polinesso.[28] To be sure, Dalinda appears to reflect perfectly the famous Lacanian statement that desire is always desire of the Other. The desiring
subject, Lacan writes, wishes to embody the Other's desire and be what
the Other desires. But in Dalinda, this desire to be desired soon takes a
masochistic twist, because she realizes, to her dismay, that the desire of
the Other is not for her but for another person. In other words, through
Polinesso's request, Dalinda understands that she is either undesired or
desired only as long as her relationship to him is a triangular one in which
she obliterates her own (unloved) self by impersonating the third (loved)
person in the triangle. Dalinda of course is in a state of total mental abjection and deludes herself that a rendezvous as a disguised Other with her
ambiguous lover is unimportant. Ariosto portrays her as sadly aware of
her status of self-loss and self-separation ("Io che divisa e sevra / e lungi
era da me" ["I, being quite divorced from my true self"]; 5, 26), but unable to escape being victimized because, as she herself puts it, she feels too
much love: "Vedi s'in me venuto era arrogante, / s'imperio nel mio cor
s'aveva assunto" ("Judge you how he lorded it over me and ruled in my
heart"; 5, 12). In Lacanian terms, Dalinda is the hysteric who chooses to
suffer for the sake of the Other's desire. Her agency gone, she finds satisfaction in Polinesso's satisfaction and sees her own needs as unimportant
or impossible to fulfill: "Io, ch'era tutta a satisfargli intenta, / né seppi o
volsi contradirgli mai, / e sol quei giorni io mi vidi contenta, / ch'averlo
compiaciuto mi trovai" ("Now to please him was all my care; I could not
have found it in me to thwart him; those were days when I was only
happy if I had earned his favour"; 5, 15). True, there is some power in
martyrdom, and Dalinda may have justified to herself this masochistic
course of action as a means of persuading Polinesso to appreciate her

acquiescence to the assignation. Essentially, however, this posture requires the cancellation of her ego. The masquerade created to gain access to man's desire in effect makes woman renounce her own desire. Dalinda's masquerade brings to mind Nietzsche's remark that women are always and everywhere acting: they give themselves even when sexually giving themselves.

There is, however, a different reading of Dalinda's masquerade that I would like to offer, one that can be seen, in a sense, as self-empowering. Dalinda masquerades as Ginevra, I argue, not simply to accede to Polinesso's request, but because she herself does not mind assuming her mistress's identity, jumping class and rank at the same time. In other words, I set aside for a while man's customary centrality in any discourse of female desire and give the story back to woman. Since Ginevra is Dalinda's ideal ego-image, the impersonation of the other should fulfill in Dalinda, I think, some of her unconscious desires.

Ginevra has all the qualities that make a woman desirable: she is beautiful, rich, and a paragon of chastity ("di vera pudicizia é un paragone"; 4, 62). Moreover, she is wooed by two rivals ("grandi amici erano stati inante / che per Ginevra si fesson rivali" ["the two had been good friends before Guinevere made them rivals"]; 5, 27). Dalinda, on the other hand, although beautiful, is neither rich nor chaste, and most probably not even loved: "Io non compresi / ch'egli fingeva molto, e amava poco; / ancor che li suo' inganni discoperti / esser doveanmi a mille segni certi" ("so blinded was I that I little realized how much he feigned, how little he loved, for all that his deceit should have been plain to me from a thousand obvious signs"; 5, 11). Thus, identification with an ego-ideal through clothing can suddenly gratify in Dalinda three purposes at once: first, it can make her idealize her own self by seeing an admired Ginevra in the unloved maiden she is; second, it can eliminate her rival in Polinesso's heart through the act of doubling/substituting for her; and third, it can give her the chance to move from chambermaid to princess and be praised for it.

This identification is available to Dalinda at the level of fantasy. Fantasies, Freud writes, "vary according to the sex, character and circumstances of the person who is having the phantasy; but they fall naturally into two main groups. They are either ambitious wishes, which serve to elevate the subject's personality; or they are erotic ones. . . . They are often united."[29] In the case of Dalinda they are indeed united: a fantasy of seduction allows her to position herself as a superior woman, a phallic mother figure. According to Laplanche and Pontalis, the subject can play different roles in fantasy, since all desires have to be repressed.[30] Dalinda does not need to identify with a specific position or to align with one gender; she can assume both a masculine and a feminine position at will. She—a maid—can identify with Polinesso and possess, through him, a superior, loved woman.[31] She can identify with Ginevra and through her forget that she is unloved and a simple servant. In fact, Dalinda has already impersonated Ginevra prior to Polinesso's request by making love in her most secret room, "quella / che piú secreta avea Ginevra bella; //dove tenea le cose piú care, / e dove le piú volte ella dormia" ("in the most secret of fair Guinevere's rooms: / the one in which she kept her most precious possessions and where she most often slept"; 5, 8–9). This impersonation also translates into her desiring what Polinesso desires, true to the Girardian logic of mimetic desire.[32] Either identificatory position in any case is narcissistic and requires a posture of fetishistic disavowal ("I know, I am not Ginevra, but . . .").[33] I would agree here with Borch-Jacobsen that identification can come before desire and that this desire is in nature antagonistic (47).

But how can Dalinda desire what she can only wish were not true? How can she—the victim—desire to be further victimized? In other words, how can one read her masochistic position as fulfilling a narcissistic desire? In the famous dream of the beautiful butcher's wife, Freud analyzes the dream of a hysteric apparently desiring what she does not want: to give a supper party.[34] At the same time, the wife wishes to fulfill several other desires, such as her own desire for caviar sandwiches, her favorite snack, or her friend's desire for smoked salmon, which in the past her friend usually denied herself. The wife believes that her husband likes her friend, although she is thin and he prefers plump women. Freud speculates that the wife is identifying with her female friend; her inviting the woman to a dinner party would mean that she would be contributing to rendering the other plump, which in turn would make her own husband more attracted to her. By denying her own wish to have a party, the butcher's wife guarantees a hidden wish: to eliminate the rival as object of attention for her husband. As Freud writes, "My patient put herself in the friend's place in the dream because her friend was taking my patient's place with her husband and because she (my patient) wanted to take her friend's place in her husband's high opinion." Thus, "the non-fulfillment of one wish meant the fulfillment of another" (150–51).

For Freud, the wife's identification follows an Oedipal trajectory: she identifies with her same-sex rival and takes the person of the other sex as a love object. The relationship between herself and the woman friend is therefore a straight one of jealousy/rivalry. Parveen Adams, however, argues that there is an oscillation in identification on the part of the hysteric. She notices that Freud does not suggest any identification of the woman with her husband, because he would then need to posit identification along nonheterosexual lines.[35] And yet not only does the wife identify with her friend by denying both herself and her female friend a wish—a posture doubling that of the other woman, who also denies her own wish—but she identifies with her husband as well, for the same reasons. The butcher too denies himself a wish—he had expressed a desire to diet—and, in turn, has a wish denied, that of having plump women around (his wife had asked him previously not to give her sandwiches so that she would not become plumper).

In "The Direction of the Treatment," Lacan returns to the issue of identification.[36] He finds the same blind spot in Freud's theorization that Adams was later to criticize. Likewise, he argues that the wife identifies not only with her friend but also with her husband in the sense that she identifies with his desire (for her friend). As Catherine Clément puts it, "The question, 'How can another woman be loved?' . . . becomes the butcher's wife's question. . . . In order to answer it, she places herself in the masculine position and desires the other woman as her husband does."[37] But Lacan also posits a third identification: the wife's desire for the other's desire causes her to identify with the signifier of desire itself, the phallus of our story, the salmon.[38] It is at the point at which she desires not the other, but what the other desires, that the butcher's wife becomes a subject.[39]

In our case in the *Furioso*, by identifying with Ginevra, what wish could Dalinda refuse to fulfill that in turn would guarantee the fulfillment of another, deeper wish of her own? What wish could she deny both herself and Ginevra in the act of mirroring her? In wishing to be Ginevra by wearing her clothes, Dalinda seems to deny herself the deeper wish of being loved, which she sees as utterly elusive: "vedi se deve, per amare assai, / donna sperar d'essere amata mai" ("Judge whether a woman who has loved greatly can hope to be loved in return"; 5, 72). But this wish to be Ginevra also paradoxically fulfills an opposite wish: not to be Ginevra. After all, Dalinda wants Polinesso to love her and not her mistress. But only by appearing to be Ginevra can she hope that Polinesso will stop desiring the other and start loving her. How can Dalinda wish to be like Ginevra, given their different social status? She can do it, I submit, by appearing to be her while not acknowledging her own subversion. As she emphasizes in telling her story, it is Polinesso's desire, not her own, that makes her embrace the masquerade: "pigli ogni vesta / ch'ella posta abbia, e tutta te ne vesta. // Come ella s'orna e come il crin dispone, / studia imitarla, e cerca il piú che sai / di parer dessa" ("I would have you take up every garment she has put off and clothe yourself in them. / Be careful to copy the way she adorns herself and wears her hair, and try to imitate her as closely as you can"; 5, 24–25). What desire does she share then with Ginevra? We know that Ginevra desires Ariodante and does not wish to be loved by Polinesso. In wanting to satisfy Ginevra's desire not to be desired by Polinesso, Dalinda literally embodies Ginevra's desire. Finally, by playing Ginevra for Polinesso's sake, Dalinda both gratifies his wish and denies its truthfulness. No substitution would suffice, in fact, if Polinesso were truly in love with Ginevra, but Dalinda seems convinced that he is only taken with her image, as he himself claims, so that her change of clothes can have a therapeutic value: through it, he will get rid of his obsession. In the end, a thoroughly masochistic masquerade becomes narcissistically gratifying, for Dalinda alone is able to satisfy everybody's fantasy—her own, Polinesso's, and Ginevra's—while denying unsavory wishes in herself and in the other two members of the triangle.

Of course, another fantasy is being satisfied through Dalinda's masquerade in this open-air stage ("rio spettacolo"; 5, 51), although only Polinesso is aware of it.[40] Unknown to Dalinda, Ariodante is watching from below, in the dark.[41] For Ariodante, who believes he is looking at Ginevra, this is first and foremost a scene of seduction, one that requires of him both a masochistic posture, if he sees himself supplanted by a rival male figure, and a narcissistic one, if he identifies with Polinesso's easy possession of a woman cast as sexually unattainable. What he sees, moreover, is a primal scene in which Ginevra, the unavailable woman/mother, is seen loved (possessed) by a man, a father figure of wealth and power. Unfortunately, Ariodante's gaze once again cancels Dalinda's "I," for subjectivity depends on the gaze of the other, and the subject is not Dalinda here, but once again an illusory signifier, the ever-present/absent Ginevra.

The Dalinda story shows that only through the masquerade of femininity and the impersonation of a desire not their own can women at times become objects of desire and reshape themselves as subjects. Only through the masquerade, moreover, can Dalinda entertain a desire of her own, that of being for a moment like a princess, and once again empower herself. But these strategies may be perceived as dangerous, for they show how shrewdly women appropriate signifiers of femininity and play them according to their own needs. By dressing as Ginevra, Dalinda does not simply defy sumptuary laws aimed at curbing personal *arrivisme*; she also, and more alarmingly, foregrounds the masquerade in terms of both class and gender and reveals the instability of either category. Each can be manipulated with imagination and cleverness because each is a cultural construct. To paraphrase Simone de Beauvoir, one is not born a woman or noble, but one becomes both. This can hardly sit well in a society energetically engaged in naturalizing gender and legislating class rigidity.[42]

Ariosto's elimination of Dalinda by making her leave Scotland thus comes as no surprise. Having created for Dalinda a self (Ginevra's) for an Other (Polinesso), he has no problems in creating yet another self, once again that of an abject: he makes Dalinda retire to a convent in the never-never land of Denmark ("per voto, e perché molto sazia / era del mondo, a Dio volse la mente: / monaca s'andó a rendere fin in Dazia, / e si levó di Scozia immantinente" ["sickened of living in the world, she turned her thoughts to God and paid her vows to Him; and, leaving Scotland without more ado, she went away to become a nun in Denmark"]; 6, 16). In the end, Dalinda survives only through a further masquerade: having once more embraced a desire that is not her own (not to be desired) in order to deny a desire of her own (to be desired/loved), she reverts to silence and refuses the symbolic altogether.

. . . . .

Gabrina is the oldest woman in the *Furioso* and, by all accounts, the most perfidious. Ariosto lacks no negative epithets to characterize her: she is an evil old woman (20, 142), treacherous (21, 12), damnable (21, 13), malignant (21, 47), and odious (21, 66). To be sure, Gabrina has behaved wickedly throughout her life, and her amorality is amply rendered in Canto 21; in this sense, her physical characterization as an old hag only reflects her moral outlook. Still, nowhere in the *Furioso* does Ariosto offer a positive image of older womanhood. Bradamante's mother, the only living mother in this romance epic, is narrow-minded and petty, and Teodora, Leone's aunt, is called a vicious old woman ("l'iniqua vecchia"; 45, 41). In his inability to characterize the aged female body in positive terms Ariosto is hardly alone. Church fathers from Saint Chrysostom to Saint Ambrose have seen decrepitude as a sign of sin and have described older men as a curse of nature. Roman writers such as Seneca and Juvenal have not been much kinder.[43] Old age was also treated punitively in the French fabliaux, as in Villon's portrait of the once beautiful seller of helmets ("belle heaulmière"), whose thighs are compared to sausages. The Renaissance worship of youth and emphasis on classical thought translated at times into attacks on old men as pedantic, lecherous, and avaricious. Women usually appeared in parodic poetry cast as old hags and witches, like Gabrina. Giovanni Pozzi argues that until the end of the sixteenth century female ugliness and female decrepitude went hand in hand; only after Tasso are there examples of ugliness associated with younger women.[44]

My concern here is not with Gabrina's maliciousness but with the reasons she causes laughter. Specifically, I concentrate on the two occasions in Canto 20 in which she encounters utter ridicule. In this canto, Gabrina is escorted by the woman warrior Marfisa, who successfully masquerades as a knight throughout the book. The pair first meet Pinabello and his companion, a lady described as beautiful but haughty and unfriendly (20, 110). No sooner does this lady see Gabrina than she starts laughing at her ugliness: "E sí come vezzosa era e mal usa, / quando vide la vecchia di

Marfisa, / non si poté tenere a bocca chiusa / di non la motteggiar con beffe e risa" ("Being ill-mannered and pert, the moment she saw Marfisa's old woman she could not refrain from laughing and jeering at her"; 20, 113). Marfisa refuses to be subjected to this outrage and claims that her lady is better-looking than the laughing one and she is determined to prove her point. Following courtly rules of engagement, she asks Pinabello for an armed encounter, the price for his defeat being his companion's clothes and palfrey. Thus, when Marfisa routs the knight, Gabrina acquires a new, more youthful wardrobe ("di quel giovenile abito volse / che si vestisse e se n'ornasse tutta" ["bidding the crone dress up in the youthful attire and all the trinkets"]; 20, 116).[45]

Four days later the two women encounter Zerbino. He too, although in a bad mood as a result of previous mishaps, cannot stop laughing at the spectacle of the old woman in her maidenly outfit. He teases Marfisa, whom he takes for a man, for escorting somebody for whose company, given her senile appearance, a knight could hardly be envied. Marfisa declares him uncourteous and her own lady beautiful. She adds that every knight would naturally try to conquer Gabrina and that Zerbino too should conform to this chivalric rule by engaging her, Gabrina's only escort, in combat: "Non vo' patir ch'un sí leggiadro aspetto / abbi veduto, e guadagnar nol tenti" ("It is intolerable that you should set eyes on so pretty a woman and yet not seek to win her"; 20, 124). If he wins, Marfisa tells him, he will gain Gabrina.[46] Zerbino tries to refuse this call to arms, since there is no pleasure in winning what is undesired, but he too is a slave to chivalric codes. When he loses, he has no choice but to escort and defend Gabrina in the name of those same codes, although the task seems hard to undertake: "Ohimé, Fortuna fella / (dicea), che cambio é questo che tu fai? / Colei che fu sopra le belle bella, / ch'esser meco dovea, levata m'hai. / Ti par ch'in luogo ed in ristor di quella / si debba por costei ch'ora mi dai?" ("'Alas, grim Fortune!' he exclaimed, 'What sort of bargain is this? You have robbed me of a lady who was the fairest of the fair and who should have been mine. And you give me this woman—do you call that a fair replacement, an even exchange?'"; 20, 132). Like Polinesso, who was saddled with a woman he did not really desire but who was available while seemingly obsessed with one he desired but found utterly unapproachable, Zerbino experiences here the incongruity of having to protect somebody he does not want while being unable to do anything for the one in his heart, Isabella.

No sooner does Gabrina exchange escorts than she takes vengeance on Zerbino for his lukewarm attitude toward her by answering his question about who defeated him ("Fa ch'io lo conosca"; 20, 129) with a cutting remark: the winner was a damsel ("Il colpo fu di man d'una donzella, / che t'ha fatto votar (disse) la sella" ["The blow which pitched you out of your saddle was delivered by a damsel"]; 20, 129). Her words recall an almost identical incident in Canto 1 in which a stunned Sacripante, disturbed while getting ready to rape Angelica, asks a messenger the identity of the knight who put a quick end to his anticipated entertainment by unhorsing him: "fa che per nome io lo conosca" ("tell me his name"; 1, 69). The messenger answers that the knight was a woman: "tu dei saper che ti levó di sella / l'alto valor d'una gentil donzella" ("You must know that the rare valour which swept you from the saddle was that of a gentle damsel"; 1, 69). Momigliano notices the connection between Angelica and Gabrina and the utter discrepancy between the two women's characterizations. One is overly pursued for her beauty, and the other cannot find a protector because of her ugliness; one functions as the ultimate object of desire, and the other causes no rivalries; one attracts awe, and the other attracts ridicule ("beffa della malvagità e bruttezza," as he puts it, 191). Gabrina is so ugly, according to the critic Julius Molinaro, that she is hanged for it; Odorico, he tells us, was "unable to endure the proximity of so ugly a woman." And he had been in her company for just a day![47]

Marfisa has no luck when she recurs to the logic of mimetic desire to prod Zerbino into a joust, for at first he refuses her challenge: "io per me non son cosí indiscreto, / che te ne privi mai; stanne pur lieto" ("I for one would not be so indiscreet as ever to wrest her from you: enjoy her company!"; 20, 122). Mimetic desire is characteristic of a good number of quests in the *Furioso*, such as those of Orlando, Rinaldo, and Sacripante; it causes macabre slaughters, such as Mandricardo's killing of Doralice's retinue in order to have her, and prompts demeaning stratagems, such as that of Polinesso. Eugenio Donato defines this type of quest as important in establishing a knight's difference from his peers. In this sense, it is not just that Angelica's beauty causes rivalries among knights, he writes; more important, rivalries are intrinsic to a knight's sense of self-definition.[48] That appeal does not work here: Zerbino has no desire to establish his difference from Marfisa or even his narcissistic sameness as a worthy knight.[49] He tells his opponent that the reason for not accepting her challenge is that he can see well and the task is not worth it: "per costei non mi tener sí cieco, / che solamente far voglia una giostra. / O brutta o bella sia, restisi teco: / non vo' partir tanta amicizia vostra" ("do not so bedazzle me with this woman as to want to fight on her account. Be she ugly or fair, keep her—I refuse to interfere in so fine a friendship"; 20, 123).

Like Dalinda then, Gabrina is not an object of desire. Rather, she is judged repulsive whether she is seen as an old woman or masquerades as a young one. She is ridiculed by both women and men for being either what she is (ugly and poor, as in the encounter with Pinabello's companion) or unlike what she is (dressed as a young damsel of means, as in the encounter with Zerbino). In the first case, Marfisa tries to remedy Gabrina's decrepitude by changing her outward aspect; in the second, by claiming that she should be envied for escorting Gabrina, since Gabrina is a woman and thus automatically an object of desire for men. In the first instance, the ridicule is of a woman by another woman; in the second, it is of a man through another (supposed) man in that Zerbino cannot understand why this knight has undertaken to protect a woman so evidently in no need of protection. Thus, in the first instance, Gabrina is laughed at because her ugliness does not sit well with a lady who regards herself as a paragon of beauty, and in the second, because her ugliness calls into question the chivalric principles of the knight escorting her. On the one hand, women laugh at her because her womanliness appears nonexistent, and thus its lack paradoxically challenges the parameters by which they are accustomed to defining their worth in society; on the other hand, men laugh at her, and at her knight, because both pretend that beauty is a natural attribute of femininity independent of age, and thus that any woman can function as an object of desire and of exchange between men. In other words, an ugly and old Gabrina unsettles both women's and men's aesthetic notions and chivalric principles.

Gabrina represents what Bakhtin would characterize as the grotesque body, a body that "transgresses its own limits."[50] For Ariosto, Gabrina's ornamented and decrepit body resembles that of a monkey: "Avea la donna (se la crespa buccia / puó darne indicio) piú de la Sibilla, / e parea, cosí ornata, una bertuccia, / quando per muover riso alcun vestilla" ("The woman [if her horny hide was anything to judge by] was more ancient than the Sybil and, tricked out as she was, she resembled a monkey that has been dressed up for a joke"; 20, 120).[51] The fact that most of the criticism in this episode centers on Gabrina's outfit is in itself hardly surprising; discourses on ornamentation have often been associated closely with discourses on femininity. For centuries philosophers and moralists have argued that a woman au naturel is preferable to an ornamented beauty, for the one in need of props not only deceives men by showing a part of herself that does not exist but may also entice them to desire this constructed surface. Thus, Christian writers from Saint Paul to Tertullian to Jerome have preached against female ornamentation for the sake of eliminating male concupiscence.[52]

When an old woman chooses ornamentation, however, as in this case, we are led to think that she appears even more unnatural and undesirable and is a proper target for ridicule. Ariosto describes Gabrina in her new finery as even uglier than before: "quant'era piú ornata, era piú brutta" ("adornments only served to enhance her ugliness"; 20, 116). Gabrina is not woman-as-lie here, because she is never mistaken for what she is not; nor is she the Nietzschean old woman as truth, for she is throughout the book the paradigmatic figure of untruthfulness and untrustworthiness.[53] Her aged and grotesque face seems in fact to constitute an uncanny experience, in Freud's sense, since the uncanny is "undoubtedly related to what is frightening—to what arouses dread and horror."[54]

Female ugliness, then, is associated with incorrect femininity, whether the woman is too decrepit to seduce or uses props to appear seductive. A famous literary antecedent of this episode occurs in the *Divina Commedia*, in Dante's dreams of "una femmina balba, / ne li occhi guercia, e sovra i pié distorta, / con le man monche, e di colore scialba" ("a woman, stammering, with eyes asquint and crooked on her feet, with maimed hands, and of sallow hue"; *Purg.* 19, 7–9).[55] This stuttering hag tries to enchant the poet only to be revealed, in a swift sadistic move, for what she is: the clothes were laid bare in front "fendendo i drappi, e mostravami 'l ventre; / quel mi sveglió col puzzo che n'uscia" ("rending her garments and showing me her belly: this waked me with the stench that issued therefrom"; 19, 31–33). In a notorious letter to Luigi Guicciardini (1509), Niccolò Machiavelli describes a similar experience of revulsion at the sight of a woman so ugly that he almost drops dead ("Omé fú per cadere in terra morto"; 26).[56] This time the excretions are displaced from bottom to top, and he can only vomit over her when the stench coming from her toothless mouth overwhelms him.[57]

Ugliness in Gabrina causes not sexual revulsion but laughter. Ugliness is not in itself a cause for ridicule, because, as Aristotle and Cicero emphasized, one usually laughs at something incongruous in the object. Many Renaissance thinkers later embraced this view. For example, in his treatise *De Ridiculis*, Vincenzo Maggi affirms that the comic ensues only when ugliness is accompanied by *meraviglia*.[58] Castiglione categorically points out that it is in bad taste to laugh at physical deformities ("le deformità del volto o della persona"; 2, 50, 159). And yet he too, through his courtly spokesman Bibbiena, sarcastically teases a woman in the *Cortegiano* who chooses ornamentation in order to seduce. She fails in her purpose, however, he writes, for she appears "empiastrata tanto, che paia aversi posto alla faccia una maschera, e non osi ridere per non farsela crepare" ("so encrusted that she seems to be wearing a mask and who dare not laugh for fear of causing it to crack"; 1, 40, 82).[59]

As we have seen through this discussion, the masquerade does not cover masculinity in Gabrina (as it does in Rivière), it does not turn her into the signifier of the desire of the other (as in Lacan), it does not camouflage a desire to make herself into the image of desire of men (as in Irigaray), it does not hide femininity (as in Montrelay) or flaunt it (as in Doane); rather, it shows precisely that she is beyond femininity. Unlike Dalinda, who is able to appear as someone else to Ariodante, Gabrina fools no one. Masked or not, she is equally repulsive. In this sense, the masquerade works to unmask her, for whereas in the past she had men do what she wanted by wearing the mask of femininity as helplessness (she convinced her husband, Argeo, to kill Filandro by claiming that he raped her, and Filandro to kill her husband by claiming that a neighbor—who turned out to be Argeo—was going to rape her), now the masquerade prompts Zerbino to say that she needs no protection because there is no femininity worth protecting. Narrative ridicule also reestablishes narrative decorum. Since Marfisa's behavior toward Gabrina gives the impression that the old crone is a moral character, Zerbino's laugh aptly addresses their mismatch.

· · · · ·

Is there, then, in the *Furioso* the possibility of defining the female masquerade in more positive terms: masquerade, for example, as resistance in Doane's sense? As we have seen, Dalinda can express her desire and her eagerness for social advancement only through the mask and can embody femininity only by playing herself as object of desire for men. Gabrina, for her part, shows that putting on the mask of femininity is so natural to women that their masquerade becomes thoroughly unsettling when, because of the ravages of time, it does not work. Perhaps we should move to Alcina's masquerade as flawless beauty queen to witness a distancing technique for women vis-à-vis the female masquerade.

Throughout her fictional life in the *Furioso*, Alcina is given every chance to construct herself as bewitching in order to entice men and further her aims: "giovane e bella ella si fa con arte / sí che molti ingannò" ("Young and fair she made herself by artifice, and deceived many"; 7, 74). For their part, men fall in love with her specifically because she embodies all their desires. But rather than losing herself in the femininity she puts on for their sake, Alcina uses the masquerade to hide and shelter a self with which she feels comfortable: that of an individual who knows how to play games, whatever they are, to her personal and political advantage. Everything she presents, therefore, is carefully invented piece by piece: "quanto / di beltà Alcina avea, tutto era estrano: / estrano avea, e non suo, dal pié alla treccia" ("Alcina's beauty was in every detail an imposture: it was wholly fraudulent. . . . Nothing, from her soles to her tresses, was natural to her"; 7, 70). In this sense, there is perhaps a different reading of the veil covering Alcina at the time of her rendezvous with Ruggiero, the veil that, as Ariosto puts it, refuses to cover whatever it is asked to cover ("il vel suttile e rado, / che non copria dinanzi né di dietro / piú che le rose o i gigli un chiaro vetro" ["the insubstantial gossamer-gown which, before and behind, concealed no more than would a pane of glass placed before a spray of roses and lilies"]; 7, 28).[60] That veil would

not be the fetishistic surface with which men wrap women in representation in order to allay their castration fear, but the distancing cover that
women defiantly put on to shelter their selfhood from male appropria-
tions. In this reading Alcina embodies the Nietzschean woman-as-lie, for
her essence is to give the appearance of having an essence. Through
adornment, Nietzsche insists, perhaps woman "seeks mastery. But she
does not *want* truth—her great art is the lie, her highest concern is mere
appearance and beauty."[61] But whereas Nietzsche needs to make woman
unconscious of her dissembling in order to circumscribe her power in the
eyes of man the philosopher, Alcina seems absolutely conscious here of
her purposes and strategies.

No wonder, then, that Ariosto sadistically rushes to punish this
woman by stripping off her veil of femininity and by uncovering ugliness
and decrepitude under a formerly perfect bodily image: "donna sí laida,
che la terra tutta / né la piú vecchia avea né la piú brutta // Pallido, crespo
e macilente avea / Alcina il viso, il crin raro e canuto, / sua statura a sei
palmi non giungea: / ogni dente di bocca era caduto" ("a woman so hideous that her equal for sheer ugliness and decrepitude could be found nowhere on earth. / She was whey-faced, wrinkled, and hollow-cheeked; her
hair was white and sparse; she was not four feet high; the last tooth had
dropped out of her jaw"; 7, 72–73). This putrefying image of a toothless
woman, no longer desirable and no longer castrating, and herself doubly
castrated, as Derrida would have it, "once as truth and once as un-
truth,"[62] harks back to Machiavelli's frightful reaction to the repulsive
image of the prostitute he so morbidly describes to Guicciardini. In both
cases the horrifying Other, "la feccia" ("dregs"; 7, 70), is unceremoni-
ously eliminated in order that the (male) narrative may continue.

• • • • •

Yet all is not told. There is in fact a woman in the *Furioso* who seems to
escape outward retribution through the masquerade. Lofty Marfisa
("Marfisa altiera"; 20, 113), who by choice would not be caught without
her armor at any time of the day or night, demonstrates in all her actions
that she does not define femininity by male standards. In the Gabrina
episode, for example, she refuses to read femininity as a mask: unlike
Pinabello's saucy damsel, who sees the value for her person of correct
femininity and complies with it (femininity as the masquerade of youthfulness), Marfisa declines to share in the merriment. With her gesture, she
insists on taking the terms of the game for real and exposes its construction. She does it through Gabrina by using what Irigaray has called mimicry, that is, an ostentatious, and thus unsettling, dressing up of woman
as embodiment of desirable femininity. That, *pace* Marfisa, Gabrina does

not become an object of scopophilic pleasure because of the accoutrements that make woman desirable, that indeed she is laughed at for pretending that it is possible, show how strongly culture defines correct femininity. That Marfisa does not accept this reading and rather enjoys this femme performance by masquerading herself as butch, as Sue-Ellen Case would want it—a protecting phallus/sword in her hand—is her way of dismantling femininity and empowering woman. For a while, at least.

Marfisa also lays bare what is at stake in the masquerade of femininity when she plays the game herself once. In Canto 26 she agrees for the first time in the *Furioso* to dress in feminine clothes in order to satisfy her male companions' playful pleas. Ariosto leaves no doubt that this is a thorough performance of femininity; Marfisa submits to it not to prove that she is a woman but to please others who want to see her dressed as such: "e ben che veder raro si solea / senza l'osbergo e gli altri buoni arnesi, / pur quel dì se li trasse; e come donna, / a' prieghi lor lasciò vedersi in gonna" ("And though she was seldom to be seen without her breastplate and other sturdy armour, today she left them off, and let herself be seen dressed as a woman as she had been asked"; 26, 69). At this point Mandricardo arrives with a firmer lance than her own ("ch'avea piú l'asta dura"; 26, 74), as Ariosto coyly puts it. He defeats all the other knights and claims her as prize since nobody is left to undertake her defense. Marfisa tells him that he can have her only through a manly engagement, sword in hand ("con la spada in mano"; 26, 82). To clarify her point, she legalistically expounds on her philosophy of self-reliance: "Io ti concedo che diresti il vero, / ch'io sarei tua per la ragion di guerra, / quando mio signor fosse o cavalliero / alcun di questi ch'hai gittato in terra. / Io sua non son, né d'altri son che mia: / dunque me tolga a me chi mi desia" ("I allow that you would be correct about my being yours by custom of war if one of these men you have overthrown were my lord or my champion. But I am none of theirs; I belong to nobody, only to myself: who wants me must first reckon with me"; 26, 79).

Marfisa can dismantle all discourses on femininity because she shows theatrically that they are based on the assumption that there is a phallus somewhere that woman will then specularize. This posited hommo-sexuality ("hommo-sexualité") at the center of any representation of desire is what Irigaray most exposes in her writing: "The feminine occurs only within models and laws devised by male subjects. Which implies that there are not really two sexes but only one. A single practice and representation of the sexual" (86). By not playing up to man, whether to secure love and class (Dalinda), to appear enticing (Gabrina), or to acquire power (Alcina), by offering her body as excessive in the very moment that she dresses it in the most proper feminine clothes, and finally by adopting an ironic stance, Marfisa is able to expose the phallus-centered and normatively heterosexual social organization that is fundamental to the literary genres in which she is made to operate: the courtly romance and the epic. To be sure, unlike Alcina, who was transformed from fantasized object of desire into repulsive and decaying matter, Marfisa incurs no actual chastisement in the text. Yet she too is punished in the long run since Ariosto keeps her solidly stuck in the realm of the comic, forever playing the nonwoman and the nonman. In a chivalric romance in which each and every narrative strand is sooner or later brought to its climactic conclusion, there is no conclusion to the Marfisa story. To "forget" to remain within a precise gender identity, to play the bigendered individual, or politically to cast biology aside, is then ultimately more costly to Marfisa than to cross-dress like the other woman warrior of the *Furioso*, Bradamante. It costs her her own story.[63]

To go back to the beginning then, we could say that there is no femininity without the mask, but the mask can be put on, paradoxically, only when there is some femininity to (re)present, some game to play for somebody else. The standard, as we would expect and as Freud would insist, is always masculine. Or, to put it as Lacan would, if the self is other to itself and is constituted through the desire of the Other, the masquerade of femininity can be put on only when there is a man at the keyhole. That in the final analysis this man may want somebody else, as in the case of Dalinda, that he may laugh at what he sees, as in the case of Gabrina, or that he would rather find nothing, as in the case of Alcina, is not as unsettling to man as not seeing any desire at all for him, as it happens with Marfisa. That there may be no phallus at the center of a (woman's) narrative is indeed the real, frightening story.

NOTES

1. An impressive array of studies on self and gender identity, and on such intriguing questions as why the Renaissance became so fascinated with related topics such as transvestism and cross-dressing, has been published in the past few years. See especially Catherine Belsey, *The Subject of Tragedy: Identity and Difference in Renaissance Drama* (New York: Methuen, 1985); Stephen Greenblatt, "Fiction and Friction," in *Shakespearean Negotiations: The Circulation of Social Energy in Renaissance England* (Berkeley: University of California Press, 1988), 66–93; Jean Howard, "Crossdressing, the Theatre, and Gender Struggle in Early Modern England," *Shakespeare Quarterly* 39 (1988): 418–40; and Jonathan Dollimore, "Subjectivity, Sexuality and Transgression: The Jacobean Connection," *Renaissance Drama* N.S. 17 (1986): 53–81. For a specific study of these

issues in the context of Ariosto's romance epic, see Valeria Finucci, *The Lady Vanishes: Subjectivity and Representation in Castiglione and Ariosto* (Stanford: Stanford University Press, 1992), chaps. 4–8.

2. There were 103 laws enacted in Venice alone during the sixteenth and seventeenth centuries. See Rosita Levi Pisetzki, *Il costume e la moda nella società italiana* (Turin: Einaudi, 1978), 30.

3. Ibid., 33.

4. James Brundage, "Sumptuary Laws and Prostitution in Late Medieval Italy," *Journal of Medieval History* 13 (1987): 343–55, p. 349.

5. Diane Hughes, "Sumptuary Laws and Social Relations in Renaissance Italy," in *Disputes and Settlements: Law and Human Relations in the West*, ed. John Bossy (Cambridge: Cambridge University Press, 1983), 66–99, p. 83.

6. Fines were levied not only against husbands, brothers, or fathers of offending women but occasionally also against dressmakers. See Brundage, "Sumptuary Laws and Prostitution," 350. Hughes argues that this legislation was aimed at curbing the aristocracy's excessive display of wealth; Brundage and Levi Pisetzki, on the contrary, see the statutes directed mainly at the moneyed bourgeoisie. Court ladies, for example, were very much free from such regulations. On the topic, see also Marjorie Garber, *Vested Interests: Cross-dressing and Cultural Anxiety* (New York: Routledge, 1992), 21–27.

7. "Le leggi suntuarie furono sempre fatte apposta per essere trasgredite anche da chi le sancisce." In Pompeo Molmenti, *La storia di Venezia nella vita privata*, 3 vols. (Bergamo: Istituto d'arti grafiche, 1906), 2:315.

8. Cited in Hughes, "Sumptuary Laws and Social Relations," 87.

9. Even during carnivals, the rare occasions on which transgressions were accepted, women found their desire to masquerade, whether as women or as men, could be thwarted. See Gian Ludovico Masetti Zannini, *Motivi storici della educazione femminile: scienza, lavoro, giuochi* (Naples: D'Auria, 1982), 277–78. He also cites (401) the seventeenth-century ordinance of the Monastero di Santa Maria Maddalena forbidding nuns to masquerade ("Niuna monacha abbia ardire d'immascherarsi nel tempo di carnevale et molto meno di farsi vedere in qualsivoglia modo fuori del suo habito"). Nuns at times masqueraded as men in conventual representations. The bishop Niccolò Sacchetti complains in a 1649 memoir that cross-dressed nuns were seen even by their cook in their rooms and during the banquet preceding their performance. See Masetti Zannini, 404–5.

10. Today female transvestism has lost much of its stigma, since women have the freedom to choose to wear or not to wear male-identified clothing. Male transvestism is, of course, another matter. On the power of clothing to shape/reshape/hide/steal/fetishize one's self, see Roland Barthes, *The Fashion System* (New York: Hill and Wang, 1983); and Eugenie Lemoine-Luccioni, *La Robe: Essai psychanalytique sûr le vétement* (Paris: Seuil, 1983). Although on the English stage women's parts were played by boys, in Italy women were already performing in female roles by 1550, no matter how many laws explicitly forbade the practice. See Molmenti, *La storia di Venezia*, 2:302–4.

11. Baldassarre Castiglione, *Il libro del cortegiano*, ed. Ettore Bonora (Milan: Mursia, 1972), 3.15.222. English text from *The Book of the Courtier*, trans. George Bull (Harmondsworth: Penguin, 1967).

12. Joan Rivière, "Womanliness as a Masquerade," in *Formations of Fantasy*, ed. Victor Burgin, James Donald, and Cora Kaplan (London: Methuen, 1986), 35–44. Freud uses the term *masquerade* twice in his writing, but not in the context of constructions of femininity. See Stephen Heath, "Joan Rivière and the Masquerade," in Burgin et al., 45–61, p. 47.

13. In *The Standard Edition of the Complete Psychological Works of Sigmund Freud*, trans. and ed. James Strachey, 24 vols. (London: Hogarth Press, 1953–79), vol. 22 (1964): 5–158, p. 131. (Subsequent references to these volumes will be indicated by the abbreviation *SE*.)

14. Friedrich Nietzsche, *The Gay Science*, trans. Walter Kaufmann (New York: Vintage Books, 1974), 317.

15. In "Displacement and the Discourse of Woman" (in *Displacement: Derrida and After*, ed. Mark Kruprick [Bloomington: Indiana University Press, 1983], 169–95), Gayatri Spivak comments: "Within the historical understanding of women as incapable of orgasm, Nietzsche is arguing that impersonation is woman's only sexual pleasure. At the time of the greatest self-possession-cum-ecstasy, the woman is self-possessed enough to organize a self-(re)presentation without an actual presence (of sexual pleasure) to represent" (170). On Nietzsche in this context, see also Heath, "Joan Rivière and the Masquerade," 51. On the pleasures of faking orgasms, see Garber's essay in this volume.

16. Jacques Lacan, "The Meaning of the Phallus," in *Feminine Sexuality: Jacques Lacan and the Ecole Freudienne*, ed. Juliet Mitchell and Jacqueline Rose (New York: Norton, 1982), 74–85, p. 84.

17. Jacques Lacan, "From Love to Libido," in *Four Fundamental Concepts of Psychoanalysis*, trans. Alan Sheridan (New York: Norton, 1977), 187–200, p. 193. As Jacqueline Rose recaps, "Masquerade is the very definition of femininity precisely because it is constructed with reference to a male sign" ("Introduction II," in Mitchell and Rose, *Feminine Sexuality*, 43). For a rebuttal and a reading of the masquerade (the term is left ungendered) as hiding the fact "that masculine sexuality is a tenuous matter," see Ellie Ragland-Sullivan, "The Sexual Masquerade: A Lacanian Theory of Sexual Difference," in *Lacan and the Subject of Language*, ed. Ellie Ragland-Sullivan and Mark Bracher (New York: Routledge, 1991), 49–80, p. 71. For other discussions on the topic, see Judith Butler, *Gender Trouble: Feminism and the Subversion of Identity* (New York: Routledge, 1990), 40ff.; and John Fletcher, "Versions of the Masquerade," *Screen* 29 (1988): 43–70.

18. Michèle Montrelay, "Inquiry into Femininity," in *French Feminist Thought: A Reader*, ed. Toril Moi (Oxford: Blackwell, 1987), 227–49, p. 239.

19. Luce Irigaray, *This Sex Which Is Not One*, trans. Catherine Porter (Ithaca: Cornell University Press, 1985), 84.

20. For the play of voyeurism and fetishism vis-à-vis woman, see the essays by Berger, Schwartz, and Enterline in this volume.

21. Mary Ann Doane, "Film and the Masquerade: Theorising the Female Spectator," *Screen* 23.3–4 (1982): 74–88, p. 82.

22. Mary Ann Doane, "Masquerade Reconsidered: Further Thoughts on the Female Spectator," *Discourse* 11.1 (1988–89): 42–54, p. 47.

23. Sue-Ellen Case, "Towards a Butch-Femme Aesthetic," *Discourse* 11.1 (1988–89): 55–73, p. 66.

24. Ludovico Ariosto, *Orlando furioso*, ed. Marcello Turchi (Milan: Garzanti, 1974). Citations in English from *Orlando Furioso*, trans. Guido Waldman (Oxford: Oxford University Press, 1983).

25. On Rinaldo's attitude, see Peter DeSa Wiggins, *Figures in Ariosto's Tapestry* (Baltimore: Johns Hopkins University Press, 1986); and Alfredo Bonadeo, "L'avventura di Rinaldo," *PMLA* 81 (1966): 199–206. On his defense of women's rights, see Mario Santoro, *Letture Ariostesche* (Naples: Liguori, 1973). The law leaves no room for the woman to tell her own truth. What is important is that a knight, by accepting the challenge, makes others believe that she is beyond reproach, whether or not she actually is.

26. Ariodante and Lurcanio reappear in Canto 18 during the Moorish Dardinello's nighttime slaughter of Christians. Dardinello kills Lurcanio, and Ariodante rushes to seek vengeance, but "Fortuna" makes them lose sight of each other (18, 55–58). The most common source for the Ginevra episode is the work of Joanot Martorell, *Tirante el Blanco* (1490). See Luigi Rajna, *Le fonti dell'Orlando furioso* (Florence: Sansoni, 1900), 149–53; and Paolo Valesio, "Genealogy of a Staged Scene (*Orlando Furioso, V*)," *Yale Italian Studies* 1 (1980): 5–31. Following on one of Ariosto's sixteenth-century commentators, Simon Fornari ("La spositione . . . sopra l'*Orlando Furioso*" [1549]), Rajna suggests that the law upon which Ginevra is to be judged has a more homey origin: Niccolò d'Este instituted in Ferrara something close to this fictional "Scottish" law when his wife, Parisina, betrayed him. Spenser uses this plot in the story of Phedon, Philemon, and Claribell in Book 2.IV of *The Fairie Queene*. Shakespeare recurs to the famous window scene in *Much Ado About Nothing*, but rather than restaging it, he has a character tell what has taken place at the window. See C. P. Brand, "Ginevra and Ariodante: A Deception Motif from Ariosto to Shakespeare," in *Essays in Honour of John Humphreys Whitfield,* ed. H. C. Davis et al. (London: St. George Press, 1975), 120–36; and John Traugott, "Creating a Rational Rinaldo: A Study in the Mixture of the Genres of Comedy and Romance in *Much Ado About Nothing*," *Genre* 15 (1982): 157–81.

27. Attilio Momigliano, *Saggio sull'Orlando Furioso* (Bari: Laterza, 1973), 182.

28. Rajna, *Le fonti*, 153. Spenser may have felt uneasy about having to portray such an abject woman, for in rewriting the story, he chose to give more credibility to the maid's acceptance of Philemon's motives for dressing up as her mistress. She would be as beautiful as her superior, he argued (*Fairie Queene* 2.IV).

29. Sigmund Freud, "Creative Writers and Day-Dreaming" (1908), in *SE* 9 (1959): 143–53, pp. 146–47. Freud arrives at a theorization of primal fantasies after renouncing his seduction theory in a famous letter to Wilhelm Fliess: "I no longer believe in my neurotica" (Sept. 21, 1897). In *The Complete Letters of Sigmund Freud to Wilhelm Fliess, 1887–1904,* ed. and trans. Jeffrey Moussaieff Masson (Cambridge: Harvard University Press, 1985), 198. On shifting positions in fantasy, see also his "A Child Is Being Beaten: A Contribution to the Study of the Origin of Sexual Perversions" (1919), in *SE* 17 (1955): 179–204. In their study on fantasy, Jean Laplanche and Jean-Bertrande Pontalis argue that original

fantasies respond to a subject's search for origins: "the primal scene pictures the origin of the individual; fantasies of seduction, the origin and upsurge of sexuality; fantasies of castration, the origin of the difference between the sexes" ("Fantasy and the Origins of Sexuality," in Burgin et al., *Formations of Fantasy*, 5–34, p. 19).

30. "To the extent that desire is not purely an upsurge of the drives, but is articulated into the fantasy," they write, "the latter is a favoured spot for the most primitive defensive reactions, such as turning against oneself, or into an opposite, projection, negation: these defenses are even indissolubly linked with the primary function of fantasy, to be a setting for desire, in so far as desire itself originates as prohibition, and the conflict may be an original conflict" (Laplanche and Pontalis, "Fantasy and the Origins of Sexuality," 26–27).

31. As Mikkel Borch-Jacobsen writes of fantasy in *The Freudian Subject*, trans. Catherine Porter (Stanford: Stanford University Press, 1988), "It is as if wish fulfillment did not so much consist in *having* the object as in *being* the one who possesses it. . . . Identification is required . . . by every instance of fantasmatic wish-fulfillment" (18). In "Group Psychology and the Analysis of the Ego" (1921), Freud uses almost the same terms to define the narcissistic ego's uncertainty between wanting to have an object and wanting to be the individual possessing it (*SE* 18 [1955]: 67–72, p. 106).

32. "The subject desires the object because the rival desires it," René Girard writes in *Violence and the Sacred* (Baltimore: Johns Hopkins University Press, 1977), 145. See also his *Deceit, Desire and the Novel* (Baltimore: Johns Hopkins University Press, 1965). Doubts have been expressed about the possibility that male and female positions may be interchangeable for Girard, since he seems to operate on the understanding that men have to be the desiring subjects. For a critique of Girard's blindness to women's desire, see Toril Moi, "The Missing Mother: The Oedipal Rivalries of René Girard," *Diacritics* 12 (1982): 21–31; and Mary Jacobus, "Is There a Woman in This Text?" *New Literary History* 4 (1982): 117–41.

33. Writing of homeovestism (same-sex transvestism), however, George Zavitzianos points out that fetishism is not a factor in impersonation: "Impersonation of the ego ideal and identification with it is a common characteristic of homeovestism, transvestism and imposture. We do not see this in fetishism. . . . I am inclined to think that in homeovestism and transvestism there is, as a rule, a fixation to the stage of 'dressing-up' games which we do not see in fetishism" ("The Object in Fetishism, Homeovestism and Transvestism," *International Journal of Psychoanalysis* 58 [1977]: 487–95, p. 494).

34. Sigmund Freud, *The Interpretation of Dreams* (1900), in *SE* 4 (1953): 146–51.

35. Parveen Adams, "Per Os(cillation)," *Camera Obscura* 17 (1988): 7–29, 11ff.

36. Jacques Lacan, "The Direction of the Treatment and the Principles of Its Power," in *Ecrits: A Selection*, trans. Alan Sheridan (London: Tavistock, 1977), 226–80.

37. Catherine Clément, *Lives and Legends of Jacques Lacan*, trans. Arthur Goldhammer (New York: Columbia University Press, 1983), 130.

38. "The woman identifies with the man, and the slice of smoked salmon replaces desire for the Other" (Lacan, "Direction of the Treatment," 262). Borch-Jacobsen criticizes Lacan's reading of the dream because it makes him "preserve the emptiness of the Desire by preventing it from being demolished, from being reduced to the demand of the other" (*The Freudian Subject*, 16).

39. As Cynthia Chase puts it by merging Lacan with Kristeva, "For *la belle bouchère*'s identification with her husband's *desire* could then be understood as a recapitulation of her identification with the mother's *desire*. The possibility of a signifier or of a subject is then situated in the identification with the desire *of* the mother, rather than with the desire *for* the woman" ("Desire and Identification in Lacan and Kristeva," in *Feminism and Psychoanalysis*, ed. Richard Feldstein and Judith Roof [Ithaca: Cornell University Press, 1989], 65–83, p. 80).

40. Laplanche and Pontalis note that fantasies are often framed (staged). On the conscious staging of this balcony scene, see Valesio, "Genealogy of a Staged Scene"; and Robert Hanning, "Sources of Illusion: Plot Elements and Their Thematic Uses in Ariosto's Ginevra Episode," *Forum Italicum* 5 (1971): 514–35.

41. On the importance of images of sight and blindness in this episode, see Hanning, "Sources of Illusion."

42. Only two other stories in the *Furioso*, those of the innkeeper in Canto 28 and of Judge Anselmo in Canto 43, are not narrated by members of the aristocracy. It is interesting, moreover, that the Dalinda story has never been referred to as such. It has come to us as the Ginevra story, although Ginevra never speaks.

43. As George Minois writes, "Lascivious, miserly, choleric, greedy and egoistical, old men were hotbeds of vice, which was all the more unforgivable in that their experience and wisdom were supposed to direct them towards the good" (*History of Old Age from Antiquity to the Renaissance*, trans. Sarah Tenison [Chicago: University of Chicago Press, 1989], 123). See also David Fowler, Lois Fowler, and Lois Lamdin, "Themes of Old Age in Preindustrial Western Europe," in *Old Age in Preindustrial Society*, ed. Peter Stearns (New York: Holmes and Meier, 1982). On old age in women, see Jacques Bailbé, "Le Thème de la vieille femme dans la poésie satirique du XVI et du debut du XVII siècle," *Bibliotéque d'Humanisme et Rénaissance* 26 (1964): 98–119; Simone de Beauvoir, *The Coming of Age* (New York: Putnam, 1972); and Kathleen Woodward, "Youthfulness as a Masquerade," *Discourse* 11.1 (1988–89): 119–42.

44. Giovanni Pozzi, "Il ritratto della donna nella poesia d'inizio Cinquecento e la pittura di Giorgione," *Lettere italiane* 31 (1979): 3–30, p. 26.

45. Pinabello's beloved will later take vengeance for this moment of debasement by establishing a custom for ladies and knights passing through her land: women forfeit their clothes, men their arms, and both lose their horses (22, 48). For more on Pinabello, see Albert Mancini, "Personaggi della poesia cavalleresca: cavalieri e villani nell'*Orlando Furioso*," in *Civiltà della parola*, ed. I. Bertoni (Milan: Marzorati, 1989), 171–88, pp. 180–82.

46. For a reading of Marfisa's playfulness and of the ironic pleasure she takes in the entire episode, see Franco Masciandaro, "Folly in the *Orlando Furioso*: A Reading of the Gabrina Episode," *Forum Italicum* 14 (1980): 56–77. For sources of this episode, Rajna mentions the French prose romance *Palamedès* (*Le Fonti*, 313–28). For a later retelling, see Spenser, *Fairie Queene*, 4, 4.10.

47. Julius Molinaro, "Sin and Punishment in the *Orlando Furioso*," *Modern Language Notes* 89 (1974): 35–46, p. 44. Ironically, Odorico was also unable to endure the proximity of a beautiful woman, for as soon as he was alone with Isabella, he tried to rape her. Wiggins argues that Gabrina is too vain and should not take offense at Zerbino's ridicule of her apparel (*Figures in Ariosto's Tapestry*, 128). In my opinion, this is not so much a question of vanity as of personal discomfort. After all, who enjoys being made a laughingstock?

48. As Donato puts it, "The dominant theme focuses more on the necessary rivalry between the various knights than upon the merits that would make Angelica intrinsically desirable. . . . The eventual possession of Angelica would be a way of establishing a difference between them, but the converse would also be true: by fighting each other they would establish a difference beyond their identity and the possession of the coveted object would ensue" ("'Per Selve e Boscherecci Labirinti': Desire and Narrative Structure in Ariosto's *Orlando Furioso*," in *Literary Theory/Renaissance Texts*, ed. Patricia Parker and David Quint [Baltimore: Johns Hopkins University Press, 1986], 33–62, pp. 36–37).

49. In rewriting Donato's logic of mimetic desire, Elizabeth J. Bellamy argues that it is their sameness rather than their difference that the knights want to secure in their jousts (*Translations of Power: Narcissism and the Unconscious in Epic History* [Ithaca: Cornell University Press, 1992], chap. 3). See also Borch-Jacobsen, *The Freudian Subject*, chap. 1.

50. Mikhail Bakhtin, *Rabelais and His World*, trans. Helene Iswolky (Cambridge: MIT Press, 1968), 26. For a Bakhtinian reading of female grotesqueness, see Mary Russo, "Female Grotesques: Carnival and Theory," in *Feminist Studies/Critical Studies*, ed. Teresa De Lauretis (Bloomington: Indiana University Press, 1986), 213–29.

51. The same connection between Gabrina and a monkey had been made earlier by another knight, Mandricardo, who also burst into laughter at the sight (23, 94).

52. Interestingly, Aquinas does not chastise as sinful old women resorting to cosmetics to cancel the ravages of time. See Brundage, "Sumptuary Laws and Prostitution," 345.

53. Nietzsche is able to give the old woman one rewarding status, that of representing truth, for only age makes woman forget her ingrained, lifelong attempts at seduction: "Up north—embarrassing to tell— / I loved a creepy ancient belle: / The name of the old hag was Truth" (*The Gay Science*, 357).

54. Sigmund Freud, "The Uncanny" (1919) in *SE* 17 (1955): 219–52, p. 219.

55. Dante Alighieri, *The Divine Comedy*, trans. Charles Singleton (Princeton: Princeton University Press, 1973).

56. "Spectabili viro L. Guicciardini in Mantova tanquam fratri carissimo," in *Lettere*, ed. Giuseppe Lesca (Florence: Rinascimento del libro, 1929), 25–28, p. 26. English translation in *The Portable Machiavelli*, ed. Peter Bondanella and Mark Musa (Harmondsworth: Penguin, 1979), 58–60. For a perceptive reading of this letter, see the essay by Schiesari in this collection.

57. "E, come prima aperse la bocca, n'uscí un fiato sí puzzolente, che, trovandosi offesi da questa peste due porte di dua sdegnosissimi sensi, li ochi e il naso, e messi a tale sdegno, che lo stomaco, per non poter sopportare tale offesa, tutto

si commosse. E, commosso, oprò sí che io le recé addosso; e cosí, pagata di quella moneta che la meritava, mi partii" (*Lettere*, 27) ("and as she opened her mouth there came from it such a stinking breath that my eyes and my nose, the two gateways of the two most outraged senses, found themselves offended by this pestilence; this was such a shock to my stomach that, not being able to bear it, it heaved so much that I vomited all over her. And so, having paid her in the way she deserved, I left" (*Portable Machiavelli*, 60).

58. Vincenzo Maggi, *De Ridiculis*, in *Il riso nelle poetiche rinascimentali*, ed. Enrico Musacchio (Bologna: Cappelli, 1985), 33–78, p. 36.

59. Being cast on the dark side of female sexuality, Gabrina is also the antithesis of the good mother. Her behavior toward Isabella in Cantos 12 and 13 is unmotherly to say the least, and that toward Filandro, with whom she has fallen in love, although he is much younger and she is already married to Argeo, has little of the maternal in it. Interestingly, Ariosto casts the triangle Argeo-Gabrina-Filandro as an Oedipal one in which the unlucky youth ("l'infelice giovene"; 21, 26) refuses to take the place of the father/husband in the mother's bed. No matter: the phallic mother pushes him to metaphorically castrate her husband by decapitating him ("con esso un colpo il capo fesse e il collo" ["With one stroke he split his head and neck"]; 21, 49), and then takes revenge for the son's unwillingness to possess her by disposing of him in the mythic way of Procne and Medea ("Progne crudel" and "Medea"; 21, 56).

60. For an allegorical reading of Alcina's veil, see Albert Ascoli, *Ariosto's Bitter Harmony: Crisis and Evasion in the Italian Renaissance* (Princeton: Princeton University Press, 1987), 162ff.

61. Friedrich Nietzsche, *Beyond Good and Evil*, trans. Walter Kaufmann (New York: Vintage Books, 1966), 163.

62. Jacques Derrida, *Spurs: Nietzsche's Styles*, trans. Barbara Harlow (Chicago: University of Chicago Press, 1979), 97.

63. For a study of cross-dressing in the *Furioso*, see Finucci, *The Lady Vanishes*, chaps. 7 and 8.

OGLING

THE CIRCULATION OF POWER

ACTAEON AT THE HINDER GATE

THE STAG PARTY IN SPENSER'S
GARDENS OF ADONIS

HARRY BERGER

OVID begins the tenth book of *Metamorphoses* by telling how Orpheus loses his wife in the underworld and how it affects him: he rejects the love of women, institutes pederasty in Thrace, and begins plinking his lyre in an open field.[1] The promise of a Thracian Woodstock pulls in an audience of shade trees, birds, and wild animals, and Orpheus sings to them of boys loved by the gods and girls inflamed by hidden lust. These are the stories we read during the remainder of the tenth book. They are bound together by misogynist, antierotic, and gynephobic themes that reflect the bitterness of the singer. The figure who links several of the stories, and who finally emerges as the singer's target when she is trapped by the consequences of her own actions and the eddying force of his ironic narrative, is Venus. It is Venus who turns the Cyprian Propoetides first into prostitutes and then into stones for denying her divinity; Venus who reverses that trick by bestowing life on Pygmalion's ivory dream virgin, Galatea, making it possible for her to found a line that includes the incestuous great-granddaughter and grandson, Myrrha and Cinyras; Venus who loves and loses their son Adonis. Galatea is both the product and the symbol of Pygmalion's misogyny: he quickly generalizes his disgust at the Propoetides' shamelessness to "the faults that nature had so lavishly bestowed on woman's mind," and gives his snowy figure a *forma* no natural woman ("femina nasci") could match.[2] Orpheus drops several clues suggesting that Venus would have done better to butt out and let Pygmalion continue in his harmless autoerotic relation with his life-size doll. When Adonis unwittingly "avenges his mother's passion" (10.524) by arousing that of Venus, his death in effect punishes the goddess for releasing Galatea from her androgenetic purity and dooming her to the curse of motherhood.

The account of the gardens of Adonis in canto vi of the third book of Spenser's *Faerie Queene* is Venus's answer to Orpheus. But of course it isn't Venus who delivers the answer; it's Spenser. Or, to be more precise, it is the narrator, whose relation to Spenser's text is the same as that of Orpheus to Ovid's text. Spenser's narrator doesn't make the distinction I do between Ovid and Orpheus.[3] He is represented as one who reads, interprets, and reacts to the Ovidian text not as a literary critic but as a cultural critic, and therefore he dissolves the particular motivated bias of the Orphean viewpoint into a more diffuse and culturally influential discourse of male chauvinism.[4] In *The Faerie Queene*, and especially in Book III, we find a citational and anthological interlace of traditional discourses—among them the Petrarchan, the Ovidian, the Neoplatonic, the chivalric, the courtly, the goliardic, and the pastoral—all represented as ideological strategies for defending or legitimating male dominance and desire, and for justifying the instrumental functions of woman in the patriarchal mode of reproduction. The object of the Spenserian critique of these discourses is the logic of the phallus, which I have elsewhere compared to the logic of Pinocchio's nose: in the latter, the more he lies the bigger it grows; in the former, the bigger it grows the more it lies.[5] In short, this is the logic of castration. Spenser's dramatization and critique of this logic in the sixth canto of Book III, and especially the reflexive irony of his narrator's knowing failure to avoid what he criticizes, are the topic of my essay. I shall explore the problems that confront the male narrator—indeed the problems displayed and performed by the narrator—as he tries to rectify the injustices of the dominant discourses by imagining an eroto-matriarchal idyll of fulfilled Venerean desire. The method informing Spenser's critique is that of conspicuous allusion. Though it is now a familiar device, and I have frequently discussed it in earlier publications, a brief comment on its recent critical history may be in order before I proceed.

Thirty years ago, one of the major efforts of New Critical practice was to distinguish the concept of allusion from that of influence; this was part of a program aimed at dissociating the work from its historical context, and the concerns of interpretation from those of literary history. Since then the meaning of allusion has been greatly enriched by four other developments. One is the reconceiving of genre as a form of intertextual discourse. The second is the related interest in exploring the interconnection and therefore the citationality of all literary texts. The third is the encouragement given by such ideas as belatedness and strong reading to the study of citational practice as a form of space-clearing parody. The fourth is the extension of these strategies beyond literary discourse to a broad range of cultural discourses whose concealed intertextual relations and fictive character may be exposed, along with their ideological interests, from the standpoint of what Althusser calls "internal distance." In the interpretation that follows, we shall see both the narrator's attempt to establish internal distance from the regime of Ovidian discourse and the obstacles placed in his way by his own subjection to the logic of castration.

Even in the happy garden state of the Variorum tradition, no one working on Book III could avoid the theme of sexual politics, but until the late

1960s there was very little public discourse or theorizing about the topic. As a result, those of us who asked Old Genius to let us out of the Variorum garden continued, mentally, to work there "without a mate." My efforts in that paradise of patriarchal pedantries were as crude as those of other Spenserians who, after venturing outside the walls that surround the "fruitfull soyle of old" criticism and sampling the cultural realities of sexual warfare, soon returned "backe by the hinder gate" into the more comfortable and familiar pieties of visionary resolutions. Since that time activities on several fronts have populated the extramural landscape with new attitudes toward and insights into the problematics of gender, generation, the family romance, the role of the reader, and the relation of Spenser's poetry to its intertextual and extratextual settings. This makes it possible for an aged boy belatedly to return to the scenes of his youthful crimes without actually returning, to stay outside the walls so as to displace his desire for Spenserian visions into the revisionary play of the poem's discursive critique of androcentric vision. Or so he hopes.

His hope, however, is mingled with the apprehensiveness caused by realizing that if he desires to defend the Spenserian narrator's defense of Venus, he too is subject to the logic of castration. He plans to guard against this by looking—or peeping—at the gardens of Adonis from the observation point provided by recent feminist critics who argue that the sixth canto constructs a virtual reader more congenial to woman's interests than to man's. He is aware that this may expose him to Actaeonic dangers, but he is willing to take the risk because he knows that after Pinocchio stopped lying the fairy did to him what Venus did to Galatea.[6] And I share his confidence. A real *puer*, however *senex*, may find new life, a life undogged by fear, unburdened by the woody growth of alien horns,[7] if only he will take the precaution of eyeing the garden not directly but in the mediating mirror of the feminist gaze. And so I hope, and in this hope I shall avail myself primarily of Maureen Quilligan's stimulating account of gendered reading in *Milton's Spenser*. I hasten to add that in using the phrase "gendered reading" I don't mean to imply that one set of responses characterizes the way women read, and another the way men read. Rather, I'm alluding to the possibility that the third book, which centers on problems of gender, generation, and sexuality, offers its readers gendered positions that correspond to those it represents.

In recent commentary, not two but three such positions have been identified (and there may be more). Quilligan, after noting that "Spenser's direct addresses to female readers are far more numerous in Book III than elsewhere throughout the poem," goes on to argue that "the male perspective on the experiences of Book III's narrative is radically censured."[8] Simon Shepherd, who represents himself as a feminist traveler, objects to this thesis and claims that "the text of *The Faerie Queene* assumes a male readership, in that it offers points of identification available to men only and objects of desire culturally designated for men rather than women. . . . In terms of pleasure and identification there is little point of entry for the woman reader."[9] Finally, according to Lauren Silberman the movement toward an androgynous discourse in III.vi creates a reader whose allegiance "transcends the partiality Spenser attributes to men."[10] My project in what follows will be to navigate among these positions and, in particular, to give Quilligan's complex argument more prime time than it gets from Shepherd, who dismisses it in a single parenthetical phrase, and who flaunts his contempt for efforts by "the academic servants of 'great Literature'" to "locate 'feminist' thought" in a narrative that "implicates the reader in some of the classic sexist ways of looking at women" (60, 79).

After the bachelor hero of Book II has been bounced off his horse, the chivalric love quest is restored in a complex form that makes the virgin the subject of desire and makes virgin power even more central than in Book I—dangerous not only to men who are overthrown by chastity's spear or undone by beauty's chase but also to those who suffer the ignominy of having to be saved or replaced by the fearless woman warrior.[11] Contemplating the story of Britomart in its general lines, how can the simple, hearty, fair-minded male reader think himself implicated in a classic sexist way of looking at women? When Britomart's desire is inscribed by Merlin in a political text, another aspect of virgin power is underlined: whether erotic or antierotic, it is a virtue necessary to male control of marriage, the institutional cornerstone on which the preservation and continuity of patriarchal order are founded. Here, perhaps, our admiration and sympathy for Britomart are crossed by just a twinge of classic sexism if we find ourselves inclined to applaud Merlin's sage advice: "Submit thy wayes unto his will," he urges her, and "his" refers both to Artegal and "eternall providence."[12]

Merlin's own submission to the Lady of the Lake adds ironic emphasis to his advice; it reminds us that since men are weak they need to inseminate strong women with the fidelity and capacity for chaste love required to guarantee orderly transmission of the phallus.[13] But of course men *are* weak, as those of us who have passed through Acrasia's bower know, and when the narrator refers to the good wizard's fall through "that False Ladies traine," we males may wonder whether he was ensnared in another seductive pietà, the dangerously ambiguous figure that conflates mothering with sexuality and death. The Acrasian shadow falling across Book III smokes the edges of the varied restatements of the pietà so that not even the witch's antitypes, Belphoebe and the great mother in her gloomy grove, are free of menace. The ministrations of maid and mother wound or enervate, inflame or infantilize, those they aspire to protect or heal or gratify. As Book III winds its readers through episodes whose turnings again and again expose the precariousness of male identity, whoever tries to identify successively with Guyon, Redcross, Merlin, Marinell, Arthur, Timias, and Adonis may be excused for succumbing to just the tiniest frisson of anxiety. On what grounds do we determine whether this sequence of locally ineffective and lyrically overmastered males constructs the reader position described by Quilligan or the one described by Shepherd?

The various episodes centered on Florimell, Malecasta, Britomart, Cymoent, and Belphoebe give diegetic continuity to an otherwise diffuse flurry of moves in a campaign against male autonomy, power, and desire. Cantos i–vi modulate from an emphasis on the flight, fear, suffering, and frustration of women to an emphasis on their self-sufficiency and power over men. After Britomart leaves the field with "all . . . in her powre," Marinell languishes on the ocean floor, Arthur stomps off in a pet, the Foster meets his just desert, and Belphoebe's *pharmakon* leaves Timias flat on the forest floor. As the woman's movement gathers force, the momentum increases with the turn backward in story time but forward in discourse time to Belphoebe's birth. This diegetic split is itself important in a poem whose broken story line is subordinated to the rhetorical transactions between narrator and reader in the *now* of discourse time, transactions that not only represent but also interpret the story. Thus if it takes an etiological flashback to advance the woman's movement, that may signify either a regressive withdrawal to an ancient vision of maternal paradise or else the need to send the Belphoebe figure back through the hinder gate so that it can be reconceived and reinterpreted—assimilated, sublated, transcended in a utopian revision of Venus. It is utopian because when Venus combines with Diana to recapture and disarm or repossess truant male desire (Cupid), she forms an alliance that temporarily diminishes the generational conflict between mothers and the loving virgins whose quest threatens maternal control of sons and lovers. By the end of canto vi one is strongly tempted to agree with Quilligan that the male perspective has been "radically censured": woman power peaks in the garden; Venus finds the maternal and erotic fulfillment she and Cymoent vainly sought in earlier episodes; not only Adonis and his Boar but also Cupid and his little family are safely back under the Mother's green thumb, along with Amoret. Thus the problem embodied as Belphoebe is resolved: because her share of Venus is muffled and repressed within the Diana function she performs, she can tend and pity the male but she can't respond to the love her tendance arouses. Her pietà is perforce a defective shadow of the one Venus attains to: a pietà of power and pity only, not of power and joy. When the narrator returns her to birth, supplies her with a Venerean twin, makes Venus temporarily overcome Diana's resistance, and sends Belphoebe out of Book III under Diana's tutelage, he releases Venus from her Belphoeban containment so that she may recapture the male desire she generates and perpetuates, may do for Adonis what Belphoebe was unable to do for Timias.[14] In her gynarchic idyll there is no need for figures of *daunger* whose chief purpose is to resist domination by male desire. Surely this can't be one of Spenser's "classic sexist ways of looking at women."

Or is it? No one says "surely" unless he isn't sure his interlocutor has been reassured by what he says. And if we look harder at the discursive structure inscribed in Belphoebe, we may find it difficult to deny the justice of Shepherd's position. It is true that she combines the resonances of Diana and Elizabeth I; but she does so under Petrarchan dispensation. As Patricia Parker notes, in developing Nancy Vickers's important insights, although the male subject in Petrarchan discourse "is always potentially an Actaeon," his vulnerable status as lover is "countered by the mastery of the poet."[15] Whatever power a Diana figure like Belphoebe has over man is a power ceded by the poets who have power over her in the sense that she is their fantasy. The ideal of the autonomous virgin is a diversionary fiction enabling the male to represent himself as a victim entitled to poetic revenge.[16]

In Book III the male origins of the fantasy are flagged in the poem by the three interconnected accounts of Belphoebe's birth. The first, which is anticipatory and is easy to overlook, occurs in the penultimate stanza of Arthur's self-victimizing complaint against foul Mother Night:

> Dayes dearest children be the blessed seed,
> Which darknesse shall subdew, and heaven win:
> Truth is his daughter; he her first did breed,
> Most sacred virgin, without spot of sin.
> Our life is day, but death with darknesse doth begin.
>
> (iv.59)

Turning from the evil matriarchy of Night to the good patriarchy of Day, Arthur speaks less of a virginlike truth than of a truthlike virgin.[17] His terms will be echoed and amplified in the stanzas of the sixth canto describing the conception of the sun's daughters. The second account occurs near the end of the fifth canto when, as Thomas Roche notes, Belphoebe's creation is "treated like that of a Platonic Idea": "Eternall God" planted her virtue in Paradise and then transplanted it "in stocke of earthly flesh" (v.52). Here, as in the first account, the mother's role is cut out.[18] The third account encodes Belphoebe's origin in poetry in the statement that "Phoebus with faire beames did her adorne," and then readmits a chastened version of the mother, whose name, Chrysogone ("golden birth"), has the force of a patronym, and signifies her subjection.

Belphoebe's birth thus betrays the "secret powre unspide" of the very male fantasy she has been invented to fend off and despise. But she can fulfill her protective function only by being created at the same time to arouse desire; otherwise she wouldn't get the chance to fend it off. This constrains her to produce the effect of Venus and Cupid in the figure of Diana, and for this reason Spenser doesn't fully extricate her from the sonneteer's famous goddess and scapegoat, the Cruel Fair. Inscribed by conspicuous allusion and exclusion in the encounter with Timias, the ghost of that Bad Lady hovers over the *Malady* produced by Belphoebe's kind and caring intervention. In the wicked medium of the poet's delighted wordplay, the energetic Belphoebe fares no better than the enervated Timias. Her hidden lord and master can't resist loading every rift with puns—and bad ones at that. While she makes Timias's wound gather and "grow hole," the effect of her "dayly plaisters" is "to save a part, and lose the whole." If we now follow Belphoebe into the sixth canto and look more closely at the third account of her birth, we may find ourselves leaning away from Quilligan's feminist Spenser and toward Shepherd's view of a poet who offers "little point of entry for the woman reader."

Although the opening stanzas of III.vi superficially portray an idyll of sexual cooperation and female parthenogenesis, a little probing uncovers a male discourse of "powre" (or *pour*) within the cornucopia of euphemisms that spill out in the second stanza:

But to this faire Belphoebe in her berth
   The heavens so favourable were and free,
   Looking with myld aspect upon the earth,
   In th'Horoscope of her nativitee,
   That all the gifts of grace and chastitee
   On her they poured forth of plenteous horne;
   Jove laught on Venus from his soveraigne see,
   And Phoebus with faire beames did her adorne,
And all the Graces rockt her cradle being borne.

This passage demands readers to pay attention to Belphoebe's horoscope, and during the years when the "faire beames" of Panofsky, Wind, Seznec, Keith Thomas, D. C. Allen, the early Gombrich, and others irradiated literary studies it was tempting to solicit help from such claims to knowledge as those made by iconography, numerology, and astrology. So, for example, almost twenty years ago one critic cast Belphoebe's horoscope in order to "validate" her "celestial heritage" by reconciling divergent interpretations and disambiguating the passage.[19] Although, as we shall see, this approach to the detection of meaning privileges the astrological

Thin Man over the textual Fat Lady, it responds to a line of exegesis thrown by the stanza itself to readers adrift in the shifting currents of Spenserian narrative. Thus the astrological critic who proposes that Belphoebe's horoscope reflects the discourse of the heavens rather than that, say, of Petrarchan lyric, only imitates a process initiated by the poem's language when it transforms the conflicts of gender and generation into a benign figure of concord under the aegis of the Olympian patriarchy. It makes those conflicts rhetorically accessible to readers inclined to seek them out, but it also establishes a high-minded vantage point for a kinder, gentler reader inclined to screen them out. From this vantage point the suspiciousness that has contaminated the reading of the last fifteen years or so can only seem perverse.

To see just how perverse, consider the "plenteous horne" in line 6. The astrologer connects the horn to the goat of Amalthea that "suckled infant Jove" and cites the ancient opinion that "the famous cornucopia is identical with the goat's horn and is discovered now in the constellation Capricorn."[20] Surely it is perverse to wonder about the nasty events behind Jove's nurture and the divine mother's effort to save her children from Saturn. It is even more perverse to sneak that allusion back through the hinder gate or over the garden wall, as critics have done more than once when they connected Saturn and his sickle or scythe with the figure of "wicked *Time*" who appears in vi.39. Surely such conjunctions dump shame and ignominy on Venus's garden state, as do several other allusions poured forth from the horn, not only to goats and satyrs but also to cuckolds. It only made matters worse when critics began reading Actaeonic sermons in horns and finding traces of male voyeurism behind every bush and before every babbling brook. Anyone who has encountered the exciting but surely perverse ideas of Nancy Vickers, Leonard Barkan, and Maureen Quilligan on this subject might be misled into seeing a pun or two in "soveraigne see," though it would be foolhardy to reduce Jove to a giggling Faunus, since he prefers to enjoy panoptic pleasures in the security of his high imperial sconce. There is safety in distance as well as in disguise—for males, at least. In the move from Jove's laughter to the scopic action first of Phoebus and then, in stanza 6, of Titan, the conception of Belphoebe gets assimilated to some famous classical fantasies of violation. That most perverse mythographer, James Nohrnberg, has folded the rape of Danae into the name and plight of Chrysogone, and noted its appearance in the tapestries of Busirane (xi.31).[21] The tapestries work as a gloss measuring the complementary intensities of violence and euphemism in the account of Belphoebe's birth; other ecphrastic episodes—the lines on Helle and Europa in xi.30—retroactively play strange tricks on the reader trying to hold fast to his kinder, gentler view of the sovereign see and plenteous horn.[22] They jeopardize the innocence of the mirth with which he learns from the astrologer that the horoscope places "Jove in Virgo" at the same time that it has Phoebus lounging in Capricorn only 120 degrees away;[23] what could he possibly be doing there?

This shimmer of Ovidian rape images blurs and destabilizes the dance that goes on in the astrological distance. It generates a mirage in which we can glimpse the swelling shape of woman's fear, and that of man's: her fear of being violated by the phallic eye, implied by Chrysogone's sequestering herself "farre from all mens vew" (iii.6); his fear of being unmanned by yielding to the desire for close encounters with Belphoeban "ympes of beautie" who subdue "royalties and Realmes" to their "willes" (v.53). And the first fear is soon justified. When Phoebus detaches himself from Belphoebe's astrological chart to turn his eye and ray on Chrysogone, that heavenly horoscope becomes an Ovidian horrorscope. By the time we slip from the poetry of Phoebus in stanza 2 to the power of Titan in stanzas 6 and 7, we realize that the statement "Phoebus with faire beames did her adorne" politely periphrases a solar rape: from a safe distance the sun god's "fruitfull ray" pierces Chrysogone's womb with "secret powre unspide" even though, like Diana, she hides from men. This miracle of distanced and furtive sex affords the god the pleasures of Actaeon without the attendant dangers, while for the nymph there is impregnation without apparent sex, without awareness, without consent or pleasure.

The slippage I mentioned actually begins to affect the narrator while he is laughing on Belphoebe in the last three lines of stanza 2, where a pronominal swerve momentarily identifies her with Venus—"Jove laught on Venus . . . , / And Phoebus . . . did *her* adorne"—and the swerve is confirmed in the mention of the Graces. As if this seductive transformation occurs too precipitously, he tries in the next stanza to chasten the image:

> Her berth was of the wombe of Morning dew,
>> And her conception of the joyous Prime,
>> And all her whole creation did her shew
>> Pure and unspotted from all loathly crime,
>> That is ingenerate in fleshly slime.
>> So was this virgin borne, so was she bred,
>> So was she trayned up from time to time,
>> In all chast vertue, and true bounti-hed
> Till to her dew perfection she was ripened.

(vi.3)

The residual touch of Venus in "berth . . . of Morning dew" leads to a sublimatory recoil similar to that which motivates Pygmalion's immaculate conception of Galatea. Here the aversion to sex seems focused primarily on the loathly crime ingenerate in the slimy female element—of which the narrator's Galatea is free because he imagines for her a mother "who by race / A Faerie was, yborne of high degree" (vi.4).

The attempted distinction between "fleshly slime" and "Morning dew" is undone by the fact that in this context both are Venerean traces—the homonymous recurrence of "dew" in the final line ironically sustains the Venus ripening within Belphoebe—and we shall see later that they are also traces of the "loathly crime" of castration to which Venus owes her dewy birth and power. But when fleshly slime snakes back in at stanza 8, it is diverted to a different order of explanation. To the bemused male reader—"him that reades / So straunge ensample"—the learned narrator offers the comfort of ethnoscience. Soberly he cites the analogy of Nilus, the fertile action of whose "fattie waves" we last saw being compared to Error's vomit in Book I. The "sacred throne" of Chrysogone's "chaste bodie" is now assimilated to the fluvial mud informed, as "men do fynd," with "Infinite shapes of creatures," and in her abjection poor Chrysogone wonders to see that throne transformed not only biologically but also rhetorically into "a belly so upblone" (vi.5, 8–9). It doesn't seem likely that the women to whom, according to Quilligan, this canto is addressed can be as pleased as the men by what "reason teacheth" (vi.8). But they can't complain about the subsequent course of the narrative. As if in reaction to Chrysogone's plight and Titan's monopoly of power, the rest of canto vi is devoted to the project of domesticating male sexuality and placing it firmly under female control. When we reach the garden, for example, we find a much improved model of parthenogenesis—a horticultural model that guarantees automatic, impersonal, nonerotic, male-free reproduction, a model that gives women the kind of reproductive freedom from the male denied to Chrysogone. "Dame Nature" presides over it at stanza 30, and at stanza 34 the God of Genesis confers reproductive autonomy on it by the verbal fiat that, uttered long ago, eliminates the need not only for a "Gardiner" but also for the solar middleman, who reappears at the end of stanza 38 only in his diminished and despicable role as a lily-killer. By the end of the journey, Adonis will have replaced Chrysogone in the passive position, and Venus will have replaced the phallic god.

It has often been said that Adonis is or has become the sun, and although this may seem incompatible with the pattern I'm discussing, a minor rephrasing that makes the statement more precise will show that it is fully compatible, and is in fact the point of the pattern. What has been displaced to Adonis is not the title or being of the sun but its function and power—the symbolic function of representing the cosmic source of physical life and light under the aspect of male virility and sexual domination. This symbolism is embedded in a biological myth, a discourse of ethnoscience, that not only reflects but reinforces and naturalizes male domination in the discourse of gender. The father of this discursive imperialism is Phoebus as the god of poetry, the patron of male imagination who is also, in his role as Belphoebe's sire, the father of another familiar genre in the discourse of gender, Petrarchism. When Venus and Adonis replace Titan and Chrysogone, their positional inversion signifies a change from one hegemonic form of the discourse of gender to its mirroring opposite. The point made by the inversion is that the generative and sexual power of the male, initially symbolized by solar aggressivity, has been resymbolized in a form that emphasizes wounded, engulfed, acquiescent passivity, a form congenial to the gynarchic idyll toward which the canto drives.

If canto vi may be said to have a "story," it is the story of the play and conflict of these opposed discourses. When the narrator calls the birth of the twins "a goodly storie" that he found "in antique books" (5–6) he cues us to its citational status, and marks it as a traditional cultural discourse. Later, he moves past the elegiac tokens of "sweet Poets verse" (45) and ascribes his account of Adonis to unspecified sources (46–48). Paul Alpers notes that the repeated hearsay formulas "remind us that the myth is a creation of many men and has taken on a life of its own," a life, he adds, that is "independent but still obviously capable of nourishing an individual poet."[24] To put this more precisely, it may be the creation of many *males*, though that has yet to be determined. My question is whether Alpers has got their relation to the individual poet right when he uses the word "nourishing." Everything "some say" and "they say" in those stanzas is consoling to partisans of Adonis, and assures them that he has escaped the "wretched fate" of the "sad lovers" who died into flowers. But doesn't that Ovidian metaphor linger on in the image of the prone Adonis? Resembling Marinell on the ocean floor and Timias on the forest floor, there he lies, ensnared with flowers like Marvell's vegetable love, or better (or worse), like the lovely vegetable Marvell's phrase so wickedly suggests and turns away from. So I am not convinced that the poet of the Adonis stanzas is exactly *nourished* by the mythic sources he mobilizes. I think it more likely that he is seeking protection from them— protection from the consequences of his own courageous quest for the woman's paradise beyond the boundaries of the domains of language use controlled by men.

If the consolation he seeks at this august moment comes from a myth created by males, doesn't that suggest a small swerve away from the goal of the quest? And incidentally, just who *is* "he"? I can go along with Alpers's view that "he" is Spenser only if I stipulate that Spenser—and by "Spenser" I mean the text I interpret—impersonates a narrator who tells stories recognizably appropriated from "antique books" and whose commitment to the values inscribed in those books the impersonator questions. Given that reservation, I accept Alpers's notion that the narrator need not be separated from his narrative, and that his comments on the stories he tells reinforce those values.[25] In canto vi the sinuous oscillation between impersonated commentary and impersonated description is at times bewildering, and in fact the very idea of storytelling is rendered extremely problematical. If a speaker informs us that he is going to "declare" a goodly story, we expect to hear about things that happen in time and space, and from the fifth stanza to the second line of stanza 19 these expectations are met. For this very reason, they are all the more frustrated by the subsequent account of the garden. One critic after another has pointed to the incongruities, the rhetorical duplicity, the bizarre disruptions of narrative and descriptive logic, that drop a kind of hinder gate between the reader and the referent of description. The referent is more clearly a place (the seminary of Nature) from stanzas 29 through 33 than it is from 34 through 38, and with the assault of Time in 39 it gathers itself back into a definite place (the hill and grove of Venus), but one that is pictorially and iconographically different from the first place. The two places are locked into positional relation to us by demonstrative shifters: the narrator and his readers are *here*, in the world, this side of the garden wall; *that* garden is *there*, vaguely *some*where—the narrator isn't telling—but definitely *else*where, except when it seems to be in, or to represent, the world, which happens between the two descriptions as well as in moments of positional and visual unclarity in the first. These changes in the account intensify what may be called *the effect of allegory*. The account has a conspicuous air of meaning or symbolizing something Big, but as the even bigger gobbets of learned commentary allowed into print testify, it would be hard to say just what that something is. The problem, then, is how to interpret this investment in mystifying discourse and, especially, how to connect it to the gender conflict the discourse vehiculates.

Let's begin, then, with the following premises: the gardens of Adonis passage both invites and frustrates visualization; it raises from the verdure of description a mist of overlapping allegories that invite but resist rational paraphrase; it diffuses these effects of allegory in a haze of allusions to a variety of mainstream texts and traditions. Let's also premise that the effect of allegory changes with the introduction of the *mons Veneris* in stanza 43. An iconography that couples the bodies of the goddess and her garden within an Ovidian framework differs from one whose terms and images touch off sparks of Platonic, Aristotelian, Neoplatonic, Augustinian, hexameral, cosmographic, eschatological, and—last but not least—antifeminist discourses. Finally, let's remember the old tradition that compares man to woman as reason to passion, soul to body, spirit to matter, culture to nature, and head to torso; and in connection with that let's recall the specific claim, most notably expressed in the *Symposium*, that the creation of poems, laws, ideas, and other products of the mind or spirit (philosophies and cosmologies, for example) is preferable to the creation of babies. This dream of male parthenogenesis ingeniously excludes the female other while appropriating her generative power and nurturant role through metaphoric sublimation. Such tactics are familiar wherever the gendering of male children involves their being weaned by initiation or education from the woman-dominated household to the extradomestic world dominated by men.

From what I have just said, it may seem that I think the more heavily allegorized seminary of Nature described from stanzas 30 through 38 appeals to male readers, while the account of the more sensuous, passionate, and bodily pleasance of Venus appeals to female readers. That deduction would not be entirely correct. It could even be totally wrong if the claim was ascribed to my belief that women go for more concrete description and less abstract allegory than men because they are naturally more sensuous and emotional and stupid. That isn't it at all. My reasons are not based on difference in nature; they are not even culture-specific but Book III–specific and canto vi–specific.

The position of female reader engendered by the poem is one anyone can apply for and fill so long as s/he sympathizes with the desire to escape from the predatory or narcissistic or patriarchal scenarios women find themselves inscribed in during the first five cantos; to escape from the pains mothers and virgins were forced to suffer or take under the pressure of chivalric, dynastic, and erotic initiatives; to withdraw into a garden that holds out the promise of autonomy, fulfillment, and power. The applicants for the position don't want a garden that will dissolve into allegory once they get there, especially the sorts of allegory, or phallegory, that would reinscribe them in hierarchies congenial to the male imagination. So they want a real *hortus conclusus* with real groves and real flowery beds and boys and birds safe behind a real double wall secured by the golden locks and iron bolts of a real hinder gate.

The position of male reader engendered by the poem is a little more challenging. Its applicants will endorse what woman wants because they're decent and fair-minded, having been fashioned by the poem in virtuous and gentle discipline; they are true gentlemen, whatever their gender. But they are still troubled by bad dreams; the old gynephobia won't go away, and even as they applaud the progress of Venus into the gloomy grove atop her real garden, the narrator keeps pricking them with image-darts that bear the traces of primal terrors. So surely they can be forgiven if they respond with gratitude to such minims of allegorical sublimation as the glimpse of "the Father of all formes" in stanza 47.

This, then, is how I propose to treat the relation of the narrative as rhetoric to the engendering of the reader. Let's look first at what happens between stanzas 30 and 33:

In that same Gardin all the goodly flowres,
    Wherewith dame Nature doth her beautifie,
    And decks the girlonds of her paramoures,
    Are fetcht: there is the first seminarie
    Of all things, that are borne to liue and die,
    According to their kindes. Long worke it were,
    Here to account the endlesse progenie
    Of all the weedes, that bud and blossome there;
But so much as doth need, must needs be counted here.

It sited was in fruitfull soyle of old,
    And girt in with two walles on either side;
    The one of yron, the other of bright gold,
    That none might thorough breake, nor ouer-stride:
    And double gates it had, which opened wide,
    By which both in and out men moten pas;
    Th'one faire and fresh, the other old and dride:
    Old *Genius* the porter of them was,
Old *Genius*, the which a double nature has.

He letteth in, he letteth out to wend,
    All that to come into the world desire;
    A thousand thousand naked babes attend
    About him day and night, which doe require,
    That he with fleshly weedes would them attire:
    Such as him list, such as eternall fate
    Ordained hath, he clothes with sinfull mire,
    And sendeth forth to liue in mortall state,
Till they againe returne backe by the hinder gate.

After that they againe returned beene,
    They in that Gardin planted be againe;
    And grow afresh, as they had neuer seene
    Fleshly corruption, nor mortall paine.
    Some thousand yeares so doen they there remaine;
    And then of him are clad with other hew,
    Or sent into the chaungefull world againe,
    Till thither they returne, where first they grew:
So like a wheele around they runne from old to new.

                                                    (vi.30–33)

As the narrator begins to describe a scene that will embody a gynarchic perspective on generation, desire, and pleasure, he uses names (Nature and Genius) that carry strong allusions to *The Complaint of Nature*, *Cosmographia*, and *The Romance of the Rose*. This allows the suspicion that the gynarchic perspective is circumscribed by that of the male tradition in terms of which it is conveyed. The terms include the antifeminism of Genius's speech in the *Romance* and the problem of sodomy about which the Nature of Alanus complains. In different ways, both encode resistance to the very gynarchic idyll the stanzas celebrate.[26] Hence if this intertextual network evokes a thought of matriarchal utopia, it is a limited matriarchy. Nevertheless, my sympathy with the maternal perspective on the life cycle moves me to discount the vaguely misanthropic description of the activities assigned the garden's first male figure, but not without first indicating what is misanthropic about them.

The double nature of Old Genius, like his double gates, signifies not merely that he is both birthgiver and deathgiver, but that he is a deathgiver *because* he is a birthgiver. The sad antithesis of stanza 31—"faire and fresh" versus "old and dride"—seems to prejudice the description of the gatekeeper to whom the dark side of Dame Nature's reproductive power is displaced: Old Genius is bound by his epithet more closely to the "old and dride" than to the "faire and fresh." The rhetoric stabs with increasing force at the folly of the desire to leave the garden for the world: from "fleshly weedes" to "sinfull mire" to "fleshly corruption," and from "mortall state" to "mortall paine." The naked babes who long for this fate do so only because the promise of new life is coupled with the eradication of old knowledge. The emphasis tilts from departure to return, and the cycle is reversed as if to undo the harm—to "make-it-unhappened" (*Ungeschehenmachen* again). The wheel of desire *runs* back toward the garden from old to new. "Leeve mooder, leet me in," and when she does, it takes the returned veterans "Some thousand yeares" to recover.[27]

This is a parent's golden-age view of the life cycle. It does not take much probing to expose the strains and transgressions smoothed over by the incantatory flow of echoing words and phrases that celebrate the idyllic dream of reversal: the strains of sexual and generational warfare, the elision of sexual with generational desire. The pejorative epithets suspended in the flow encapsulate in generalized form the bitterness of the elder's view of life as loss, a bitterness that elsewhere in Spenser is composed of nostalgia for lost youth, envy of those who have it, anger at their prodigal misuse of it. The bitterness in this passage seems directed against the folly of the naked babes' desire of incarnation: they pester Genius for "fleshly weedes," and "weedes" is still redolent of the fragrance of those that "bud and blossome" in stanza 30; he rewards them instead with "sinfull mire" and sends them "forth to live in mortall state" until they have had enough and learned their lesson. This bitterness can easily be assimilated to the narrator's partisan representation of Nature and Venus. You can, for example, associate it with the mother's judgment on those who are foolish enough to leave their vegetable bliss in the womb for the autonomy of gendered life in a man's world, the life in Jove's iron age and under his "soveraigne see." The enclosed garden is introduced as a place that commemorates loss—"called is by her lost lovers name" (29)—and then, in stanzas 30–33, is depicted as a place walled in against loss, isolated from the male- and death-dominated "world" of "mortall state." The theme of the mother's loss of power over her child, the center of the previous episode involving Venus's search for Cupid, modulates into the theme of the lover's loss of her beloved.

The elision of these two themes affects the description in stanza 31. James Nohrnberg and David Miller have discussed the importance of incestuous desire in Book III, and in lines 5 through 7 of that stanza there is a hint of sexual intercourse that adumbrates the two perspectives, maternal and filial, on the mother's desire.[28] The hint is dropped partly by the use of the term "men" in line 6; this is the only occurrence of that word in the description of the garden and its occupants, and though the usage seems generic it momentarily narrows the range of Nature's creatures to the human race and its dominant gender (in stanza 35 forms "fit for reasonable soules" are mentioned). The perspectival difference is produced by the ambiguous relation of the two contrasting pairs coupled in lines 6 and 7: "By which both in and out men moten pas; / Th'one faire and fresh, the other old and dride." The featured aspect is the fantasy of reversal and promise of rebirth: you enter the garden old and dried, and leave it fair and fresh. But the parallel position of the clauses—"in" lines up with the pre-caesural "faire and fresh"—momentarily muddies that message. If you are fair and fresh when you go in through the wide-open gates, and old and dried when you leave, that is clearly another story: the story of the threat or fear of maternal eroticism, of the mother's power to enfeeble, desiccate, and reduce her "men" to impotence. Again, this is only a momentary effect, and the reading is of course ruled out by what follows. But if you have registered it, it may affect the connotative value you give to the naked babes who want out in stanza 32, and who seem importunate about it by the time their desire is matched by its first rhyme-word. The price of the rebirth the garden promises is perpetual infantilization, life as a vegetable. From the standpoint of the male reader, the only safe position in that maternal paradise is the one occupied by Old Genius, whom Nohrnberg calls "a slightly dissociated *puer senex*" (532) and whose two natures as womb and tomb porter are liminal parentheses: they bracket out those stages of the male life cycle during which the mother's control over her sons and lovers could be more effectively resisted.

This diminution of the male conforms with the logic of idyllic desire, which is autonomous desire, desire of escape from the power of the other. *Idyll* means "little picture" (*eidyllion*), and its logic drives the imagination toward the closure of spatial enclosure, the conclusion of the *hortus conclusus*. Accordingly, idyllic narrative drives toward the visualization or description of a place apart from others, securely removed from the world's grasp. I emphasize this drive because it contrastively highlights the meaning of the rhetorical strategy that resists it.[29] Thomas Roche was one of the first to demonstrate that the rhetoric of stanzas 31–33 denies precisely the visualization that the narrator pretends to offer, and David Miller has more recently shown how the ambiguous "barrage of doublings" in stanza 31 "dis-locates" what the narrative presumptively locates.[30] The ambiguity continues in the first two lines of stanza 32, "He letteth in, he letteth out to wend, / All that to come into the world desire," where letting in and letting out both seem to denote coming into the world. Of lines 6 and 7 in stanza 33 A. C. Hamilton notes that the disjunctive "Or" is puzzling because "*and* sent into the chaungeful world againe" would make more sense.[31] Nothing in the passage suggests that "clad with other hew" indicates an intra-garden alternative to being sent out, so we are left with the possibility that the two lines express synonymous alternatives, which means that the garden and the world must be the same. This dissolution of boundaries is contained by the shifters—"that" in line 2, "thither" in line 8—but, as we'll see, the boundaries break down from stanzas 34 through 38 and do not get securely reestablished until the counterfactual subjunctive that exorcises Time in stanza 41 modulates into the indicative mood. Then, as the fantasy is actualized, the garden's body solidifies, becomes an icon of the goddess's body, and forms the uncanny place elsewhere that protectively enfolds her triumphant idyll.

In the first section of this essay I stated that I would present the gardens of Adonis passage as Venus's answer to the misogynist, antierotic, and gynephobic discourse Ovid assigns Orpheus in *Metamorphoses* X. But I also stated that since the answer was delivered by a male narrator his critique might be vulnerable to the effects of the logic—the logic of Pinocchio's nose, or of castration—it targets. This hypothesis, which has been tested in the preceding pages of interpretation, will obviously affect my response to the conflict about gender positions I reported in the second section—Maureen Quilligan's claim and Simon Shepherd's denial that Book III of *The Faerie Queene* privileges the female perspective and censures the male perspective on its narrative. The reading developed in the subsequent sections indicates a strong preference in both its author and Spenser's narrator for the position Quilligan advocates. But it also testifies to a kind of backlash, a subversive countermovement of gynephobia generated by the narrator's drive to visualize and actualize the fantasy of Venerean gynarchy. Though this aspect of the reading may seem to implicate the reader "in some of the classic sexist ways of looking at women" (Shepherd, 79), it actually has very little in common with Shepherd's simplistic argument and terse rejection of the alternative. My debts are all to Quilligan, and an important part of any critical debt is gratitude for the chance to differ, the chance to find, in the paradise of interpretive desire, a little corner all one's own. And this is all I seek as I turn to give Quilligan's reading the attention it deserves.

Quilligan argues that "the safest vantage point for viewing" what happens in the gardens "is that of Venus herself—that is, the female perspective." The male viewpoint is "potentially endangered by" the vision of "Venus's awesome power over Adonis," so that "the most comfortable and unthreatened viewpoint" on the gardens is that of a female reader (193, 196).[32] Quilligan finds this message inscribed in the moment of the meeting between Venus and Diana at which the Actaeon allusion is displaced to Venus. Here, as she notes in a more recent essay, Spenser "conspicuously rewrites tragedy out of the famous moment by removing the potential for sexual violation." These perceptions compose into a powerful and original interpretation, one that has forced or enabled me to revisit III.vi after many years of complacency with what I thought was an adequate if youthful vision of the canto. Under her tutelage I have discovered, like other reentry students, that all has changed, and that these ancient glittering eyes must learn to see differently. Therefore I hope it will not be misconstrued as patronizing if I suggest one or two small changes that will strengthen Quilligan's argument—give it more muscle, so to speak.

I begin by interrogating the status she assigns the name "Spenser" because she uses it frequently and casually without specifying the range of its referents or making distinctions among them, so that it isn't easy to determine whether in any particular instance she is referring to the author or the narrator and, if to the narrator, whether she views him as an innocent or a suspicious reader of the stories he tells. I have already touched on this problem above, and I'll simply repeat that since in my lexicon "Spenser" denotes the product rather than the producer of his text, it also denotes the product of interpretations of the text. The complication that bears on Quilligan's usage stems from my thesis that this product, this narrator, sometimes mimics or parodies the perspective of a traditional (ergo, male) reader whose attitudes are those of the dominant literary and cultural discourses *The Faerie Queene* represents. For example, in the sixth canto the narrator begins by sharing with *his* readers an Actaeonic prospect on the secrets of the goodly new stories he claims to have discovered in old books. When, in the seventh stanza, he says that the sunbeams pierced Chrysogone's womb "With so sweet sence and secret power unspide," the "sweet sence" must—since Chrysogone sleeps through it—be Titan's, and the narrator seems in describing Titan's secret pleasure to be identifying himself with it.[33] At such moments I'm not sure he could be said to be making an appeal to female readers, and this leads to another revision of Quilligan's thesis. Her statement that in canto vi we "look at female power from a peculiarly female perspective" (197) seems to collapse the distinction between the narrator and the implied reader. I would prefer to say that we look at female power from the peculiarly male perspective of the narrative occasionally addressed to female readers to whose interests it is clearly sympathetic. This revision in fact reinforces and renders more consistent Quilligan's claim that the male viewpoint on the garden is represented as threatened by its vision of female power. But to say this only leads me to wonder whether what I am doing for, or to, Quilligan is a clue to what the narrator is doing for, or to, his female readers. For the consequences of my revision differ from those she adduces.

By way of making my own position clear, let me reaffirm my commitment to the notion that canto vi is trying to give the woman's cause a better than even break. Speaking for myself, I want Venus to have everything that is coming to her, and I commend the narrator for wanting the same. But wanting it is one thing, and responding to what transpires when you make it happen is another. My point is that if Quilligan likes the garden as much as she says Spenser's female readers do, she and they may be tempted to like it more than they should—or at least with more unqualified enthusiasm than I think is warranted by the narrator's responses to the woman's fantasy of paradise he gradually builds up to. The garden, she claims, celebrates "the cosmic legitimacy of the female Eros's triumph over a male Thanatos" (196). It clearly does, and even as I applaud this outcome I have to admit that I find it a little scary. Nor am I relieved by her attempt to assure me that "the garden's eroticism should not be read as dismemberment" after reminding me that Venus's cave has been described by Lauren Silberman as "the vagina dentata." I take some heart, but not too much, from her view of the garden as "a vision of male sexuality brought safely and creatively under the control of an awesome female power," but her comment that "the anatomical allegory plays out [a fantasy] . . . of female control over everlasting sexual communion" leaves me vicariously exhausted (195–96). So I am forced to wonder whether my reaction merely betrays my own anxiety or whether I can find any justification for it, any echo of it, in the narrator's discourse. The examples I have chosen to discuss are admittedly one-sided since they include some of the more lurid passages in the stanzas (34–38) that follow the account of Old Genius at the garden gate.

Critics have often been puzzled by the way Spenser uses the philosophical buzzwords "substance" and "form" in the sequence that moves from the God of Genesis (34) through the description of the cosmic womb (36) to the news that the bits of unchanging substance, feminized in stanza 38 ("her hew," "her temper"), put on and wear out variable forms. I think it's less puzzling if we see it as an example of a familiar and relevant effect: the effect of "symbolic inversion," which Stallybrass and White more pointedly describe as "a generalized economy of transgression and of the recoding of high/low relations," though a recoding that retains the same hierarchic structure of inequality.[34] The biblical image of creative autonomy as the legacy of the Father—"the mightie word, / Which first was spoken by th'Almightie lord" (34)—is recoded in stanzas 36 and 37 as an exercise of maternal power. Now it isn't the inversion itself that makes me uneasy. I praise and admire it as a long-delayed acknowledgment of Mother's share in the hexameral achievement, a share concealed by the tradition of hexameral discourse. But I can do this only as long as I keep a safe Platonic distance between me and the substance of the text. If I draw too close I begin to feel the need of an ounce of civet. What the text discloses may not be hell, may not be the sulphurous pit, but it's pretty bad.

> For in the wide womb of the world there lyes,
> In hatefull darknesse and in deepe horrore,
> An huge eternall Chaos, which supplyes
> The substances of natures fruitfull progenyes.

> (36)

This begins to sound a little like Arthur's fantasy of Night, "foule Mother of annoyance sad" (iv.55). I hear the "deepe hor*rore*" of the phallic mother's savage beasts. I think also of previous touches of aversion in the references to "fleshly slime" in stanza 3, "mud" in stanza 8, and "sinfull mire" in stanza 32—touches, to put it more forcefully, of *abjection* in the precise sense given that term by Julia Kristeva. And things are not made easier by the invasion from inner space that follows in stanza 37:

> All things from thence doe their first being fetch,
> And borrow matter, whereof they are made,
> Which when as forme and feature it does ketch,
> Becomes a bodie, and doth then invade
> The state of life, out of the griesly shade.

It is soothing to learn, if only for a moment, that the *things* have some power: they can fetch their first being and borrow their matter. But as soon as they do, they open themselves up to predation. The "plenteous horne" of Belphoebe's horoscope has become a fearsome *copia*, an invasion of maternal body-snatchers, a monstrous forcing-bed, the implacable force of an inexhaustible reproductive power flooding the world with her grisly hungry stuff, catching and consuming the forms of individual things. And I am truly scared.

But no matter. To return to our goodly story: at stanza 38, with woman securely on top, the chastened masculine viewpoint is inscribed in the Platonic nuance and courtly flourish of the elegiac phrase "that faire flowre of beautie." The transgressive logic of the passage might suggest that even the *idea* of beauty falls prey to the incessant metamorphoses of the maternal invaders. But this possibility is immediately blocked by the simile that follows: the image of the lily undone by "the sunny ray" displaces blame to the power that pierced Chrysogone's womb; Titan's "fruitfull ray" is readmitted only as a destroyer. I suspect Spenser's female readers would be pleased by this development, as well as by the appearance of the new scapegoat it introduces in stanza 39: wicked Time flailing rabidly away with his scythe and flaggy wings. I do not share their complacency. Expelling the lethal power of the mother's fertility onto that figure slanders my sex, converts my fear to anger, and prompts a thought of revenge. If you can't enjoy their joy or youth, if you can't stem the killing force that through the green fuse drives the flower, then cut them down. I sympathize with wicked Time as I think Milton did, and in his behalf I say this to Venus's "deare brood": "League with you I seek, / And mutual amity so strait, so close, / That I with you must dwell or you with me." Evil be thou my good.

This bitter moment represents the cost of the effort to imagine "male sexuality brought safely and creatively under the control of an awesome female power." I repeat Quilligan's phrase here because I think my reactions to canto vi bear out her stunning insight into gendered reading, and I also think they reflect the discursive reactions that produce and are objectified in the figure of Time. What Time signifies is a mutability not limited to mortality. It extends to losses and deprivations of other kinds. He is, both objectively and subjectively, a figure of castration. His scythe, his flaggy wings, his "malice hard," proclaim his draconian or Saturnine affinity to the class of envious have-nots that people Spenser's poetry—to the bitter elders, for example, and the guardians of the law whose fear of Venus makes them stoic censors in Book IV. His destructive frenzy repeats that of Guyon in the Bower of Bliss. He is recalled in the wild Boar's cruel tusk and malice, also in "the winged boy" who "hath with spoiles and cruelty / Ransackt the world" (49), and will again, when Venus's great enemy reappears in the figure of Busirane. Time is like one of the nodal points in a network whose synapses fire off in different parts of *The*

Faerie Queene, and the charges he bears suggest that Quilligan's phrase could well supply the network with its name: The Endangered Male Viewpoint.

As if relieved by the explosive and frenzied materialization of Time, the narrative sympathetically reverts to the perspective of Venus. The mantle of motherhood is transferred from dame Nature to Venus after the lethal effects of unrestrained fertility have been transferred from the cosmic womb to Time, whose enmity now justifies the continuing exercise of reproductive power. Before turning to the Venerean climax of the canto, I would like to review the goddess's progress through the sixth canto. When the canto begins, she is confined to her planetary role under Jove's "soveraigne see." We next find her in her Uranian "house of goodly formes and faire aspects." In both of these textual sites she serves "high God" as one of the instruments through which he exercises his creative power, either as a planetary influence or as a generative but desexualized principle of the World Soul. Trapped in that refined form she has a hard time commanding the obedience of the male desire her fatter incarnation gives birth to. She can regain control of Cupid only by leaving her patriarchal house and descending—or regressing—to her Pandemic and Ovidian avatars, and by co-opting Diana in a mythological conjunction that will shift the balance of power. This happy if suspect negotiation facilitates the successful journey to her bower of bliss. She receives the title of "great mother" in stanza 40 (not before) and soon thereafter regains her fabled fatness by sheltering in the dilated landscape of her own body, where she rules unchallenged.

At this point, since I seem to be turning Venus into a dramatic character, I should probably issue a disclaimer in the spirit of Paul Alpers. Let me reassure you, therefore, that I think of Venus only as a symbol, a kind of intertextual allusion. The denotation of the name "Venus" doesn't have to be restricted to, say, a goddess or a planet or the World Soul, or to a symbol of beauty, of woman's desire and desirability, of her dangerous erotic and creative power, and so forth. "Venus" may also denote a second-order symbol of discourses that produce and deploy the figure. That is, representing Venus may be a way to represent and parody the discourses that represent Venus. And those discourses are expressions not merely of male desire, but of the discursive regime we somewhat loosely call "patriarchal."[35] The demystification of that regime can be found oddly enough within the very traditions that perpetuate it. John Hankins's traditional survey of the traditions behind Spenser shows that although mythographers and others depict Venus as a goddess they interpret her as an alienated figure of the masculine role in procreation.[36] Like the roiling sea-cradled sex of the castrated father from which she is born,

Venus is a projection, an ejaculation, of male fantasy. The product of a castration, she is constituted and empowered by the seminal spume of desire, and then externalized as its object and cause. (She is, in that respect, the daughter of her own son.) Her dangerous phallic power, her power both to generate and to castrate, derives from the Oedipal scene of her birth. The complex of fears and desires condensed in her figure are repeatedly repressed in discourses that purge it of Oedipal terrors by various strategies of allegorization, countertextual strategies that dissociate the castration from the birth and reposition both in such safer sites as cosmology, cosmogony, and theology.[37] When Spenser begins his Venus canto with allusions to two of those purged Venerean sites, the planetary and Neoplatonic contexts mentioned in stanzas 2 and 12, he marks the target of a textualizing discourse that will restore to the rarefied Venus both her "copious fertility" and her "threatening . . . sexuality."[38] Her progress through the partitions of the canto's citational field gives fullest scope to a fantasy of what women do in men require—and seldom find— the lineaments of gratified desire. Yet at the same time, the canto registers the threat, the risk, to a narrative viewpoint engendered by the very discourses it opposes. The threat is inscribed in the teller's rhetorical and narrative inventions. These are organized as a dialectic between, on the one hand, the increase and integration of woman's powers and, on the other, increasing signs of male anxiety, resistance, malice, and, finally, submission to a climactic moment of generative sexuality, a submission that remains, nevertheless, serrated by hints of terror and symbolic castration.

As this climax approaches, the narrative shifts attention from Venus's reproductive power to sexual pleasure, and to an image of perpetual communion that, although it implies reproduction, carefully excludes mention of its pains and labors; it isn't Venus who has the babies. The logic of this withdrawal to erotic play enacts that of the song of the Rose in the Bower of Bliss (II.xii.74–75). In the climactic image of redundant *jouissance* Venus modulates back into her Ovidian form so as to "reape sweet pleasure of the wanton boy" (46). This is clearly a benign revision of Malecasta's tapestry Venus, conflating that figure with the great mother, and its echoes of the Bower of Bliss make it a benign revision of Acrasia. Nevertheless, the Malecastan and Acrasian overtones, along with their dangers and ambiguities, adhere to the revision. They draw the figure of Venus back into the system of erotic discourses that edge her with menace. The beautiful reaper is the antithesis of the grim reaper, but she remains a reaper; she does Time's work, and the boar's. Or *they* do *her* work. While the poetry of her wish-hill excludes one after another fragmentary image of male threat—sharp steel, wicked beasts, "*Phoebus* beams," and "Aeolus sharp blast"—in the cave beneath her landscape body Time's "malice hard" has become internalized as the prisoner or property of the phallic mother.

In Lauren Silberman's fine reading of the passage, "the boar returns as the agent of castration" in an image that "promises Adonis's safety while figuring forth the *vagina dentata*, ultimate expression of Venus's fearsome power" (271). That reading is supported, I think, by the pun in the phrase "with his cruell tuske him deadly cloyd" (48). Since "cloy" means not only to pierce but also to surfeit or satiate with sweetness, to gratify beyond the limits of desire, it isn't inconceivable that the phrase conceals a subversive comment on the statement that Venus "when ever that she will, / Possesseth him, and of his sweetnesse takes her fill," or on the statement that "he may not / For ever die," even if he should want to (46–47). Adonis's share in this pleasure is described in an oddly qualified way: "Joying his goddess and of her enjoyd." The goddess is the primary subject of both verbs.[39] When Adonis momentarily merges with the boar in stanza 48, there is a question, intensified by the syntactic inversion in line 7 ("That her sweet love his malice mote avoyd"), as to whose malice it is, and who or what's doing the avoiding—or voiding—to what or whom. These confusions are not resolvable, and they have the effect of clogging, or cloying, the path to decisive acceptance or wholehearted approval of Venus's triumph. In such moments the narrative perspective seems trapped in ceaseless oscillation between the desire and the fear of Venus, between the desire to promote and proclaim woman's right to unencumbered fulfillment and the anxiety that, projected in the figure of Adonis, is not fully allayed by all the nice things Poets and others say.

Silberman differs from Quilligan in hypothesizing a male reader: "The text . . . creates a reader who is anything but partial, who by a courage that is moral as well as sexual transcends the partiality Spenser attributes to men." She commends this reader for "facing the threat to which hierarchy and exclusion attest" (271). But her focus on the reader, like Quilligan's, blunts what I take to be the force of Spenser's Venus canto, which derives from the male narrator's viewpoint. The text creates a narrator who is anything but impartial not only because he inscribes the male fear of abjection in his celebration of Venus's triumph but also because he justifies the fear by the way he characterizes that triumph. For he represents it as a one-sided, absolute, and premature desire for closure, a hegemonic fantasy of maternal eroticism, or erotic maternalism. He motivates the fantasy, indeed justifies it, as a reaction to the spectacle of predatory, unstable, and self-protective male behavior in the earlier cantos, a reaction also to the cosmic imperialism of male desire and fantasy suggested by the sixth canto's discursive sampler. Spenser's discourse of

Venus is a contestatory discourse that talks back to the Ovidian source it alludes to as it does to all the other "antique books" glanced at or referenced in the sampler. Yet at the same time, the narrator marks the extremism of that reaction by displaying the anxiety that founds and sustains the contested master discourses. Thus the breakdown that occurs in the next six cantos is latent in the self-divided narrative of this one, and Busirane's hall of horrors in cantos xi–xii is only the climax of a process of backlash already at work in that self-division. Perhaps that is why the endangered male viewpoint dramatized in canto vi finds its specular complement in the endangered female viewpoint dramatized in cantos xi–xii. From vii through xii the narrative teeters crazily through a funhouse full of sexual freaks, a mob of lechers, deviants, rapists, monsters, whores, and sadists rushing by with the verve of a Russ Meyer production. This narrative conforms to and illustrates the logic of castration. From canto viii on the males try ever more busily—because ineffectively—to dominate, violate, and terrorize, or merely defend themselves against, female figures. The repeated pattern of male behavior in these cantos is the shift from weaker to more aggressive forms of violence, and from victimization to tyranny: the shift, for example, from the hapless witch's son to the hyena-like monster that feeds on women's flesh; from the Squire of Dames and Argante's other victims to Ollyphant; from the fisherman to Proteus, Malbecco to Paridell, and Scudamour to Busirane. Castration is inscribed in the reliance of helpless males on the cross-dressed virgins—Palladine (vii.37, 43–44, 52) and Britomart—whose investment parodies the gender roles of chivalric discourse. The cantos that follow Venus's garden idyll pour forth from their "plenteous horne" such an ingenious array of threats and lets to the male will that it is no wonder the legend of chastity eventuates in the *busy reign* of terror.

NOTES

1. This is a revised and expanded version of the Kathleen Williams Lecture delivered at the Spenser at Kalamazoo meeting on May 7, 1988. It gives me pleasure to thank Professor Regina Schwartz for suggestions that made the task of revision much easier.

2. Ovid, *Metamorphoses* X (Cambridge: Harvard University Press, 1946), II, 64–117. For a more detailed discussion, see my "Orpheus, Pan, and the Poetics of Misogyny: Spenser's Critique of Pastoral Love and Art," *English Literary History* 50 (1983): 27–34.

Pygmalion is both creator or "father" of Galatea and her lover. The relation is in that respect incestuous, and thus Myrrha's desire for her father is a "genealogically" motivated mirror image of her ancestral origin.

3. On the equation of narrator with narrative see my "Narrative as Rhetoric in *The Faerie Queene*," *English Literary Renaissance* 21 (1991): 3–48, especially 11–13 and 41–45.

4. This representational practice is more extensively discussed in Berger, "'Kidnapped Romance': Discourse in *The Faerie Queene*," in *Unfolded Tales: Essays on Renaissance Romance*, ed. George M. Logan and Gordon Teskey (Ithaca: Cornell University Press, 1989), 208–58.

5. See "From Body to Cosmos: The Dynamics of Representation in Precapitalist Society," *South Atlantic Quarterly* 91 (1992): 582–86.

6. On Actaeon in Spenser, his contemporaries, and his predecessors see Leonard Barkan's brilliant "Diana and Actaeon: The Myth as Synthesis," *English Literary Renaissance* 10 (1980): 317–59; Maureen Quilligan, *Milton's Spenser: The Politics of Reading* (Ithaca: Cornell University Press, 1983), 166–69 and 191–99; and Quilligan, "The Comedy of Female Authority in *The Faerie Queene*," *English Literary Renaissance* 17 (1987): 165–67. See also "'Kidnapped Romance,'" 254.

7. Cf. Ovid, *Metamorphoses* III.139–40.

8. *Milton's Spenser*, 188.

9. Simon Shepherd, *Spenser* (New York: Harvester Press, 1990), 58. Shepherd identifies himself as "an anti-heterosexist, anti-patriarchal man, who has worked in close and creative political alliances with feminists"—but who is not, he adds, "a woman" (59). In a review of this book Raymond Waddington complains that its "viewpoint is so resolutely that of the yobbo student sprawled in the back row that interest quickly fades" (*Studies in English Literature* 30 [1990]: 180). I am more partial to Shepherd's politics than I suspect Waddington is, and my chief quarrel with the book is that its investment in close reading is too halfhearted to support its arguments or justify its dismissive and contentious tone.

10. Lauren Silberman, "Singing Unsung Heroines: Androgynous Discourse in Book 3 of *The Faerie Queene*," in *Rewriting the Renaissance: The Discourse of Sexual Difference in Early Modern Europe*, ed. Margaret W. Ferguson, Maureen Quilligan, and Nancy J. Vickers (Chicago: University of Chicago Press, 1986), 271. Pamela Joseph Benson defends the view that Spenser's treatment of woman and women in Book III is only superficially profeminist but actually conservative: "Rule, Virginia: Protestant Theories of Female Regiment in *The Faerie Queene*," *English Literary Renaissance* 15 (1985): 277–92. David Lee Miller seconds this view in *The Poem's Two Bodies: The Poetics of the 1590 "Faerie Queene"* (Princeton: Princeton University Press, 1988), 215–81, especially 215–24. Arguing for "the subordination of the feminine in Spenser's allegory," Miller takes issue with Quilligan's position in *Milton's Spenser*, which he sees as "compelling evidence of the literary canon's continuing power to co-opt representations of the feminine on behalf of a patriarchal ideology" (217). The view to be developed in the present essay will in effect cut between Quilligan and Miller. For an interesting account of gendered writing in Book III influenced by Quilligan and Silberman, see Susanne Lindgren Wofford, "Gendering Allegory: Spenser's Bold Reader and the Emergence of Character in *The Faerie Queene* III," *Criticism* 30 (1988): 1–21.

11. This sentence is borrowed with slight alteration from "'Kidnapped Romance,'" 247.

It accords with the logic of Britomart's search for Artegall that she unhorses two Anteros figures—Guyon and Marinell—and thus symbolically lowers male resistance to female desire. At the same time, her threat to Cymoent—overthrowing Marinell is the first step in releasing him from maternal domination—leads to a renewal of maternal solicitude that recurs in Belphoebe in canto v and in Diana and Venus in vi.

12. All quotations of *The Faerie Queene* are from Spenser's *Faerie Queene*, ed. J. C. Smith (1909; rpt. Oxford: Clarendon Press, 1961), 2 volumes; hereafter cited in the text. I have normalized *j*'s and *v*'s.

13. Borrowed from "'Kidnapped Romance,'" 249.

14. Notice that in the encounter between them (vi.16–28) Diana is unarmed—without her hunting implements—and is thus parallel to Verdant with his "suspended instruments" in II (see Patricia Parker, *Literary Fat Ladies: Rhetoric, Gender, Property* [New York: Methuen, 1987], 54–66). She lacks her normative male power and responds to Venus as if the latter is a male, an Actaeon (see references to Quilligan in note 6 above). This, added to the anomalous reconciliation between the two traditionally antagonistic forces, suggests a potential and unusual threat to male power and security. The narrator sets up the danger as a premonitory feint and then reassuringly returns Venus and Diana to their traditional postures when Venus subordinates them both to male hegemony ("We both are bound to follow heavens beheasts, / And tend our charges with obeisance meeke," vi.22). After this they find the twins and take up nurturant duties.

15. See Parker, *Fat Ladies*, 62.

16. A. Leigh DeNeef has convincingly demonstrated how Spenser's techniques produce the illusion of an autonomous virgin and stress her illusoriness: *Spenser and the Motives of Metaphor* (Durham: Duke University Press, 1982), 115.

17. For a parallel discussion see "'Kidnapped Romance,'" 251.

18. Thomas P. Roche, Jr., *The Kindly Flame: A Study of the Third and Fourth Books of Spenser's "Faerie Queene"* (Princeton: Princeton University Press, 1964), 107.

19. Richard J. Berleth, "Heavens Favorable and Free: Belphoebe's Nativity in *The Faerie Queene*," *English Literary History* 40 (1973): 481.

20. Ibid., 485.

21. James Nohrnberg, *The Analogy of "The Faerie Queene"* (Princeton: Princeton University Press, 1976), 564.

22. Tormented by Cupid, Jove,

> leaving heavens kingdome, here did rove
> In straunge disguize, to slake his scalding smart;
> Now like a Ram, faire *Helle* to pervart,
> Now like a Bull, *Europa* to withdraw. . . .

23. Berleth, "Heavens Favorable and Free," 489.

24. Paul J. Alpers, *The Poetry of "The Faerie Queene"* (Princeton: Princeton University Press, 1967), 328.

25. See my "Narrative as Rhetoric," 11–13.

26. The implications of sodomy are broader than those vaguely glanced at in the reference to "the hinder gate"; but even if the reader picks up connotations of same-sex desire, the interpretive framework gives it a specific significance here: autonomy from the other and from heterosexuality.

27. Noted by Nohrnberg, *Analogy*, 529.

28. See Nohrnberg, *Analogy*, 436; and Miller, *Poem's Two Bodies*, 279–80.

29. The text, as we shall shortly see, interferes with the very visualization it encourages. On the metaphorics and politics of spatialization, see Louis Marin, *Utopics: Spatial Play*, trans. Robert A. Vollrath (Atlantic Highlands, N.J.: Humanities Press, 1984), especially pp. 33–60.

30. Roche, *Kindly Flame*, 119–22; Miller, *Poem's Two Bodies*, 254.

31. A. C. Hamilton, ed., *Spenser: The Faerie Queene* (1977; rpt. New York: Longman, 1980), 361.

32. See also "Comedy of Female Authority," 164–67.

33. Contrast, for example, the account of Venus's rape of Adonis in Malecasta's tapestry (III.i.34–38): there Venus kidnaps the poor young boy and furtively takes advantage of him. Titan's rape is no less furtive or forceful, but those qualities are rhetorically muffled, and it gets more sympathetic press from the narrator, who describes it in romantic and procreative terms. Of course the narrator both distances himself from Venus's rape and scapegoats it by assimilating it to Malecasta's desire and representing it as an ecphrasis, which is a way of putting it in scare quotes.

34. Peter Stallybrass and Allon White, *The Politics and Poetics of Transgression* (Ithaca: Cornell University Press, 1986), 19.

35. See "'Kidnapped Romance,'" 238–39, n.29.

36. See John Erskine Hankins, *Source and Meaning in Spenser's Allegory: A Study of "The Faerie Queene"* (Oxford: Clarendon Press, 1971), 241–46.

37. Conspicuous sublimation—that is, mystification and evasion—of the Hesiodic story of Aphrodite's birth begins with Plato, most prominently in the *Symposium*. One has only to probe a little way beneath the surface of suave speechmaking in that dialogue to find the flood of apprehensions that shakes the homosocial confidence of the symposiasts: the desire of lovers to throw off the yoke of fathers, parents, and the patriarchal *oikos*; the attempt to overthrow the myth celebrating woman's (Aphrodite's) power over male desire by distinguishing a higher, Uranian, Aphrodite who presides over all-male attachments; the fears implicit in that attempt, which registers the Hesiodic association of Aphrodite with the nightmare of terrible fathers hating, burying, swallowing their sons, of the son mutilating the father, of the paternal phallus begetting the archetypal seductress who will enact his revenge by her ability to disempower and emasculate his sons.

The story of the twin Aphrodites, and of the sublimated Uranian twin whose genesis is carefully dissociated from the scene of castration, is picked up by Plotinus in *Enneads* 3.5.2. Plotinus's straight-faced misreading of Platonic and Socratic irony is reinforced by his indifference as to whether Ouranos or Kronos is the heavenly Aphrodite's father. This text, along with adjacent sections, is the mediating source that affects both Ficino's and Pico's treatments of the twin goddesses. As Edgar Wind demonstrates, while discussing the sources of Botticelli's painting, Pico and Poliziano mention the scene of castration primarily to minimize and metaphorize it away (*Pagan Mysteries in the Renaissance* [New Haven: Yale University Press, 1958], 115–20). In Ficino's commentary on the *Symposium*, the castration of Ouranos is mentioned in 5.12, and carefully insulated from the discussions of the birth (6.7) and the twin Venuses (2.7).

38. The quoted phrases are Patricia Parker's, *Fat Ladies*, 18.

39. A. C. Hamilton (*Spenser*, 364) glosses "Joying" as "enjoying," and I suppose one could also render "of her enjoyd" as "made joyous by her." Though my reading of the episode leads me to give primacy to one pair of alternatives in this range of possibilities, the range itself allows for the confusion and oscillation I mention below.

EMBODIED VOICES

PETRARCH READING (HIMSELF READING) OVID

LYNN ENTERLINE

WRITING IN THE NAME OF LOVE

ETRARCH'S complex encounter with Ovid's *Metamorphoses*, as Renaissance literary critics know well, left an indelible mark on the history of European representations of the poet—particularly as that poet represented himself, or herself, as the subject of language and of desire.[1] In rereading and rewriting Ovidian stories, Petrarch necessarily worked through a relationship fundamental to the *Metamorphoses*'s poetic project: the mutually constituting, and mutually interfering, relationship between rhetoric and sexuality. Any attempt to account for Ovid's place in the *Canzoniere*, therefore, will implicitly be commenting on rhetorical and erotic problems that ramify, extending throughout the mythographic lexicon of Renaissance poetic self-representation.[2] In order to examine how the rhetoric of Ovidian eroticism affects Petrarch's portrait of himself in love, I consider several Ovidian characters crucial to Petrarch's representation of himself as a "martyr" to an idol "sculpted in living laurel" (12.10; 30.27): Apollo, Pygmalion, Narcissus, Actaeon.[3] In this essay, I ask several related questions: Precisely how—and with what formal and libidinal effects—does Petrarch read Ovid? What does that reading suggest about the relationship between language and sexuality in the *Canzoniere*? And what does Ovid's presence in the *Canzoniere* mean for the Petrarchan subject, particularly when the poet who would rival Pygmalion is tormented by language as well as desire? For Petrarch, like Apollo, gets his laurel leaf—a signifier in return for his impossible demand—but as soon as he reaches the tree, he finds only "such bitter fruit" that his "wounds" are more aggravated than comforted (6.13–14).

The characteristic turn to Petrarch's Ovidianism that affected the way future writers appropriated the *Metamorphoses,* of course, was his project of adapting Ovidian figures to his own epideictic purpose by turning them into figures of his own story. The sheer metamorphic virtuosity of Petrarchan autobiography in the first canzone (23) suggests how profoundly autobiography would become, in the poetry of "Petrarchism," a gravitational center anchoring the difficult, often violent, certainly labile relationship between rhetoric and sexuality in the *Metamorphoses*. But Petrarch, by writing that the "first laurel" casts its shadow over all other "figures" (23.167–69), defines himself through a desire that Ovid saturates in the vagaries of language. The story of Apollo and Daphne—as the god of poetry violently, erotically, but nonetheless poetically "breathes" down her neck and yearns to "arrange" her tangled hair—concisely captures Ovid's penchant for turning stories about bodily "form" into commentary on poetic form. For Ovid characterizes the extremity of Daphne's reluctance linguistically—"immediately, the one loves but the other flees *the name* of love"—just as he turns her "beauty" to poetically useful purpose: Daphne's *forma* provokes the god of poetry; it is her *figura* that she prays to lose (I. 489, 530, 547). Indeed, the struggle between "the one and the other" (*alter* and *altera*) becomes as much one of the god of poetry's ability to *persuade* Daphne as to catch her. But his prayer breaks off with words "imperfect," for though he "would have said more," she runs away too quickly. In this metarhetorical scene of failed persuasion, Ovid systematically couples the erotic story with various aspects of rhetorical speech. He turns to trope by making Daphne's *figura* the body and the "figure" that the god of poetry wants—Apollo's similes being the verbal means deployed to lay his hands on that figure—and shifts from tropological to semiotic self-reflection when Apollo plucks the laurel, the sign for poetry.[4] His ensuing paean then plays on the much loved palindrome in Latin on the words for love and for Rome (AMOR- ROMA) after he plucks the laurel leaf from another anagram: the branches, or RAMOS, of her tree. That one needs to account for the collapse of the rhetorical and the sexual becomes somewhat brutally clear when one remembers that Latin writers use *ramus,* or branch, as a euphemism for the penis.[5] Following in Apollo's footsteps, Petrarch too would generate poetry from anagrammatic play on the actual letters of his laurel tree.[6] Ovid's text, in forging a connection between body, desire, and language—witness the frequent metalinguistic puns on *forma, figura,* and *membra*—constantly confronts the violence latent in both rhetoric and sexuality. Yet the *Canzoniere* poses a question underlying the *Metamorphoses* with new urgency: in Petrarch's internal landscape of Ovidian stories, the question becomes, what precisely is the poet's place, as a subject, in relation to the often violent interplay between language and *eros*? The much studied figure of Actaeon, suspended between his vision of beauty and the dismemberment attending his loss of voice, attests eloquently enough to the complexity of this intersection in both poems: "and still I flee the belling of my hounds" (23.160).

Although numerous artists in the *Metamorphoses* become surrogates for the narrator,[7] and such stories as Apollo's or Pygmalion's seem to comment on and to complicate that narrator's continuing and intense self-reflection, Ovid nonetheless distances himself from the erotic component of his own stories. No longer declaring himself, however ironically, "master" of erotic experience (*magister* in the *Ars Amatoria*) or victim of love (as in the *Amores*), the narrator of the *Metamorphoses* weaves no erotic fiction for himself. The narrator's distance—his habit of directing attention away from eros and violence as content to the violence and erotics of signification—is differently worked into the texture of Petrarch's exclusively, even obsessively, poetic relationship to Laura. Of course, his allusions to the *Metamorphoses* shape a persona very different from Ovid's narrator, for Petrarch weaves a new, suffering "voice" by directing Ovidian irony against himself. In the *Canzoniere* a distance seems to surface *within* the poetic subject, pitting the self against itself, rather than, as in Ovid, *between* the narrating subject and his erotic stories.[8] In Petrarch's hands, Actaeon's dismemberment becomes an emblem of his internal condition. Such a distance within—named by turns error (*errore*) or exile (*'l duro esilio*)—might, in a Christian vocabulary, be called a sense of sin. In psychoanalytic terms, it might be called the effects of denial or the splitting of the subject.[9]

By shifting to a psychoanalytic account of the signifying subject, however, I aim to do more than experiment with another way of reading Petrarch's self-alienation. Looking behind the Augustinian frame for Petrarch's linguistic and erotic predicament to focus instead on the Ovidian figures with which Augustine may seem to be at odds, I am emphasizing the aspect of Petrarch's self-portrait that transgresses the theological discourse within which his semiotic and erotic project is often read. I stress the Ovidian texture of Petrarch's "martyrdom" to a figure and bring psychoanalytic theory to bear on that intertextual relationship in order to explore the complex connection between rhetoric and sexuality without subsuming one to the other. But I am also suggesting something specific about the Petrarchan subject: precisely by reaching back to Ovidian metamorphosis as a way to counter the discursive logic of conversion, memory, and right reading that governs "Augustinus's" understanding of the self,[10] Petrarch's specifically autobiographical revision of Ovidian stories paradoxically produces a discourse of the self in love that looks forward to the alienated linguistic subject, and the story of its desire, adumbrated by recent psychoanalytic theory. Where in the *Secretum* Augustinus says of his conversion "I was transformed into another Augustine" (*transformatus sum . . . in alterum Augustinum*), one realizes when reading canzone 23 that in calling this a transformation, Petrarch uses the very verb that evokes Ovid's metamorphoses: *trasformare*.[11] In contrast to a past split that produced two Augustines—*transformatus sum* signaling the difference between a narrating and a narrated self—the poet-as-Actaeon writes, "I *am* transformed" (159). He thus modifies the temporality of Augustine's autobiographical division into two selves with an Ovidian representation of subjectivity *as* crisis: the poetic subject is caught in a continual process of metamorphosis, "a mean between living and dead" (*mezzo . . . tra vivo et morto* 89). Neither this nor that, the poet rivals many an Ovidian subject's anguish when caught between forms. A *spirito doglioso,* he is trapped in a process of self-alienation that includes the very process of writing about that self: "I shall speak the truth; perhaps it will appear a lie, for I felt myself drawn from my own image and into a solitary wandering stag from wood to wood quickly *I am transformed (mi trasformo) /* and still I flee the belling of my hounds" (159–60). The difference between *transformatus sum* and *trasformo* marks a shift from autobiography divided between a narrated and a narrating self to autobiography as a continuing process of metamorphosis in which the self's alienation through transformation includes the very attempt to write a history of the self. This continuing disjunction emerges most forcefully in the *Canzoniere* as forgetting and repetition. Both suggest that the self's inability to totalize or transcend—an inability modeled on time's differential movement in Augustine's *Confessions*—is the condition of memory and of writing.[12] The effect of this transforming process becomes most resonant for a psychoanalytic understanding of the signifying subject when Petrarch, complaining of martyrdom, claims he can neither relinquish the "one" figure that torments him nor remember, though he try, the whole of his own history: "And if here my memory does not aid me as it is wont to do, let my torments excuse it and the one thought which alone gives it such anguish that it makes me turn my back on every other and makes me forget myself beyond resistance" (15–20). With this painful fixation on an idolized sign that forces the self to "forget" itself we might compare Freud's theory of the unconscious—the blind spot that nonetheless shapes one's desire.

In the *Confessions,* the autobiographical text that profoundly influenced Petrarch's poetic practice, Augustine represents desire as cause and effect of language: for Petrarch, as for Augustine, "language engenders desire, and it originates in desire."[13] But the question still remains how one is to read this language. For the sense that language both constitutes and impoverishes the self—which Petrarch certainly shares with Augustine—fuels many of Petrarch's favorite stories from the *Metamorphoses.* Throughout Ovid's poem, some kind of figure, representation, or sign intervenes between a subject and his or her world, forever altering that relationship. In the stories of concern here, an *imago* "like a statue" (*signum*) falls between Narcissus and any other lover, a statue (*simulacrum*) falls between Pygmalion and womankind, and a laurel leaf as a sign for poetry bars Apollo from the beautiful figure of his desire. While such intervention directs attention to the beauty of the "form" in question, the subject's captivation with this form also gives rise to an absence—or better, an indefinite postponement—that nonetheless seems to constitute the subject. Thus Apollo becomes "himself"—produces an epideictic poem rather than *verba imperfecta*—when he receives a signifier in return for his demand for love. In the scene anticipating Petrarch's conversion of Laura as absent referent into linguistic absence, the only thing the god actually gets for the body he demands is the laurel leaf as "his" signifier. Daphne's resistance, we might say, is moved within, displaced in the scene's seeming resolution, for this signifying "closure" withholds as much as it gives. As the leaf replaces Daphne's body—the literal object Apollo said he wanted—a certain refusal of his demand is reified, turned into a signifier. The laurel leaf signifies poetry and, since it is part of an etiological story, its origin in Daphne's refusal. When the laurel replaces bodily form, the poem shifts attention from the absent referent to the absence that constitutes signification.[14] The Ovidian narrative crucial to Petrarch's self-portrait shadows the displacements founding desire in language when Apollo stops demanding an object (even as a tree she recoils from his kisses) and turns his demand for love into discourse, which takes the form of a poem in praise of something *other* than Daphne (Rome).

Addressing himself to this question of desire in language, John Freccero offered a powerful account of Petrarchan idolatry by reading the linguistic condition of the self in Augustinian terms, contrasting the *Canzoniere* with Augustine's attempt to render the world intelligible by grounding language and desire in God as "the ultimate end of desire." To Augustine, Petrarch's pose would be "deliberately idolatrous," challenging the allegorical project of right reading: on Freccero's account, Petrarch undermines the "fig tree," the allegorical conversion story, by remaining with the laurel, the "autoreflexive" story of idolatry. Deploying the distinction between right and wrong reading in *De Doctrina Christiana,* he writes that Petrarch is self-consciously guilty of enjoying what he should use: "to deprive signs of their referentiality and to treat poetic statement as autonomous, an end in itself, is [Augustine's] definition of idolatry." Freccero thus reads Petrarch's idolatry—his dream of "an autonomous universe of autoreflexive signs"—according to a "theological problematic."[15] But the *Canzoniere,* I have been suggesting, offers another frame of reference for reading linguistic idolatry: the rhetorically self-conscious world of the *Metamorphoses,* whose characters appear in the cycle as so many figures for the laurel, the "first figure" of the poet's adoration (23.167). When Petrarch represents his own condition through Pygmalion's formally mediated fascination with himself—*operisque sui concepit amorem* ("with his own work he falls in love" X.249)—his allusion to the elaborately and explicitly sexual rendition of "idolatry" in the

Ovidian sense makes critics think again about the discourse of verbal fetishism. For Petrarch concludes the paired sonnets on Simone Martini's painting of Laura by alluding to a distinctly sexual subtext for his love:

Quando giunse a Simon l'alto concetto
ch'a mio nome gli pose in man lo stile,
s'avesse dato a l'opera gentile
colla figura voce ed intelletto,

di sospir molti mi sgombrava il petto
che ciò ch' altri à più caro a me fan vile.
Però che 'n vista ella si monstra umile,
promettendomi pace ne l'aspetto,

ma poi ch' i' vengo a ragionar con lei,
benignamente assai par che m'ascolte:
se risponder savesse a' detti miei!

Pigmaliòn, quanto lodar ti dei
de l'imagine tua, se mille volte
n'avesti quel ch' i' sol una vorrei!

When Simon received the high idea which, for my sake, put his hand to his stylus, if he had given to his noble work voice and intellect along with form, he would have lightened my breast of many sighs that make what others prize most vile to me. For in appearance she seems humble, and her expression promises peace; then, when I come to speak to her, she seems to listen most kindly: if she could only reply to my words! Pygmalion, how much you must praise yourself for your image, if you received a thousand times what I yearn to have just once! (78, translation modified)

Petrarch compares this visual *figura* to the poet's written *figura*, the "idol sculpted in living laurel." As is usual with Petrarch's veiled eroticism, "that which" Pygmalion "received a thousand times" seems not to refer to sexual favors (which crown Pygmalion's activities in the *Metamorphoses*), but merely to the lady's verbal response. When he turns away from the blunt sexuality of Ovid's scene, that which the poet would have "just once"—words—seem themselves to become erotic. As with Apollo, Petrarch substitutes words for sexual relations. But in a further turn toward Pygmalion's love for his sculpted *simulacrum*, linguistic form usurps bodily form when this verbal artist makes words themselves the objects of his desire.

It is because of Pygmalion's rather startling literary career, the sheer persuasiveness of his poetic-erotic project, that I think a feminist and psychoanalytic reading is called upon to study the considerable literary appeal of fetishism. For feminist criticism, as many have argued, might have

much to gain by reconsidering the poetic inscription of subject-object relations according to a linguistically attuned psychoanalytic theory. By
means of this fetish, Laura is preserved, as Daphne for Apollo, or the
statue for Pygmalion, for her lover's exclusive "use"—a use that conforms itself with stunning instrumental virtuosity (and considerable
Ovidian irony) to exactly the shape imposed by the subject: like wax, the
statue warms to Pygmalion's fingers, becoming "usable through use itself" (*ipsoque fit utilis usu*, X.286). In his apostrophe to Pygmalion,
Petrarch figures an Augustinian understanding of idolatry through an in-
tensely Ovidian meditation on the self's love for the figures of its own
making. In Ovid's poem, Petrarch discovers not only idolized or reified
signs (Augustine's sense of idolatry), but a peculiarly self-reflexive idolatry: in the stories of Narcissus and Pygmalion, the fixated subject is himself the author of the figure or sign he adores. In the *Secretum*, Petrarch
makes amply clear that for him Pygmalion's fixation on the ivory image
of his own making recapitulates the predicament of Narcissus, captivated
by the "image" of his own "form" (III.416). In Ovid's text, Narcissus's
story does obliquely anticipate Pygmalion's sculpture: Narcissus freezes
before his *imago* and is himself compared to a statue, "a figure (*signum*)
formed from Parian marble" (419). The precise symmetry of these two
stories, in which either the loving subject or the beloved object may be a
marble statue, anticipates the mirroring reversals that characterize the
relationship between Laura and her author. Where looking at this sign or
figure (*signum*) prompts Narcissus to declare *ipse ego sum* only to dissolve in tears, Petrarch depicts himself as one similarly fascinated, to his
harm, by an image. And so Augustinus refers to Simone's painting when
he rebukes Franciscus not merely for loving an image for its own sake,
but for loving himself, as poet, in that image: "What could be more senseless (*insanius*) than that, not content with the presence of her living face,
the cause of all your woes, you must needs obtain a painted picture by an
artist of high repute, that you might carry it everywhere with you, to have
an everlasting spring of tears, fearing, I suppose, lest otherwise their foun-
tain might dry up?"[16] In this fetish, Narcissus and Pygmalion meet. Once
again, Petrarch turns a dense Ovidian image to autobiographical account
(weeping before a painting). In sonnet 78, moreover, the poet's imagined
attempt to speak to the painting reminds us that these two stories were
also about rhetoric, as both Ovidian lovers attempt to persuade, to in-
voke, or to move the image into a response by some kind of speech.
Where Narcissus pleads his case with the *imago* itself, Pygmalion strikes
upon a happier idea, turning away from the image to pray to Venus for a
woman "like" his ivory maiden. In both cases, Ovid closely records the
actual words the lover speaks to hold onto the image of which he is the
author.

Such a fantasy as that of Pygmalion's animating success implicates the artists who use him in the very narcissistic relationship they outline. Ovid turned a story about a king in love with a statue into a story specifically about an artist's love for his own work; his version makes Pygmalion's a story about the artist's "escape into creative art from the defects of reality."[17] He then places Pygmalion's successful artistic endeavors in the frame of Orpheus's song: the sculptor's desire and his success in giving life by giving form thus become part of the wishful *fort-da* game of Orpheus's own desire. Orpheus, for his part, is one of the poem's most prominent figures for the rhetorical achievement to which the narrator aspires.[18] In a similar, artistically self-reflexive move, Petrarch compares Pygmalion's desire to his own and in so doing eroticizes his own words. But he does far more than this. In sonnet 78, Pygmalion himself turns into a very precise version of the poet. He becomes a love poet in the *epideictic* tradition. To Petrarch, Pygmalion's pleasure is more than pleasure: *Pigmalión, quanto lodar ti dei / de l'imagine tua* (literally, "Pygmalion, how much you must praise yourself for your image" [12]). This *"lodar ti dei"* casts Pygmalion in Petrarch's image, reminding the reader that Petrarch is indeed the poet of praise, the one who derives his poems and the name of his object from the same word: *lodare*, or the Latin *laudare*, is the etymological and literal basis for the changes on *laura* that generate the figures of the *Canzoniere*. Petrarch thus becomes a consummate Pygmalion, as had Ovid before him, by reshaping a previous story into one made better because reconstituted in his image and thus made "useful through use itself."

ACTAEON EGO SUM   *blazon*

Though the *Canzoniere*'s structure of address gave a distinctive turn to the conventions of erotic description by which male poets in the Renaissance fetishized and dismembered the female body,[19] these conventions owe much to Ovid's rhetoric of the body. As soon as Apollo looks on Daphne, a *blason* seems to emerge: "He gazes at her hair . . . he looks at her eyes gleaming like stars, he looks on her mouth . . . he praises her fingers and her hands and her arms . . . what is hidden, he believes even better" (I.497–502). This amorous look—and the enumeration of eyes, lips, fingers—would generate a long and varied literary history of erotic idealism. But it is important to remember that the *Metamorphoses* regularly fragments the human body and that dismemberment produces effects as horrifying as Apollo's gaze is idealizing. Thus Ovid frames Pygmalion's love for his *simulacrum* by recalling Actaeon's fate: when Pygmalion's narrator, Orpheus, dies, he is compared to "a doomed stag in the arena" falling "prey to dogs."[20] Whether violent (the death of Actaeon or Orpheus) or erotic (Apollo's lingering enumeration), dismemberment is one of the *Metamorphoses*'s chief (dis)organizational principles as the narrator "turns his mind to tell of bodies changed into new forms" (1.1).

Petrarch reworks Ovid's rhetoric of body parts by incorporating it into the epideictic strategies of poetic autobiography. He captures the aesthetics and the violence of dismemberment in Ovid's poem: praising the body of Laura, like Apollo praises Daphne's, as so many beautiful parts, he also takes the story of Actaeon as his own. Where a fantasy of the *corps morcelé*—the "body in bits and pieces"—informs the *Canzoniere*'s dismembered subject and fetishized object, so it frames the seemingly happy story of Pygmalion's *simulacrum*, for his narrator's *membra* are scattered, torn apart by instruments also "scattered" across the landscape (X.35, 50).[21] As Nancy Vickers suggestively argues in comparing Freud's theory of castration to Petrarch's "scattered rhymes," dismemberment and fetishism are part of the same amatory and defensive process.[22] According to Freud's simultaneously sexual and signifying etiology, Pygmalion's exclusive love for his statue, the object of his own making, would be a fetishistic love for a substitute—a transference of significant value from a prized body part to an external object that is henceforth required for gratification. Thus Pygmalion's *simulacrum* and Petrarch's *figura* eclipse the subject's interest in any other erotic investment: all pleasure (corporal or aesthetic) is invested in this idol alone. Pygmalion's ivory maiden permanently replaces womankind in her maker's eyes; Petrarch is "governed" by Laura's veil only.[23] But as Freud makes clear, the fetish works precisely to defend against dismemberment—specifically, the dismemberment of castration. And it is this form of dismemberment, Vickers suggests, that the rhetoric of bodily fragmentation seems both to evade and to evoke.

What psychoanalytic theory shares with Ovid's and Petrarch's Pygmalion is a sense that while the fetish reveals much more about the loving subject than about the object with which he is captivated—remember that in Ovid the *simulacrum* is not named, while in Petrarch she takes her name from *his* rhetorical activity of praise—the fetish so absorbs the subject because it compensates for a profound disappointment with the "defects of reality." As we shall see, both Ovid's and Petrarch's Pygmalions suggest that the loving subject rejects the real world as deficient, incomplete. For Freud, of course, the fetish is both a memorial to, and an attempt to cover up, a particular lack that affronts the young boy's narcissistic investment in the form of his own body: the fetish replaces "a quite special penis that had been extremely important in early childhood but was afterwards lost. . . . [I]t is a substitute for the woman's (the mother's) phallus which the little boy once believed in and does not wish to forego." Symbol and symptom, the fetish signifies the price of masculine identity, for masculinity achieves its (always contradictory) coherence by acknowledging the law of exogamy. This taboo on incest, in turn, is personified in "the father." The fetishist, however, "attempts to substitute the rules of his own desire for the culturally predominant ones."[24] As his object-sign acquires "value" and "significance" by displacement, his devotion becomes an "artful" evasion of what the child "ascribes" to the father's "role."[25] A symbolic substitute—and symptom of a culturally demanded renunciation only nominally accepted—the fetish works by contradiction: it both affirms and denies the traumatic loss that it replaces (and preserves).

For Vickers, the "scattered rhymes" work according to this logic of fetishism, denying the very dismembering the poet practices and to which he alludes: "[W]oman's body, albeit divine, is displayed to Actaeon, and his body, as a consequence, is literally taken apart. Petrarch's Actaeon, having read his Ovid, realizes what will ensue: his response to the threat of imminent dismemberment is the neutralization, through descriptive dismemberment, of the threat. He transforms the visible totality into scattered words, the body into signs; his description, at one remove from experience, safely permits and perpetuates his fascination." The subject's memory (the play on *membra/ri-membra*) and the "body" of his poems are constituted by signs that "re-member the lost body" and thus, "like fetishes, affirm absence by their presence."[26] Here it is important to remember that the male child's "troubling encounter with intolerable female nudity" (103) is a cultural encounter with woman's body as it is read—and *given* significance—as "lacking parts." Woman's body is interpreted, that is, according to the taboo that legislates exogamy and that the sheer weight of cultural practice personifies in the father. If Freud's little boy sees a woman's body as dangerously mutilated, he does so because that body is offered to him to read as it has been rendered legible for him by a symbolic, not a natural, order. Legislated, that is, as that which comes to represent all those losses under the sign of what he may *yet* lose if he does not obey the law.[27] A symbolic cover for the lack the "male" subject wants to refuse but must "know" just the same to become socialized, the fetish allows him to love women by occluding their difference. The fetish is riddled with ambivalence, a historical relic of the narcissistic subject's attempt to retain his pleasure without submitting to the law of sexual difference through which "he" may come to be.

The Lacanian proposition—that sexual difference be read literally—is concisely distilled in the differential, enunciative structure through which the *Canzoniere* so persuasively transmitted Ovidian stories: difference between *io* and *voi* depends on a difference between *lauro* and *laura*.

Pygmalion's fetish, however, would signal a certain resistance to the meaning attributed to this differential structure. And the *Canzoniere*'s figures do indeed dismantle any simple gender identity: as both Giuseppe Mazzotta and Nancy Vickers rightly stress, the images for possible gender positions remain remarkably fluid.[28] In canzone 29, the poet becomes Dido: "My thoughts have become alien to me: one driven like me once turned the beloved sword upon herself" (29.36–39). Or in canzone 23, giddy transformations of gender are nonetheless articulated within a binary structure that shapes the fictions of a self represented as "male" or "female" by turns.[29] Read psychoanalytically, dismemberment and idolatry suggest that the formal relationships of Petrarchan (and, by extension, Ovidian) poetics implicate the libidinal, and thus *social*, history of two different subjects resisting a tradition that is extremely consistent—rigid even—when it comes to the representation of sexual difference. But that entanglement of formal and historical concerns, however, will not be the history of conscious understanding (a history of ideas), but rather a study of its disruption—of the effect of a subject as it is produced in (an unpredictable) relation to a larger discursive field that is already laden with the weight of tradition.[30]

Like the story of Actaeon's dismemberment, Pygmalion's idol has struck many as having a phallic resonance.[31] In Ovid, Pygmalion's artistry is caused specifically by a flaw in womankind: after "seeing" female sexual crimes (the prostitution of the Propoetides), he carves his statue out of "disgust" for the "faults nature had so liberally given the female mind" (10.243–45). In the *Canzoniere*, Petrarch renders his idolatry less specifically and rather more retroactively than Ovid's Pygmalion. But he nevertheless effectively conveys the sense that he finds the rest of the world impoverished by comparison: in his state of arrested infatuation, the poet "breathes many sighs," that, to him, "make what others most prize vile" (78.5–6). In the fiction of sonnets 77 and 78, of course, the poet is commenting on a painting of Laura by someone else's hand. Because he must distinguish Simone from other painters who have won fame "in the art of looking" in order to praise him as a painter of Laura (77.2, 5–14), the poet's explicit disdain is turned against a vague, general group of "others."

> s'avesse dato a l'opera gentile
> colla figura voce et intelletto,
>
> di sospir molti mi sgombrava il petto
> che ciò ch'altri à più caro a me fan vile.
>
> . . . if he had given to his noble work voice and intellect along with form, he
> would have lightened my breast of many sighs that make what others prize
> vile to me (78.3–6)

This broad censure may include Simone's *figura*, the visual image being inferior to the poet's *figura*. Turned into a vague "something dear" or valuable "to others," that which is "vile" to the poet may also be understood specifically—that is, as other women, particularly in a poem that ends with an apostrophe to the artist who was "disgusted" with the female mind. But Pygmalion's particular distaste seems to have turned into a far more general disgust with worldly things. The poet's sweeping revulsion seems to have been produced by occluding its origin in the very specific distaste of Ovid's Pygmalion for what nature gave womankind; these lines seem to fashion the poet's disappointment by alluding only very evasively to Pygmalion's generative misogyny. True to the split in fetishistic pleasure, the poems to his painted idol affirm and deny their origin. Sonnet 78 relies on the Ovidian text, with its very specific reason for Pygmalion's creative act, and deflects attention from it by referring so very generally to "that which others most prize" as "vile to me." Similarly, Petrarch's self-designation as an Actaeon suspended *before* mutilation by his hounds hints at these contradictory, but nonetheless entangled, attitudes. Though invoked, Actaeon's dismemberment is never recounted in the *Canzoniere*; this suspension renders his fate all the more indelibly as a dark subtext resonating beneath or beyond the cycle.

Taboo, and the punishment for violating it, informs the libidinal scene of both poems. As is frequently noted, Pygmalion's love for the image of his own making is not only fetishizing, it is incestuous. The artist himself does not "dare say" in his prayer what he really wants (*timide . . . non ausus . . . dicere* 274–76), and the desire of Myrrha for her father retrospectively casts some doubt over her grandfather's desire. When lying to her father to say she would like to marry someone "like" him, Myrrha quotes the words of her grandfather, Pygmalion, turning the narrative back on itself: Pygmalion's prayer, *"similis mea," dixit "eburnae,"* reappears in her metrically identical answer, *"similem tibi" dixit at ille* (X.276, 364). Pygmalion and Myrrha employ the language of substitutes in order to avoid saying what is prohibited—that neither wishes, in fact, to enter into the play of substitutions at all.[32] This sense of violation, moreover, informs the visual and the vocal imagination of both poems. Petrarch's very rhymes, of course, violate Diana's injunction against speaking about what he has seen ("Make no word of this" [23.74]). Similarly, Ovid's story of Pygmalion exists precisely because of a violated prohibition on looking: for Orpheus takes over the narrative of the poem, and tells the story of Pygmalion, only because he has lost Eurydice by disobeying Pluto's injunction not to "look back." We are thus able to read the narrative of Book X in the first place only because Orpheus disobeyed an injunction not to look. Recall, too, that the Actaeon story, central to the rhetorical and phantasmatic work of the *Canzoniere* and echoed in the death of Orpheus, revolves around a taboo against looking. As Vickers suggests, criminal offense hangs heavy in the air when Diana forbids the intruder to speak about what he has, mistakenly, seen: "You would now tell the story of me seen before you, my robe put aside, if it were permitted that you be able to tell it" (III.192–93). The mountain on which unlucky Actaeon is torn to pieces is already "stained with the blood of many slaughtered beasts"; nymphs smite their breast and cry out when he enters the grove (143, 178). In the *Canzoniere*, not only does the poet as Actaeon stumble on what he should not see, but he writes poems about what he should not tell.

As Freud conceived it, a fetish is a contingent, foundationally *accidental* object attached to the traumatic scene of castration. Few texts, I might add, stress as repeatedly as the *Metamorphoses* that the occurrence and the object of desire are accidental: in the continuing narrative of that *amor sceleratus habendi* ("cursed love of having" 1.131), the emphasis falls heavily on the sheer transgressive force of *amor* rather than on the many objects desired. A statue or an image, that is, can become just as desirable as another human, and those human forms designated as forbidden by "law" easily become erotic.[33] In the story Petrarch chooses to represent his own desire, of course, the bad luck of stumbling across Diana naked proves fatal. *Fortuna* and *error*, the Ovidian narrator tells us, rather than *scelus* are to blame. And so, in the *Canzoniere* too, it is "the contingency of the encounter, the involuntary experience that Petrarch stresses."[34] Freud's account of fetishism is comparable to Ovid's and Petrarch's unlucky Actaeon because it is the accidental quality of the traumatic scene that founds the possibility of the "perception" of castration: "The setting up of the fetish seems to take its cue from a process which is reminiscent of the halt made by memory in traumatic amnesia. Here too interest stops on its way, perhaps at the last impression before the uncanny, traumatic one is seized as a fetish."[35] In Freud's exposition, a threat alone—and the eventual traumatic inscription in the subject of sexual difference as castration—produces in *some* males the socially sanctioned "normal" result of heterosexual desire. Thus I understand the ideological persuasiveness of the "experience" or "perception" of castration, or of the "truth" of sexual difference, according to a view of sexuality's traumatic and social character as set forth by Slavoj Žižek: "Ideology is not a dreamlike illusion that we build to escape insupportable reality . . . it is a fantasy-construction which serves as a support for our 'reality' itself: *an illusion which structures our effective, real social relations and thereby masks some insupportable, real, impossible kernel.*" Not only will subjects never have a nonimaginary relation to their real conditions of existence (Althusser), but their representations (such tenacious "fantasy-constructions" as the Diana-Actaeon story) structure social relations so effectively precisely because they offer a means of evading or "masking" trauma—which, in Žižek's terms, amounts to the construction of the unconscious in the subject around the Law's "senseless" and "non-integrated" "injunction."[36]

Further reflection on the relationship between the poetic "I" and his linguistic practice suggests that Petrarch's verbal fetishism occludes another disappointment: although the beloved, like Daphne, disappears as the cycle's absent referent—her body ceding place to his letter—Petrarch's language is itself marked by the very absence it decries in the real world. Citing Freccero's assessment that Petrarch's language is "idolatrous in the Augustinian sense," Thomas Greene stresses that his remains a self-consciously failed attempt. Where Freccero allows that "pure auto-reflection of the sign" is impossible, Greene observes that "the question is whether this service" to the signifier *laura* "ever really works." Though Petrarch attempts to "create" himself in relation to the signifier, *laura*, "one might argue rather that he creates himself out of *failed* signifiers."[37] When it comes to *laura*, his *ingegno* and *arte* are somehow "lacking" (308.12–14). Her absence as referent returns to haunt the language of the cycle as language's own lack: poetic-erotic melancholy repeats thematically as an erotic story what happens in actual semiotic practice.[38] Petrarch's differential signs—the difference between *lauro* and *laura*, or between *velo* and *vela* as self-reflexive signs for poetry—repeat the differential structure of the cycle itself. In an observation that describes Petrarch's lyrics in terms reminiscent of de Saussure's definition of the sign as a relational entity produced from a synchronic network of differences, Mazzotta writes: "each poem's autonomy is unreal . . . the origin of each lyrical experience lies always outside itself . . . and each reverses and implicates others in a steady movement of repetition." Rendering the logic of differentially produced signs explicit, the cycle evokes "plenitude and wholeness" only as they vanish; "emblems of origin" remain "unavoidably elusive."[39]

Such language about language as something that fails, or as a structure without an origin, suggests a further connection between the *Canzoniere* and psychoanalytic theory. First, Lacanian theory and Petrarchan practice converge around the dismembered body "in bits and pieces" not simply as a theme or a symbol for erotic danger and desire—Actaeon as motif—but around the weaving of this story of sexual difference (as male visual trauma) into a specifically linguistic problem of meaning and structure.[40] In both, a synchronic network of differential, interdependent signifiers constitute a system in which any one element is meaningful only in relationship to what it is not. Absence haunts the erotic and the linguistic self-understanding of the cycle; the loss in one reflects loss in the other. The poetic form that most succinctly captures such a conception of semiotic functioning in the *Canzoniere* is, of course, the sestina. The signifier, Lacan insists, is constituted in its absence from itself, an absence in which the subject, as a "speaking subject," is utterly implicated. It is in the translation of a linguistic into a sexual scene that Lacan locates the work of culture: "[T]he phallus is our term for the signifier of his alienation in signification," by which he means to suggest that "it is in the *name of the father* that we must recognize the *support* of the symbolic function which, from the dawn of history, has identified his person with the figure of the law."[41] On this account of the signifying subject, Petrarchan self-consciousness concerning his words' failure, his own linguistic "exile," receives the support of "the name of the Father" in the form of Actaeon and the prohibition on the female body in the form of a naked Diana.

Ovid and Petrarch place particular stress on the linguistic crisis from which dismemberment follows, or better yet, to which it is compared. As we saw earlier, Petrarch's allusion to Actaeon's vision replaces a past conversion into two selves (*transformatus sum*) with a continuing crisis of metamorphosis (*trasformo*). This Ovidian crisis includes the attempt to write an autobiographical account of the self's continuing alienation from itself. After he "stood to gaze on" the only sight that "appeases him," the poet undergoes a transforming process continuous with the moment of writing:

> . . . l'acqua nel viso co le man mi sparse.
> *Vero dirò; forse e' parrà menzogna:*
> *chi' i' sentì trarmi de la propria imago*
> et in un cervo solitario et vago
> di selva in selva ratto *mi trasformo,*
> et ancor de' miei can fuggo lo stormo.
>
> . . . she sprinkled water in my face with her hand. *I shall speak the truth,*
> *perhaps it will appear a lie, for I felt myself drawn from my own image* and
> into a solitary wandering stag from wood to wood quickly I am transformed
> and still I flee the belling of my hounds (23.153–57).

In a canzone whose every word transgresses the foundational command "make no word of this," the poet's own shape is drawn, like his words, away from its "proper image" (*la propria imago*). No sooner is he returned to his earthly body (*terrene membra,* 151) than he must flee his hounds; no sooner does he most wish to coincide with his utterance than his words appear to lie. Where the speaker remarks that he was returned to his body only that he might suffer more (152), the dual figure of the *imago* also implies that the language in which he finds himself serves the same purpose—to increase his torment. Drawn from a *propria imago*, an "image" in both a linguistic and a corporal sense, the poet uses bodily disfigurement to figure the linguistic error of which the poem speaks and from which it cannot escape (*Vero dirò; forse e' parrà menzogna*). For as itself a poetic figure, the vanishing "proper image" reinscribes the very problem to which it refers.

In Ovid's text, dogs tear Actaeon's flesh because he cannot say his own name—because Diana's prohibition interferes between the subject and a language that, quite literally, is no longer merely his instrument, no longer the transparent medium of his intention: "He longs to cry out, 'I am Actaeon (*Actaeon ego sum*). Know your master.' But words fail his spirit (*uerba animo desunt*); the air resounds with barking" (III.229–30). This is the linguistic crisis that becomes the very condition of poem 23: "Make no word of this." The horror in Ovid's scene is attached, as much as anything else, to the way the sound of human words recedes before the sound of hounds barking. But, as Lacan would suggest of this not-speaking, "no one would think of that . . . if there weren't beings endowed with an apparatus for giving utterance to the symbolic . . . so as to make one notice it." One might ask, why are animals represented as beings that don't speak? Because of the human habit of projecting itself as a signifying subject: "You only know what can happen to a reality once you have definitively reduced it to being inscribed in a language."[42] Because his mouth changes to a stag's, Actaeon cannot pronounce his *nomen* and the subject is lost before the barbarity of the nonsignifying animal world. Further, it is on the change in the shape of Actaeon's lips that the representation of canine "reality" hangs: before Actaeon's metamorphosis, each dog achieved a quasi-human status because he, too, bore a name given by his master. Ovid draws out the pathos of the hunter hunted, increasing the barbarity by citing every name no longer available to Actaeon: "While he hesitates he sees his hounds . . . Melampus and keen-scented Ichnobates are the first to give signals by barking . . . then others run faster than the quick wind: Pamphagos and Dorceus and Oribasos . . ." and so on (206–25). At the intersection between human and nonhuman, the signifying and the nonsignifying, the dogs appear all the more inhuman precisely because, once personified by names and trained by "signals," they now devour the speaker who defined each in a community founded on a rudimentary sort of language. When *Actaeon ego sum* literally fails to work, the dogs lapse back into a state understood only in relation to not-speaking, or "known," as Lacan puts it, once "reduced to being inscribed in a language." In this soon to become emblematic crisis of identity, we should recall Lacan's position that the subject represents itself as a subject for "the Other," which is not another subject, but another signifier. This is what Actaeon is trying to do—to use a signifier (Actaeon) to represent himself, as a subject, for another signifier (in this case, the other names for his hounds). But all he gets in return is barking because his lips cannot form that word and the dogs, once personified through signifiers of their own, literally cannot recognize the "sound" that "though not human, is still one no deer could utter" (*gemit ille sonumque, / etsi non hominis, quem non tamen edere possit / ceruus* 237–39). If one is defined retroactively as a subject by means of the differential movement of the signifier within a system of exchange with other speakers, it is because one's address to another requires the impersonal intervention of the Other. In this intervention, the fact of getting an answer or meeting with silence on the part of the actual interlocutor is beside the point: it is to the chain of signification in which both parties are assumed to be embedded, as subjects, that the signifier is addressed.[43]

The proper name—crucial to Actaeon's linguistic impasse—is also crucial to Ovid's representation of his place as a subject, as author, in his text. For Ovid often inscribes his own name in his work: *Ars Amatoria* ends with *Naso magister erat*. At the end of the *Metamorphoses*, he imagines his own permanence by way of signifiers: his name (*nomen*) and his work (*opus*) will survive because readers will read his text aloud. In the *Tristia*, he compares himself to Actaeon as someone who saw something he shouldn't only to distinguish himself as one who managed to achieve a name "heard" by a "crowd of learned men": *turbaque doctorum Nasonem nouit et audet* (II.119–20). In claiming a place as author, Ovid repeatedly represents himself as a signifier—a *nomen* heard throughout the world. In both the *Metamorphoses* and the *Tristia*, moreover, he offers this signifier to an audience who, in contrast to Actaeon's hounds, are fully signifying subjects (readers who read, a crowd that "hears). Like Petrarch, who represents himself as a *lauro* in poems addressed to a *laura*, Ovid's favorite way to represent himself as author is to represent himself as a signifier for the Other.

Actaeon's failure to control language—his being controlled by the words usually taken to be instruments of the mind—is woven into a story of a prohibited looking that "causes bodily dismemberment. As Jane Gallop observes, "castration for Lacan is not only sexual . . . it is also linguistic: we are inevitably bereft of any masterful understanding of language, and can only signify ourselves in a symbolic system that we do not command, that, rather, commands us."[44] The Symbolic order is for Lacan a "phallic" order because linguistic absence is grafted onto a culturally organized sexual "absence." Such a theory could find few stories more apt than Actaeon's. The subject's sudden, unexpected imprisonment by the language that "he (mistakenly) assumed to be secondary or instrumental to thought is precisely what both the Petrarchan and the Ovidian Actaeon, in different ways, enact. But in taking up Actaeon's story as a figure for his own as a poet—which Ovid does in the *Tristia*, Petrarch in the *Canzoniere*—each represents the condition of the poetic subject so that, as Žižek puts it, "the subject of the signifier is a retroactive effect of the failure of its own representation . . . *the failure of representation is its positive condition.*"[45] It is not that there is more to "Actaeon" than he can say, that he exists somehow more completely outside the distortions of language. Rather, it is because he must represent himself as a signifier for another signifier—for the Other—that the lack which founds the possibility of this exchange becomes the "positive condition" for his existence as a subject.[46] The structure of address (Actaeon's to his hounds, Ovid's to his readers, Petrarch's to Laura) introduces the lack in the signifier by referring to the Symbolic network of language that "is the condition of the possibility of both parties to the exchange. From a Lacanian perspective, then, it is no accident that the subject's precipitation in such a differential structure—his alienation from "him"self in signification—is rendered as a sexual story about seeing the female body as a trauma leading to a phantasm of the viewer's dismemberment. Nor is it an accident that so many future self-defining male writers used Actaeon's predicament as an emblem for their own condition. That story, however, would be precisely a "support" lent to the absence necessary to symbolic functioning, a support in which culture has, in practice, identified the "person" of the father "with the figure of the law" (though it need not). In Ovid's text, the scattered members of Pygmalion's narrator, Orpheus, recall those of Actaeon and qualify Pygmalion's happier fate. These *membra* remind one that culture's foundational story of sexual difference informs not only the erotic but also the linguistic project of both poems. That this horrible fate transcends personal pathology is suggested by the ever increasing popularity of Actaeon as a figure for expressing the inner condition of "man."[47]

The stories of Actaeon and Pygmalion suggest that the different forms of the human body—as given meaning by cultural laws—continue to cast a shadow over what might seem to be the most abstract formal, linguistic, and rhetorical concerns of both poems. Actaeon's story collapses bodily dismemberment into the disappearance of a name (in Ovid) or into the foundational distortions of poetic "images" (in Petrarch). Each poem reads the first in terms of the second, inscribing the accidental sight of a naked woman into "male" subjectivity realized *as* linguistic crisis. So, too, both Pygmalion stories weave desire into linguistic or rhetorical self-reflection, attesting to the body's continuing pressure on each poem's figurative strategies. In *The Ego and the Id*, Freud wrote that "the ego is first and foremost a body-ego." Of this evocative comment, Laplanche elaborates that the ego is an imaginary organ, a "projection or metaphor of the body's surface" that "is constituted outside of its vital functions, as a libidinal object." This body-ego would take its shape, moreover, "from the perception of a fellow creature," which "perception," I have argued,

is inseparable from the social codes of sexual difference that "give perception meaning.[48] A certain phantasm of the body's unity structures the
subject's perception—but also its symbolic activity. In both poems, I suggest, it is in the recurrent images of dismemberment, as well as in Pygmalion's fetishized statue, that one may recognize the ego of the writing
subject.[49]

But it seems to me crucial, nevertheless, to distinguish between an actual fetish and these poems about verbal fetishism. For according to psychoanalytic theory, the fetish would be the one substitute that "freezes the
signifying process, denying the "senseless" injunction of the letter that
"offers the female body to the male subject-in-the making as the visual
explanation for his traumatic inscription in language. Founded on an initial substitution, a fetish allows the subject to fix on *one* image as that
which cannot be substituted for others like it. This refusal of substitution
is, of course, a refusal to enter into the network of language's structure of
deferral and difference. But the fetish, initially a substitution, does not
continue in a tropological sequence: thus, as Julia Kristeva argues, a fetish
"is not a sign," nor can a sign be a fetish. In *The Revolution in Poetic
Language*, she asks, "isn't art the fetish par excellence, one that badly
camouflages its archaeology?" If entry into the Symbolic requires obedience to the Law-of-the-Father, she further asks, doesn't the subject continue to believe that "the mother is phallic, that the ego—never precisely
identified—will never separate from her, and that no symbol is strong
enough to sever this dependence?" For her, though "the subject of poetic
language clings to the help fetishism offers," nonetheless it is a symbolic
subject; though the "poetic function" may "converge" with fetishism, "it
is not identical to it." In contrast to a fetish, the poetry continues to signify. In the *Canzoniere*, of course, Laura's veil is never stripped away. In
the *Metamorphoses*, it is only as a *simulacrum* that the maiden may be, as
it were, "seen" in the narrative *nuda*; once she becomes flesh, the narrative glances away. This *simulacrum* may be "seen" at all, it seems, because it signifies the desire of its narrator, Orpheus. "The text is completely different from the fetish because it signifies . . . it is not a substitute
but a sign (signifier / signified) and its semantics unfurled in sentences."[50]
Because it "signifies the unsignifying," a text is still a sign even as it gestures to the other side of signification. On such an understanding of linguistic subjectivity, and of the difference between fetishism and poetic
language, I would suggest that these seemingly fetishized female figures be
read as signs pointing to the cultural conditions legislated for becoming a
"speaking-subject." They are assigned a peculiar place: these idols become signs of what the culturally fashioned male subject of poetic language must renounce if "he" is to accede to symbolic form. Diana, Eurydice, Pygmalion's maiden, Laura: over and over in the *Metamorphoses*

and the *Canzoniere*, female forms become signifiers for what is in excess of signification. But the female "form" thus positioned only returns as a remainder that "represents what is missing in language, and thus in the subject. Female form, that is, is not merely turned aside on the threshold of the linguistic. Her form returns from this initial turning aside to represent that (enabling) absence that is the "positive condition" of the poetic "speaking" subject. The absence of Laura—but also of Eurydice—always informs the fantasy of Pygmalion's love for a nameless, living idol. Both Ovid's and Petrarch's Pygmalion suggest that although the poet's voice may be empty, it is not, however, disembodied.

NOTES

1. I would like to thank Patricia Rosenmeyer, Bryan Wolf, Marguerite Waller, Peter Brooks, and Wayne Koestenbaum for their enlightening comments and many helpful suggestions while I wrote this essay. In its final stages, this essay also benefited from the comments of the Works in Progress Group at Yale, particularly those of Heather James.

2. Most recently, see Lawrence Kritzman, *The Rhetoric of Sexuality and the Literature of the French Renaissance* (Cambridge: Cambridge University Press, 1991); and Ann Rosalind Jones, "New Songs for the Swallow: Ovid's Philomela in Tullia d'Aragona and Gaspara Stampa," in *Refiguring Woman: Perspectives on Gender and the Italian Renaissance*, ed. Marilyn Migiel and Juliana Schiesari (Ithaca: Cornell University Press, 1991). For discussions of Ovid and Petrarch, see Leonard Barkan, *The Gods Made Flesh: Metamorphosis and the Pursuit of Paganism* (New Haven: Yale University Press, 1986); Robert Durling, *Petrarch's Lyric Poems* (Cambridge: Harvard University Press, 1976); and Sara Sturm-Maddox, *Petrarch's Laurels* (University Park: University of Pennsylvania Press, 1992).

3. Unless otherwise noted, quotations and translations of Petrarch are from Robert M. Durling, *Petrarch's Lyric Poems: The Rime Sparse and Other Lyrics* (Cambridge: Harvard University Press, 1976), and quotations of Ovid are from W. S. Anderson, *Ovidius Metamorphoses* (Leipzig: Teubner, 1977). Translations of the *Metamorphoses* are mine.

4. For a similar reading, see Lavinia Lorch, "Human Time and the Magic of the Carmen," *Philosophy and Rhetoric* 15, 4 (Fall 1982): 262–71.

5. See Frederick Ahl's detailed account of anagrams in *Metaformations* (Ithaca: Cornell University Press, 1985). See J. N. Adams, *Latin Sexual Vocabulary* (London: Duckworth, 1982): he cites *ramus roborascit*, "his branch is hardening."

6. Ovid also plays with the letters of *laurus*: struck by a golden arrow (*aura*tum est, 470), the god seeks to touch her hair, blown about by the breeze (dabat *aura* capillos, 529), gets the *laurus*, and sings a song in praise of Rome. For Petrarch's revisions, see #5, 23, 30, 194, and 196–98.

7. See E. W. Leach, "Ekphrasis and the Theme of Artistic Failure in Ovid's *Metamorphoses*," *Ramus* 3 (1974): 102–42; and Donald Lateiner, "Mythic and Non-Mythic Artists in the *Metamorphoses*," *Ramus* 3 (1974): 1–31.

8. For example: *Ne pur il mio secreto e 'l mio riposo / fuggo, ma più me stesso* ("Nor do I flee my secret place nor my rest, but I flee more from myself" [234.9–10]).

9. See Thomas Roche, *Petrarch and the English Sonnet Sequences* (New York: AMS Press, 1989). For analysis of the splitting of the subject as a defense, see David Rodowick, *The Difficulty of Difference: Psychoanalysis, Sexual Difference & Film Theory* (New York and London: Routledge, 1991).

10. I refer to Augustinus's position in Petrarch's *Secretum*, which is to be distinguished from Saint Augustine's own project. Were one to read Saint Augustine's text carefully (particularly in terms of the address to God that frames it), his autobiographical subject would look rather less stable than Petrarch would have it. On the difference between Augustinus and Saint Augustine, see Charles E. Trinkaus, *In Our Image and Likeness: Humanity and Divinity in Italian Humanist Thought* (Chicago: University of Chicago Press, 1970).

11. *Secretum*, in *Prose*, ed. G. Martellotti, P. G. Ricci, E. Carrara, and E. Bianchi (Milan: Sansoni, 1955), 156–58. All citations are to this edition. Critics often note that Petrarch disrupts the Augustinian autobiographical narrative of conversion he invokes. See Robert Durling, *The Figure of the Poet in Renaissance Epic* (Cambridge: Harvard University Press, 1965), 84; Giuseppe Mazzotta, "The *Canzoniere* and the Language of the Self," *Studies in Philology* 3 (1978): 271–96; and Marguerite Waller, *Petrarch's Poetics and Literary History* (Amherst: University of Massachusetts Press, 1980), 21, 56, and 91. Although Augustine is not mentioned, a good recent discussion of what the split self implies for the subject of autobiography is Vincent Crapanzo's " 'Self'-Centering Narratives," *Yale Journal of Criticism* 5, 3 (Fall 1992): 61–80.

12. Both the *Secretum* and "The Ascent of Mont Ventoux" attest to the enormous effect that Augustine's reflections on time had on Petrarch's representation of himself. See Victoria Kahn, "The Figure of the Reader in Petrarch's *Secretum*," *PMLA* 100 (1985): 154–66, for an acute account of Petrarch's relation to Augustinian definitions of reading, memory, and self. In the *Secretum*, she argues, the text that might seem a place to "preserve memory" in fact becomes a "means of self-forgetfulness." She adds that, important for this analysis of Petrarch's verbal fetishism and Pygmalion's place in that fantasy, the *Secretum* itself becomes an "object of desire" (160).

13. Mazzotta, "The Language of the Self," 291. See also his recent discussion of Petrarch's "disjunctive consciousness" in sonnets 77 and 78 in *The Worlds of Petrarch* (Durham and London: Duke University Press, 1993), 28–29.

14. As Lacan puts it, the signifier, like the purloined letter, "will be and not be where it is, wherever it goes" ("Seminar on 'The Purloined Letter,' " *Yale French Studies* 48 [1975]: 54).

15. "The Fig Tree and the Laurel: Petrarch's Poetics," in *Literary Theory/ Renaissance Texts*, ed. Patricia Parker and David Quint (Baltimore: Johns Hopkins University Press, 1986), 22.

16. Translation by William H. Draper, *Petrarch's Secret* (London: Chatto, 1911), 134. All subsequent citations are from this translation unless otherwise noted. Mazzotta similarly observes, "Like Narcissus, who gazes at his reflected image—discovers that he, too, is a shadow—Petrarch looks at Simone's painting of Laura and "sees" in it his own mute reflection" (*The Worlds of Petrarch*, 31).

17. See H. Frankel, *Ovid: A Poet Between Two Worlds* (Berkeley and Los Angeles: University of California Press, 1945), 96; and G. Karl Galinsky, *Ovid's Metamorphoses: An Introduction to the Basic Aspects* (Oxford: Basil Blackwell, 1975), 30.

18. A detailed demonstration of this part of my argument lies beyond the scope of this essay. In a book I am writing on the relationship between body and voice in the *Metamorphoses* and Renaissance texts indebted to it, I argue that Ovid's stories of desire complicate the narrator's attempt to claim a place as "author" by means of a kind of "metempsychotic" poetics of animation in which Ovid seeks to transcend linguistic (as well as corporal) form through the hallucinated presence of a "voice."

19. See Kritzman, *The Rhetoric of Sexuality*, 6. The most extensive, and influential, treatment of dismemberment in the *Canzoniere* remains Nancy Vickers's "Diana Described: Scattered Woman and Scattered Rhyme," in *Writing and Sexual Difference*, ed. Elizabeth Abel (Chicago: University of Chicago Press, 1982), 95–110. For an account of the *blason* in terms of property relations, see Patricia Parker, *Literary Fat Ladies: Rhetoric, Gender, Property* (London and New York: Methuen, 1987), 126–54.

20. XI.24–27. Vickers compares Actaeon, Orpheus, and Pentheus in "Diana Described," 99–100. Ovid's preoccupation with *mutatas formas corpora* has the uncanny habit of returning: Quintillian, for instance, excuses Ovid's rhetorical excess because of the necessity of "collecting exceedingly diverse" material into "the semblance of a unified body" (*Institutio oratoria* IV.1.77).

21. Jane Gallop comments, "The *corps morcelé* is a Lacanian term for a violently nontotalized body image, an image . . . accompanied by anxiety" (*Reading Lacan* [Ithaca: Cornell University Press, 1985], 79).

22. "Diana Described," 103–5.

23. *Canzoniere*, 11.12. See "Fetishism" and "The Splitting of the Ego in the Defensive Process," in *Sexuality and the Psychology of Love*, trans. Robert Strachey (New York: Macmillan, 1963). References are to this translation, modifications noted where made. Freud writes that "the devotees of fetishes regard them as abnormalities, it is true, but only rarely as symptoms of illness; usually they are quite content with them or even extol the advantages they offer for erotic gratification" ("Fetishism," 214).

24. Constance Penley, *The Future of an Illusion: Film, Feminism, and Psychoanalysis* (Minneapolis: University of Minnesota Press, 1989), 27.

25. "The Splitting of the Ego," 222–23 and 221. "The boy did not simply contradict his perception, hallucinating a penis there where none was to be seen, but undertook a displacement of value [*Wertverschiebung*], transferring the significance of the Penis [*die Penisbedeutung*] to another part of the body" (222; translation modified). For original, see "Die Ichspaltung im Abwehrvorgang,"

Studienausgabe, 12 vols. (Frankfurt: Fischer Taschenbuch, 1982), III.393. German texts are cited from this edition. On the "role of the father," see "Fetischismus," 387–88.

26. "Diana Described," 103 and 104–5. To those familiar with Petrarch and Petrarchan criticism, Kaja Silverman's "Lost Objects and Mistaken Subjects: Film Theory's Structuring Lack" sketches a movement in 1980s film theory concerning fetishism similar to the one from Freccero to Vickers—although, because Freccero turns away from Freud and Vickers does not make use of Lacan, the relationship between a semiotic and a psychoanalytic theory of the "speaking subject" has not been developed as extensively in the criticism of Petrarch as it has in the critique of film (*Wide Angle* 7, 1 and 2 [1985]: 14–29). From the semiotics of film as a language constructed around lack or absence (of the referent, the site of production, or of the subject of enunciation) to a rethinking of that lack in filmic signification as one that takes place *for* the subject, one can hear an echo of the theory in "The Fig Tree and the Laurel." Thus Petrarch constructs an effect of poetic "presence" in relation to the fetishized veil, a symbol of the lack constituting his own autobiographical discourse (Laura becomes the single, privileged, missing "referent"). In describing the veil as a "fetish," Freccero makes a move comparable to that of Stephen Heath, who argues that the cinematic subject is installed in relation to the fetish ("Lessons from Brecht," *Screen* 15, no. 4 [1980]: 107–8), though he explicitly turns away from any engagement with the comparable linguistic analysis of subjectivity developed in psychoanalytic and film theory. This engagement is left to Vickers, whose Freudian account of fetishism argues that castration is central to Petrarch's "scattered rhymes." In contrast to film theory, however, Vickers does not join the sexual and the linguistic through Lacan's work on "castration" as the *cultural* imposition of the Oedipal story on the displacements necessary to linguistic functioning.

27. In *Sexuality and the Psychology of Love*, Strachey translates, "the fetish itself has become the vehicle both of denying and of asseverating the fact of castration" (218). "The fact of castration" is the translator's wording; Freud writes only "castration" (*Studienausgabe* III.387). In both "Fetishism" and "The Splitting of the Ego," castration is socially constructed—the traumatic recognition of a *taboo*, not an unmediated encounter with the female body. As Freud suggests, the threat "by itself" might not "produce a great impression" (*für sich allein muß nicht viel Eindruck machen*); the sight alone of the female genitals "might" convince him of the possibility (*von einer solchen Möglichkeit überzeugen können*)—but he might "draw no conclusion from this alone" (III.392). What Freud studies is the social and psychic *construction* of *die Realität der Kastrationsgefahr*. This construction is produced for the subject when taboo and memory coincide: meaning is transferred to a sight that first meant nothing. The joint work of taboo and retrospection produces the verdict of "reality" or fact, and fetishism reveals that this "fact" is something that *may or may not* be believed. Either a little boy disregards what he "sees," or a previously "harmless" scene is revived in memory and recognized, the second time, as a threat because a look and a prohibition "happen" to coincide: "the little boy believes that he now understands" (*Der Knabe glaubt jetzt zu verstehen*). See Jean Laplanche's study of temporality and the production of "meaning" for the traumatized sexual subject in *Life and Death in*

Psychoanalysis, trans. Jeffrey Mehlman (Baltimore: Johns Hopkins University Press, 1976), 35–47 and esp. 40.

28. Vickers, "Diana Described," 104. In "The *Canzoniere* and the Language of the Self," Mazzotta tellingly writes of #52: "If the analogy between Actaeon and the poet collapses as the poet does not look at the goddess, he now insinuates he is like Diana. The shift of perspective is hardly surprising in Petrarch's poetry: he often casts himself, as is well known, in the role of Apollo and, in the same breath, casts Laura as the sun. *The shift implies that the categories of subject and object are precarious and reversible.*" He then argues that the strictly differential nature of this subject/object, male/female relationship also produces an internal split: "the shift insinuates a doubleness at the moment in which the self is constituted: *Petrarch is at the same time both Actaeon and Diana but he is also neither, a double, like the two foci of an ellipsis always implicating each other and always apart*" (283–84, emphasis mine).

29. See Rodowick, *The Difficulty of Difference*, 68, and Janet Bergstrom's "Enunciation and Sexual Difference" (*Camera Obscura*, nos. 3–4 [Summer 1979]: 33–70) for insightful work on the bisexual mobility and contradictory multiplicity of subject positions in psychoanalytic work on fantasy.

30. See Slavoj Žižek, who stresses the insistence of synchronic structures and the contingency of any new intervention in those structures: analysis "produces the truth; that is, *the signifying frame which gives the symptoms their symbolic place and meaning.* As soon as we enter the symbolic order, the past is always present in the form of historical tradition and *the meaning of these traces is not given; it changes continually with the transformations of the signifier's network.* Every historical rupture, every advent of a new master-signifier, changes retroactively the meaning of all tradition, restructures the narration of the past, makes it readable in another, new way" (*The Sublime Object of Ideology* [London: Verso, 1989], 56, emphasis mine).

31. A number of scholars suggest Pygmalion's name (*pygmaios*) evokes a "phallic dwarf": see Franz Bömer, *P. Ovidius Naso, Metamorphosen,* vol. 5 (Heidelberg: Heidelberg University Press, 1969), 93; and Ahl, *Metaformations,* 256–57.

32. See, for example, J. Hillis Miller, *Versions of Pygmalion* (Cambridge: Harvard University Press, 1990).

33. One continually reads, "one day x happened to be somewhere and saw y. . . ." Not only does desire not conduct itself along heterosexual lines or according to the demand for exogamy, it doesn't always stick to the human (e.g., Pygmalion loves a statue, Narcissus an *imago*). Orpheus, the "author" for "giving his love to tender boys," sings of Jove's love for Ganymede, Phoebus's for Hyacinthus, Pygmalion's for his own work, Myrrha's for her father, and Venus's for the child of that incestuous union, Adonis, because of the interference of her own son. One may, however, discern a certain logic to this labile erotic slippage. As in Freud's thesis of "polymorphous perversity," Ovid does provide a framing, organizational sign by which to measure Book X's shifting erotic objects: Hymen connects Book X to Book IX because of the marriage of a woman to a man-turned-woman (Iphis to Ianthe). Referring to Pasiphae's love for a bull, Iphis claims that her passion for another woman is yet "more mad" than that (9.737–38). Thus

same-sex love between women is "mad" because it lacks a penis; that love must nonetheless be interpreted in relation to that missing organ—a signifier for what *amor* means. A phallic ordering of sexuality represents one woman's love for another as "more mad" than that of a woman for a bull.

34. Mazzotta, "The *Canzoniere* and the Language of the Self," 284.

35. "Fetishism," 217; translation modified. *Studienausgabe* III.385–86.

36. *The Sublime Object of Ideology*, 45 and 37. Žižek asks how an external "symbolic machine" becomes "the place where the fate of our internal, most 'sincere' and 'intimate' beliefs is in advance staged and decided," and trauma becomes the mechanism by which the unconscious is constituted as a social "affair of obedience to the dead, uncomprehended letter." For him, trauma is the condition of the subject's "unconscious economy." His revision of Althusserian "interpellation" clearly pertains to Freud's theory that the subject recognizes what it means to be "male" (and what it means for his mother to be a "woman") because of the trauma called "castration": "How does the Ideological State Apparatus . . . 'internalize' itself; how does it produce the effect of ideological belief . . . [or] recognition of one's ideological position? . . . This external 'machine' of State Apparatuses exercises its force only in so far as it is experienced, in the unconscious economy of the subject, *as a traumatic, senseless injunction*. . . . It is precisely this non-integrated surplus of senseless traumatism which confers on the Law its unconditional authority. . . . Far from hiding its full authority, this traumatic, non-integrated character of the Law is a positive condition of it" (*The Sublime Object of Ideology*, 43 and 37, emphasis mine). With similar emphasis on the subject's traumatic insertion into the Symbolic order, Laplanche argues that it is the disjunction between the intelligible and the as yet unintelligible, the "senseless," that characterizes Freud's understanding of any subject's entrance into sexuality. In Laplanche's linguistic account of "latency," the interference between the not-yet significant and the significant inducts the always unprepared subject into the system of sexual meanings, an interference that makes traumatic the necessarily "retrospective" work of rendering sexuality legible (*Life and Death in Psychoanalysis*, 35–47 and esp. 40).

37. "Within the limits of this book," he writes, the lady "is never created." *Laura* is "unable to create her supposed lover as laureate . . . the closed system of an autonomous universe remains permanently out of reach" (*The Light in Troy: Imitation and Discovery in Renaissance Poetry* [New Haven: Yale University Press, 1982], 115).

38. See my "'Myself/Before Me': Gender and Prohibition in Milton's Italian Sonnets," in *Milton and the Idea of Woman*, ed. Julia Walker (Urbana: University of Illinois Press, 1988), 32–51.

39. Giuseppe Mazzotta, "Petrarch's Song 126," in *Textual Analysis: Some Readers Reading*, ed. M. A. Caws (New York: Modern Language Association of America, 1986), 125, 129, and 130.

40. In *S/Z*, Barthes writes of fetishism in *Sarrasine*: "the sentence can never constitute a total; meanings can be listed, not admixed: the total, the sum are for language the promised lands, glimpsed *at the end* of enumeration. . . . As a genre, the *blazon* expresses the belief that a *complete* inventory can reproduce a total body . . . description . . . accumulates in order to totalize, multiplies fetishes in

order to obtain a total, defetishized body; thereby, description *represents* no beauty at all: no one can *see* La Zambinella, infinitely projected as a totality impossible because linguistic, *written*" (trans. Richard Miller [New York: Hill and Wang, 1974], 114).

41. First quotation: "Desire and the Interpretation of Desire in *Hamlet*" as reprinted in *Literature and Psychoanalysis: The Question of Reading: Otherwise*, ed. Shoshana Felman (Baltimore: Johns Hopkins University Press, 1982), 28. Second quotation: *Ecrits: A Selection*, trans. Alan Sheridan (New York: W. W. Norton and Co., 1977), 67, emphasis mine. See "L'instance de la lettre" (*Ecrits*, 493–528) and "La chose freudienne" (*Ecrits*, 414–15) for a summary of the "gap" or "béance congénitale" in man's "natural relations" as translated by "*l'omniprésence pour l'être humaine de la fonction symbolique.*"

42. *The Seminar of Jacques Lacan: Book II, The Ego in Freud's Theory and in the Technique of Psychoanalysis 1954–55*, trans. Sylvana Tomaselli (New York: W. W. Norton and Co., 1988), 238 and 239.

43. See *Ecrits: A Selection*, 40.

44. *Reading Lacan* (Ithaca: Cornell University Press, 1985), 20.

45. *The Sublime Object of Ideology*, 175. Compare here Thomas Greene's observation that "one might argue" that Petrarch "creates himself out of failed signifiers."

46. One might compare the similar formulation by Nicholas Abraham and Maria Torok—that to become a subject, one must join a linguistic exchange within a community of "empty mouths" (*L'Ecorce et le noyau* [Paris: Aubier-Flammarion, 1978], 268).

47. Ovid's Actaeon appealed widely to male writers representing internal states. See Ioan Couliano's discussion of Actaeon's role in Giordano Bruno's *Eroici Furori*, in *Eros and Magic in the Renaissance*, trans. Margaret Cook (Chicago: University of Chicago Press, 1984), 72–80. But Actaeon's accidental vision proved useful in a yet larger cultural domain than the lyric. As Wendy Wall demonstrates, early book prefaces represented reading as "voyeurism," thus "mediating and suppressing" a set of cultural anxieties released by printing technology ("Disclosures in Print: The 'Violent Enlargement' of the Renaissance Voyeuristic Text," *Studies in English Literature* 29 [1989]: 53). For her, Actaeon's presence in prefatory material figures and deflects the anxieties of the new democratizing, anti-aristocratic trade in books; making the reader a voyeur allows an "aristocratic" disavowal of the stigma of print while also constituting a marketing strategy.

48. *Life and Death in Psychoanalysis*, 82–83.

49. See *The Seminar of Jacques Lacan: Book II*, 166–67.

50. *The Revolution in Poetic Language*, trans. Margaret Waller (New York: Columbia University Press, 1981), 65–67.

THROUGH THE OPTIC GLASS

VOYEURISM AND PARADISE LOST

REGINA SCHWARTZ

> He sees you when you're sleeping
> He knows when you're awake,
> He knows if you've been bad or good,
> So be good for goodness' sake.

> Read in such a way that the invisible becomes visible, the
> transcendent, historical; the sacred icon, a cultural image . . .
> Milton's poem becomes as powerful an instrument for the
> undoing of the cultural economy inscribed in it as it was
> for its institution—more powerful, indeed, than
> less "pure" forms of patriarchal currency.
> (Christine Froula, "When Eve Reads Milton:
> Undoing the Canonical Economy")

*P*ARADISE LOST is a poem in which everyone seems to be looking at everyone else—Satan, God, Eve, Adam, the narrator, us—and all the while, they are looking back. Throughout our reading, we are directed to follow someone else's line of sight: through the eye of Satan, we "behold / Far off th' Empyreal Heav'n" and we first see "this pendant world"; joining Satan's gaze, we first view Paradise, eyeing Adam and Eve askance with his/our jealous leer. When the Almighty Father "ben[ds] down his eye, / His own works and their works at once to view," we bend down our eye with his, and it happens again when he/we behold our two first parents, survey Hell and Chaos, and watch Satan in the "precincts of Light," ready "to stoop with wearied wings, and willing feet / On the bare outside of this World" (3.73–74).[1] Early in the poem, then, Satan is looking at Heaven and Earth as God is looking at Satan—who is looking at Heaven and Earth—and we are implicated in all of these gazes. It is more complicated still, for while the narrator is blind, he also sees, and we join the drama of an unseeing narrator who nonetheless tells all he sees.

Even the Fall itself, which, biblically speaking, should be the story of the temptation to taste (or touch, as Eve exaggerates the command), lays surprising stress on the temptation to see. In the rhetoric of synesthesia that marks the scenes of temptation and fall, seeing continually emerges as the key sense; indeed, Milton comes close to telling us that this is sin enough, to rewriting the Genesis tradition to make the sin looking rather than eating: "Fixt on the Fruit she gaz'd, which to behold / Might tempt alone" (9.735–36). In the temptation scene, the serpent tries to trick Eve by inciting her supposed wish to be an exhibit: "one man except, / Who sees thee? (and what is one?) who shouldst be seen / A Goddess among Gods" (9.545–47). Eve dismisses that ploy as "overpraising," only for the serpent to tempt her with the obverse wish—to be a voyeur.

> he knows that in the day
> Ye Eat thereof, your Eyes that seem so clear,
> Yet are but dim, shall perfetly be then
> Op'n'd and clear'd, and ye shall be as Gods.

> (9.705–8)

These words win all "too easy entrance" into her heart. Eve seems to be succumbing to the power the gaze could offer her: Eve, first the object not only of the "gaze admiring" and "gaze insatiate" of the serpent but also the one "all things living gaze on" (the word *gaze* is repeated like a refrain in Satan's opening temptation speech to Eve), now seizes that position of voyeur: "Fixt on the Fruit she gaz'd." Finally, Eve's heightened appetite at the hour of noon, the smell of the fruit, and the desire to touch or taste, solicit "her longing eye" (9.743). It turns out that in his emphasis on seeing, Milton is true to Genesis after all, where the serpent's explanation for the prohibition is that "God knows that when you eat of it your eyes will be opened and you shall become as gods" (Gen. 3.5), and the immediate consequence of the transgression is the "opening of eyes": "Then the eyes of both were opened, and they knew that they were naked" (Gen. 3.7). With all these voyeuristic temptations and wishes, it is no wonder that our first parents immediately cover themselves up with fig leaves.

But despite the evidence that this is a poem preoccupied with voyeurism (among other things), the dynamics of specularity in *Paradise Lost* challenge any conventional understanding of what voyeurism might mean.[2] If the scopophilic drive is a will to dominate, how is such domination possible when the object itself is inaccessible, distorted and disappearing in the very act of perceiving? If subjects and objects are constituted by the act of seeing—the subject sees and the object is the focus of sight—what happens when the watching subject is watched and the object of sight looks back? Such questions push psychoanalysis, willingly or not, into the realm of politics, where insights into the complexities of the gaze could enable objects of sight to begin to reclaim their gaze—or, at least, their subjectivity.

STARGAZING

When Augustine condemned astronomers for their efforts to master the heavens, he offered the analogy of a spider entangling its victim in its web, calling curiosity the "lust of the eye." *Paradise Lost* is brimming with lustful eyes. In Milton's poem, the figure of the astronomer is not distinguishable from that of the voyeur—nothing is more forbidden than the heavens—and if voyeurism brings the seamy side of observation and knowledge-seeking into view (i.e., power), so does astronomy. Speculations of the "new science" mattered far more in the Renaissance than one would predict of abstruse scientific hypotheses about the motions of remote heavenly bodies, and they mattered so much because those theories did not reinscribe patterns of dominance encoded in theocentrism; they challenged them. If Milton, as he claimed in *Areopagitica,* visited Galileo, he found a terrible demonstration of retaliation by the powers-that-be against such a challenge: he found his Tuscan voyeur of the heavens as a blind man imprisoned by the Inquisition. Years later, blind and imprisoned, Milton will depict both an intrusion upon the heavenly sanctuary and the divine defense against it: the only laughter in all of *Paradise Lost* is provoked by astronomers trying to master the secrets of the heavens (8.71–84). Such efforts at mastery are contemptible, his Deity would sneer with sadistic laughter: "Ha Ha, I can see you but just try to see me" or, better, "You'll show me yours, but if you think I'll show you mine, think again." The presence of Galileo in *Paradise Lost*— his enigma heightened because he is the only contemporary Milton mentions in the epic—invites not only speculation about astronomy, then, but also questions about power and its abuses, desire and its frustrations, questions that resurface each of the many times the poem fixates on the stars.[3]

This version of the epic's preoccupation with looking—peering at the heavens—is inaugurated in the poem by Galileo in a simile comparing Satan's shield to the moon, which the "Tuscan artist" looks at through his optic glass. Needless to say, the description of Galileo gazing at the moon is prompted by still another gaze: we are looking at Satan. Our voyeuristic eye follows Satan moving toward the shore with his "ponderous shield," "massy, large and round," but then we turn away from watching Satan to watch Galileo. That is, Galileo, voyeur of the heavens, also becomes an exhibit, seen by us, and it is only after we have spotted him that we move in, our eye joins his own, and they share the same line of sight toward the moon. Having redirected our vision from Satan and his shield to the moon, "to descry new lands, / Rivers or mountains in her spotty globe," we become identified with the Tuscan artist, spectators looking through an optic glass of our own.

He scarce had ceas't when the superior Fiend
Was moving toward the shore; his ponderous shield
Ethereal temper, massy, large and round,
Behind him cast; the broad circumference
Hung on his shoulders like the Moon, whose Orb
Through Optic Glass the Tuscan artist views
At Ev'ning from the top of Fesole,
Or in Valdarno, to descry new Lands,
Rivers or Mountains in her spotty Globe.

(1.283–91)

To summarize this logic, the complete movement of our gaze in the passage is from looking at Satan to looking at Galileo to looking at the object
of Galileo's sight. But that isn't quite right either, for the simile compli-
cates things further. As our eye follows Satan moving toward the shore
with his shield, our line of sight is *analogous* to Galileo's line of sight as
he looks at the moon, and the force of that analogy is to establish, not
sequence, but simultaneity: *even as* Galileo is watching the moon, we are
watching Satan, specifically his shield, which is "like the moon." That
means both that we are made a spectator of Galileo (he is our exhibit) and
that we are made to identify with Galileo (we are the same voyeur he is,
gazing at the heavens), and when we take the logic of the simile to heart,
we are not only shifting back and forth between these positions, we are in
both positions at once: we look *at* Galileo and *as* Galileo, and that is one
of the eerie senses in which the object of our sight looks back at us.

In several important ways, a conventional pseudo-Freudian understanding of voyeurism is challenged in this passage. First, the successful
voyeur supposedly watches unseen, but Galileo is not hidden from view,
for someone else—God, the narrator, and the reader—is always watching
him watch. Second, voyeurism suggests positioning a subject and an object, but our example demonstrates how unstable any such positioning
necessarily is when the "subject" is both looking at the "object" of sight
and identifying with it. Which orb is spotty after all? This shifting is ac-
counted for in Lacan's elaboration of the Freudian mechanism of reversal. In "Instincts and Their Vicissitudes," Freud describes how the voyeur
and the exhibitionist change roles in response to fear of object loss. Fearing he will lose the object of his sight, the voyeur inevitably wants to be
the object himself. Lacan's contribution is to see this shifting as continual,
to see the positions as so unstable that they cannot really be fixed positions at all.[4] Any fixed positioning as voyeur or exhibitionist is also challenged on another front: according to Edward Branigan, the first stage in
a cinematic point-of-view shot must be to situate the spectator at point A
before situating the object at point B, in order to establish the line of sight

from point A to point B.[5] But we do not know where Galileo is. Is he looking from the top of Fiesole or from the valley of the Arno? We do know that his gaze sparks projections: from a mountain or in a river valley, Galileo sees (of all things) mountains or rivers when he looks at the moon. But wait, are those spots mountains, or are they rivers?—it turns out that the object is as unstable as the subject. Yet somehow Galileo is granted a line of sight, even though we do not know where he is or what he sees and where *it* is.

The case of Galileo also suggests that the voyeur cannot successfully possess the object of his sight because what he sees is at best a fabrication, an idealized image composed at an ideal point in a telescope, another fabrication. When Milton alludes to the astronomer as the "Tuscan artist"—the only use of *artist* in all his poetry—he chooses a word whose multivalence casts long shadows in this poem. In the Renaissance, *artist* could mean both a master of the liberal arts, a philosopher, and someone who has practical rather than theoretical "arts"; by the time Charles was executed, *artist* suggested an untrustworthy master of artifice. Galileo is not just the artificer of his optic instrument; there is, as Donald Friedman points out, more than a hint that he has fabricated those moon spots.[6] In contrast to the trustworthy vision of Raphael, "the Glass / Of Galileo, less assur'd, observes / Imagin'd Lands and Regions in the Moon" (5.261–63). That wonderful line joins things-observed to things-imagined unproblematically. Milton seems to suggest—and Lacan would agree—that for the astronomer, and the voyeur, to observe *is* to imagine.

Starlight

Paradise Lost is brimming with lustful eyes. For all of the ways that Galileo challenges the clichés of voyeurism-as-aggression and exhibitionism-as-passivity, there is plenty of evidence for such formulas elsewhere. Satan as voyeur/aggressor and Eve as exhibit/victim virtually allegorize those notions. Satan approaches Paradise as a predator, "nearer to view his prey, unespi'd." His eyes become weapons, metonymically, the paws that would tear Adam and Eve to pieces.

> about them round
> A Lion now he stalks with fiery glare,
> Then as a Tiger, who by chance hath spi'd
> In some Purlieu two gentle Fawns at play,
> Straight couches close, then rising changes oft
> His couchant watch, as one who chose his ground

Whence rushing he might surest seize them both
Gript in each paw:

(4.401–8)

Next, Satan resolves, "with narrow search I must walk round / This Garden, and no corner leave unspi'd" (4.528–29). Making those rounds with "sly circumspection" (the sly voyeur would himself be hidden), he intends to master all he surveys. That mastering, destructive aim of his gaze is perhaps clearest when Satan watches Paradise from a special position of concealment: perched as a cormorant on the Tree of Life, he "only us'd / For prospect, what well us'd had been the pledge/ Of immortality" (4.199–201). Why should *immortality* be the antithesis of *prospect*? Why, unless Satan's line of sight is the antithesis of life, unless, that is, the gaze of Satan is lethal. His sightings—Satan will inhabit more predatory creatures to spy "unespi'd"—are offered less as the prelude to attacking his prey than as the first phase of his attack.

Freud joined his discussions of voyeurism and exhibitionism to another pair, sadism and masochism. Like sadism, the look is an effort to master, to possess, as the devils intend to "possess / All as [their] own" (2.365–66), but the mechanism of reversal that turns the sadist into the masochist also turns the voyeur's gaze toward its object back upon himself.[7] While he goes on to insist that the active stage is primary (first we look, then we want to be seen), Freud argues elsewhere for the primacy of narcissism: we *begin* by directing our gaze at ourselves, and only then do we direct it outward—like Eve, looking first at herself in the pool, and only later at Adam.[8] In her temptation dream, Satan begins by tempting Eve to want to be the object of more gazes (playing, we could speculate, on the fact that she began life as the object of her own gaze, making the object position a familiar one for her).[9] The sexual overtones of gazing upon her, and thereby devouring her, are not very subtle.

Heav'n wakes with all his eyes,
Whom to behold but thee, Nature's desire,
In whose sight all things joy, with ravishment
Attracted by thy beauty still to gaze.

(5.44–47)

But as the dream proceeds, instead of being looked at, Eve does the looking, gazing first at the tree and then at the one standing beside the tree who "on that Tree also gazed" (5.54–57). The very process of temptation describes the reversal Freud characterizes, from Eve as seen object to Eve becoming the voyeur herself. "Taste this," says Satan, "and be henceforth among the Gods / Thyself a Goddess . . . and see / What life the Gods live

there, and such live thou" (5.76–81). Eve tastes and Eve sees: transported
up to the clouds, she sees below "a prospect wide and various." If Satan
began by luring Eve into the familiar narcissistic desire to be an exhibit,
he concludes by holding out to her a very different temptation: the temptation of voyeurism. Eve wants to seize the spectatorial position, to gaze
upon that prospect wide and various, and by that gaze to master all she
surveys. Her punishment is the inevitable terror for being caught in the
act of looking. In this sense, the myth of the Fall in *Paradise Lost* is made
to enact the male dread of woman seizing her own gaze: she must be
condemned to death for her desire.

All of this is classic—too classic—and yet the same dynamic is fully
elaborated in the temptation itself, the waking one. The serpent spies Eve,
the hand of Eve—revealed and hidden provocatively among the roses—
but once he has made her the object of his stupefied gaze, he works to get
Eve to look at *him*: he "Curl'[s] many a wanton wreath in sight of Eve, /
To lure her Eye" (9.517–18). The serpent rears up, with

> Circular base of rising folds, that tow'r'd
> Fold above fold a surging Maze, his Head
> Crested aloft, and Carbuncle his Eyes;
> With burnished Neck of verdant Gold, erect.
>
> (9.498–501)

"Look on me" (9.687), says this phallus, late voyeur-become-exhibition-
ist. She looks, and then, as in her dream, her gaze moves from the serpent
to the object of his sight: "Fixt on the Fruit she gaz'd." In the scene, Satan
has virtually caught her eye, and possessing it, he directs it where he
chooses. Her point of view is now Satan's. Again, Satan has turned Eve-
the-exhibit into Eve-the-voyeur, for once he fixes her/his gaze on that
fruit, she must possess it, just as Satan possesses her. And once again, her
punishment suits her crime: having dared to look, she must suffer exposure. Eve becomes aware that she is naked.

One of the things that is wrong with this reading is that it presumes,
like the bulk of film criticism on spectatorship, that voyeurism is sadistic.
It complies—hook, line, and sinker—with the limited understanding of
looking as active domination. Laura Mulvey's influential essay "Visual
Pleasure and Narrative Cinema" divided looking into the male gaze and
the female image;[10] ever since, voyeurism has been largely gendered as a
male perversion, one the entire cinematic apparatus is complicitous with,
addressing voyeuristic male spectators with voyeuristic male characters
by means of a voyeuristic male camera. Female spectators are left only to
identify with the victims or the victimizers. "Confronted with the classical
Hollywood text with a male address, the female spectator has basically
two modes of entry: a narcissistic identification with the female figure as

spectacle, and a 'transvestite' identification with the active male hero in his mastery."[11] Since 1975, much of film theory has been engaged in refining and revising Mulvey's thesis on the role of female spectatorship (including Mulvey's own revision).[12] In particular, the cases of films that were explicitly made to address women and the spectatorship of lesbian and gay male audiences have gone far toward qualifying these assumptions.[13] But while the biological reductionism of sexual difference has been critiqued, and cinematic identification has come to be understood as far more complex and fractured, the basic assumption—that looking is sadistic—has gone largely unchallenged.[14] When critics do take the sadism out of spectatorship, it is only to replace it with male masochism. According to that account, the spectator submits himself to the overwhelming presence on the screen, reentering a preoedipal phase of attachment to the mother. But to substitute masochism for sadism, and preoedipal for oedipal, does little to break down those binary oppositions; besides, the analysis still conforms to the dictates of oedipal logic, a logic that has created "preoedipal" as pre-itself. Surely, understanding the spectator's response—male or female—as masochistic is no more liberating than understanding it as sadistic. We can look back, we can even look first, and we need not be sadists to do so.

Nonetheless, there has been a stubborn tendency to see spectatorship sadistically and to see that observation as politically liberating. The following remark is indicative: "Unfortunately, Silverman's essay, like Studlar's, ultimately refuses to cede any importance to sadism in the male viewer's response."[15] Why is this unfortunate? What is gained by seeing specularity as sadistic? Why not understand the spectator as implicated in a mode of looking and in a series of looks that do not polarize power and that therefore do not empower anyone sadistically? The tenacity of film criticism to grasp spectatorship as sadistic is all the more surprising given that its own discourse is deeply Lacanian; it is Lacan's notion of the gaze that set these questions into motion, his categories of the symbolic and imaginary that have been the context for the discussions, and his vocabulary that has dictated the terms. What, then, has happened to Lacan's insight that when we look, we both identify with and are alienated from the image that confronts us?[16] Crudely put, any act of looking involves too much narcissism for the model of voyeurism-as-domination to hold—unless we are talking about self-aggression, in which case we may as well call it masochism, or passivity. To be a little less crude and a little more Lacanian: the subject not only produces images of objects; the subject is illuminated by objects, by the light emitted by objects. In that sense, the object looks back. Hence, Lacan's story of the fisherman who pointed out to him a sardine can floating on the water: "Do you see that can? Do you see it? Well, it doesn't see you!" But for Lacan, "It was looking at me at the level of the point of light, the point at which everything that looks at me is situated."[17]

Freud also muddles the opposition between voyeurism and narcissism. Offering an excursus about scientific methodology in the midst of "On Narcissism," he expresses apprehension about theorizing in the absence of *observable* data, "of abandoning observation for *barren theoretical controversy*" (my italics).[18] Freud is telling us that he is attached to external objects rather than that he is narcissistic, and the evidence for his object-libido is the stock he puts in observation of external phenomena, over against absorption in his own internal ruminations. Defining megalomania as "the over-estimation of the power of one's mental acts," he associates such megalomania with the withdrawal from the external world—with, that is, narcissism. In other words, even Freud's oppositions do not square: on the one hand, he lumps together voyeurism, sadism, and activity, and on the other, he joins exhibitionism to masochism and passivity. But how can observation—wherein knowledge is *constrained* by the external world—belong in that active, sadistic category, and narcissism with its "*omnipotence* of thought" belong in the passive, masochistic one? Beats me—or do I beat it?

STAR-STRUCK

What about Satan's predatory gaze? Couldn't the gaze of Satan be a powerful symbol of male domination, and therefore serve as confirmation that the ideology of the poem endorses such domination? In *Paradise Lost*, the polarization of voyeur/victimizer/man over against exhibit/victim/woman is attached most persistently, as we have seen, to Satan, to the temptation of Eve, and to the Fall. Satan does not only prey upon Eve; his impulse to polarize power begins when he regards the Son's elevation as his own reduction—Satan's is an entire discourse of victims and victimizers—and the Fall is a fall into that classic (and Satanic) version of voyeurism in which looking (and curiosity) is destructive. The distinction between prelapsarian and postlapsarian looking is made graphic in the scene where Eve "minister'd naked" at the luncheon on the grass of Adam and Raphael. The fallen narrator knows all about predatory gazes and projects back onto the occasion the perspective that would turn Eve into a topless and bottomless waitress. And then, the Miltonic "but" shakes off the voyeuristic fantasy, protesting that "then" is not now, even as the protest heightens his delight, veiling his object of desire with that vast distance imposed by the Fall.

> Meanwhile at Table Eve
> Minister'd naked, and thir flowing cups

With pleasant liquors crown'd: O innocence
Deserving Paradise! if ever, then,
Then had the Sons of God excuse to have been
Enamour'd at that sight; but in those hearts
Love unlibidinous reign'd, nor jealousy
Was understood, the injur'd Lover's Hell.

                                                    (5.443–50)

Perhaps voyeurism is so thoroughly implicated in the Fall because Milton understands the Temptation *as* the temptation of voyeurism—that is, the temptation to polarize power. In this sense Milton may give predatory voyeurism that fatal role, not in order to punish women for their desire for it, but in order to critique such voyeurism altogether. The aggressive gaze is not only Eve's, nor is it fatal only for Eve; it is the cause of all our "death and all our woe." Eve's error may not be seizing the gaze but interpreting it (like so many film critics) as polarizing power into victims and victimizers. At the moment of her fall, Eve interprets divine looking in just that way:

And I perhaps am secret; Heav'n is high,
High and remote to see from thence distinct
Each thing on Earth; and other care perhaps
May have diverted from continual watch
Our great Forbidder, safe with all his Spies.

                                                    (9.811–15)

A newly fallen Eve must hide since her Forbidder has all the weapons. Like Satan, she feels continually watched in a perpetual prison, and her only hope of freedom lies in the Forbidder diverting his gaze or having his vision clouded for reasons that have nothing to do with her.

Still, classifying the scenes of sadistic looking as "fallen" or, in contemporary parlance, "perversions" begs the question of whether seeing is sadistic, positing, as it does, that there is a bad kind of seeing in the fallen world and a good kind of seeing once-upon-a-time. It turns out that even these fallen voyeuristic scenes are not so straightforward, for the aggression of the voyeur is challenged on other fronts, familiar from the example of Galileo. Someone is watching Satan watch Eve, someone is watching Eve watch Satan, someone is watching Adam watch Eve, and someone is watching Eve watch Adam. The reason that, theoretically, the voyeur's pleasure depends upon his hiding, upon his seeing without being seen, is that the very character of his aggression is to turn the object of his sight into just that, an object; if he were simultaneously seen, then he too would be reduced to an object, of another's gaze. But all of the voyeurs in *Paradise Lost* suffer precisely this dilemma—God is watching his creatures, the narrator is watching God and his creatures, and the reader is watching them all—and that is another reason why the temptation of voyeurism, the temptation to master, is never wholly achieved. Someone else is *always* watching.

But if sadism is constrained by another's sadism—by someone else watching the voyeur watch—then aggression is not denied; it is only deferred. Wouldn't the last one in this chain of sight be the master? Depending upon our framework, this "fourth look"—as Paul Willemen calls it to distinguish the watcher watching the watcher from the other three looks in cinema[19]—this gaze can belong to God, to the narrator, or to the reader. Within the story told by the epic narrator, God is the Transcendental Voyeur, ever watchful of the watchers watching, so that for all his efforts at concealment, Satan is fully exposed to the all-seeing eye of Heaven. And Eve's reflexive guilty response to her crime—her hope that she has not been seen, that "other care perhaps / May have diverted from continual watch / Our great Forbidder"—is not simply projection; in a parody of the earlier exhibitionist wish to be seen a goddess among the gods, Eve *is* seen by God, "for what can scape the eye of God all-seeing?" Adam's shame is expressed, as we know, by the urge to hide to avoid the gaze of another; he calls upon pines to cover him, leaves to cover him, until the robe of righteousness is offered by the Son of God to cover him—and his private parts—from the sight of his Father. It turns out that God is the supreme voyeur, watching unseen, possessing all he sees, his all-seeing eye circumscribing the power of the other voyeurs. But in the wider context of the epic itself, that position is reserved for the narrator, who even watches God watching, and whose gaze Milton makes an explicit theme. In the larger context still—our experience of the poem—we are in that privileged last position. We watch the narrator watch God watch; theoretically, that makes the reader the arch-voyeur, the tyrant of tyrants of tyrants. Power has so amassed by the time it has been seized by the voyeuristic reader that it is surprising that her mere glance doesn't ignite the epic. Surely, the notion of reading as devouring, of interpreting as mastering, will come as little surprise to most literary critics; our scrutinizing gazes have so dissected *Paradise Lost* for several centuries that it is a wonder there is anything left. But there is. And so the image of a reader smug in her awareness that she sees and knows more than either Milton's narrator or his God—attractive as it may be—may need qualifying.

Where does this chain of deferred spectatorship really lead? To start with the Almighty Looker, what does God see when he bends down his eye on his works, but himself? Milton's theology makes that clear: "God shall be all in all" (3.341), "from whom / All things proceed, and up to him return" (5.469–70). God's first extensive gaze on his world can easily be read as God checking himself out, surveying his parts—Earth, Hell, and Chaos—to see what is happening on each of his regions.

Now had th'Almighty Father from above,
From the pure Empyrean where he sits
High Thron'd above all highth, bent down his eye,
His own works and their works at once to view.

(3.56–59)

Or if we prefer to think of the Eternal One temporally instead of spatially, we can catch him peering at himself that way too, "from his prospect high, / Wherein past, present, future he beholds" (3.76–77). If God is the Transcendental Voyeur, he is also the Transcendental Exhibit, for while the "invisible king . . . hath suppressed in night" his hidden secrets not to be scanned, he has also expressed himself, "shown himself," in creation, where he writes them for all to see in the "book of knowledge fair." Furthermore, while the watching Father is concealed behind skirts "dark with excessive bright" (even the seraphim must veil their eyes), he has expressed the "effulgence of his glory" in his visible Son, "in whose conspicuous count'nance, without cloud / Made visible, th'Almighty Father shines" (3.385–86).[20] For that matter, what is the object of the narrator's gaze, if not his work and their works? The narrator even makes it doubtful that he looks outward for this vision: physically blind, he directs his sight inward for this poem.[21] And surely the lessons of reader-response criticism prevent us from assuming naively that the reader acts upon an object/text that is distinct from herself or, for that matter, from her cultural context. But to say that the reader, narrator, and God are only looking at themselves, that the voyeur is only watching her/himself, is to elide the distinction between subject and object that any notion of aggression depends upon. It is just that comfortable distinction that Milton prohibits us from making: how can there be a cast of victims and victimizers when it is not possible to determine clearly where God ends and his objects of sight begin, where the narrator ends and his delineations of the cosmos begin, and where the reader ends and her visions of all of the above begin?

Raphael tells Adam that the heavens are more like the earth than it is generally believed, just as Galileo's discovery of the earth in the moon confirms that "ultimately one found in the stars things that could be looked for on Earth."[22] Here, Raphael voices this eerie identification of the subject and the object in cosmic terms: "though what if Earth / Be but the shadow of Heav'n, and things therein / Each to other like, more than on Earth is thought?" (5.574–76). Disturbingly enough, Raphael also says the opposite: "Heav'n is for thee too high / To know what passes there" (8.172–73). Here, the spectator and the object of sight are not thoroughly entangled but are completely separated, so much so that they are inaccessible to one another. And that remoteness is another constraint on aggression: the Tuscan artist cannot possess what he cannot see. The inaccessibility of the object of desire has also been underscored by Lacan: "Generally speaking, the relation between the gaze and what one wishes to see involves a lure. The subject is presented as other than he is, and what one shows him is not what he wishes to see."[23] This lure is an image—whether in the telescope, on the cinematic screen, on the printed page, or in the mind. Satan does not see Eve, he sees an image of Eve, and her hand, both concealed and revealed, offers testimony only to the image. Galileo does not see the moon, he sees an image in his optic glass, and the telescope—the very instrument that brings the moon so near—also makes it hopelessly remote by distorting it, imaged or imagined: "The glass / Of Galileo, less assur'd, observes / Imagin'd Lands" (5.261–63).

If the lenses of the telescope represented to Bacon an advancement in man's dominion over nature, they were also a reminder that our sight is always deceived and our mastery is always frustrated. The lens is no more trustworthy than our unaided eye, for adjustments in the angle of refraction produce only more images. Any sense of expansive "epistemological privilege" gained by the invention of the telescope was counterbalanced by the sense that neither the eye nor optic instruments can penetrate the vast heavens.[24] Historically, the reception of the telescope—the refusal of Galileo's colleagues to look through it or to believe what they saw—made it evident that seeing was not what counted. According to Hans Blumenberg, "Through the offer of the telescope, the fact that one can refuse to see, and deny that one has seen, and dispute the possibility of ever seeing, and wish that one did not have to see, became, as a human and a historical possibility, the acute incentive to expect less from bringing forward immediate intuitive evidence." What was needed to conquer the heavens "could never be demonstrated by observation or experiment, with whatever equipment."[25] Along with optic instruments, the Renaissance fascination with perspective in the visual arts heightened the awareness that images are distortions. "To see a thing 'in perspective' is to see it from the proper vantage point, at a sufficient distance to make it fully manifest or properly set in its context, to see it clearly, unambiguously, in short, truly."[26] But because perspective depends upon a rigidly fixed point of view, upon only one of an infinite number of positions (as perspective's spatial plenitude reminds us), all of that clarity instantly dissolves if the spectator moves. Like the telescope, the arts of illusion suggested not only confidence in "seeing truly" but also confirmation that our vision is imperfect and limited.

Understanding vision as limiting access, rather than granting it, is as old as Plato. But Plato wanted it both ways: if the senses were untrustworthy, nonetheless sight also allowed perception of the visible world, even, in his theory of recollection, of the Forms. This entailed a deeper and familiar paradox. Perception involved the identification of subject and object, the "meeting of like to like," and this meeting entailed both the active streaming of light toward the object and the active streaming of light *from* the object. Objects "look back," rather like the Lacanian sardine can:[27]

> So when there is daylight around the visual stream, it falls on its like and coalesces with it, forming a single uniform body in the line of sight, along which the stream from within strikes the external object. Because the stream and daylight are similar, the whole so formed is homogeneous, and the motions caused by the stream penetrate right through the body and produce in the soul the sensation which we call sight.[28]

For Plato, when we see we do not only penetrate objects; we are penetrated by them. With Descartes, however, seeing becomes exclusively passive—our lenses receive images. But then the contradiction grew intolerable: how could he reconcile a passive optics with the will to regard knowledge as dominating? The solution was to sever the mind's eye from the body's eye; if physical sight was passive, inner sight was still active.[29] In Descartes, "Those [things] are purely intellectual which our understanding apprehends by means of a certain inborn light, and without the aid of any corporeal image."[30] This split may remind readers of *Paradise Lost* of the blind prophet who sees with inner light, but it is at odds with Miltonic ontology, wherein matter and spirit are undivided. Rather than making physical sight passive and spiritual sight active, Milton sees in the more Platonic sense of extramission and intramission, looking at a world that looks back.

STAR-CROSSED

Throughout this rhetoric, the voyeur and the astronomer are linked by a suspiciously gendered vocabulary: nature-as-woman-as-object is to be dominated by the scientist-as-man-as-observer. The heavens must be penetrated. An oedipal reading of this gendered world would suggest that the man must separate from Mother Nature, and once he has won independence from her, he is free to look at/violate her. The image of the astronomer seems to fit that paradigm perfectly, since he is attached to his telescope at a safe distance from the object he simultaneously penetrates. Then, too, Milton's moon is a woman. For argument's sake, let's try on the hypothesis that the gaze is male after all. Is Eve allowed to look in the same way the others do? Does she have her own gaze? In "Missing Mothers/Desiring Daughters," Naomi Scheman argues that films that seem to be exceptions to the rule of being governed by the male gaze (films in which women are allowed to look to their heart's content) are singularly marked by "the double state of motherlessness (neither having nor being one)" required of their heroines.[31] This blotting out of maternity—or in the case of melodrama, the rupturing of the mother/daughter relation—signals how threatening the preoedipal attachment of mother and daughter is to structures of male domination and explains the demand that women abandon their mothers to submit to male desire. Eve is motherless, like the comedic heroines who are constructed by male desire, but unlike them, Eve *literally* comes into existence "only in relation to her father's desire for her," needing to "acknowledge him as her one true parent."[32] And because her parent is also her husband, Eve is taught, from birth on, to respond to male desire (hence, she is born sexually mature): she is created by Adam as the object of his desire, and she is re-created by Satan as the object of his desire. But what does *Eve* want? Milton's scant attention to that question yields the answer to be herself, and he depicts that desire as a fatal narcissism she must be "saved from" by a harsh warning voice and a male hand that seizes her and forcibly wrenches her away from what she really wants, her own image, to submit to another "less winning soft, less amiably mild, / Than that smooth wat'ry image" (4.479–80). Henceforth, she obeys: "I yielded, and from that time see / How beauty is excell'd by manly grace" (4.489–90). Having thus capitulated to male desire, she becomes vulnerable to the host of male gazes that inhabit the epic, including the narrator's: she "half imbracing lean'd / On our first Father, half her swelling Breast / Naked met his" (4.494–97). That must explain why Eve is the one who is selected to be tempted by the exhibitionist wish. That must explain why Eve is the one who wants to look, to reclaim her desire, and that must explain why Eve, when she does seize the spectatorial position, must be punished—with death, yes, but also with childbearing. Eve's maternity comes into the world as a curse. The woman's preoedipal attachment to her mother is so threatening to the patriarchy that would wrench her from it that Eve cannot have a mother at all, and her own mothering must be painful.

I am not going to rewrite this skewed story to redeem Eve, to give her back her gaze, partly because my whole discussion above of the dynamics of the scopic drive is intended to show that she never lost it and that such biological reductionism teaches us little about gender difference.[33] I will only add that such a reading strikes me as being thoroughly complicitous with the very oedipal logic it means to critique, for it, like the model of female sexuality it depends upon, is an account of Eve's development within the context of the male (dominating) gaze. Eve resists being assimilated to such patriarchal logic; she resists it, as all Milton readers know well, when she refuses to succumb to Adam's desire that she work at his side, and she resists it when she chooses to eat the apple Satan offers her. Victims are not granted such choice. In these scenes Eve voices the same logic that God does and that Milton does in *Areopagitica* to defend her freedom and her desire:

> If this be our condition, thus to dwell
> In narrow circuit strait'n'd by a Foe,
> Subtle or violent, we not endu'd
> Single with like defense, wherever met,
> How are we happy, still in fear of harm?
>
> (9.322–26)

Victims are not given such lines. Instead, because her narrative is framed, I am going to look at the figure who narrates her story, asking whether the gaze of the narrator, like that of the cinematic apparatus, is the male gaze.

Any account of voyeurism in Milton must come to terms with the narrator's looking, especially with how Milton characterizes it in his invocations. Politically disempowered, blind and imprisoned, the narrator expresses his sense of victimization: "On evil days though fall'n, and evil tongues; / In darkness, and with dangers compast round, / And solitude" (7.26–28). He portrays himself as the exhibit before a deity that is all-seeing—"Heav'n hides nothing from thy view"—and he conjures his audience, fit though few. He visits a lamp that may illuminate him, but that does not enable him to see—"Thou / Revisit'st not these eyes, that roll in vain / To find thy piercing ray, and find no dawn" (3.22–24). Descriptions of Milton's ideology of male domination must survive this narrator's complaint that he is not only denied sight, he is denied the gaze. As Modleski concludes of Hitchcock's films, "The strong fascination and identification with femininity revealed in them subverts the claims to mastery and authority not only of the male characters but of the director himself."[34] At the core of Milton's myth of the Fall is Adam's identification with Eve, an attraction that makes him fail to embrace that "masculine autonomy" Raphael instructs him in. "Fondly overcome by female charm," that is, thoroughly feminized, our first man drags the whole race of men after him into the "emasculinization" of mortality. When the narrator does dare to look, it is with the fear that he will be punished, as Eve is, for his guilty seeing—"May I express thee unblam'd?"—and he only takes a peek with many nervous allusions to safety (3.21; 7.15,24) and with a masochistic identification with the specter of Orpheus torn to pieces by the wild rout. Can we trust this complaint, or is the narrator really masking his voyeurism, an insistent wish to "see and tell of things invisible to mortal sight"? Or conversely, is his ambition to look a defense against, not exactly victimization, but an exhibitionism that is tied to those familiar characterizations of Milton's egotism? Even overtly, the blind narrator's response to his unseeing exhibitionism is not only to feel victimized. He defends himself in the poem in the same way that Milton defended himself in *The Second Defense of the English People* against his enemies' charge that his blindness was punishment for his political heresy: he claims that his blindness is better than their sight. That boast that his darkness is superior sounds like the predictable reaction to being an exhibit. Now the narrator has become the powerful voyeur, swollen with that ambition familiar from Milton's youth to "at Heav'n's door / Look in, and see each blissful Deity."[35] William Kerrigan and W.B.C. Watkins have commented on the "phallic aggression" conferred on images of seeing throughout the poem.[36] But if these invocations become occasions for the narrator to enact the polarizations of aggressive voyeur and passive exhibit, of sadism and masochism, it is only to reject those formulas. His sight depends upon the light looking inward—"So much the rather thou Celestial Light / Shine inward, and the mind through all her powers / Irradiate"—to enable him to see outward—"There plant eyes, all mist from thence / Purge and disperse, that I may see and tell / Of things invisible to mortal sight" (3.51–55). In his formulation, this narrator is illuminated *so that* he can see. The epic begins, "What is dark in me, / Illumine." This is not the depiction of a passive victim peered at through the keyhole; this is a portrayal of an active exhibit, one presaged in Milton's early, remarkably telling expression of his ambition: "I have some naked thoughts that rove about / And loudly knock to have their passage out."[37] And yet, for all his thundering aggression, the maturer Tuscan artist peers through his optic glass "less assur'd" to imagine *Paradise Lost*.

NOTES

A version of this essay was read at the Third International Milton Symposium in Florence, Italy, in June 1988, and at the Newberry Milton Seminar in Chicago in May 1989. I want to thank the members of those audiences for their many helpful responses and James Kincaid for inspiration. An earlier version of this essay was published as "Rethinking Voyeurism and Patriarchy: The Case of *Paradise Lost*," *Representations* 34 (Spring 1991). It is reprinted here with the permission of University of California Press.

1. All references to *Paradise Lost* are to *John Milton: Complete Poems and Major Prose*, ed. Merritt Hughes (Indianapolis, 1957).

2. Some of the poem's other myriad concerns, psychoanalytic and theological, and their relation to scopophilia are elaborated in Schwartz, *Remembering and Repeating: On Milton's Theology and Poetics* (Cambridge, 1988; reprint, Chicago, 1993). More on the relation between psychoanalysis and theology is in Schwartz, "The Toad at Eve's Ear: From Identification to Identity," in *Literary Milton*, ed. Diana Trevino Benet and Michael Lieb (Pittsburgh, 1994).

3. Star- (or moon-) gazing occurs again in the temptation dream, in the temptation itself, in a key dialogue between Adam and Eve, and in a lengthier discus-

sion between Adam and Raphael. In a broader sense, the heavens are the focus of Raphael's attention as he tells of the rebellion in heaven and the Creation, and the object of the narrator's gaze as he recounts the divine council. When the narrator's Muse is given a proper name, it is Urania, the muse of astronomy. But Milton is not just fixated on the stars for their own sake (although that is no small focus in an era when the astronomical theories of the "new science" were the subject of hot debate), and his Adam does not only ask how the stars move in the skies—he asks about the limits of knowledge.

4. Sigmund Freud, "Instincts and Their Vicissitudes," in *The Standard Edition of the Complete Psychological Works,* trans. James Strachey, 24 vols. (London, 1953–74), 14:109–40; Jacques Lacan, *The Four Fundamental Concepts of Psycho-Analysis,* ed. Jacques-Alain Miller, trans. Alan Sheridan (New York, 1978), 78. Lacan would regard fixation in voyeurism as a denial of the movements of substitution and repression characterizing shifts in positioning. The Lacanian "gaze" suggests a whole system of shifts in voyeurism and exhibitionism—not strictly visual—in a largely unconscious discourse. See Robert Con Davis, "Lacan, Poe, and Narrative Repression," *Modern Language Notes* 98, no. 5 (1983): 983–1005.

5. Edward Branigan, "Formal Permutations of the Point-of-View Shot," *Screen* 16, no. 3 (Autumn 1975): 54–64.

6. Donald Friedman, "Galileo and the Art of Seeing," in *Milton in Italy,* ed. Mario Di Cesare (Binghamton, N.Y., 1991), 170. Further discussions of the "optic glass" include William Madsen, *From Shadowy Types to Truth: Studies in Milton's Symbolism* (New Haven, 1968), in the context of accommodation; William Kerrigan, *The Sacred Complex,* in the context of the primal scene; and John Guillory, *Poetic Authority: Spenser, Milton, and Literary History* (New York, 1983), in the context of history and intention.

7. Freud outlines the stages: 1) scopophilia as an activity directed toward an extraneous object; 2) abandonment of the object and a turning of the scopophilic instinct toward a part of the subject's own person, therewith a transformation to passivity and the setting up of a new aim—that of being looked at; 3) the institution of a new subject to whom one displays oneself in order to be looked at ("Instincts and Their Vicissitudes").

8. Sigmund Freud, "On Narcissism: An Introduction," in *Standard Edition,* 14:67–104.

9. I owe that suggestion to Jonathan Goldberg.

10. Laura Mulvey, "Visual Pleasure and Narrative Cinema," *Screen* 16, no. 3 (Autumn 1975): 6–18.

11. Ibid., 9.

12. Revisions include Laura Mulvey's own, "Afterthoughts on 'Visual Pleasure and Narrative Cinema' Inspired by *Duel in the Sun,*" *Framework* (1981); and Mulvey, "Changes," *Discourse* 7 (Fall 1985): 11–30. The literature has been listed in Mandy Merck, "Difference and Its Discontents," *Screen* 28, no. 1 (Winter 1987): 2–9, and reviewed in Tania Modleski, *The Women Who Knew Too Much: Hitchcock and Feminist Theory* (New York, 1988), 1–15. Since the earlier version of this essay was published (as "Rethinking Voyeurism and Patriarchy: The Case of *Paradise Lost,*" *Representations* 34 [Spring 1991]), the dominating power of the male gaze has come under increasing critique while conversely the

power of the female gaze has been under reassessment. See especially Kaja Silverman, *Subjectivity at the Margins* (New York, 1992), which helpfully distinguishes the Lacanian gaze from the look; and Barbara Freedman, *Staging the Gaze, Postmodernism, Psychoanalysis, and Shakespearean Comedy* (Ithaca, 1991), 47–77.

13. Mary Ann Doane, *The Desire to Desire: The Woman's Film of the 1940s* (Bloomington, Ind.,1987); E. Ann Kaplan, *Women and Film: Both Sides of the Camera* (New York, 1983); Michelle Citron, Julia Lesage, Judith Mayne, B. Ruby Rich, and Anna Maria Taylor, "Women and Film: A Discussion of Feminist Aesthetics," *New German Critique* 13 (Winter 1978): 83–107.

14. D. N. Rodowick's critique is more helpful: he recognizes that looking contains both active and passive forms, and he points out that Mulvey has left no place for the feminine subject in her scheme. He also points out that Freud is even less willing than Mulvey to reduce "male" and "female" to biological difference: "The Difficulty of Difference," *Wide Angle* 5, no. 1 (1981): 4–15. See also Edward Snow's "Theorizing the Male Gaze: Some Problems," *Representations* 25 (Winter 1989): 10–41. I am heartened to read in his analysis of Velázquez's *Rokeby Venus,* "Nothing could better serve the paternal superego than to reduce masculine vision completely to the terms of power, violence, and control" (31); I am disappointed that the alternative he hails is a version, albeit a subtle one, of "pre-oedipal contentment" (40).

15. Modleski, *Women Who Knew Too Much*, 12. Reference to Kaja Silverman's essay is to "Masochism and Subjectivity," *Framework* No. 12 (1980): 2–9.

16. Even the mirror stage describes a subject recognizing (or misrecognizing) herself through an image that simultaneously alienates it and hence, potentially, confronts it: who is the voyeur and who the exhibit in such a mutual identification/confrontation? See also Jacqueline Rose, *Sexuality in the Field of Vision* (London, 1986), 174.

17. Lacan, *Four Fundamental Concepts*, 95.

18. Freud, "On Narcissism," 77.

19. Paul Willemen, "Letter to John," *Screen* 21, no. 2 (Summer 1980): 53–65, in response to John Ellis's "On Pornography" in the previous issue, discusses the "fourth gaze" (the first three being the looks of characters in the film, the camera's look, and the viewer's look) as bringing the scopic drive into focus. At first, Willemen sees this as destabilizing the voyeur in pornography: "the viewer also runs the risk of becoming the object of the look, of being overlooked in the act of looking" (56). But then he lapses into the voyeur-as-sadist logic that allows him to say, "In the vast majority of porn, women are the space on which male pleasure and phallic power is inscribed" (60).

20. Buck McMullen has pursued this dynamic in an unpublished essay, "Blindness and the Book of God," written for a graduate Milton seminar. He comes to the suggestive conclusion that the Son, as the seen God, is given up or sacrificed in the object position in order for the Father to remain concealed: "To be seen is, to the voyeur, the ontological equivalent of death, and this seems to be precisely what God the Father is asking of God the Son when he asks for volunteers to redeem man" (21). See also McMullen and James Kincaid, "Tennyson, Hallam's Corpse: Milton's Murder, and Poetic Exhibitionism," *Nineteenth-Century Literature* 45, no. 2 (September 1990): 176–205.

21. See Lacan, *Four Fundamental Concepts*, 80–90. "The phenomenologists have succeeded in articulating with precision, and in the most disconcerting way, that it is quite clear that I see *outside*, that perception is not in me, that it is on the objects that it apprehends. And yet I apprehend the world in a perception that seems to concern the immanence of the *I see myself seeing myself*" (80–81).

22. Hans Blumenberg, *The Genesis of the Copernican World*, trans. Robert Wallace (Cambridge, Mass., 1987), 675.

23. Lacan, *Four Fundamental Concepts*, 104.

24. Ernest Gilman, *The Curious Perspective* (New Haven, Conn., 1978), 31, 47.

25. Blumenberg, *Genesis of the Copernican World*, 390, 394.

26. Gilman, *Curious Perspective*, 29.

27. Plato and Lacan are ultimately at odds, however. For Lacan, subject and object are structural positions that reverse, and that reversal entails a surprise; see *Four Fundamental Concepts*.

28. Plato, *Timaeus*, 45c–d.

29. I am indebted to the discussion of vision and epistemology by Evelyn Fox Keller and Christine Grontkowski, "The Mind's Eye," in Sandra Harding and Merrill Hintikka, eds., *Discovering Reality* (Dordrecht, W. Germ., 1983), 207–24. See Toril Moi's trenchant critique of the ideological implications of Keller's epistemology as partaking in a kind of "cultural essentialism" of fixed gender-identities, "Patriarchal Thought and the Drive for Knowledge," in Teresa Brennan, ed., *Between Feminism and Psychoanalysis* (New York, 1989), 189–205.

30. Rene Descartes, "Meditation 5," in Elizabeth S. Haldane and G.R.T. Ross, eds., *Philosophical Works of Descartes*, 2 vols. (Cambridge, 1934), 1:41.

31. Naomi Scheman, "Missing Mothers/Desiring Daughters: Framing the Sight of Women," *Critical Inquiry* 15, no. 1 (Autumn 1988): 62–89.

32. Ibid., 71.

33. The literature of defense on women and Milton is extensive. It includes Diane McColley, *Milton's Eve* (Urbana, Ill., 1983); Barbara Kiefer Lewalski, "Milton on Women—Yet Once More," *Milton Studies* 6 (1974): 3–20; Joan M. Webber, "The Politics of Poetry: Feminism and *Paradise Lost*, *Milton Studies* 4 (1980): 3–24; and in a different key, Joseph A. Wittreich, *The Feminist Milton* (Ithaca, 1987). On the other side, see Christine Froula, "When Eve Reads Milton: Undoing the Canonical Economy," *Critical Inquiry* 10 (1983): 321–47; and Mary Nyquist, "The Genesis of Gendered Subjectivity in the Divorce Tracts and in *Paradise Lost,*" in Margaret Ferguson and Mary Nyquist, eds., *Remembering Milton: Essays on the Texts and Traditions* (New York, 1987), 99–127. Froula, invoking the cultural hierarchy of invisibility over visibility, claims that Adam is presented as invisible and Eve as visible. Nyquist's essay reproaches Milton for offering us an endorsement if not a celebration of women's subservence to men in marriage. On the other side, Lewalski, Webber, and McColley have defended Milton, offering the contexts of genre conventions, history, and sociology to demonstrate that Eve "is not relegated to the domestic sphere, nor [is] her creativity confined to her maternal role; rather, she—'accomplisht Eve' (IV, 660)—shares and participates in the full range of human activities and achievements" (Lewalski, "Milton on Women," 8–9).

However vigorously upheld, arguments on both sides are cast within the same frame, one in which what "patriarchy" means is self-evident and what constitutes oppression is clear and unproblematical. But the terms in the formulation "Men own the gaze" deserve more careful reflection in the light of the complexity of gender constructions and the dynamics of specularity. I would not argue that the poem is either fraught with or free of patriarchalism; once the dynamics of power are reconceived as not polarizing a world into victimizers and victims, the tired question of Milton's old-fashioned patriarchalism must be displaced by another inquiry.

34. Modleski, *Women Who Knew Too Much*, 3.

35. John Milton, "At a Vacation Exercise in the College," in Merritt Y. Hughes, ed., *Complete Poems and Major Prose of John Milton* (New York, 1957), pp. 30–32, lines 34–35.

36. William Kerrigan, *The Sacred Complex* (Cambridge, Mass., 1983), 159. Kerrigan has written a powerful and provocative analysis of the relation between the Freudian primal scene and guilty seeing in chapter 4, "The Way to Strength from Weakness," 127–92, part of the male oedipal journey he describes as the "psychogenesis of *Paradise Lost*." Kerrigan's distaste for Lacan is elaborated in "Terminating Lacan," *South Atlantic Quarterly* (Fall 1989): 993–1008.

37. Milton, "At a Vacation Exercise," lines 23–24.

LOVING AND LOATHING

THE ECONOMICS OF SUBJECTION

LIBIDINAL ECONOMIES

MACHIAVELLI AND FORTUNE'S RAPE

Juliana Schiesari

A S AN AID to feminist criticism, psychoanalysis can help bring out
the gender relations in texts. As a critical partner in psychoanalytic
interpretation, gender studies can reveal the unconscious forces
at work in texts. As a focus of investigation, the Renaissance offers a
privileged vantage point on the development of modern subjectivities and
gender identities. Far from being anachronistic, feminism and psychoanalysis discover the historical roots of their analytical material clearly
elaborated in works of the early modern period. As I have argued repeatedly, the triangular exchange between feminism, psychoanalysis, and Renaissance studies is one necessarily *transformative* of each of those fields
as well of their interrelation (typically and unfortunately adversarial).[1]
The paradigms of Freudian interpretation are as altered by recent feminist
rereadings and reappropriations of the psychoanalytic corpus as they are
by their application to a time and a culture where the sense of self was
without doubt very different from that of the modern subject and where
Oedipal rivalries, neurotic behaviors, and unconscious desires may not
have functioned in the same way. In a similar manner, fixed notions of
gender identity are challenged by an attention to the psychoanalytic distinction between imaginary and symbolic determinations of subjectivity
and by research into a period where the exact status of the role and privileges of women remains a subject of considerable debate today and which
varied enormously from region to region and from one social rank to
another. Finally, Renaissance texts said to be incomprehensible, or even
in some of the stranger cases, accepted by literal-minded readers as anecdotal fact, can become all the more readable with the help of feminism
and psychoanalysis.

One such difficult text is Machiavelli's December 8, 1509, letter to
Luigi Guicciardini, brother of the eminent historian Francesco Guicciardini. This letter describes a bizarre sexual encounter with a woman living
in a half-buried house run by another woman who sells and cleans shirts.
Curious to know who this woman is, since the whole episode occurred in
the dark, Machiavelli lights a lamp and discovers her to be a loathsome
old hag who so disgusts him he vomits all over her. The letter then closes

with some odd and cryptic remarks about his desire to return to Florence to traffic as a chicken merchant ("vorre pur giunto ad Firenze fare qualche trafficuzzo. Ho designato fare un pollaiolo").[2]

Critics of Machiavelli have avoided this embarrassingly vulgar and outrageous text either by simply not talking about it, pretending that it holds no significance in the opus of the sixteenth century's greatest political thinker, or by treating it at face value as an unqualifiedly autobiographical and referentially bound description of a real experience between an old prostitute and a hapless Machiavelli in need of much desired male sympathy after his encounter with her. Either way, however, what is successfully expunged is the letter's symbolic quotient, and of course its possible commonality with other aspects of Machiavelli's work.

Rather than an accurate portrayal of some real occurrence, the preposterous events as described in the text sound more like fantasy or dream narrative. Now, my remark in no way impinges upon whether the historical Machiavelli did or did not have this strange experience with a woman in Verona. What matters is that his description of the episode—"real" or not—is *already* a fanciful or phantasmic interpretation of it. It is a text written *to* someone, Luigi Guicciardini, and couched in a language and style for his benefit. And inasmuch as it is a text, it is also eminently in the service of unconscious processes such as displacement, condensation, and representational conditions, and therefore most suitable for a psychoanalytic interpretation. And despite the traditionalist charge that psychoanalysis is a reductionist search for penis symbols and Oedipal complexes, a psychoanalytic approach may turn out to be more adept at revealing a motivational coherence between this and other texts of the Machiavellian corpus than would a supposedly literalist acceptance of Machiavelli's wild story that surreptitiously invents all kinds of motivations and explanations for his behavior.

A case in point is Wayne Rebhorn's reading of the letter in his prize-winning *Foxes and Lions: Machiavelli's Confidence Men.*[3] For Rebhorn, Machiavelli's "encounter with an old prostitute" is an act of "desperate lust" that issues forth into an experience of "humiliation and degradation" for him (242–43). Insisting at length upon Machiavelli's humiliation at the hands of this woman, while downplaying the letter's presentation of "the sexual act essentially as an assault" upon her (242), Rebhorn then proposes to read Machiavelli's "unattractive gesture" of vomiting over the woman as "an act of personal purgation" in response, "perhaps unconsciously," he adds, to her humiliation of him (243). While Rebhorn's reading has the merit of acknowledging the "symbolic" dimension of the letter, notably that of the woman's role as a "scapegoat" for Machiavelli's own "disgust with himself" (244), it remains entrenched in a naive historicism that freely attributes psychological motivations that excuse or mitigate Machiavelli's behavior by reading the letter solely from its author's viewpoint. Sexual violence is simply an expression of "desperate lust," and Machiavelli's revolting, degrading treatment of the old woman is justified by his own feelings of being humiliated by her. Yet while the letter opens with an admission of Machiavelli's lack of sexual success, his "lust" or "foia" appears as no more than temporarily desperate. Nor does Machiavelli admit anywhere in the text to feeling "humiliated and degraded" as opposed to merely disgusted by the old woman. The sophisticated but traditional biographical reading results in projecting psychological states onto the author in order to explain away his behavior, thereby rendering it more sympathetic (at least to a male readership). Rebhorn's Machiavelli appears as a rather pathetic victim of women, and his regurgitational "triumph is, however, very limited and imperfect, for the social and political dimensions of the degradation which figure in Machiavelli's experience were in no way affected by his final treatment of the old woman" (244). In other words, his behavior is taken to be understandable but ineffectual, an unfortunate but unsurprising clash with the feminine that is of no import for the "real" world of relations between men. Nonetheless Rebhorn goes far beyond any other critic in attempting to deal seriously with this text.

More typically, male critics have deployed defense or distancing mechanisms, or what Barbara Spackman has called a "prophylaxis,"[4] in order not to have to read or interpret the letter or what the letter says. Pasquale Villari says that the text "would be preferable to entirely ignore [sic]" and " makes us deplore that a man no longer in his youth, father of a family, husband of an affectionate wife, could even jestingly dip his pen in rank impurity."[5] At the other extreme but no less unconsciously avoiding the text is Charles D. Tarlton, who finds that "the description is funny and grotesque . . . and it is impossible not to laugh"; from this Tarlton cheerfully concludes that Machiavelli had numerous "experiences with prostitutes" and that "he was a good man with a foul joke."[6] Mark Hulliung likewise refers to the letter as being "so uproariously comical and grotesque that it proves [Machiavelli] is unbeatable as a teller of tall tales."[7] While for Peter Bondanella and Mark Musa, the "unusual portrait of a grotesque prostitute [is] a figure no doubt born of an authentic experience and Machiavelli's vivid imagination," Sebastian de Grazia concludes that "the tale is a popping concoction," a rhetorical and stylistic exercise written to Luigi Guicciardini, who "had encouraged his friend [Niccolò] to give reign to whimsy in writing."[8] Although it would be interesting to psychoanalyze these critics in terms of what they have to say about Machiavelli's letter, I would like to insist rather on their combined inability and / or refusal, with the possible exception of Rebhorn, to offer any coherent interpretation of this text.

I would therefore like to reread the text of Machiavelli's letter from a woman's perspective and with the hermeneutical assistance of psycho-analysis. I thus hope to offer a more complex reading that will also draw more suggestive connections between Machiavelli's unconscious motivations and the wider political and literary production credited to his name. The letter begins thus:

> Affogàggine, Luigi; e guarda quanto la fortuna in una medesima faccenda dà ad li huomini diversi fini. Voi fottuto che voi havesti colei, vi è venuta voglia di rifotterla, e ne volete un altra presa. Ma io, stato fui qua parecchi dì, accecando per carestia di matrimonio, trovai una vecchia che m'imbucatava le camicie, che sta in una casa che è piu di meza sotterra, né vi si vede lume se non per l'uscio: e passando io un dì di quivi, la mi riconobbe e factomi una gran festa, mi disse che io fussi contento andare un poco in casa, che mi voleva mostrare certe camicie belle se io le volevo comperare.

> [Damn it, Luigi; see how much with one blow fortune gives different ends to men. Once you fucked her you felt like fucking her again, so you want another go at her. But I, having been here several days, going blind in the absence of the marriage bed, came across an old woman who washed my shirts; she lives in a house that is practically underground, and the only light that comes in is from the door. I was passing by there one day, and she recognized me and made a big fuss over me; she said that if I wished, she would show me some beautiful shirts that I might want to buy.]

The opening vulgarity and invocation of the addressee immediately and "phatically" situate the letter in the realm of an exclusively male discourse about sexuality—or what today passes for locker-room talk. That the topic of discussion is then quickly brought to that woman called Fortune is of no small consequence for the author of *Il Principe* and indeed for an understanding of the ensuing sexual narrative. From the start, Fortune is a highly overdetermined figure: not only is *she* the figure of Lady Luck, since it is through her that men have diverse ends, but as luck and as fortune she is also the figure for something unquantifiable that has quantifiable effects, hence the opening adverb of *quanto* (how much). It is precisely the multiple aspect of fortune in Machiavelli's text that, I believe, is crucial to understanding the relation of fortune, and for that matter, money and luck, to femininity. The capriciousness of good fortune is misogynistically metaphorized as the capriciousness of women. Either way, wealth or good fortune or sexual favors are understood as arbitrary gifts bestowed by a mysterious agent, an unfathomable Other. Either way, what is denied is the possibility of systemic social relations that would determine the distribution of wealth, power, and sexual privilege. In other words, what the overdetermined figure of *fortuna* screens is the existence of class and gender hierarchies. Misfortune is the result not of nascent capitalism or masculine privilege but of one's "lot." But if one's lot depends upon the female notion of *fortuna*, it remains to be determined which aspect—wealth or woman—metaphorizes the other. Does the overt misogyny displace an economic anxiety? Or is the apparent arbitrariness of fortune a screen for the fear of sexual difference, a projection of the phallic mother onto the generalized realm of exchange? Fortune is most certainly a woman, as Hannah Pitkin has superbly demonstrated in her book by that title, but is woman also not, as Carla Freccero has suggested, in a determinative relation to the system of economic exchanges that comprises fortune and wealth?[9] In the late feudal society of Machiavelli's time, women were not just commodities passed between men in the "traffic" of patriarchal culture, but they were also a unique means of access to greater power and riches if a man married a woman of higher rank. In other words, women were not just objects of exchange or even potential subjects of exchange or even alienated labor, but—to use the current language of the stock market—they were investment vehicles, that is, commodities bought with wealth on the basis of their production of future wealth, such as municipal bonds or mutual funds. In the case of a late feudal woman, her investment value would be realized by her giving birth to a male child capable of ruling the various fiefs and terrains of father *and* mother under a single family name and title. Is fortune not, in psychoanalytic terms, precisely the figure that *condenses* these economic as well as sexual anxieties?[10]

This condensation of fortune's multiple senses is corroborated in Machiavelli's letter by his ensuing admiration for Luigi Guicciardini's good luck in being able to fuck women and then to want to fuck them again, as opposed to Machiavelli's own misfortunes at being sexually deprived, or as he says, "going blind in the absence of the marriage bed" [accecando per carestia di matrimonio]. Grammatically, however, the same lines can be read as referring to Luigi's successful ability to keep fucking fortune herself, that is, turning things to his own advantage, while Machiavelli, and this is to look ahead to the story he is about to tell, can't seem to fuck fortune without being fucked in turn, and so losing his desire. Thus, to reiterate the letter's opening sentence, fortune with the same blow strikes men in different ways.

To continue our reading of the letter, what I am proposing is that we read this figure as one predicated on an unconscious struggle with economy and with sexuality. As we have seen, the letter states that in the absence of his marriage bed Machiavelli is going blind (*accecando*), a probable euphemism for masturbation, and that one day he found an old lady who washed his shirts (*imbucatava*) and who lived in a scarcely lit house that was "more than half underground." As he passed by her place, she recognized him and asked him to go inside her home with her since she wanted to show him some beautiful shirts that she thought he might want to purchase. Here, the link between women and economy becomes more pronounced, establishing equivalences that rewrite the figure of fortune in terms of an unconscious struggle between economy and sexuality, for this laundress makes her living not only from a commercial, mercantile activity, cleaning and whitening other people's dirty laundry, but also from selling beautiful shirts. Furthermore, the letter seems to situate the relation between fortune, money, and exchange within a feminine realm. This "market" economy, of course, hinges upon a libidinal one, since so far the whole little narrative is framed around Machiavelli's envy for Guicciardini's good luck that he is fucking. Machiavelli presents us with the fantasy of one man's sexual wealth and plenitude contrasted to another man's impoverished lack of it. Or, as the old proverb goes, "Chi fila ha una camicia, e chi non fila ne ha due" [He who weaves has a shirt, and he who does not weave has two].

The laundress stands as the mediator between extremes, as the operator of their exchange, between darkness and light, dirty and clean, between the sign that is money and the commodity that is its referent, and to the extent, as we shall see, that she is also a procuress, between desire and its satiety. For her, fortune is not some mysterious effect but a gainful strategy. She is not the awed victim or beneficiary of a mysterious power but an active agent in a process of quantifiable conversion (the exchange of goods or services for money) that effectively gives different results to different people "by the same stroke." Just as the half-buried placement of her house reproduces the liminal space of transaction, so too does it stand in its dark, earthy, cavelike enclosedness as a metaphor of the female sex. And in fact the writer's entrance into that house to "buy a shirt" turns out to be his willing or unwilling acceptance of an act of prostitution, a transaction that effectively condenses the sexual and the economic with its exchange of money for bodily pleasure. Not that the writer remains unaware of the sexual nature of his penetration into the dark abode even in his supposed innocence: "Onde io, nuovo cazo me lo credetti" [I believed her—innocent prick that I am]—presumably, only a new, inexperienced prick would fail to understand what this sale of a shirt would really mean.

Once having entered, he saw a woman sitting in a corner with a towel on her head. The old lady took him by the hand and led him to her, saying: "Questa è la camicia che io vi voglio vendere, ma voglio la proviate prima, e poi la pagherete" [This is the shirt I wish to sell you, but I want you to try it on first, then you can pay for it]. Now, if the image of this self-described young *cazo* entering into the dark, subterranean house of a woman can count among the most banal of sexual images, the alternative one of a shirt to be put on, an image that refigures the sexual act as one in which the male organ is wrapped or enclosed within the female body, already prefigures the reversal to be operated upon the young prick that is Machiavelli. Even the old woman's cocksureness, if you like, in inviting Machiavelli to try out the merchandise *before* paying for it bespeaks an enormous confidence in her "product," that is, she knows full well what she is doing when she tells the young prick the "shirt" is one he really ought to try on first. In fact, the old laundry woman vanishes, leaving our hero in the dark with the other woman. And, in order to shorten the story, says Machiavelli, he fucked her once, and even though he found her thighs were wrinkly, her cunt wet, and her breath stunk, so much was the desire that he had that he kept on fucking her (". . . pure rimasto solo con colei ed al buio, perché la vecchia si uscì subito di casa e serrò l'uscio, per abbreviare, la fotté un colpo e benché io le trovassi le coscie vize et la fica umida e che le putisse un poco el fiato, nondimeno tanta era la disperata foia che io havevo, che la n'ando"). Machiavelli's expression "che la n'ando," also implies a violence to his act that skirts the limit between "consensual" sex and rape.

After he had sated his lust, he desired to see this "merchandise" [questa mercantia] that he had "tried on" in the dark, so he took a "brand from the fireplace next to [him] and lit a lamp that was above it" [E facto che io l'ebbi, venendomi pure la voglia di vedere questa mercantia, tolsi un tizione di fuoco d'un focolare che v'era e accesi una lucerna che vi era sopra]—all of which implies that the inside of the house was not as dark as he claims. Holding the lamp up to the woman's face, he says, "I almost dropped dead, so ugly was that woman" [Omè, fu per cadere in terra morto, tanto era bructa quella femina]. The portrait Machiavelli then provides is that of a grotesque hag, whom he describes in traditional medieval terms starting from her hair down and passing through the features of her face, stopping however at her Adam's apple.

> E se le vedeva prima un ciuffo di capelli fra bianchi e neri cioè canuticci e benché l'avessi el cocuzolo del capo calvo, per la cui calvizia ad lo scoperto si vedeva passeggiare qualche pidocchio, nondimeno pochi capelli e rari le aggiugnevano con le barbe loro fino in su le ciglia; e nel mezzo della testa piccola e grinzosa haveva una margine di fuoco, ché la pareva bollata ad la colonna di Mercato; in ogni puncta delle ciglia di verso li occhi haveva un mazzetto di pelli pieni di lendini; li occhi li aveva uno basso e uno alto et uno era maggiore che l'altro piene le lagrimatoie di cispa ed enipitelli di pilliciati: il naso li era conficto sotto la testa arriciato in sù, e l'una delle nari tagliata piene di mocci; la bocca somigliava quella di Lorenzo dei Medici, ma era torta da uno lato e da quello n'usciva un poco di bava, ché per non haver denti non poteva ritener la sciliva; nel labbro di sopra haveva la barba lunghetta ma rara: el mento haveva

lungo aguzato, torto un poco in su, dal quale pendeva un poco di pelle che le adgiugneva infino ad la facella della gola.

[The first thing I noticed was a tuft of hair, half white and half black, and although the top of her head was bald, which allowed you to observe a number of lice taking a stroll, nevertheless a few hairs mingled with the whiskers that grew around her face; and on top of her small, wrinkled head there was a scar-burn which made her look as if she had been branded at the market; her eyebrows were full of nits; one eye looked down, the other up, and one was larger than the other. Her tear ducts were full of mucus and her eyelashes plucked; her nose was twisted into a funny shape, the nostrils were full of snot, and one of them was half cut off; her mouth looked like Lorenzo de Medici's, but it was twisted on one side and drooled a bit since she had no teeth to keep the saliva in her mouth; her upper lip was covered with a thin but rather long moustache; her chin was long and sharp, pointed up, and from it hung a bit of skin that dangled to her Adam's apple.]

Although Machiavelli's horror is that of discovering the merchandise/ woman to be very different from what he had assumed her to be—a reversal that corroborates the old laundry woman's symbolic power as an agent of exchange but that is also the source of many male critics' sympathy for a "humiliated" Machiavelli—the actual portrait of the ugly prostitute is a fascinating compendium of contradictory traits beginning with her tuft of hair "fra bianchi e neri." But she is also then described as half-bald, a feature that recalls a long iconic tradition of representing Fortuna or the associated being of Occasio as bearing a long forelock with the back of the head being bald.[11] Fortune, of course, was also often represented as having two faces, designating her malevolent as well as benevolent aspects. Here, of course, the ideal ugliness portrayed by Machiavelli is but the reverse aspect of the well-known portraits of ideal beauty found in medieval romance.

Machiavelli's whore has a scar on her head that looks like "she had been branded at the market" [ché la pareva bollata ad la colonna di Mercato], ignominiously stamped as a commodity or object of potential exchange, the emblematic punishment for prostitution. Like the stamping of a bill or the striking of a coin, the branding explicitly marks placement within the circulation of the market. In the case of the woman stamped as commodity, her circulatory value is paradoxically lowered by the mark— unlike a standard commodity, whose identification and marking as a commodity make it marketable. Ideally, a woman/commodity must not appear to be one; to be desirably exchanged she must be a "priceless" commodity, one that is implicitly exchangeable but not explicitly included within the general circuit of exchange. In fact, the explicit mark on the prostitute's body, the brand, excludes her from the desired exchange for wealth and power that is associated with marriage and relegates her to the margins of the social.

In this text, though, women appear both as the object and the subject of exchange, further determining—negatively—the commercial world as a symbolically feminine one. For the economic scandal of prostitution is that the woman/commodity can sell herself; its ethical and political scandal is that anything and anybody can be bought and sold. Needless to say, the commercial exchange of prostitution merely makes explicit what is already the case (albeit repressed) throughout the society at large. Anyone can be bought and sold or, as Machiavelli should know, bribed or manipulated by a shrewd prince; and one of women's few possibilities of manipulating the symbolic to their advantage is to take the apparently contradictory position of being at once the object of an exchange between men and the subject who is a trading partner in that exchange. But such a generalized realm of exchange where women are traders just as much as men, and where men are exchanged as much as women, can appear only as negative and scary to a Machiavelli shocked by the "merchandise" he has "bought," shocked to discover that he is being used as much as he uses the other. Whence the unpredictable contrariness of *fortuna*, its mysterious and monstrous contradiction.

Such contradictions abound in the details of the portrait he makes of the hag: one eye looks up and the other down, with one being larger than the other; one of her nostrils is "half" cut off; her mouth is twisted on one side. Even more interesting, the woman has masculine characteristics: whiskers on her face and a mouth that looks like that of Lorenzo de Medici, of all people.[12] Finally, the description of her mouth and chin reads more like a description of the male sexual organ: her mouth "was twisted on one side and drooled a bit since she had no teeth to keep the saliva in her mouth; her upper lip was covered with a thin but rather long moustache; her chin was long and sharp, pointed up, and from it hung a bit of skin that dangled to her Adam's apple" [era torta da uno lato e da quello n'usciva un poco di bava, ché per non haver denti non poteva ritener la sciliva; nel labbro di sopra haveva la barba lunghetta ma rara: el mento haveva lungo aguzato, torto un poco in su, dal quale pendeva un poco di pelle che le adgiugneva infino ad la facella della gola]. This salivadripping, upward-tilting "mento" with a fleshy sack of skin swinging below it anamorphically reveals in the lowest part of Machiavelli's portrait an image of what the Romans called the *mentula*. In psychoanalytic terms, Machiavelli comes face to face with a degraded phantasm of phallic femininity, a confrontation that leaves him stunned ("adtonito") before this monster ("questo mostro"). According to him, she realized that he was stunned and was about to ask what was wrong with him. However, since she was "scilinguata," stuttering or literally without a tongue, she could not speak. What comes out instead is a waft of such bad breath from her toothless mouth that he is completely repulsed and throws up all over her, saying that he was thus able to "pay" her with his vomit instead of with money, "pagata quella moneta."

Now, if the hag's toothless mouth is, as Barbara Spackman has eloquently argued, a displacement upward of the *vagina dentata*, Machiavelli's regurgitational aggressivity is also quite clearly a displaced ejaculation, which condenses that young prick's befuddled combination of fear, disgust, and erotic excitement.[13] Indeed, he had noted the bad breath earlier on, even before his initial copulation with the prostitute, but it had not at that time prevented the violent expression of his "foia." It is only when the phallic contradictoriness of the woman becomes manifest—her "foul" mouth, for example, recalling in shape that of Machiavelli's future lord, Lorenzo de Medici—that desire becomes foreclosed as disgust, as *sdegno*. Then, in a fit of postcoital rage against this monstrous woman bearing the face of symbolic authority, does Machiavelli realize he cannot fuck fortune without being "had" by a woman. He notes the final disappearance of his "foia," at least as long as he is in Lombardy. In a reference to the letter's opening line, he says his friend can thank God for "the hope of finding such pleasure again," while he too thanks God for "having lost the fear of ever again having such displeasure." Interestingly, now, though, by avoiding any traffic in or with women, the mysterious but quantifiable effects of fortune are superseded by the good graces of God the father, as a pagan, feminine symbolic is overturned by a Christian, patriarchal one. And interestingly enough, the letter closes with greetings sent to a number of male friends as well as Machiavelli's plans for the money that will remain to him after his trip. He says he would like once again to be back in Florence to do some "traficuzzo," namely to be a chicken merchant, and have a "maruffino" overlook his business. Whatever Machiavelli may mean by his claim to own a "henhouse," we have clearly returned from a world of threatening female power to a boys-only club of commercial associates. Evidently, selling chickens is less worrisome than buying women.

Rather than being simply an anecdotal account of Machiavelli's secular side—"impossible not to laugh," says one critic—the letter, written incidentally on the feast day of the Immaculate Conception, stages the fear of a feminine symbolic order, one where the distinctions between political economy and sexual economy, subject of exchange and object of exchange, masculinity and femininity, are blurred. On a more general and abstract level, the letter allows us to understand such different moments of Machiavelli's thought as his suspicion of women, especially older, more ambitious ones, as well as his inability to theorize the role of economic factors—despite his acknowledged brilliance at explicating the ruses of pure power.[14] Chapter 26 of *Discourses* III (*Discorsi*) offers a good example, as illustrated by its very title: "Come per cagione di femine si rovina uno stato" [how a state is ruined because of women]. Machiavelli begins by recounting the fall of Ardea as described by Livy in the fourth book of his *Histories*. Briefly, a kinsman seeking to marry off a rich woman in his charge received offers to marry her from two men, one plebeian, the other a nobleman. The woman's family was quickly split between her tutors, who favored the plebeian, and her mother, who sided with the noble suitor; but more gravely the entire town split along class lines, between "tutta la Nobilità . . . in favore del nobile, e tutta la plebe in favore del plebeo." Civil war broke out, and neither side being able to prevail, each called in help from outside: the plebs from Volschius and the nobility from Rome. Unsurprisingly, the latter side won out, and the entering Romans had the "leaders of the sedition" executed while quieting the city down ("composono le cose di quella città"). The lesson drawn by Machiavelli is that the Ardeati make a crucial blunder not only by allowing this family spat over a woman's betrothal to escalate out of all proportion but also, and more devastatingly, by requesting outside help, which is an inescapable prelude and pretext for their ensuing servitude at the hands of the "helpful" outside power: "i [Ardeati], per avere lasciato crescere quella gara intra i loro cittadini, si condussero a dividersi infra loro, e volendo riunirsi ebbono a mandare per soccorsi esterni, il che è uno grande principio d'una propinqua servitù" (380) [the Ardeati, for having allowed this dispute to grow among its citizens, become divided among themselves, and wishing to reunite, had to send for outside help, which is a great principle for swift servitude]. Insisting on this tactical mistake in an otherwise overblown debate over a woman, Machiavelli nonetheless fails to note that this civil war is no mere factional strife but, for lack of a better word, a veritable class struggle ignited by what is rather clearly an economic issue, a wealthy dowry for whoever gains the hand of this "femmina *ricca*" in matrimony. In other words, the investment potential of that woman/commodity is extremely high whether it be for the class that aspires to greater privileges or the one that seeks to preserve, if not increase, the powers and privileges it already has. (Not that the woman's desires are given any account: she remains nameless throughout the narration, and we are not even told her fate at the end.) The plebs' case is not that of a faction which is an equal partner or adversary in the civil war but that of an oppressed group engaged in "sedition," the word used to characterize the uproar once at the beginning and again at its close when the Romans punish its leaders. In any case, Machiavelli's misogynistic anecdote reveals a blindness to the role of political economy.

It is once again as if the failure to understand the situation of women is equivalent to the failure to see the political implications and consequences of the rules of commercial exchange.

More dramatically, Machiavelli here sees women as nothing more than potential troublemakers whose entrance upon the public stage can only spell downfall for state rulers. Even the case of the Lucretia legend, celebrated in Machiavelli's time and others as the *foundational* moment in the rise of Roman republicanism, appears to Machiavelli as but the precipitating event in the downfall of the Tarquins.[15] Woman thus remains a solely negative force, whose mere appearance requires an aggressive response such as the one he advises in the penultimate chapter of *Il Principe*, where the relation between woman and fortune becomes once more explicit:

> Io iudico bene questo, che sia meglio essere impetuoso che respettivo, perché la fortuna è donna: ed è necessario, volendola tenere sotto, batterla e urtarla. E si vede che la si lascia più vincere da questi che da quelli che freddamente procedono. E però sempre, come donna, è amica de' giovani, perché sono meno respettivi, più feroci, e con più audacia la comandono.

> [I certainly think that it is better to be impetuous than respectful, because fortune is a woman, and if you want to hold her under your will, it is necessary to beat her and push her around. And it is clear that she lets herself be more easily overcome by such impetuous men than by those who proceed coldly. Since fortune is a woman, she is friendly towards young men, because they are less respectful, are more ferocious, and command her more boldly.]
> (p. 82)

These well-known and often commented upon lines can be read at this point in our analysis not only in conformity with the chapter in the *Discourses* but also as a secondary revision of the letter to Guicciardini, which conversely can be read as a grotesque parody of what Machiavelli here says young men should do to fortune. Bluntly stated, Machiavelli's advice is that women like to be raped. The language here is less vulgar but the sense is just as violent as in the letter to Guicciardini. And if young men are favored, it is certainly not because they are more handsome or physically stronger but because they are "less respectful" and "more ferocious." Fortune, like woman, prefers to be "manhandled"—or at least prefers that to the cold ("fredda"), dispassionate manner of a calculating seducer. This alternative—to be raped or to be used—is hardly a woman's choice. Violence against women, thus metaphorized, translates of course into an opportunistic public policy, one dedicated to the same Lorenzo de Medici whose mouth appeared in the description of the hag/prostitute. And if Machiavelli learned anything from writing that letter, it was that impetuousness is better than respect. In fact, he would have gone away from that scene quite content had he not insisted on a better look at the woman, had he not wanted that *re-spettare* in the literal sense of the word. And it is by in-specting that "merchandise" with his new gaze that he loses all respect for her and treats her with the supreme disrespect of repaying her services with his vomit. Such "repayment" cannot really control or "command" fortune; it can only react more or less pathetically to the way fortune has disposed of him, to the prior action of a powerful if denigrated female figure.

Machiavelli's anxiety about powerful women is also his anxiety about a changing economic order whose new capitalist rules he can comprehend only as the mysterious workings of Lady Luck. Like pagan Fortuna, women are unpredictable and incomprehensible (and not necessarily) human beings who throw the social order into chaos, but are certainly not political subjects who might have their own specific grievances with, and reasons for, resisting the condescending "good sense" the patriarchal order metes out to them. Should they appear in a temporarily empowered role as the controlling agent in some symbolic or commercial exchange, that role is given a negative cast by their horrified or disgusted depictment as whoring old hags who are as unpredictably vindictive as fortune herself. For Machiavelli, the worlds of commerce and of women are equally incomprehensible in their subservience to Fortuna, whence the demand for the corrective *virtù* of "great men" who understand power and fear not the use of force—be it in the form of words or ideology, as lions or as foxes.

NOTES

1. See the introduction to my book *The Gendering of Melancholia: Feminism, Psychoanalysis, and the Symbolics of Loss in Renaissance Literature* (Ithaca: Cornell University Press, 1992), pp. 1–32.

2. For Machiavelli's letter, as well as for later citations from *Discorsi* and *Il Principe*, I use Mario Bonfantini's edition of Niccolò Machiavelli, *Opere* (Milan: Riccardo Ricciardi, 1954), pp. 1088–90. Translations with some modifications come from *The Portable Machiavelli*, ed. and trans. Peter Bondanella and Mark Musa (New York: Viking, 1979), pp. 58–61.

3. Wayne Rebhorn, *Foxes and Lions: Machiavelli's Confidence Men* (Ithaca: Cornell University Press, 1988), pp. 242–44.

4. See Barbara Spackman, "Inter Musam et Ursam moritur: Folengo and the Gaping 'Other' Mouth," in *Refiguring Woman: Perspectives on Gender and the Italian Renaissance*, ed. Marilyn Migiel and Juliana Schiesari (Ithaca: Cornell University Press, 1991), pp. 19–34. In analyzing macaronic poetry, Spackman says, "These texts are about the *volgare* in more than the linguistic sense, how-

ever; and while recent studies have examined one of these senses in focusing on the 'realistic' representation of peasant life in macaronic poetry, they have left untouched what is perhaps most 'vulgar.' Philology has thus served as a sort of prophylaxis, protecting critics from the . . . theme of female sexuality, . . . in which the muse is whore and the grotesque body female" (pp. 19–20).

5. Pasquale Villari, *The Life and Times of Niccolò Machiavelli*, trans. Linda Villari (London: Ernest Benn, 1891), p. 470.

6. Charles D. Tarlton, *Fortune's Circle: A Biographical Interpretation of Niccolò Machiavelli* (Chicago: Quadrangle Books, 1970), p. 133.

7. Mark Hulliung, *Citizen Machiavelli* (Princeton: Princeton University Press, 1983), pp. 112–13.

8. Bondanella and Musa, *Portable Machiavelli*, p. 58; Sebastian de Grazia, *Machiavelli in Hell* (Princeton: Princeton University Press, 1989), p. 126.

9. Hannah Pitkin, *Fortune Is a Woman: Gender and Politics in the Thought of Machiavelli* (Berkeley: University of California Press, 1984). See Carla Freccero's excellent analysis of how gender and economy are "interstructured" in Western discourse and especially the importance of Renaissance discourse on family and gender structures to the rise of capitalist economic relations in "Economy, Woman, and Renaissance Discourse," in *Refiguring Woman*, pp. 192–208. For a provocative reading of this particular letter of Machiavelli's in terms of gender and politics, see Linda L. Carroll, "Machiavelli's Veronese Prostitute: *Venetia Figurata?*" forthcoming in *Proceedings of the Twenty-Fourth Annual Conference*, ed. Richard Trexler, Center for Medieval and Renaissance Studies, SUNY Binghamton.

10. On the relation between family, women, and economy much has been written. In addition to Freccero, I will cite only some of the more crucial studies: Gayle Rubin, "The Traffic in Women: Notes on the Political Economy of Sex," in *Toward an Anthropology of Women*, ed. Rayner Reiter (New York: Monthly Review, 1975), pp. 157–210; Cristiane Klapisch-Zuber, *Women, Family and Ritual in Renaissance Italy*, trans. Linda Cochrane (Chicago: University of Chicago Press, 1985); Stanley Chojnacki, "The Power of Love: Wives and Husbands in Late Medieval Venice," in *Women and Power in the Late Middle Ages*, ed. Mary Erler and Maryanne Kowaleski (Athens: University of Georgia Press, 1988), pp. 126–48; Lauro Martines, "A Way of Looking at Women in Renaissance Florence," *Journal of Medieval and Renaissance Studies* 4 (1974): 15–28; and Judith Brown, "A Woman's Place Was in the Home: Women's Work in Renaissance Tuscany," in *Rewriting the Renaissance: The Discourses of Sexual Difference in Early Modern Europe*, ed. Margaret W. Ferguson, Maureen Quilligan, and Nancy J. Vickers (Chicago: University of Chicago Press, 1986).

11. Howard R. Patch, *The Goddess Fortuna in Mediaeval Literature* (Cambridge: Harvard University Press, 1927), pp. 116–17.

12. Valeria Finucci has noted that in *La Mandragola* a similar description occurs in reference to Callimaco.

13. Spackman, "Inter Musam et Ursam moritur," p. 20.

14. See Pitkin's analysis of Machiavelli's fear and awe of older women (*Fortune Is a Woman*, pp. 118–69).

15. Stephanie Jed, *Chaste Thinking: The Rape of Lucretia and the Birth of Humanism* (Bloomington: Indiana University Press, 1989). I wish to thank Myra Best for focusing my attention on this text during conversations with her in Ithaca, New York.

FEMALE FRIENDS AND

FRATERNAL ENEMIES IN

AS YOU LIKE IT

WILLIAM KERRIGAN

*A*S YOU LIKE IT is clearly less menacing than the dramas that surround it in the canon, including the comedies yet to come, and I
treasure it for just this reason. Beginning with *Hamlet*, though of
course with prior intimations, through to the *consummatum est* of *Timon
of Athens*, plenty of stage time is given to what Wilson Knight used to call
"the Shakespearean hate-theme"—poisoned idealism, anger at ingratitude and trust betrayed, misanthropy, world-hatred, sex-disgust, everything high and sweet collapsing into a chaos without distinction.[1] The
Shakespearean hate-theme is a fearsome thing. Nothing and nobody
stands in the way of it. As soon as triggered, it leaps from the particular
to the global, and blasts away, in great pulsating tirades of poetic fury, at
the very designs of nature and civilization. It speaks through Hamlet in
most of the soliloquies, his enraged rejection of Ophelia's virginity, and
the dagger-talk to his mother, through Othello, Lear, Coriolanus, and
Timon, but finally it seems to be free of character or dramatic motive,
hovering about the work of this period as an almost impersonal force,
like pressure seeking outlets.

Fraternal rivalry, the "primal eldest curse" of *Hamlet*, is one of those
outlets. Shakespeare writes the success story of a "band of brothers" in
Henry V, then he relates the failure of a conspiracy of brothers in *Julius
Caesar*, and then—assuming the correctness of the Evans chronology[2]—
he writes *As You Like It*, which opens in a world torn by fraternal strife.
The late Sir Rowland de Boys had three de Boys and has left the family
lands and most of their money to Oliver, who now mistreats his youngest
brother, Orlando, refusing him funds, denying him an education, and
making him eat with the servants. So far as inheritance went, this was, as
Louis Montrose has reminded us, the "courtesy of nations": primogeniture, the right of the firstborn to the family title and estates.[3] Younger
sons of the aristocracy were indeed, like Orlando, resentful. Some became
wastrels. Others became lawyers, clergymen, and civil servants. For such

careers education was a prerequisite; hence Oliver's peculiar nastiness in refusing to educate his youngest brother.

Oliver de Boys even strikes Orlando de Boys while calling him a "boy" (1.1.52).[4] The blow precipitates a wrestling match. When next Orlando wrestles, the treacherous Oliver will have chosen a proxy—Charles, the Ultimate Warrior of the Normandy World Wrestling Federation, a brother-killer, who warms up for Orlando by tearing three of them to pieces.

Elder brothers despise younger brothers. When attention shifts to the dukedom, we learn that the direction of such hostility can be reversed. "What's the new news at the new court?" Oliver asks (1.1.96–97). Charles's reply is metadramatic: "There's no news at the court sir, but the old news. That is, the old Duke is banished by his younger brother the new Duke." The new news is the old news, a younger brother deposing his elder. The new news will go on being the old news as late as *The Tempest*, where younger brother Antonio usurps the dukedom of Prospero. Some things never change.

But villainy is a plodder in *As You Like It*. Oliver shows little agility in preparing Orlando's downfall. He simply gives Charles an account of his own character—envious of others, a backstabber, a plotter against his brother—and attributes it to Orlando. The height of his villainy is a plan to torch Orlando's bedroom; Richard III would have done better than that. Nor will Duke Junior put the murderous machiavel to school. When he realizes that Orlando is the son of Rowland de Boys, a great favorite with Duke Senior, his sibling hatred flares anew, and soon lights on his niece Rosalind, whom up to now he has appeared to love.

All of this is old news, business as usual in Shakespeare. Male aggression divides kingdoms, friends, lovers, and families. Passages of social criticism elsewhere in the play remind us of other typical symptoms of male contentiousness: the new self-interestedness with which men move upward in hierarchies, forgetting the antique bonds of service, as represented here by Adam; the ingratitude of friends; the pompous rigor with which insults are registered on the way to fighting a duel. Men seem to be making a mock of civilization. Old news.

What feels new, though it isn't quite, is the extraordinary closeness of Celia and Rosalind. Begun in the cradle, it has almost magically survived the hostility between their fathers. In *A Midsummer Night's Dream*, Hermia and Helena are "sweet playfellows," bosom companions, before love rivalry divides them.[5] But the friendship of Rosalind and Celia is presented as mysteriously exceptional: ". . . for the Duke's daughter her cousin so loves her, being ever from their cradles bred together, that she would have followed her exile, or have died to stay behind her. She is at the court, . . . and never two ladies loved as they do" (1.1.107–12). Their loves, a courtier remarks, "are dearer than the natural bond of sisters" (1.3.266). There does not appear to be, in other words, a standard model for this intimacy. No other women have loved this way. The love is dearer than that between sisters. Dearer, I wonder, because it is without rivalry?

For language such as this describing a bond between two people, begun in what is virtually a twinning in childhood, then continued into young adulthood, we have to jump ahead to Leontes and Polixenes in *A Winter's Tale*. That childhood friendship was broken by the "fall" of sexuality; women came between the two men, as they do again in the unfolding romance. Leontes' jealousy is a dark variant on the catfighting scenes in *A Midsummer Night's Dream*: narrative's sharpest way of dividing two friends is to have one of them suppose that the other has stolen his or her beloved. But the friendship between Celia and Rosalind, as we will see, is made exempt from this fate.

Rosalind has been called the wittiest woman in the canon. A wit can make do with a simpleton, but give a wit an answerably witty companion, as Shakespeare has in pairing Rosalind with Celia, and the result is a magnificent picture of great but unsentimental intimacy. The three or four scenes between Celia and Rosalind seem to me much the most beautiful things in the play. The way, never ceasing to score quips and quibbles, they still manage to adjust each other's emotions in benign directions, correct imbalances, get at the hard truths behind circumlocutions—it's a marvel! Shakespeare, who had two sisters and two daughters, observed well. Did Touchstone train these female wits? It seems likely that they trained him, for they are completely his masters in the Shakespearean art of verbal fencing.

When they hit the road for Arden and Duke Senior, soon to be followed by Orlando and Adam, we feel that they really do go "To liberty, and not to banishment" (1.3.134). They are too fine for Duke Junior, with his ridiculous claim that Rosalind in her wit and grace makes Celia seem a "fool." In fact, a fool is too fine a thing for the vain and witless Duke Junior to understand. Celia reiterates the preciousness of their bond:

> If she be a traitor,
> Why so am I. We still have slept together,
> Rose at an instant, learn'd, play'd, eat together,
> And whereso'er we went, like Juno's swans,
> Still we went coupled and inseparable.[6]

(1.3.68–72)

And thus are born Ganymede and Aliena, brother and sister.

You have to make some choices in reading Shakespeare. The historical evidence is not decisive one way or the other, but the stakes are high, for on these choices depends the Shakespeare you experience and interpret. Some recent critics have made much of the fact that female roles were taken by men or boys on the English Renaissance stage.[7] They claim that there is always a certain metadramatic awareness of this; an aura of homoerotic flirtiness or knowingness surrounds feminine roles in Shakespeare, and comes to the fore with special intensity when cross-gender disguises are donned. It may seem to confirm this view that Rosalind takes the name of Ganymede, Zeus's cupbearer, the mythic prototype of the glamorous homosexual boy. But the historical evidence is never decisive, especially in the realm of myth. Maybe Shakespeare just kept the name from his source, Lodge's *Rosalynde*, where Ganymede was a better-motivated choice, since Rosalynde played the part of a page, not a brother. A male homosexual name could be thought appropriate to Shakespeare's Rosalind/Ganymede in the sense of "destined never to love a woman," the truth that she will stage for Phebe later in the play.

The larger question at stake is whether Shakespeare made good in dramatic terms on his mimesis of women—and whether, on the other side of the stage, his audience was willing to accept boy actors as women, even when these women in turn disguise themselves as boys.[8] Whipping up an artificial campiness around the feminine characters in *As You Like It* would erode the dramatic solidity of female friendship, to my mind a main source of the comedy's goodness.[9] The play does indeed accumulate a charge of homoerotic feeling, but it is not to be enjoyed as readily as some modern interpreters imagine. Work must be done before the epilogue, where "Rosalind" is clearly a male actor's female part, releases a homoeroticism kept largely in check during the comedy proper.

Though all the world's a stage, and men and women the players, Jacques's famous speech is about, narrowly, the ages of *man*. But in my view *As You Like It* is more profoundly concerned with the ages of woman, and with the place that might be assigned in the ages of woman to the radiant friendship (more than kin, and more than kind) of Rosalind and Celia.

But I have neglected to mention what happened before their exile to Arden. There would be no comedy without it: Rosalind and Orlando have fallen in love at first sight. The tongue-tied Orlando is "thrown down" and "overthrown": wrestling, with its fraternal rivalry and male violence, has been metaphorically transformed into love. The women in turn accept the metaphor, and it becomes part of their witty intimacy.

Celia. Come, come, wrestle with thy affections.
Ros. O they take the part of a better wrestler than myself.

(1.3.20–22)

It is surely a portent that Orlando gets tongue-tied the moment he falls in love. Rosalind gives him a chain, perhaps actually places it around his neck, and Orlando finds himself transformed into "a mere lifeless block": "Can I not say, 'I thank you'?" (1.2.239). A moment later he has no difficulty in saying "I thank you sir" to Le Beau (1.2.257), yet the on-slaught of love renders him speechless. It's the usual Petrarchan pattern, to be sure; but given his devotion to *this* woman, the fastest mouth in the play, Orlando's weighted tongue foretells that he will be the submissive partner in his love match. Maybe it also implies a degree of ingratitude due in part to his immaturity; since the death of his father, no one has given him anything. He has in particular complained of not receiving an education. Orlando will certainly be schooled in the discourses of court-ship and marriage when Dr. Ganymede, the magical love counsellor of Arden, is finished with him.

The play is interested in time and how time can be divided, distin-guished, and periodized. Jaques notes that "we ripe, and ripe, / And then from hour to hour, we rot, and rot. / Thereby hangs a tale" (2.7.26–28). Eventually the tale of ripening and rotting gets told, in Jaques's famous speech on the seven ages of man.[10] Rosalind is several times made to dis-play the traditional lover's trait of impatience. In one of her wit lessons for Orlando she compares various subjective experiences of time to the gaits of a horse. A maiden rides the hours between her betrothal and her wedding at a "hard trot," because her impatience makes her uncomfort-able. Orlando, in the end, is exhausted with delay: "I can live no longer by thinking" (5.2.50).

Yet we feel in Rosalind herself a drive contrary to this conventional impatience. She clings to her disguise and uses it more often and with more dedication than the plot itself requires. Why is she so concerned, when she faints over Oliver's presentation of the bloody handkerchief, that this feminine swoon will give her away? Beyond that, why does she swoon at all?[11] Because her anger at Orlando's lateness is instantly trans-formed, by the handkerchief, into anxious concern? It has crossed my mind that two things cross in the mind of Rosalind. The bloody handker-chief evokes both the violence done to Orlando and a sweeter violence that Orlando will do to her—the consummation of the wedding sheets: that which, in other words, she ought to be impatient for, but which in fact she appears to be warding off through the intrigues of her disguise. "O ominous!" Rosalind declared when first aware of Orlando's presence in the forest, "he comes to kill my heart!" (3.2.242). The handkerchief presents to her in one anamorphic image the pictures of killing her be-loved and marrying (being killed by) her beloved, his blood spilt and her blood spilt. That conjunction knocks her out.

Comedies are mechanistic. Beloveds are found early in the play. They endure complications. Then, with some element of surprise, Jacks have their Jills, and the marriages crank into line. Viola in *Twelfth Night* is caught passively in her disguise, like patience on a monument smiling at grief, yet we never feel that her will is somehow resisting the mechanism of the plot. Her passivity can be viewed as a faith that "time," the comic plot, "must untangle this, not I" (*Twelfth Night* 2.2.39). But Rosalind seems freely to indulge in her disguise, to *explore* it, and for a time this indulgence acts as a drag on the destined resolution of the comedy.

Why? First of all, obviously, Orlando is undergoing a love test. Several Renaissance gender clichés operate in *As You Like It*. One of them is that women talk a lot, say whatever is on their minds—Rosalind mentions that one, and realizes how well it fits her. Another is a cliché about men, that they break vows made to women during courtship. This stereotype is alluded to early in the play, in one of Celia's speeches after Orlando's victory at the wrestling match: "If you do keep your promises in love / But justly, as you have exceeded all promise, / Your mistress shall be happy" (1.2.232–35). So Rosalind's doses of acid truth for Orlando are in part meant to test his fidelity. She induces him to make promises—that, for instance, he will appear at a certain time. Transgressions are punished, for they represent metaphorically the possibility of breaking love oaths. Perhaps, too, the charade of purporting to cure Orlando's love continues a pattern established the very first time she sees him; when they fell in love at first sight, she was also on a mission to dissuade him (from wrestling), and failed. Wrestling becomes courting: maybe she liked the fact that she failed to move him. Maybe she relishes, in Greenblatt's term, the friction.[12]

Usually we are meant to feel at the end of a comedy that the young have been freed from their complications and are now ready, with marriage, for a deeper happiness, something of great constancy. But Ganymede's scathing love cures feature some fairly chilling looks at the treacheries possible in marriage. Maybe Rosalind clings to her disguise because, as certain feminist readers have suggested, it removes her from the standard positions of the gender system. According to Catherine Belsey, devices such as the Ganymede disguise have "momentarily unfixed the existing system of differences, and in the gap thus produced we are able to glimpse a possible meaning, an image of a mode of being, which is not a-sexual, nor bisexual, but which disrupts the system of differences on which sexual stereotyping depends."[13] On this view, Rosalind/Ganymede enters a state of liminality, neither man nor woman, betwixt and between, and in this state enjoys the freedom to stock her spirit with novel perspectives.

I find a great deal to recommend this view, though I am not sure that Rosalind's state really is outside the Renaissance gender system, which is maybe not so pitiless or clear-cut as some feminists suggest. Courtship itself—which is certainly part of the gender system, and in comic drama has a whole genre given over to it (comedies end in marriage: another way of saying this is that comedies are typically about courtship)—is after all a liminal state, and is represented as such throughout Shakespearean comedy. During courtship some of the major dichotomies in life are experienced at the same time. The participants in a wooing may exchange vows and love tokens, at once married and not married; in the Renaissance this sort of doubleness flourished in the time between troth-plight (*sponsalia per verba de futuro*) and the exchange of performative vows completing the marriage (*sponsalia per verba de praesenti*).[14] Wooers are also chaste and sexual, settled and unsettled, adult and not fully adult, sane and mad.

Courtship, moreover, in Shakespeare as in our own day, can involve a feeling of being in disguise. Receiving a quick or sudden love puts one into a disguise: this person does not know you, and couldn't possibly love *you*, so it must be that some disguised version of yourself is loved. Even when love is gradually rather than suddenly declared, both parties often have a sense of slowly undisguising themselves as the relationship moves toward the ideal of full revelation. The true state of the courtship must also, for a time, be kept from other people. Thus Donne, in "Lecture upon the Shadow": "So whilst our infant loves did grow, / Disguises did, and shadows, flow, / From us, and our care; but, now 'tis not so." During courtship, then, identity can mutate into a series of pretenses.

Of course the ordinary liminality of courtship does not include female/ male, as it does for Rosalind. Or does it?

There seem to be two conditions that must be met before, imaginatively, Rosalind will be ready to doff her disguise. One of them is satisfied when she encounters Phebe and Silvius acting out the familiar Petrarchan scenario of an extravagantly dogged male pursuing a coldly unyielding woman. Rosalind has no sympathy for this form of female superiority, though it is, in the abstract, not unlike what she has been imposing on Orlando. Maybe her chiding words to Phebe are in the manner of a self-repudiation. The content of her intervention, in any case, is a spirited attack on Phebe's self-love, which she interprets as the consequence of Silvius's misplaced devotion. Ganymede gives voice to an anger that the Petrarchan male, nourishing his obsession, keeps under wraps; this scolding induces Phebe's sudden crush on Ganymede. "It is a pretty youth," Phebe declares, "—not very pretty— / But sure he's proud, and yet his pride becomes him. / He'll make a proper man. The best thing in him / Is his complexion; and faster than his tongue / Did make offence, his eye did heal it up" (3.5.113–17). Ganymede is not yet a man in the dazzled eyes of Phebe, and for this reason, the speech implies, is not enslaved by female beauty; Ganymede retains sufficient pride of his own to rebuke her feminine pride, rather than begging her to relent like the Petrarchan Silvius.[15] Phebe also senses a femininity in the body language of Ganymede, a friendliness of eye and gesture that "heals up" the sting of his rebuke. We might conclude that this crush somehow "completes" Rosalind, rounding out her liminality. She's looked at love from all sides now: as a woman, she enjoys the reciprocal love of a woman (Celia) and a man; as a man, she is loved by a woman (Phebe) and (in the game being played with Orlando) by a man.

The second condition for dropping the disguise seems to be the appearance of a male lover for her soul mate Celia.

Freud's recurrent problem in his four famous papers on female psychosexual development, and the main reason for the continual revisions of his theories, lies in his inability to understand how the little girl gets into an oedipal position.[16] For a heterosexual boy, the love object remains constant from cradle to grave: the mother, the sexualized mother of the Oedipus complex, and metaphorical derivatives of the mother in courtship and marriage. But the little girl, to emerge from childhood with a heterosexual disposition, has somehow to shift her love from the mother to the father. How can this happen without some traumatic disappointment with her mother, or with femininity itself? Throughout his life Freud kept trying to figure out how this shift might typically occur. Though the plot kept changing, the major scene remained the same. Somehow this shift must involve an injury to the girl's narcissism.

In *Paradise Lost* Milton anticipates Freud on this question. Eve's famous narrative of the first human courtship in Book 4 of the epic shows us that, even in Eden, the first suitor had a rival in Eve's own image, which is her first love. In loyalty to this primal affection, she does not fall in love at first sight, but rather turns and runs away.[17]

It is harder for a woman than it is for a man to realize that she needs the opposite sex to complete her. Here, I think, we are close to the heart of the Celia/Rosalind twinship. As in girlhood, so on the verge of courtship and marriage: the Rosalind/Celia relationship is puberty's renegotiation of the old attachment to the early mother. They jest about suitors, sexuality, having babies, but they are not, at the beginning of the play, courted. How could they be, when they are inseparable, waking together and eating together? Men will inevitably divide them. Their friendship is an attempt to achieve a completeness and self-sufficiency right on the threshold of mature sexuality—and as such this friendship does not really want to deal with the fact that maturity has to involve its dissolution. The moment Rosalind falls in love with Orlando, the friendship appears to receive its death notice. It has survived the violent rivalry of fathers, but now, with heterosexual love on the horizon, it seems to be doomed.

We see no signs of jealousy in Celia, though she is sometimes bored with Rosalind's Orlandoizing and appalled at her accounts of feminine treachery. In his book *The Theater of Envy: William Shakespeare*, René

Girard concedes that the Rosalind/Celia relationship is a notable exception to his theories of mimetic desire.[18] There ought to be rivalry here.
There ought to be rivalry the very moment that Rosalind tells Celia to
"Let me love him for that [because he is deserving], and do you love him
because I do" (1.3.34–35). Their friendship does not obey the ordinary
laws of human relationship in Shakespeare.[19] But Girard, rather than interpreting this suspension of the ordinary, gets worried about his theory;
instead of suffering the scandal of an exception, he blames the idiocy of
the pastoral genre, too stupid to allow for conflict, devises a convoluted
scheme in which mimetic desire governs the play after all, and winds up
with the exception proving the rule. But the plot of *As You Like It*, with
the promise of goodwill evident in its title, moves to protect this friendship from internal as well as external disruptions. Celia need not be jealous; the plot will provide. With the appearance of a reformed Oliver,
both women can simultaneously, in a twinned marriage ceremony, make
the transition into adulthood, choose marriage over female friendship,
yet at the same time elevate their cousinhood into sisterhood, becoming
aunts to each other's children. A pair weds a pair. For the friendly cousins
to marry brothers—and better than that, brothers who have settled their
sibling rivalry—is the best-case situation for preserving their old oneness
in the adult context of marriage. Resentments that divided their fraternal
fathers have already been ironed out in their fraternal husbands.

Let me put this another way. Courtship is a time of liminal experimen-
tation for a woman—both Shakespeare and Milton know this, and since
they do, it cannot be altogether outside the gender wisdom of the Renaissance. Let's suppose that courtship in Renaissance culture has its own
gender channels. Men declare their love openly, enjoying what Cressida
terms "men's privilege / Of speaking first" (3.2.127–28); if they are
tongue-tied and cannot speak, they as it were write poems and hang them
on trees. They let women know. But women do not ordinarily profess
their hearts. They are courted, and during this time remain ambiguous,
disguised, undeclared, and undivulged. It is understood in these cultural
arrangements that the resolution of the courtship, its success or failure, is
a woman's call. Finally she declares her heart, and it is either at one with
the man's declared love or it is not. Courtship is the time of woman's
greatest power and liberty.[20] It is for her to decide *when the comedy will
be over*. Moreover, this is probably the most important decision of her
life. The comedy of courtship is a realm of female supremacy—she's the
monarch of the play, as it were, and calls the shots.

Marriage, typically in Shakespeare, is a realm of male supremacy. But
this comedy seeks to mediate courtship and marriage. Rosalind arranges
a marriage that, so far as possible, will allow the liberty of courtship—

whose main expression is the relationship with Celia—to survive the end of the comedy. The rebuke to feminine pride that Freud posited at the threshold of the female Oedipus complex, and the echo of that rebuke at the threshold of courtship, when feminine friends must partially give way to male lovers, are deflected onto Phebe. The play gives to *her* the castrating disillusionment of trying to make a woman do for a man. In Rosalind and Celia, Shakespeare builds a nest for feminine pride, bestows the gift of mutual wit to prevent that pride from becoming pathological, and in the end folds friendship into heterosexual marriage. When the forthcoming nuptial arrangements are repeated before Duke Senior, Rosalind and Celia leave the stage together, and soon return, Rosalind having discarded her hose and doublet, with the figure of Hymen, who then performs the only marriage ceremony wholly completed on Shakespeare's stage.[21] Their entrance with Hymen in tow is a crowning emblem of the comic transformation of their friendship. Hymen unites rather than severs them.

The absence of the hate-theme clears a space for this triumphant empathy. But a full analysis of the achievement must include the comedy's successful defensive measures for denying a purchase to wrath and rant.

In the plays that lead up to *As You Like It*, Shakespeare avoids serious conflict with the father. Precisely that avoidance is the watchword of Henry V's career. As a young man he acts a prodigal. But at the end of *Henry IV, Pt. 1*, he rescues his father in battle; at the end of *Pt. 2*, he repudiates Falstaff, assimilating his father's disapproval; finally, in *Henry V*, we see him fulfilling his father's political ambitions, right down to wooing Katherine with the thought that one of their sons might lead a crusade (5.2.206–10). As Shakespeare planned *Julius Caesar*, he edited out Plutarch's suggestion that Caesar was Brutus's father.[22]

Rosalind remarks at one point: "why talk of fathers, when there is such a man as Orlando?" (3.4.34–35). But in fact the paternity of Orlando is early on presented as the rationale for her love. Rosalind feels free to love Orlando because Duke Senior loved Rowland de Boys. This relayed affection also bears upon Oliver's hostility toward his brother. He professes to resent the younger man's natural gentility and charisma. But I think we can be certain that another way to describe his envy is that Orlando (but not Oliver) has inherited the bearing and the grace of his father; Orlando himself says that the "spirit of my father" (1.1.70) compels him to rebel against his ill-treatment by Oliver. So Rosalind, in loving Orlando, repeats in the sphere of heterosexual love her own father's love for Rowland de Boys. Duke Senior sanctions or, better, initiates her love.

The prominence of fraternal rivalry at the beginning of the play serves to close off the possibilities for cross-generation hostility. Oliver does not curse Sir Rowland for failing to transmit his natural endowment to him; all his aggression is subsumed in his hatred for Orlando. The one exception is Celia, who rejects Duke Junior in accompanying Rosalind to the forest of Arden. Shakespeare disposes of this conflict with the deus ex machina of Duke Junior's instantaneous fit of monastic penance, brought on by his encounter with an old religious man. This, combined with Oliver's abrupt submission to the spirit of his father as embodied in Orlando, squares things with the paternal generation. At the end of the play there is no reproach whatsoever for fathers. We certainly sense that such themes are straining to get out, and they will, though somewhat disguised, in *Hamlet*. Reading the plays in sequence, it seems clear that Shakespeare, as Barber and Wheeler maintain, is laboring mightily to postpone *Hamlet*.[23] The paternal outlets of the hate-theme are sealed off by the end of *As You Like It*.

The escape from tragedy is of course embodied in a place, the forest of Arden. Early in the play, Rosalind and Celia debate the correct way of distinguishing between the realms of nature and fortune, that housewife at her wheel. Fortune is said to supply the gifts of the world, whereas nature bestows the "lineaments" (1.2.41) of one's fundamental endowment. Shakespeare will be preoccupied for the rest of his career with various conceptions of nature.

No doubt Arden to some extent is nature. The exiled courtiers talk about suffering weather and the changing seasons. They debate with Jaques about man's place in nature—about, for example, whether men should live on fruit or venison. But if we take Arden in this way, we must be struck by the fact that the exiles' relationship to this nature is transformed utterly by their literacy. The whole question of man's relationship to nature is a pastoral question—and thus a question whose precondition is literacy. In the "uses of adversity" speech, Duke Senior concludes that "our life, exempt from public haunt, / Finds tongues in trees, books in the running brooks, / Sermons in stones, and good in everything" (2.1.15–17). Arden is a text, something read. So is Jaques; Duke Senior now and then browses him: "I love to cope him in these sullen fits, / For then he's full of matter" (2.2.67–68). Indeed, there are poems on the trees.[24]

Arden is a forest of literacy, teeming with heteroglossia. Amiens sings a song celebrating the movement from corrupt court to nature; Jaques inserts a verse ridiculing the stupidity of anyone who would abandon wealth and ease to live in a forest. Song, mock-song. Orlando puts up his Rosalind poems; Touchstone proceeds to grind out mock-Rosalind poems. Even the vicar is named Martext. There's a resident satirist in Jaques, who has his own love affair with the resident fool. The horns of the deer inevitably, given language, are transferred from nature to culture, to branch out as the horns of the cuckold—horns that any married man must be prepared to wear. The comic and satirical scenes tend to assume the exhaustive structure of encyclopedia entries: on the kinds of melancholy, the strides of time, the seven varieties of insult, the seven ages of man. Philosophy and theology are sent up. There are burlesque versions of Caesar's "I came, I saw, I conquered," Troilus and Cressida, Hero and Leander. Ovid's myths are also burlesqued, as when Orlando tells Jaques to look at his image in a pond. There are lawyer jokes, priest jokes, rich-man jokes, lover jokes, simpleton jokes, women jokes, men jokes, fool jokes, and so on. "Nay then God buy you, and you talk in blank verse," says Jaques, talking in blank verse. The fool compares his state to Ovid's exile, and Phebe, a rustic shepherdess, quotes Marlowe: "Dear shepherd, now I find thy saw of might, / Who ever lov'd that lov'd not at first sight"—a heroic couplet, the form in which Marlowe wrote *Hero and Leander*. Arden is less nature than a heteroglossic rap on nature—an adventure in the forms and counterforms of literate life.

The followers of Jaques Lacan maintain that language is paternal, a system we are inserted into by virtue of oedipal castration. But of course that isn't true. Nothing that Jaques says is altogether true. Language is embryonically a part of the mother/infant dyad. Infants are bathed in language, and the first distinct signifiers are gradually differentiated from this global immersion in baby talk, body talk, clucks, goo-goos, coochie-coos, lullabies—the "blooming buzzing confusion" of William James.[25]

I almost hesitate to say it, because it is such an obvious point, and so comically open to any interpretation whatsoever, but this forest where maybe you should kill deer, and maybe you shouldn't. . . . Shakespeare's mother came from a prominent family of landowners in Stratford, and her name was Mary Arden.[26] Shakespeare's grandfather cultivated Arden forests as a tenant farmer. Can it be incidental that Shakespeare writes his mother's maiden name when Englishing Ardennes? With all the literacy in *As You Like It*'s Arden, does the play contact an early mother there, a set of problems that stand prior to conflict with the father?

Sibling rivalry must surely predate the Oedipus complex for Shakespeare. I think it has its roots in being displaced at the breast, as a new baby usurps the mother's central affections while her former darling stares in envy at the new arrival occupying his one-time place.[27] Duke Junior claiming the manor for himself might be read as the younger brother displacing the older. If we shift to the sibling feud in the de Boys family, Oliver forcing his younger brother to eat with the servants seems from this perspective an appropriate revenge. In the same spirit, one could read Duke Senior's migration to Arden as a wishful undoing of this primal usurpation. Junior has the dukedom, but Senior has the mother—Mother Earth, Mother Nature, Mother Arden.

Both sets of exiles discover that, in order to get to Arden, one must nearly starve; hunger in infancy is what calls forth the mother, transforming her absence into presence. These cues suggest that the flight to Arden is at some level a flight to the mother of infancy.

But this early mother also has her terrible aspects; she is a devourer, engulfer, smotherer. I see her in the "suck'd and hungry lioness" (4.3.126), more dangerous than the snake, who lies in wait for the sleeping Oliver:

> Under an old oak, whose boughs were moss'd with age
> And high top bald with dry antiquity,
> A wretched ragged man, o'ergrown with hair,
> Lay sleeping on his back. About his neck
> A green and gilded snake had wreath'd itself,
> Who with her head, nimble in threats, approach'd
> The opening of his mouth. But suddenly
> Seeing Orlando, it unlink'd itself,
> And with indented glides did slip away
> Into a bush, under which bush's shade
> A lioness, with udders all drawn dry,
> Lay crouching head on ground, with catlike watch
> When that the sleeping man should stir; for 'tis
> The royal disposition of that beast
> To prey on nothing that doth seem as dead.
> This seen, Orlando did approach the man,
> And found it was his brother, his elder brother.
>
> (4.3.105–20)

An impotent father presides. The "old oak" overseeing this extraordinary scene evokes a very old man, like the oak in Jonson's "To the Immortal Memory and Friendship of . . . Sir Lucius Carey and Sir H. Morison" that falls "a log at last, dry, bald, and sere."[28] This is the father sans everything, reduced to an emblematic presence only. But men of such antiquity, according to the logic of the seven ages, reencounter their opposites in "second childishness" (2.7.165). Events transpiring beneath the tree bear the stamp of relived infancy. The oak is bald, the man beneath "o'ergrown with hair." Yet in the drama unfolding below, in the ground-level realm of second childishness, the "dry" of the treetop reappears as the "dry" udders of the lioness. Oliver has neither youth nor age, but a pre-dinner sleep of exhaustion, dreaming on both.

The scene bristles with maternal menace. All the players are dry and hungry. In this "wretched ragged man" we have for the third time confirmation that exiles to Arden arrive there in a state of near starvation. As he sleeps, ancient nightmares—the "indented" and "catlike" totem animals of the maternal hate-theme—seem to materialize about him. Choking or poisoning might be the aim of the female snake wound around Oliver's neck, reminiscent of the chain Rosalind gave to his younger brother after the wrestling match.[29] "Nimble in threats," she moves toward the mouth in a deadly assault on the first site of mother/infant merger, later the first site of ego boundaries, and still later the site of speech. What does the snake intend to do before it slithers away at the appearance of Orlando? Her prey is in need of nourishment; the maternal beast waiting in the bush is sucked and hungry. The blasts of the winter wind, in one of Arden's songs, are "not so unkind / As man's ingratitude" (2.7.176).[30] I think the snake threatens to enter his mouth and bite an ungrateful tongue, a tongue like Orlando's earlier in the play, that cannot say, when a woman puts the gift of a chain around his neck, "I thank you." Reimagining the chain as a snake, this scene projects that ingratitude back into the preliterate recesses of psychic time as a motive for maternal vengeance and therefore also as a deep motive for the speechless ingratitude of mature males, whose tongues are weighted with the unconscious stings of infantile revenge tragedies. Unlike the snake, who threatens a motionless prey and slinks off when disturbed by Orlando, the "royal disposition" of the beast crouching in the bush's shade—a regressive figuration of the classic *vagina dentata*—requires animated game, the pleasure of a kill. The lioness "with udders all drawn dry" is a nightmare out of Melanie Klein, a talionic mother who will devour her child because, in that child's primitive fantasy world, he has devoured her.[31]

Twice Orlando turns his back on the endangered brother. But "kindness" and "nature" defeat revenge and justice (4.3.128–30). Orlando saves his brother from the lioness, at the cost of being wounded himself, and immediately the sibling rivalry is over. They weep to hear each other's story; after a brief audience, Duke Senior formally assigns the duties of hospitality for the newcomer to his "brother's love" (4.3.144). As Oliver was excessive in hostility, so now he is excessive in beneficence: he will give Orlando the estates, and live in Ardenic bliss with his beloved Aliena.

In sum, the older brother forgives the younger brother because the younger has rescued him. I think this is a dramatic representation of one of the earliest checks against all-out sibling rivalry. That new brother has taken my place; see how Mother dotes on him, when she should be doting on me. But on the other hand, there is the counterthought we have come to expect in the reversible intellectual structures of Arden: it is good to be free of that mother, to mourn my losses and become an independent self. The usurper is also a liberator. I will no longer be engulfed. The new baby has pushed me toward my future.

The fear of being engulfed by a primeval mother might translate, on a much later plane of psychic development, into a dread of being overmastered by the wit and bossiness of a dominant wife. Maybe that is yet another reason why the wound ends the masquerade and rounds off the love test: by surviving the onslaught of the most savage early mother, the hungry dry-dugged lioness, Orlando has proven himself fit for marriage to a Rosalind.

After which, an epilogue of elaborate pointlessness:

> It is not the fashion to see the lady the epilogue; but it is no more unhandsome than to see the lord the prologue. If it be true that good wine needs no bush, 'tis true that a good play needs no epilogue. Yet to good wine they do use good bushes; and good plays prove the better by the help of good epilogues. What a case am I in then, that am neither a good epilogue, nor cannot insinuate with you in the behalf of a good play? I am not furnished like a beggar, therefore to beg you will not become me.

Strictly from hunger, Rosalind's epilogue seems condemned to offer and then to undermine rationales for itself. Yet the logic of the play is still subliminally at work in this self-thwarting appendage. An impulse to epilogue seems at war with an impulse to anti-epilogue. Rosalind is pretending to a great deal of trouble in asking for the audience's gratitude. By the end we realize that the epilogue cannot request this gratitude without first delivering to its audience the comedy's mixed sexual messages. Before the comedy can receive its due, theater must come clean.

As is conventional in epilogues, the play is reduced to an object of primitive judgment. Like wine, it is either good or bad, to be spit out with hisses or taken in with applause. And in fact things look bad for *As You Like It* in this suspended state between fiction and fact, performance and reception: Rosalind has neither a good epilogue for a bad play nor a good epilogue for a good play. It would certainly be a good epilogue for my interpretation if this lighthearted condemnation of the comedy could be associated with the primitive object encountered in the forest of Arden. Metaphorically a bush (the ivy sprig, traditional sign of the vintner) and a woman, the prologue may indeed remind us of "Into a bush, under which bush's shade / A lioness. . . ." That may seem a stretch. But when the epilogue discovers a raison d'être, it has to do with kissing, bringing mouths together without hatred or reproach:[32]

> My way is to conjure you, and I'll begin with the women. I charge you, O women, for the love you bear to men, to like as much of this play as please you. And I charge you, O men, for the love you bear to women—as I perceive by your simpering none of you hates them—that between you and women the play may please. If I were a woman, I would kiss as many of you as had beards that pleased me, complexions that liked me, and breaths I defied not. And I am sure, as many as have good beards, or good faces, or sweet breaths, will for my kind offer, when I make curtsy, bid me farewell.

This is *As You Like It.* What women like in the play, they should equate with the love they bear to men; what men like in the play, they should equate with the love they bear to women. Dr. Ganymede is on the audience's case: liking the play is equivalent to heterosexuality; the gravity of the genre produces marriages. But this heterosexual declaration is followed by an evocation of male fellowship.

The fear of being engulfed by a primeval mother might also translate, on a much later plane of psychic development, to a fear of being drawn into dangerous fantasies by a masterful work of art. The epilogue banishes this fear in jovial acceptance. Ganymede's insistence that Orlando treat him as Rosalind echoes the male actor's insistence throughout the performance that the audience treat him as Rosalind. Exposing this similitude, the epilogue balances the theme of female friendship with good spirits between men. There is one final undermining in the offer to kiss pleasing mouths: "If I were a woman. . . ." He is not. The woman-man that has been "Rosalind" here divides into a role and an actor; our lady the prologue is our lord the prologue. After heterosexuality has been linked to the liking of the play, after the male actor has expressly disengaged himself from the female role, homosexual desire surfaces in the kisses that he in playing she would plant on the audience's most attractive faces.[33] *As You Like It* has met and survived the hungry lioness; homosexuality holds no terror, since the imago that might compel it has been overcome. Written by a male, performed by males, and ultimately addressed to males, the play has as its bottommost wish the desire to cleanse and reaffirm the realm of the oral, blocking out the hate-theme at its source. Even if the good comedy is bad, it will be good. Even if the heterosexual desire celebrated in the play is homosexual desire, it will be good. As the comedy itself becomes a primitive object in its epilogue, the very idea of a primitive object becomes comic—a thing created by men for the entertainment of men. With a most flirtatious curtsy the actor exits to applause, having shown to the limits of Shakespeare's imagination that men can reconfigure their dread of women.

NOTES

1. G. Wilson Knight, *The Wheel of Fire* (rpt. London: Methuen, 1986), p. 236.
2. I refer to the sequence given in G. Blakemore Evans et al., eds., *The Riverside Shakespeare* (Boston: Houghton Mifflin, 1974), pp. 47–56.
3. Montrose, " 'The Place of a Brother' in *As You Like It*: Social Process and Comic Form," *Shakespeare Quarterly* 32 (1981): 28–54. I have some local disagreements with Montrose. For example, I see no evidence that Orlando is bitter about the *principle* of primogeniture. His allusion to the "courtesy of nations" is

not sarcastic (Montrose, 31, 32, 36); he instead resents the particular indignity of his treatment at the hands of Oliver. Stressing the social elevation of Orlando through his marriage to Rosalind, Montrose believes that the play appeals to the grudges of younger brothers. Moreover, he assumes that Renaissance attitudes toward primogeniture were governed by self-interest, younger brothers resenting it, eldest brothers favoring it. I therefore find it odd that he never mentions, even in passing, Shakespeare's own status as an eldest brother. This oversight may count as an aporia, since it is impossible to see how Shakespeare, given Montrose's belief in the necessary self-interestedness of social attitudes, could have sympathized so fully with younger brothers. But the major problem with the Montrose essay is that his approach via primogeniture all but ignores the heart of the play: the friendship between Celia and Rosalind. Orlando is actually a rather dull character, and the best bits in the first two acts (which Montrose admits are his primary focus) concern the radiant female friends. Toward the end of this essay I will offer some psychoanalytic suggestions about the treatment of fraternal rivalry in *As You Like It*.

4. All citations of the play are from Agnes Latham, ed., *As You Like It* (London: Methuen, 1975).

5. One also thinks of the female community gathered around the princess in *Love's Labour's Lost*, though Boyet is so prominent in their scenes that they have scant opportunity to converse with one another, the opening of 5.2 being the lone exception. Perhaps a better example of the power of female unity is *Richard III* 4.4, where the three queens make common cause against Richard, weave their curses together, and imaginatively put an end to the Wars of the Roses.

6. The coupled swans recall Spenser's "Prothalamion," probably written in 1596. For other sources, consult *The Works of Edmund Spenser: The Minor Poems*, Vol. 2, ed. Edwin Greenlaw, Charles Osgood, Rederick Padelford, and Ray Heffner (Baltimore: Johns Hopkins University Press, 1947), pp. 667–73. The image foreshadows the union of friendship and marriage at the entrance of Hymen in Act 5.

7. Examples may be found in Lisa Jardine, *Still Harping on Daughters: Women and Drama in the Age of Shakespeare* (New York: Columbia University Press, 1983), pp. 9–36; and Stephen Orgel, "Nobody's Perfect, or Why Did the English Stage Take Boys for Women?" *South Atlantic Quarterly* 88 (1989): 7–29.

8. The alternative, as Robert Kimbrough suggests in "Shakespeare's Androgyny Seen Through Disguise" (*Shakespeare Quarterly* 33 [1982]): 17–33, is that almost all of the plays would have to have been treated as farce (p. 17).

9. A review of the early criticism of the play reveals that my main predecessor in this view is H. N. Hudson. An appreciation of the Rosalind-Celia friendship shines through the haze of his Wordsworthian prose. "Instinct with the soul of moral beauty and female tenderness, the friendship of these more-than-sisters 'mounts to the seat of grace within the mind.'" He finds sisterhood in the very serenity of Arden: "the graces of art and the simplicities of nature meet together in joyous, loving sisterhood." *Shakespeare: His Life, Art, and Characters*, 4th ed., rev.; 2 vols. (Boston: Ginn and Company, 1891), 1:346, 349.

10. C. L. Barber, *Shakespeare's Festive Comedy* (New York: Meridian Books, 1963), p. 226.

11. On swooning in medieval romance and Shakespearean comedy, see the interesting remarks of E. E. Stoll in *Shakespeare Studies* (New York: Macmillan, 1927), pp. 40–42.

12. Stephen Greenblatt, *Shakespearean Negotiations* (Berkeley: University of California Press, 1988), pp. 66–93. "And the effect of her humour," the foreshadowing Hudson writes of Rosalind, "is, as it were, to *lubricate* [his emphasis] all her faculties, and make her thoughts run brisk and glib" (*Shakespeare*, 1:345).

13. "Disrupting Sexual Difference: Meaning and Gender in the Comedies," in John Drakakis, ed., *Alternative Shakespeares* (London: Methuen, 1985), p. 190. See also, in the same volume, Jacqueline Rose's "Sexuality in the Reading of Shakespeare: *Hamlet* and *Measure for Measure*." Belsey's view that something prototypically "feminist" emerges from woman-into-man disguises in Shakespeare runs counter to that of Linda Woodbridge in *Women and the English Renaissance: Literature and the Nature of Womankind, 1540–1620* (Urbana: University of Illinois Press, 1986), pp. 154–55. Robert Kimbrough discusses the controversy in *Shakespeare and the Art of Humankindness: The Essay toward Androgyny* (Highlands, New Jersey: Humanities Press, 1990), pp. 101–5.

14. On the oddities of marriage law, consult Frederick Pollock and Frederic Maitland, *The History of English Law*, 2 vols. (rpt. Washington, D.C.: Lawyers' Literary Club, 1959), 2:368–99.

15. In a comparable scene in *Twelfth Night* (1.5.238–58), Viola/Caesario first (unlike Rosalind/Ganymede) praises the beauty of Olivia, then (like Rosalind/Ganymede) indicts her pride. Like Phebe, Olivia clearly prefers this freedom from enamorment to Orsino's Petrarchan enslavement.

16. These essays, cited from James Strachey, ed. and trans., *The Standard Edition of the Psychological Works of Sigmund Freud*, 24 vols. (London: Hogarth Press, 1953–74), are "On the Sexual Theories of Children" (9:207–26); "The Dissolution of the Oedipus Complex" (19:172–79); "Some Psychical Consequences of the Anatomical Distinction Between the Sexes" (19:243–58); and "Femininity" (22:112–35). Scorned by the first generation of academic feminists, these papers have recently been hailed by some members of the second and third generations—an event so momentous as to have made the cover of *Newsweek* in 1991. See the introductory matter in Elisabeth Young-Bruehl, ed., *Freud on Women: A Reader* (New York: Norton, 1990).

17. Interpretations of Eve's courtship from a Freudian point of view may be found in Mark Edmundson, *Towards Reading Freud: Self-Creation in Milton, Wordsworth, Emerson, and Sigmund Freud* (Princeton: Princeton University Press, 1990), pp. 57–86; William Kerrigan and Gordon Braden, *The Idea of the Renaissance* (Baltimore: Johns Hopkins University Press, 1989), pp. 201–3; and my "Gender and Confusion in Milton and Everyone Else," *Hellas* 2 (1991): 195–220.

18. (New York: Oxford University Press, 1991), pp. 92–105.

19. So far is Celia from jealousy that she plays the priest in the mock wedding of 4.1.118–24.

20. Several points in this account of courtship are illustrated in one of Cressida's speeches:

If I confess much you will play the tyrant.
                    . . . See, we fools!
Why have I blabb'd? Who shall be true to us
When we are so unsecret to ourselves?—
But though I lov'd you well, I woo'd you not;
And yet, good faith, I wish'd myself a man,
Or that women had men's privilege
Of speaking first.

                                        (3.2.118–28)

Carol Thomas Neely, in *Broken Nuptials in Shakespeare's Plays* (New Haven: Yale University Press, 1985), pp. 6–22, offers a brief and historically informed account of the "deidealization" to which married women are subjected in Shakespeare. Recent generalization about this subject is too often guided by Lawrence Stone's *The Family, Sex and Marriage in England 1500–1800* (New York: Harper and Row, 1977); I suspect that the balanced views of Keith Wrightson, *English Society 1580–1680* (New Brunswick: Rutgers University Press, 1982), pp. 89–117, are more trustworthy.

21. Ann Jennalie Cook, *Making a Match: Courtship in Shakespeare and His Society* (Princeton: Princeton University Press, 1991), p. 223. Cook also stresses the unreality of the marriage, its distance from contracts and settlements. Property came under English common law, which preferred that it be exchanged in public; thus brides were customarily endowed at the church door (Pollock and Maitland, *History of English Law*, 2:374–75).

22. Ernest Jones, *Hamlet and Oedipus* (New York: W. W. Norton, 1949), pp. 121–25.

23. C. L. Barber and Richard P. Wheeler, *The Whole Journey: Shakespeare's Power of Development* (Berkeley: University of California Press, 1986), pp. 237–42.

24. Dryden was dead wrong in supposing that Shakespeare "needed not the spectacles of Books to read Nature"—D. Nichol Smith, ed., *Shakespeare Criticism 1623–1840* (London: Oxford University Press, 1963), p. 16.

25. For a distinguished psychoanalytic discussion of this point, see Hans Loewald's "Primary Process, Secondary Process, and Language," in Joseph H. Smith, ed., *Psychoanalysis and Language* (New Haven: Yale University Press, 1978), pp. 235–70.

26. William George Clarke seems to have been the first to note, in his edition of 1864, that Arden "was the maiden name of his very own mother—Mary Arden, whose ancient family derived their name" from the forest of Arden in Warwickshire; see Richard Knowles, ed., *A New Variorum Edition of Shakespeare's As You Like It* (New York: MLA, 1977), p. 556. James Joyce includes the association in the great "Shakespeare chapter" (9) of *Ulysses*, ed. Hans Walter Gabler (New York: Random House, 1986): "—As for his family, Stephen said, his mother's name lives in the forest of Arden" (p. 171). Barbara Bono has also argued for this connection; see "Mixed Gender, Mixed Genre in Shakespeare's *As You Like It*," in Barbara Lewalski, ed., *Renaissance Genres: Essays on Theory, History, and Interpretation* (Cambridge: Harvard University Press, 1986), p. 194.

One should also consult the long note on "forrest of Arden" in H. H. Furness, ed., *As You Like It* (New York: Lippincott, 1890), pp. 16–18.

27. Gilbert would have been the usurping brother in Shakespeare's own childhood. Though one cannot rule out the possibility of a wet nurse, I strongly suspect that Mary Arden nursed her own children. The smothering fantasies discussed by Rothenberg (see note 29) might have resulted from Mary Shakespeare's feeling that, having lost Joan in 1559 or 1560 and Margaret in 1563, she would need to provide her next child with a great deal of nourishment in order for it to survive infancy. I will extend these comments in a forthcoming book, *Hamlet's Perfection*. The locus classicus for the idea of a sibling rivalry originating in being replaced at the breast is Augustine's *Confessions* 1.7.

28. *Ben Jonson: The Complete Poems*, ed. George Parfitt (New Haven: Yale University Press, 1975), p. 213. "Under an old oak, whose bows were mossed with age" gives prominence to "old," which refuses to submit to metrical law. One commentator (see Furness, *As You Like It*, p. 241) "cannot believe that in an otherwise deftly wrought and perfectly rhythmical passage, Shakespeare would load a line with a heavy monosyllable, entirely superfluous to any purpose other than that of marring the description and making the verse halt."

29. Montrose, in " 'The Place of a Brother' " (p. 50), connects the snake to the chain Rosalind gave to Orlando at their first meeting. Celia later recalls it when trying to identify for Rosalind the lyricist of her name: "And a chain, that you once wore, about his neck" (3.2.178). For infantile fantasies about choking and smothering in Shakespeare, see Alan Rothenberg, "Infantile Fantasies in Shakespearean Metaphor: (1) The Fear of Being Smothered," *Psychoanalytic Review* 60 (1973): 205–22; and "The Oral Rape Fantasy and Rejection of the Mother in the Imagery of Shakespeare's *Venus and Adonis*," *Psychoanalytic Quarterly* 40 (1971): 447–68. Rothenberg does not suggest an etiology for this complex of fantasies in Shakespeare, but see note 27.

30. Wilson Knight (cited in note 1) always assumed that anger over ingratitude was at the heart of the Shakespearean hate-theme, in part because he was the only major critic of his generation to accept the centrality of *Timon of Athens* to Shakespeare's tragic phase. See Viola's contempt for ingratitude above all other vices in *Twelfth Night* 3.4.363–66.

31. One thinks here of the bear in *The Winter's Tale*; see Murray Schwartz, "*The Winter's Tale*: Loss and Transformation," *American Imago* 32 (1975): 158–59.

32. I have discussed some of the roles of kissing in Renaissance lyric poetry in "Kiss Fancies in Robert Herrick," *George Herbert Journal* 14 (1990/91): 155–71.

33. I am anticipated by, among others, Leslie Fiedler, *The Stranger in Shakespeare* (New York: Stein and Day, 1972), p. 47, and Stephen Dedalus in Joyce's *Ulysses*, p. 157: "But his boywomen are the women of a boy. Their life, thought, speech are lent them by males." On the female dislike of kissing men with beards and bad complexions see *Much Ado About Nothing* 2.1.26–28, Marston's *The Dutch Courtesan* 3.1.10ff., and the ninth lyric of Jonson's "The Celebration of Charis." The rejection of these men in the audience, the men that he in playing she would not wish to kiss, might be taken as a comic version of the wound the lioness inflicts on Orlando.

DREAMING ON

UNCANNY ENCOUNTERS

FROM VIRGIL TO TASSO

THE EPIC TOPOS AS AN UNCANNY RETURN

Elizabeth J. Bellamy

I T IS ONLY RARELY," writes Freud in "The Uncanny," "that a psy-cho-analyst feels impelled to investigate the subject of aesthet-ics. . . ."[1] Here Freud, despite his reliance on Sophocles' *Oedipus Rex* and Shakespeare's *Hamlet* as the "specimen stories" of psychoanaly-sis, would seem (coyly?) to suggest that there is no necessary and inherent point of intersection between literature and psychoanalysis. But Shos-hana Felman has argued that literature, even more than simply having an unconscious that psychoanalysis then reveals, can, in its turn, serve as *"the unconscious of psychoanalysis . . .* that literature *in* psychoanalysis functions precisely as its *unthought."*[2] Literature, in other words, can at times constitute an ineffable nodal point (a kind of Freudian *Knäuel*), or tangle, that renders psychoanalytic interpretation overdetermined—or, as Freud writes in *The Interpretation of Dreams*, that "resists unravel-ing."[3] "Fiction," writes Hélène Cixous in a similar vein, "*is the very strange thing . . .* fiction pointing toward the unknown."[4]

What makes fiction "the very strange thing" that points toward the unknown is, of course, its ongoing engagement with the uncanny. Noting that aesthetic treatises have traditionally been concerned only with "what is beautiful, attractive and sublime,"[5] Freud proposes instead a study of the *Unheimliche*—or the quality of being frightened—and also, we may infer, the way its literary representations present a kind of unconscious for psychoanalysis itself. For Freud, the quality of being frightened is as inherently an *aesthetic* response as it is a psychic one: "The uncanny as it is depicted in *literature . . .* merits in truth a separate discussion. Above all, it is a much more fertile province than the uncanny in real life."[6] But as Cixous warns, Freud's essay "The Uncanny" cannot thereby be viewed as a unified discourse because there can be no aesthetic delineation of what she terms the "nature of incertitude."[7] Throughout Freud's essay, the concept of the *Unheimliche* is developed not so much through precise definition as through a kind of agglutinative adding on of diverse (yet ultimately interrelated) psychic experiences: the uncanny as, at one and the same time, narcissism, fear of death, the return of the repressed, anxi-ety, castration, ambivalence, terror, uneasy anticipation, animism, doubt.

In its often massive overdeterminations, the *Unheimliche*, then, constitutes a kind of unassimilated psychic residue—the point at which fiction,
as its own kind of uncanny reality, resists interpretation.[8]

Thus if, as Felman contends, literature and psychoanalysis can mutually enrich one another through shared processes of interpretation, they
can also undo one another by the overdeterminations accruing within the
interpretive detours and indirections that constitute their structural limits. In *Beyond the Pleasure Principle*, Freud reveals his anxieties about the
interpretive deferrals of overdetermination: "The indeterminacy of all
our discussions that we call 'metapsychological' is of course due to the
fact that we know nothing of the nature of the excitatory process that
takes place in the elements of the psychic systems, and that we do not feel
justified in framing any hypothesis on the subject. We are consequently
operating all the time with a large unknown factor—a capital X—that we
are obliged to carry over into every new formula."[9] If psychoanalytic interpretation *is* inevitably overdetermined, then how do we interpret literature when it structures itself on "elements of psychic systems" that supposedly frame the limits of the literary "subject"? This question will be
addressed later in more detail. For the time being, suffice it to say that we
can propose Freud's concept of the *Unheimliche* as just such a "capital
X" that overdetermines the intersection between literature and psychoanalysis.

But the principal question I would like to address in this essay is: what
(over)interpretive framework is needed to comprehend the phenomenon
of the uncanny as the "return of the repressed" when that "return" takes
place within the broader scope of literary history? It can be argued that
literary history (like a kind of Lacanian unconscious) is not a repository
of "meaning" as such, but rather an ongoing process of signification
whose effects are not always subject to authorial control. Can we say that
literary *history*, more authoritatively than simply "literature" itself,
serves as the unconscious of psychoanalysis—as, indeed, the "uncanniest" of the hiding places for the *Unheimliche*? I would like to consider
the literary history of epic and, in particular, the extent to which its recurring *translatio topos* of the bleeding branch from Virgil to Tasso serves as
the site not just of epic history's return of the repressed, but as, in some
sense, its ongoing *repression* of the return of the repressed.[10] In perhaps
his most fundamental attempt at defining the uncanny, Freud, quoting
Schelling, offers the *Unheimliche* as *"the name for everything that ought
to have remained . . . secret and hidden but has come to light."*[11] The
oddly ethical valence of Schelling's "ought" is vividly illustrated by the
topos of the bleeding branch as epic history's paradigmatic return of the
repressed. There is something about these macabre branches, painfully
oozing blood and uttering human lamentations, that somehow *ought* to

have remained secret. The supernatural spirit of Virgil's Polydorus, staining the ground with his own gore, *ought* to have remained buried in its obscure Thracian mound. But his ululating moans and mangled roots persist in making their ghostly returns to constitute epic history's privileged mise-en-scène of dread and ontological uncertainty—and a drama so hermeneutically overdetermined that, as part of its *resistance* to interpretation, it also manifests an *insistence* on returning to the site of terror. Indeed, through an examination of this topos throughout the literary history of epic, we will come to see that Freud's concept of the *Unheimliche* is an aestheticization of the psychic and interpretive complexities of the repetition compulsion itself.

In its daemonic and repetitive reanimations of the dead, the *translatio topos* of the bleeding branch prompts consideration of a far-reaching question: how should interpretation accommodate not just epic, but the larger scope of the literary history of epic? Or, more fundamentally, what can this topos tell us about where the moment of interpreting epic *begins*? If literary history if constituted sequentially, or diachronically, then in a literary historical approach to the interpretation of epic, the full meaning of an epic topos can be revealed only *retroactively*. What the particular topos of the bleeding branch demonstrates is that within the literary history of epic, interpretation "originates" only *nachträglich*—only in the temporally indeterminate (and distinctly psychic) space of the repetition compulsion. If, as Freud argues, the *Unheimliche* consists (uncannily) of its own etymological doubling-back onto the *Heimliche*, then the *Unheimliche* always returns ("home-like") to its "origins" as a topos; the uncanny is, in short, always predicated on repetition. But if the recognition of a topos is always already belated, then this temporally curious process of *Nachträglichkeit* necessarily postpones the final moment of interpretation. The crucial question for fully understanding the literary history of epic, then, is: how do we interpret the "meaning" of an epic topos? As we shall see, for the epic hero who suddenly encounters the uncanny man-plant, the moment is always *unheimlich*; but for the reader of the literary history of epic who recognizes the topos (belatedly) this moment of recognition is distinctly *heimlich*. Like the uncanny itself, a topos is, to echo Freud, "nothing new or alien, but something which is familiar and old-established in the mind and which has become alienated from it only through the process of repression."[12] How, then, are we to interpret this ambivalent intersection of the *Heimliche* and the *Unheimliche* when the repressed makes its return as an epic topos? To answer this question, we must move to a detailed consideration of trees and branches as "the very strange thing" of the literary history of epic.

The extent to which trees and branches can serve as the "unthought" of psychoanalysis is itself uncannily alluded to by Cixous when she refers to the "enigmas and apparitions" of the *Unheimliche* as, specifically, a "display [of] branches."[13] In another of his often tentative definitions, Freud characterizes the uncanny as "what arouses dread and horror"[14]—and that which persistently arouses "dread and horror" within the literary history of epic is, quite simply, trees and branches. The topos of the bleeding branch "originates" with Virgil, who chooses to begin his account of the founding of Rome on a note of fear and anxiety. In a Thracian grove, Aeneas, in the process of making a sacrifice to Venus, attempts to pluck a branch from a myrtle bush and is suddenly confronted with "horrendum et dictu uideo mirabile monstrum" [an awful omen, terrible to tell (3.26)].[15] As Aeneas breaks off the leafy frond, black blood oozes from the roots and drips onto the ground. Even as he feels a *frigidus horror* (29), Aeneas tears at a second shoot—and then a third; but the branches of the bush are eerily resistant until a voice cries out: "quid miserum, Aenea, laceras?" [Why are you mangling me, Aeneas? (41)]. Even as the branch speaks, Aeneas's own terror is speechless: "hic confixum ferrea texit / telorum seges et iaculis increuit acutis" [I was astounded, and my hair / stood stiff, my voice held fast within my jaws (45–46)]. The horrifying *anima incarcerata* reveals its identity as Priam's son Polydorus, a (distinctly *heimlich*, or "home-like") Trojan brutally murdered by the king of Thrace.[16] The unnerving episode concludes with renewed funeral rites for Polydorus and Aeneas's determined departure from the haunted Thracian grove—an episode rendered no less disquieting just because the bush stakes a claim to an identity that was once human.

There is no known source for Virgil's incarceration of Polydorus in a bush, and thus the uncanny in epic originates in a broken frond. Moreover, Aeneas's subsequent encounter in Book 6 with the renowned, but enigmatic Golden Bough demonstrates that much of the hero's celebrated *pietas* persists in centering on uncanny encounters with branches and trees. Surely one of the stranger mysteries of the *Aeneid* is the episode of the Golden Bough, situated as it is on the very threshold of psyche and history.[17] Aeneas cannot descend into the Underworld (and its prophecy of the future founding of a Roman *imperium*) without the bough, but it is mysteriously secreted in a dark, shadowy grove in an *arbore opaca* (136); like the *Unheimliche* itself, it is "[c]oncealed, kept from sight."[18] Charles Paul Segal has perceptively argued that "the whole Golden Bough episode is hardly necessary to advance the plot and in fact . . . effects only its retardation—all the more reason for seeking its significance in a symbolic rather than purely narrative function."[19] Not simply aesthetic (or "symbolic"), however, the Golden Bough is distinctly *uncanny*. Simultaneously beautiful and ghostly, partly hidden and partly giving off a golden hue, the bough is neither fully metallic nor fully organic (as a *ramus humum* [196]). Its eerie sheen (its *discolor auri aura* [204]), contrasting with the dark-leaved ilex, embodies the uncanny itself—both natural and yet beyond nature, both benign and yet somehow ineffably threatening.[20]

Not simply what Freud might designate a "thing of terror,"[21] the Golden Bough is uncontrollably overdetermined—a space of "unthought" that resists interpretation, indeed "the very strange thing" that is literature itself. Though the bough, as the Sibyl tells Aeneas, is uncannily self-renewing when plucked, it also strangely, if only momentarily, resists breaking off: "corripit Aeneas extemplo, avidusque refringit /cunctantem, et vatis portat sub tecta Sibyllae" [And at once Aeneas plucks it / and, eager, breaks the hesitating bough / and carries it into the Sibyl's house (210–11)].[22] Like the branches of the myrtle that enclose the spirit of Polydorus (the very branches that Aeneas attempts repeatedly to pluck), the Golden Bough, despite the Sibyl's assurances that it would snap easily, and despite Aeneas's eager alacrity, mysteriously resists breaking off—and it is at this point that we can see emerging (retroactively) a topos of not simply the bleeding branch, but also of the *resisting* branch. And, in the dim light of the resistant (*cunctantem*) Golden Bough, we can now pose (belatedly) some questions that underscore just how difficult it is to interpret the preceding Polydorus episode. What, exactly, does the man-tree represent for Aeneas? Is Polydorus, as Freud might venture to interpret, a mirror of Aeneas's own narcissism? Is Aeneas's need to attempt a breaking off of the branch not once, not twice, but three times a kind of sadistic "insurance against the destruction of the ego"?[23] Is Aeneas's affective terror itself a fear of castration—a fear that uncannily reflects back to Aeneas his own death anxiety? Why is the myrtle branch itself so strangely resistant to breaking off (or to castration)? Is the branch's resistance to castration in effect a resistance to Aeneas's narcissistic attempt to recuperate a sense of wholeness for himself through the fragmentation of the other?

In this enactment of dread and doubt, the answers to these questions must, of course, remain elusive because, in the broken branch, we have reached one of those symptomatic sites where psychoanalytic interpretation is overdetermined by literature—for the *Unheimliche* is far more complex than simply a kind of castration anxiety or a manifestation of narcissism. We should be reminded, in this context, that when the branch of Polydorus makes its repressed return in the form of the Golden Bough, the bough also resists, if only momentarily. And it is as if, within the bounds of this "topos of resistance," the epic branch becomes established as the site where fiction itself resists interpretation. The bough must be snapped from its tree before it can yield the "truths" of Aeneas's destiny—but even then it yields no "truths" other than its own irreconcilable contradictions. To echo Segal, the bough fails to advance the plot. It is simply *there*—the "very strange thing" of literature—serving no other purpose than to offer resistance: physical resistance to Aeneas's attempt to break it off, hermeneutic resistance to interpretation, but also a site of *insistence* as a return to the epistemological incertitude so ambiguously posed by the man-tree Polydorus. What the overdetermined and unanswered questions posed earlier demonstrate is that literature, as the "unthought" of psychoanalysis, cannot unravel, but can only further obfuscate the complexity of the *Unheimliche*.

The uncanny Golden Bough is also a harbinger of death, for even as Aeneas searches for it, he and his men happen upon the body of Misenus, another of the *Aeneid*'s many corpses from the fall of Troy, and once Hector's comrade. As they build a burial altar for Misenus, once again trees unexpectedly (compulsively?) become the focus of the narrative, and it is in this digressive episode that we can see why the *Unheimliche*, as Freud contends, always returns us to an "old, animistic conception of the universe":[24]

> tum iussa Sibyllae,
> haud mora, festinant flentes aramque sepulcri
> congerere arboribus caeloque educere certant.
> itur in antiquam siluam, stabula alta ferarum;
> procumbunt piceae, sonat icta securibus ilex
> fraxineaeque trabes cuneis et fissile robur
> scinditur, aduoluunt ingentis montibus ornos.
>
> (176–82)

> [Then they rush to carry out,
> in tears, the Sibyl's order, strive to heap
> an altar for his tomb, to build it high
> to heaven, searching through the ancient forest,
> deep dens of animals. The pitch pines fall;
> the ilex rings beneath ax strokes; their wedges
> now cleave the trunks of ash and splintering oaks.
> They roll the giant rowans down the mountain.]

As the Trojans hack aggressively at the trees of the Avernus wood, they experience none of the *frigidus horror* felt by Aeneas after he assaulted the fronds of Polydorus's myrtle. Yet, as the trees fall noisily and heavily to the violent, colonizing strokes of the ax (even as the wood's animals are forced to flee), the passage suggests reluctance, resistance, protest. At one point, Freud describes the *Unheimliche* as "intellectual uncertainty whether an object is alive or not";[25] and for the reader, if not for Aeneas, every tree branch in the forest would seem to have become an anthropomorphized Polydorus protesting its violent castration. After Aeneas plucks the Golden Bough, the Trojans resume the building of Misenus's funeral pyre. And once again, there is the suggestion that the animated trees are not participating willingly in their own destruction. One of the trees used in building the pyre is a *cineri ingrato*, glossed by R. G. Austin as "the ash that gives no thanks," almost as if, as Austin notes, "the cremation is anticipated."[26] And thus, somehow, in the interpretive space circumscribed by this topos of protest, that is, by Aeneas's aggressive grasping *(corripit)* of the Golden Bough, by the bough's resistance to seizure *(cunctantem)*, and by the resisting *(ingrato)* ash's protest, lies the Freudian *Knäuel*, the "capital X" of overdetermination. There is something in the resisting branches of the forest of Avernus that lingers as the evanescent *unthought* of interpretation.

In these three episodes from the *Aeneid* that we have discussed, the *Unheimliche* reveals itself to originate in the trees' animate (though futile) resistance to aggression. And in this context, we might also briefly consider Book 8 of Ovid's *Metamorphoses* (though not within the bounds of the literary history of epic, nevertheless an important document of uncanniness in the *translatio topos* of the resisting tree), where the arrogant Erysichthon, Aeneas-like, impiously violates an ancient grove sacred to Ceres. He singles out for destruction a huge oak that is *una nemus* [itself a grove (744)],[27] dwelling-place of Ceres' hamadryads. As Erysichthon's ax is poised to strike,

> et pariter frondes, pariter pallescere glandes
> coepere, ac longi pallorem ducere rami.
> cuisus ut in tronco fecit manus impia vulnus,
> haud aliter fluxit discusso cortice sanguis.
>
> (759–62)

> [The holy tree
> Shuddered and groaned, and every leaf and acorn
> Grew pale and pallor spread on each long branch.
> And when his impious stroke wounded the trunk,
> Blood issued, flowing from the severed bark.]

What Erysichthon's act of aggression demonstrates is that the blood-soaked and mutilated tree will always make its uncanny return in the form of resistance, but a resistance that is itself an *insistence* on making its return as a painful protest—that is, protest as the literary animism of the sort that constitutes the *unthought* of psychoanalysis.

But to return momentarily to the *Aeneid*, one could argue that, despite the horror of Polydorus and the enigma of the Golden Bough, the uncanny animism of Virgil's trees is most vividly demonstrated by a large, shady elm, the dwelling-place of empty dreams (*somnia uana*) that stands on the pathway to the waters of Acheron:

> multaque praeterea uariarum monstra ferarum
> Centauri in foribus stabulant, Scyllaeque biformes,
> et centumgeminus Briareus, ac belua Lernae
> horrendum stridens, flammisque armata Chimaera,
> Gorgones Harpyiaeque et forma tricorporis umbrae.
> corripit hic subita trepidus formidine ferrum
> Aeneas, strictamque aciem uenientibus offert;
> et ni docta comes tenuis sine corpore uitas
> admoneat uolitare, caua sub imagine formae,
> inruat, et frustra ferro diuerberet umbras.

(285–94)

> [so many monstrous shapes of savage beasts
> are stabled there: Centaurs and double-bodied
> Scyllas; the hundred-handed Briareus;
> the brute of Lerna, hissing horribly;
> Chimaera armed with flames; Gorgons and Harpies;
> and Geryon, the shade that wears three bodies.
> And here Aeneas, shaken suddenly
> by terror, grips his sword; he offers naked
> steel and opposes those who come. Had not
> his wise companion warned him they were only
> thin lives that glide without a body in
> the hollow semblance of a form, he would
> in vain have torn the shadows with his blade.]

Despite the Sibyl's assurance that the elm tree's disembodied, chimerical spirits *(tenuis sine corpore uitas)* are incorporeal—scarcely more than products of the imagination—in the animistic world of the *Unheimliche* they are frighteningly real to Aeneas, who ironically grips (*corripit*, 290) his sword with the same aggressive force with which he snatches (*corripit*, 210) the Golden Bough just moments earlier. In "The Uncanny," Freud links animism with "the subject's narcissistic overvaluation of his own mental processes."[28] Here the *Unheimliche* is perceived by Freud as a privileged symptom of narcissism; and in Virgil, if the elm of *somnia uana* appears to be bristling with animistic spirits, it is because the tree becomes the chosen projection of Aeneas's "own mental processes." Thus Aeneas, in some sense repressing the confrontation with his own narcissism that constituted the terror of his earlier encounter with Polydorus, now strangely persists in "overvaluing" the animistic potential of the Avernus wood—an unpredictable act of narcissism confirming trees as "the very strange thing" of epic.

The episode of the Avernus wood initiates a topos within the literary history of epic—the topos of the haunted, animistic wood where epistemological uncertainty holds sway in the absence of any "reality" provided by the Sibyl's commentary. Despite the anti-Virgilian impulses of his first-century *De Bello Civili*,[29] Lucan enacts a return to the animistic wood of Avernus—a return that, as we shall see later, will prove to have profoundly influenced Tasso. And it is in this return that we can see, once again, how a topos is always "originated" (belatedly). In Book 3 of Lucan's epic, Caesar and his men are stalled outside Marseilles. Concluding that he needs to build assault towers to storm the city's fortifications, Caesar sends his men into the nearby forest to cut down trees for wood. But Caesar's axmen soon discover that the forest is haunted:

> Hunc non ruricolae Panes, nemorumque potentes
> Silvani Nymphaeque tenent, sed barbara ritu. . . .
>   . . . nec ventus in illas
> Incubuit silvas, excussaque nubibus atris
> Fulgura: non ullis frondem fraebentibus auris,
> Arboribus suus horror inest. . . . Iam fama ferebat
> Saepe cavas motu terrae mugire cavernas,
> Et procumbentes iterum consurgere taxos. . . .
> Sed fortes tremuere manus, motique verenda
> Maiestate loci, si robora sacra ferirent,
> In sua credebant redituras membra secures.

(402–31)

> [Here there lived no nymphs, no Pan-like god of the country,
> No wood deities like Silvanu: only barbaric,
> Sinister rites of worship. . . .
> No breeze ever fanned the leaves of the trees, but they rustled,
> Even so, with their own mysterious tremors. . . . And legend
> Told of shuddering earth, of groans from underground caverns,
> Yew trees crashing down and then regrowing. . . .
> Caesar's soldiers were tough, but they shrank from the awe-inspiring
> Atmosphere of the place and believed, if they struck at the sacred
> Trunks, that the axe would bounce and rebound on the limbs
>   of their wielders.][30]

In this passage, we are presented with a vivid illustration of Freud's hypothesis that the *Unheimliche* always represents a "narcissistic overvaluation" of one's mental processes. More than simply believing that spirits inhabit the trees surrounding Marseilles, the soldiers fear that their aggressive axes will actually rebound with the force of the trees' vengeance to cut off their own limbs. But eventually their fear of Caesar's anger, vented with an ax on a nearby oak, takes priority over their fear of the haunted wood; and the axmen, in a passage directly reminiscent of Aeneas's felling of the trees for Misenus's tomb, complete their (murderous?) task:

> Procumbunt orni, nodosi impellitur ilex,
> Silvaque Dodones, et fluctibus aptior alnus,
> Et non plebeios luctus testata cupressus,
> Tum primum posuere comas, et fronde carentes
> Admisere diem. . . .

(440–44)

> [So down came crashing the ash trees,
> Down came the gnarled ilex. And the wood of Dodona, the oak tree,
> Alder, resistant to sea, and cypress, whose presence in graveyards
> Signifies a tomb of more than plebeian importance—
> All for the first time ever were robbed of their foliage.]

Again, we are mysteriously presented with the topos of arboreal resistance. Lucan's alder can protect itself against the ravages of salt water, but it is doomed to fall in reluctant silence to the cleaving axes of Caesar's soldiers. Were the soldiers right to hesitate initially in their refusal to cut down the trees? *Are* there indeed spirits inhabiting the trees? In the absence of the Sibyl's assurances, how can one be certain they are not?

In "The Uncanny," Freud at one point depicts the *Unheimliche* as a walk in the woods: "So, for instance, when . . . one has lost one's way in a mountain forest, every attempt to find the marked or familiar path may bring one back again and again to one and the same spot. . . ."[31] Epic narrative frequently retraces a labyrinthine path through a Wandering Wood—and not surprisingly, then, it is in the uncanny and literally "familiar" (i.e., spirit-inhabited) forest of Canto 13 of the *Inferno* that Dante encounters epic's now paradigmatic return of the repressed, a return so self-conscious of its literariness that it becomes a virtually theoretical exploration of what constitutes the uncanniness of an epic topos. In the pathless, forbidden Wood of the Suicides, where there is "non fronda verde, ma di color fosco" [foliage . . . not verdant, but merely black (4)], Dante's guide Virgil warns his charge to be observant: "però riguardo ben; sì vederai / cose che torrien fede al mio sermone" [Therefore look carefully and you will see / things in this wood, which, if I told them to you / would shake the confidence you have placed in me (20–21)].[32] Thus the burden of interpreting this return to a mysterious wood is shifted from Virgil's guiding commentary to the confirmations of Dante's own inadequate sensory powers. As we saw in the woods of Marseilles in Lucan's *De Bello Civili*, epistemological doubt can be dispelled, if only momentarily, by a simple blow from Caesar's ax; but Virgil intends for the Wood of the Suicides to become for Dante a subtle, deductive test of belief, of certitude, of *fede*. In this uncanny episode of *fede*, Dante is left to test for himself Freud's conjecture that the *Unheimliche* is always a product of "intellectual uncertainty whether an object is alive or not." In effect, Dante must test for himself the veracity of an epic topos.

Virgil warns Dante to look out for strange apparitions, but, seeing no humans, the poet hears only cries of lamentation (*sentia . . . trarre guai* [22]) issuing from the tenebrous trees. The complex intersubjectivity of Dante's elegant conceit of doubt and second-guessing ("Cred'io ch'ei credette ch'io credesse / che tante voci uscisser, tra quei bronchi . . ." [I think perhaps he thought that I was thinking / those cries rose from among the twisted roots . . .]) underscores the psychic "nature of incertitude" that constitutes this test of phenomenality. Urging Dante to trust his own senses in this wood of error, Virgil then directs his charge to break off one of the branches of *un gran pruno*. Unlike the fronds of Polydorus's myrtle or the Golden Bough, the branch breaks off easily; but the topos of the painful protest is renewed when the trunk cries out, "Perchè mi schiante?" [Why do you tear me? (33)], even as the mangled branch becomes stained with black blood.[33]

If, as we have seen, the essence of the *Unheimliche* is that which "ought to have remained . . . secret and hidden but has come to light," then we can only note with dread the reanimation of Polydorus in the many *uomini-piante* of the Wood of the Suicides.[34] And for the reader, the episode is all the more uncanny because, ironically, it is all the more familiar. We recognize, for example, the predictable return of the affective response of frozen fear, almost as if Dante had caught a glimpse of the castrating Medusa's head itself. When the branch speaks, Dante is immobile: "ond'io lasciai la cima / cadere, e stetti come l'uom che teme" [Startled, I dropped the branch that I was holding / and stood transfixed by fear . . . (44–45)]. The terror of Dante's response to the branch arises because it is almost as if something in the funeral rites of Polydorus had been left unmourned—not fully worked through—and hence the return of the repressed as the *uomo-pianta* that must compulsively "act out" its pain. Eventually the tree identifies itself as Pier delle Vigne, once-powerful adviser to Frederick II of Sicily, who committed suicide after being accused of treachery.[35]

But once again, as was the case with Polydorus, mere revelation of a human identity does little to unravel the uncanny overdeterminations of the episode. We must, for example, consider the significance of the fact that the branch of Pier delle Vigne's tree is broken off not unwittingly, but rather as part of a calculated test of *fede*. In fact, we could argue that because Dante is urged to do what Aeneas did in ignorance, the episode unfolds as nothing less than the constituting of epic literary history itself.

It begins with Virgil claiming that he is unable simply to *tell* Dante about the mysteries of the wood. And it ends, amidst the eerie ululations of the bleeding branch, with Virgil's rationalization to delle Vigne that his pain is the necessary result of Dante's epistemological uncertainty that an animistic wood can exist:

> "S'elli avesse potuto creder prima, . . . anima lesa,
> ciò c'ha veduto pur con la mia rima,
> non averebbe in te la man distesa;"

(47–51)

> ["O wounded soul,
> could he have believed before what he has seen
> in my verses only, you would yet be whole."]

If only Dante had believed, insists Virgil, what he had read in the *Aeneid*—if, in effect, Dante had not dismissed (repressed?) the horror of the *anima incarcerata* Polydorus as merely "fictive"—then the uncanniness of the return of the repressed would not have had to be restaged, and delle Vigne would not have had to cry out in pain.[36] In the Wood of the Suicides, then, delle Vigne's painful protest, "Perchè mi schiante?," becomes nothing less than the structural foundation of the literary history of epic, validating, if only *nachträglich*, the broken, bleeding branch as, in some sense, the "origin" not of epic, but of the literary history of epic. The bleeding branch as the privileged *cosa incredibile* of the Wood of the Suicides may have no other "meaning" than to affirm (retroactively) the bleeding branch of the *Aeneid* as "the very strange thing" of Virgil's narrative; ironically, Virgil's contrived test of *fede* and phenomenality in the *Inferno* ensures that there is such a "strange thing" as literary history itself.

The return of the repressed that constitutes literary history can only be an uncanny moment. If literary history is a re-cognition or re-membering of its own origins (in *la mia rima*, as Virgil notes), then such a process can only ever be uncanny. "Dismembered limbs," writes Freud, ". . . have something peculiarly uncanny about them."[37] And Cixous, taking her cue from Freud, describes the *Unheimliche* thus: ". . . in the end, the *form* of a *body* of *examples* emerges but without 'revealing' itself, a form of forms, a body which returns to its *dismemberment*."[38] Within Cixous's characteristically elliptical description of the *Unheimliche*, we can see that in the mangled branch as the "form of forms" of the uncanny, the literary history of epic always "returns to its dismemberment." But as a distinctly *affective* topos, the epic branch also elicits fear and dread—the site of resistance to interpretation and understanding, and the site of a "forgetting" to "re-member" these same *dis*-membered and severed branches as the revenants of the literary history of epic.

It is almost as if Virgil is setting out to prove that recognition of a topos eases (interpretive) anxiety and ambivalence. But the *Unheimliche* is, perhaps, never so much a crisis of perception as it is in the *Inferno*, Canto 13. Despite Virgil's efforts to fix the ontological status of the *uomo-pianta* that stands before Dante, it remains *la cosa incredibile*, "the very strange thing" that, although vulnerable to breaking off, resists interpretation—resists, in its dismemberment, the kind of "re-membering" that would render the trees of epic less uncanny.

If Dante's treatment of the topos of the broken branch is a careful presentation of the crisis of perception, Ariosto's "return" to this privileged site of the repressed in epic literary history in his *Orlando furioso* serves as his anticipation of a particularly pertinent question that Cixous's asks of the uncanny: "how many repetitions are necessary before distress turns into comedy?"[39] Much of the narrative of Ariosto's sprawling epic unfolds within the dilatory space of the *selve e boscherecci labirinti* of romance. And perhaps because the *Furioso* maintains such a close and literal proximity to trees (because its eccentric narrative refuses to repress the enigma of trees as "the very strange thing" of the literary history of epic), Ariosto's romance narrative demonstrates far less anxiety about the overdeterminations of the *Unheimliche* than anything we have seen previously in epic history. Ariosto's continuation of the *translatio topos* of the bleeding branch is not structured as an uncanny moment for epic, but is rather wholly in keeping with the breezy sophistication and wry poetic omniscience that control the tone of his vastly ironic poem. If for Virgil, Lucan, and Dante, the topos of wounded trees is always the *unheimlich* site of dread and horror, for Ariosto the topos is reduced to the occasion for comic absurdity.[40] We can pick up in Canto 6, where the luckless Astolfo has been transformed by the enchantress Alcina into the by now all-too-familiar *verde mirto*. But whereas Polydorus and delle Vigne suffer the (always uncanny) return to their dismemberment, Ariosto's treatment of Astolfo refuses the pain of mutilation. When Ruggiero unwittingly tethers the hippogryph to one of the animate myrtle's branches, the beast becomes so frightened that the *uomo-pianta* is ludicrously reduced to little more than a pile of leaves—scarcely evocative of the terror of the oozing blood found in the episode's sources. When the *mirto offeso* speaks, the poet likens the release of Astolfo's voice, pseudo-comically, to a log hissing on a fire (27)—a far cry, tonally, from the vividness of Dante's analogy (40–42). And finally, the affective topos of the fearful response, in the past the very "essence" of the *Unheimliche*, is reduced to mere comic amazement on Ruggiero's part: "e poi ch'uscir da l'arbore s'accorse, / stupefatto restò piú che mai fosse" [when he realized that it issued from the tree, he was no little astonished (29)].[41] In the sheer absurdity of Astolfo's status as a *corpo orrido et irto* (a soul in a "spiky, contorted body" [30]), we realize that the *Unheimliche* simply cannot flourish within a poetic sensibility that privileges comic realism over dread and horror. It is as if Ariosto consciously set out to depict the point at which a topos may have "returned" to its own repression once too often.[42]

Insofar as Ariosto considers a more thoughtful and complex situating of trees within the literary history of epic, we must turn not to the Astolfo episode, but rather to the poet's extensive account of the onset of his central protagonist Orlando's *furore*. For Ariosto, if the trees and branches of epic do have a psychic resonance, it is not to be found in the often enigmatic anticipation and dread of the *Unheimliche*, but rather in the more explicit pathology of madness, vividly demonstrated by Orlando's celebrated insanity when he realizes that his beloved Angelica has run off with the foot soldier Medoro. In Canto 23, in a passage familiar to readers of epic, Orlando, searching for Angelica, happens upon a grove of trees, where the names Angelica and Medoro are inscribed in her handwriting on the tree trunks. The amorous *scritti* of the trees, then, serve collectively as a kind of perverse Tree of Knowledge, convincing (and maddening) proof of Angelica's betrayal of Orlando. But Orlando cannot bear to accept the truth of these arboreal inscriptions.[43] Whereas the trees of Virgil, Lucan, and Dante become mirrors of ontological uncertainty (of the uncanniness that arises from doubt and ambivalence), Ariosto's trees become the site of an exquisite irony at the expense of the uncanny trees of epic. No longer the site of the *Unheimliche*, the *scritti* of Ariosto's trees serve instead as the site of epistemological *certainty*; but what is particularly ironic is Orlando's desperate efforts to transform the trees into uncanny sites of doubt and uncertainty. Refusing to believe that Angelica has betrayed him, Orlando attempts several strategies of disavowal—of what can more accurately be termed a kind of Freudian process of "derealization":

Va col pensier cercando in mille modi
non creder quel ch'al suo dispetto crede:
ch'altra Angelica sia, creder si sforza,
ch'abbia scritto il suo nome in quella scorza.

(103)

[He searched in his mind for any number of excuses to reject what he could not help believing; he tried to persuade himself that it was some other Angelica who had written her name on the bark.]

Orlando then attempts to persuade himself that "Medoro" is simply an-other name for himself: "Finger questo Medoro ella si puote: / forse ch'a me questo cognome mette" [Can she perhaps be inventing this Medoro? Perhaps by this name she means me (104)].[44] Unlike the topos of the haunted wood, Ariosto's trees are "animated" not with chimerical spirits, but with the imaginative efforts of Orlando to "derealize" the truth that confronts him. When these psychic processes of derealization eventually fail and Orlando is forced to face the truth of the trees, he becomes insane, throws off his armor, smears his body with dirt, and goes on a rampage of total eco-destruction—including a savaging of the trees of the sur-rounding countryside that serves as a virtual parody of the epic topos of the destruction of the resistant tree:

> ch'un alto pino al primo crollo svelse:
> e svelse dopo il primo altri parecchi,
> come fosser finocchi, ebuli o aneti;
> e fe' il simil di querce e d'olmi vecchi,
> di faggi e d'orni e d'illici e d'abeti.
> Quel ch'un ucellator che s'apparecchi
> il campo mondo fa, per por le reti,
> dei giunchi e de le stoppie e de l'urtiche,
> facea de cerri e d'altre piante antiche.
>
> (134–35)

[at one jerk he rooted up a tall pine, after which he tore up several more as though they were so many celery-stalks. He did the same to oaks and ancient elms, to beech and ash-trees, to ilexes and firs.]

Here the epic topos of sadistic aggression against an animate wood be-comes Orlando's pathological "solution" to the problem of trees that "failed to be *not uncanny enough* to suggest the doubt and ambivalence that could have preserved his psychic wholeness. But Ariosto's character-istically detached and editorial response to Orlando's excess is, in the final analysis, simply to acknowledge that trees are the inevitable locus of madness:

> Varii gli effetti son, ma la pazzia
> è tutt'una però, che li fa uscire.
> Gli è come una gran selva, ove la via
> conviene a forza, a chi viva, fallire.
>
> (24.2)

[Various are love's effects; but from one source all issue, though they lead a different way. He is, as 'twere, a forest, where perforce who enters its re-cesses go astray.]

The trees that are carved with Angelica's *scritti* effect a linking of epic woods with the concept of poetic "truth" in ways that might have been more than a little suggestive to Ariosto's Ferrarese successor, Tasso. (For that matter, the latter poet's very name, "Torquato Tasso," or "twisted yew tree," is an *unheimlich* anticipation of the extent to which trees will become the guiding obsession of the *Gerusalemme liberata*.)[45] For Ariosto, the trees of epic are always sites of authorial control—but for Tasso, these same trees become perhaps the most uncanny and overdetermined locus in all of epic literary history.

If for Freud the uncanny, as a distinctly aesthetic concept, was, like the beautiful or the sublime, deserving of its own treatise, Tasso's two prose documents on the composition of the epic, the *Discorsi Dell'arte Poetica* (1587) and the *Discorsi del Poema Eroico* (1594), can be read together as a virtual countertreatise to Freud's essay—almost as if the poet were seeking a theory to ensure that the *Unheimliche* cannot make its repressed return in epic. In these two works, Tasso meticulously outlines his theory of epic, in which history is privileged as its proper subject matter because history is *true*. Tasso's persistent concern for what constitutes epic "truth" leads him to caution against a *gran commodità di fingere*: in effect, Tasso counsels that the psychic lures of the *Unheimliche* must be suppressed through an emphasis on the *verisimile* in epic poetry as that which is "propria ed intrinseca dell'essenza sua." One of the greatest challenges for the epic poet, as Tasso perceives it, is to achieve a harmonious joining of the *verisimile* with the potentially uncanny devices of the *maraviglioso*, a difficult poetic task never achieved by the likes of Ariosto, whose fantastic hippogryph, in Tasso's estimation, points to a poetic failure to accommodate the wondrous unobtrusively into epic. For Tasso, the *verisimile* and the *maraviglioso*, though "diversissime," must, like the genres of epic and romance, be joined together in "un'azione medesima."

Tasso's plan for his *Liberata*, then, is to transform the uncanniness of trees *(i miracoli del bosco)* into emblems of the verisimilar in epic—in effect, to counter the uncanny *translatio topos* of the eerie tree by accommodating it into that which is "propria ed intrinseca" to epic poetry. In the second book of his *Discorsi del Poema Eroico*, Tasso warns against the "incanti . . . ne la selva che ingannanò con delusioni" [the enchantments in the woods, deceiving with illusions].[46] At another point he expresses his concern that "la materia [of poetry] è simile ad una selva oscura, tenebrosa e priva d'ogni luce" [the material (of poetry) is like a dark forest, murky and without a ray of light]. Here Tasso is suggesting that if the poet does not exert a self-conscious control over the proliferation of *meraviglie* in epic, then inevitably the uncanniness of the *selva oscura* will overtake any attempt at poetic "truth." Tasso's goal for his own epic, then, is nothing less than to purge the literary history of epic of its ongoing compulsion to return to the uncanniness of animistic trees.

The extraordinary ambition of the *Liberata* can perhaps best be measured by Tasso's plan for the "delivering" of Jerusalem from the pagans. In a direct borrowing from Lucan, Tasso depicts Goffredo, leader of the Crusaders, as deciding to storm Jerusalem not immediately upon the Christian soldiers' arrival at the city's gates, but only after the careful construction of siege towers as a weapon of assault. The trees in the wood surrounding Jerusalem, then, become the strategic key to Goffredo's military decision to assault Jerusalem in a distinctly "epic" (i.e., a distinctly *Pharsalian*) way. No longer simply the uncanny, marginalized, and abandoned locus of animate mystery, the Jerusalem wood is slated by Tasso to become the pivotal site of epic victory.

As part of his self-conscious strategy to chase the uncanny *meraviglie* of epic from his trees, Tasso seeks to confine the absurd fantasies and chimeras of Virgil's Avernus wood to Plutone's hell:

> Qui mille immonde Arpie vedresti, e mille
> Centauri, e Sfingi, e pallide Gorgoni,
> molte e molte latrar voraci Scille,
> e fischiar Idre, e sibilar Pitoni,
> e vomitar Chimere atre faville,
> e Polifemi orrendi, e Gerioni;
> diversi aspetti in un confusi e misti.
>
> (IV.5)

> [Here might you see a thousand filthy Harpies and a thousand Centaurs and Sphinxes and pale Gorgons: a myriad ravenous Scyllas howling and Hydras hooting and Pythons hissing and Chimaeras belching forth black flames; and horrible Polyphemuses and Geryons; and in strange monstrosities, not elsewhere known or seen, diverse appearances confused and blended into one.][47]

In a dramatic demonstration of the "anxiety of influence" in epic, Tasso in effect banishes Virgil's entire haunted wood to hell in an authoritative and ambitious gesture of "de-animating" the highly unstable woods of the literary history of epic. Consequently, when Goffredo's axmen reach the Jerusalem wood, they exhibit none of the fearful ambivalence of Caesar's soldiers in the *De Bello Civili*:

> L'un l'altro esorta che le piante atterri,
> e faccia al bosco inusitati oltraggi.
> Caggion recise da i pungenti ferri
> le sacre palme e i frassini selvaggi.
>
> (III.75)

[One man spurs on another to cut down the trees, and to do unwonted outrages to the wood. The sacred palms fall, cut by the cleaving steel, and the woodland ashes.]

In the context of the epic topos of the haunted wood that we have been examining, the *inusitati oltraggi* inflicted by Goffredo's axmen on the Jerusalem trees assume a far-reaching significance. Throughout the literary history of epic, the topos of aggression against the animistic and resistant tree has served as the predictable site of the uncanny flourishing of narcissism—specifically the "overvaluation of one's own mental processes," whose narcissistic projections create, perhaps tautologically, the psychic space of fear and anxiety of animation. The *inusitati oltraggi* of Goffredo's axmen, however, become Tasso's own quasi-sadistic guarantor of "truth" and the banishment of narcissism in epic poetry. Because Tasso has ensured that the woods are free from spirits, the Crusaders' aggression against the trees presumably takes on not a psychic, but a solely military significance.

In so doing, Tasso believes that he has, in effect, successfully interpreted the "meaning" of the epic topos of the animate tree—and hence his attempt to write the marvels of the tree out of the literary history of epic. It is as if Tasso seeks ambitiously to annihilate the *nachträglich* retroactions of epic history and to proclaim his Jerusalem wood as the point at which the interpretation of epic can "originate." But despite the ambition of his epic poetry (despite his attempt to subsume all of epic literary history under the de-animated woods of Jerusalem), what Tasso does not fully reckon with is the ongoing persistence of literary history itself as the unconscious (the *unthought*) of interpretation—and, indeed, as the "uncanniest" of hiding places for the *Unheimliche*. As we have seen, the *Unheimliche* is always predicated on repetition; it always returns to its origins as a topos. Thus, when the wayward Tancredi is sent into the Jerusalem wood to cut down its trees for siege towers—when, in effect, the epic poet "returns" to a topos in order to annihilate it—what is left unanticipated are the consequences of the "return" of a topos to its own (oddly indestructible) dismemberment.

In Canto 13 of the *Liberata* (the same canto in the *Inferno* where Dante encounters the *uomo-pianta* delle Vigne), we come to see the *Unheimliche* as, more than ever, "the name for everything that ought to have remained secret and hidden." As part of the pagans' counterstrategy against the Christians, the Jerusalem wood now teems with the evil enchantments of the sorcerer Ismeno—enchantments that frighten Goffredo's axmen from inflicting their *inusitati oltraggi* on the trees. Tancredi, still grief-stricken from his unwitting slaughter of his beloved Clorinda on the battlefield, volunteers to cut down the trees; and thus it is encumbent on Tancredi's blow of the ax (like Caesar's and Char-lemagne's before him) to collapse the *verisimile* of epic and the *mara-viglioso* of romance into "un'azione medesima." The episode is well known to readers of epic and requires only a brief summary, for as Tan-credi enters the enchanted *selvaggio orrore*, the reader is confronted with descriptions so familiar they are virtual clichés. The wood is "inviluppato e fosco" [tangled and dark (37)], and "fremere intanto udia continuo il vento" [meanwhile he heard the wind continually moaning (40)]. When Tancredi hacks at a tall *cipresso*, the *recisa scorza*, or "split bark," bleeds, and from it issues the pained voice of Clorinda as "un indistinto gemito" [a muffled, sorrowing groan (41)]. He "tutto si raccapriccia" [is com-pletely horrified (41)]. And finally, like Aeneas, Tancredi, fearful but committed to aggression, "pur rinforza / il corpo" [even redoubles the blow (41)].

The poet's strategy is seemingly to render the *selvaggio orrore* so recog-nizably clichéd that Tancredi's fear of its animism will be interpreted as a wrongful and misguided (and narcissistic) response to the uncanny. To echo my earlier point, it is as if Tasso believes the reader, if not Tancredi, will interpret the "meaning" of an uncanny topos as that which is not *propria ed intrinsica* to the *essenza* of epic poetry. In this celebrated epi-sode, Tasso is, in effect, demanding that epic interpretation "begin" with the *end* of the *translatio topos* of the bleeding tree. But the clichés of the topos, as that which "ought to have remained secret and hidden," trans-form themselves into eloquent reminders that no "return" (especially to an animate wood) is ever a simple matter. Indeed, one could argue that it is the very predictability of these formulaic descriptions that works against Tasso. What the poet cannot fully reckon with is the possibility that the topos of sadistic aggression against the animate tree will always (uncannily) insist on its own return to the topos of the resisting branch— in this particular case, a resistance to the collapsing of the *verisimile* and the *maraviglioso* into "un'azione medesima."

Thus, of even greater psychic significance than the *micidial* Tancredi's "return" to the murder of his lover may be Tasso's own "return" to the *translatio topos* of the bleeding tree.[48] One question that the episode poses is: can a "return" ever be fully conscious? When the palms and ashes fall helplessly to the *inusitati oltraggi* of Goffredo's axmen earlier in Canto 3, Tasso should perhaps have been content with this authoritative effort to "write" the animate tree out of epic. Instead, his poetic ambition not only re-enchants the Jerusalem wood, but also dictates an ambitious but overdetermined "return" to the site of dismemberment. Tasso begins, unwittingly, to illustrate Cixous's point that the *Unheimliche* "*refers* to no more profound secret than itself."[49] The only interpretive revelation of this episode is that there may be no "meaning" other than Tasso's own decision to return to an animate wood. Among the *segni ignoti* of the tall *cipresso* that Tancredi assaults is an inscription that warns: " 'non dée guerra co' morti aver chi vive' " ("the living ought not wage war with the dead" (39)]. To wage war *co' morti* is always to blur the distinctions between the animate and the inanimate. It is, in short, to release the mysteries of the uncanny—and to enact a "return" that inevitably becomes the *unthought* of interpretation (or, in Tasso's case, the *unthought* of poetic ambition). The living *ought* not to wage war with the dead. And the *Unheimliche* trees of epic *ought* to have remained "secret and hidden." These repetitive "oughts" converge in the *selvaggio orrore* to demonstrate that a "return" to a topos is never without its psychic consequences.

But in the midst of this discussion, what has become of Felman's claim that literature is the *unconscious* of psychoanalysis? We may say that psychoanalysis explicitly meets the *translatio topos* of the bleeding tree when, in *Beyond the Pleasure Principle*, the same essay in which the author posits a "capital X" as the symbolic indeterminacy of all "metapsychological" discussions, Freud identifies the point at which Tancredi "wounds his beloved once again" as "the most moving poetic picture" of the compulsion to repeat.[50] "Moving," yes—but Tancredi's assault on the tall *cipresso* is also vastly overdetermined in ways that Freud could not have foreseen. Freud's allusion to Tasso turns to the literary history of epic for what he accepts as an unproblematic illustration of the psychic phenomenon of the repetition compulsion. But if, as Felman contends, the *unthought* of psychoanalysis is its own unexamined involvement with literature, then what Freud could not have anticipated is how uncannily overdetermined any reference to the epic topos of the bleeding tree is. Let us consider the following chronology: *Beyond the Pleasure Principle* was published a year later than "The Uncanny" (published in 1920), but the former work had already been completed at the time Freud wrote "The Uncanny." One could argue, then, that the (retroactive) *unthought* of the composition of *Beyond the Pleasure Principle* is the psychic phenomenon of the *Unheimliche*—or, to put it another way, any attempt to confront and analyze the repetition compulsion can only ever itself be uncanny. The more far-reaching implication of Freud's allusion to the *Liberata* is not simply its illustration of Tancredi's compulsion to repeat his wounding of Clorinda, but more significantly, its serving as an inadvertent reminder of Tasso's own compulsion to repeat epic's "return" to its privileged site of the *Unheimliche*, the bleeding, wounded tree. Freud's allusion is to be viewed not as a straightforward example of the repetition compulsion, but rather as a vivid demonstration of how the repetition compulsion is *itself* always overdetermined by the *Unheimliche*. Any reference to the bleeding tree of epic, any allusion to fiction as "the very strange thing," can, in the end, only serve as the unconscious of psycho-analysis itself.

In "The Uncanny" Freud writes that "the realm of phantasy depends for its effect on the fact that its content is not submitted to reality-testing."[51] But the test of the *verisimile* is precisely Tasso's goal when, in Canto 18, Rinaldo enters the *selvaggio orrore* to cut down the uncanny trees once and for all. By destroying the animated woods of Jerusalem, it is as if Tasso, in response to Canto 13's ambivalent "return" to the *Unheimliche*, attempts to eradicate fiction itself as "the very strange thing." In short, the *Unheimliche* is that which resists analysis. Like the wounded *misero tronco* that houses Clorinda, it is that which "ought to have remained hidden"—but, once returned to, cannot be dispelled with the simple blow of an ax. Throughout the literary history of epic, the uncanny *translatio topos* of the bleeding branch has no interpretive "origin" other than a repetitive return to its own dismemberment. Cixous has observed that, within the realm of the *Unheimliche*, "nothing is ever sufficiently dead"[52]—not Polydorus, not delle Vigne, not Clorinda. Put another way by Cixous, "Death will recognize us, but we shall not recognize it."[53] Or maybe we should say that a *topos* will recognize us, but we shall not recognize it—especially when the "meaning" of that topos is nothing more than its own return.

NOTES

1. *The Standard Edition of the Complete Psychological Works of Sigmund Freud*, 24 vols., trans. James Strachey et al., ed. James Strachey (London: Hogarth, 1953–74), 17:219. (All references to the works of Freud are taken from the *Standard Edition*, hereafter abbreviated as *SE*.)
2. "To Open the Question," in *Literature and Psychoanalysis: The Question of Reading: Otherwise*, ed. Shoshana Felman (Baltimore and London: Johns Hopkins University Press, 1982), 10; italics Felman's.
3. *SE* 5:530.
4. "Fiction and Its Phantoms: A Reading of Freud's *Das Unheimliche*," trans. Robert Dennomé, *New Literary History* 7:3 (1976): 547; italics Cixous's.
5. "The Uncanny," *SE* 17:219.
6. Ibid., 249.
7. "Fiction and Its Phantoms," 526.
8. For a valuable discussion of the uncanny as "a certain undecidability which affects and infects representations, motifs, themes and situations" (1132), see Samuel Weber, "The Sideshow, or: Remarks on a Canny Moment," *Modern Language Notes* 88:6 (1973): 1102–33.
9. *SE* 18:24–25.
10. An overview of previous studies of the topos of the bleeding branch in-

cludes Charles Speroni, "The Motif of the Bleeding and Speaking Trees of Dante's Suicides," *Italian Quarterly* 9:33 (1965): 44–55, and a comprehensive series of articles by William J. Kennedy: "The Problem of Allegory in Tasso's *Gerusalemme Liberata*," *Italian Quarterly* 15–16 (1972): 27–51; "Irony, Allegoresis, and Allegory in Virgil, Ovid, and Dante," *Arcadia* 7 (1972): 114–34; "Rhetoric, Allegory, and Dramatic Modality in Spenser's Fradubio Episode," *English Literary Renaissance* 3 (1973): 351–68; and "Ariosto's Ironic Allegory," *Modern Language Notes* 88 (1973): 44–67. For a more recent discussion of the topos, see Shirley Clay Scott, "From Polydorus to Fradubio: The History of a *Topos*," in *Spenser Studies*: *A Renaissance Poetry Annual, VII*, ed. Patrick Cullen and Thomas P. Roche, Jr. (New York: AMS Press, 1987), pp. 27–57.

11. *SE* 17:224; italics Freud's.

12. Ibid., 241.

13. "Fiction and Its Phantoms," 539. Cixous's analogy assumes further significance when considered in the particular context of one of Freud's case histories, where not only are we tempted to complicate the overdeterminations of the *Unheimliche* even further, but also we observe the ongoing and uncanny resonances of branches. In his "Screen Memories," Freud quotes from a patient's account of a particularly vivid memory of a child "breaking off a branch from a tree while he was on a walk and of his being helped to do it by someone" (*SE* 3:319). As Freud writes, "I should be prepared to give an interpretation, if only the person concerned had not been a Frenchman . . . since what provides the intermediate step between a screen memory and what it conceals is likely to be a verbal expression. In German "to pull one out" is a very common vulgar term for masturbation. The scene would then be putting back into early childhood a seduction to masturbation—someone was helping him to do it—which in fact occurred at a later period.' " (319).

14. *SE* 17:219.

15. All citations of the *Aeneid* are from *Vergili Maronis Opera*, ed. F. A. Hirtzel (1900; reprint ed., Oxford: Oxford University Press, 1966). The English verse translation is from Allen Mandelbaum's *The Aeneid of Virgil* (New York: Bantam Books, 1971).

16. Because Polydorus was murdered for his wealth, Bernardus Silvestris glosses the name Polydorus as *multa amaritudo*, or "great bitterness": "Thus Polydorus is buried in Thrace because there is great bitterness involved in avarice—for what is more bitter than the greedy person . . ." (*Commentary on The First Six Books of Virgil's "Aeneid*," trans., intro. Earl G. Schreiber and Thomas E. Maresca [Lincoln and London: University of Nebraska Press, 1979], 20). Bernardus's allegorical interpretation of Polydorus's pain as the "great bitterness" that comes from greed seems calculated to repress the uncanny psychic valences of his return as a broken branch.

17. The initial description of the Golden Bough is preceded by the Sibyl's warning about death: ". . . facilis descensus Averni—/ noctes atque dies patet atri ianua Ditis—" [easy—/ the way that leads into Avernus: day / and night the door of darkest Dis is open (126–27)]. In this context, it is worth noting the extent to which the threshold of Virgil's Avernus is implicated within psychoanalysis. Avernus serves as the backdrop for Lacan's correction of Poe's memory in his

"Seminar on 'The Purloined Letter.'" In Poe's story, the detective Dupin, criticizing the unwary arrogance of the Minister who still believes he possesses the Queen's letter, claims that the Minister was premature to boast about his *facilis descensus Averni*" (6.126). In an editorial note, Lacan mistakenly "corrects" Poe's grammar when quoting from the Sibyl's speech to Aeneas with the curt words, "Virgil's line reads: *facilis descensus Averno*" (68n40).

18. *SE* 17:223.

19. Charles Paul Segal, "*Aeternum per Saecula Nomen*, the Golden Bough and the Tragedy of History: Part I," *Arion* 4:4 (1965): 620–21.

20. For more on the paradoxical nature of the Golden Bough, see Segal's essay. Although he never places the Golden Bough explicitly in the Freudian context of the uncanny, much of Segal's essay is a discussion of its contradictory enigmas. See also Robert A. Brooks, who has described the bough as embodying "life-in-death" ("*Discolor Aura*: Reflections on the Golden Bough," *American Journal of Philology* 74 [1953]: 271).

21. *SE* 17:236.

22. The oddly momentary resistance of the Golden Bough is remarked upon by Segal, who observes: "All the words—*corripit, extemplo, refringit*—suggest sudden, violent action and peremptory force" (633).

23. *SE* 17:235.

24. Ibid., 240.

25. Ibid., 233.

26. R. G. Austin, *P. Vergili Maronis. Aeneidos: Liber Sextvs* (Oxford: Clarendon Press, 1977), 201.

27. *Ovid: Metamorphoses*, ed., trans. Frank Justus Miller (Cambridge: Harvard University Press, 1916). The English translation is *Ovid: Metamorphoses*, trans. Rolfe Humphries (Bloomington: Indiana University Press, 1958).

28. *SE* 17, 240.

29. As the epic poet of Rome's civil wars between Pompey and Julius Caesar, Lucan can be described as an "anti-Virgil," the poet of Nero as opposed to Augustus—and a poet decidedly cynical toward the unity of a Roman *imperium*.

30. All references to Lucan are from *M. Annaei Lvcani: Belli Civilis*, ed. A. E. Housman (Oxford: Basil Blackwell, 1926). The English translation is *Lucan's Civil War*, trans. P. F. Widdows (Bloomington and Indianapolis: Indiana University Press, 1988).

31. *SE* 17:237.

32. All references to the *Inferno* are from *The Divine Comedy of Dante Alighieri*, ed. John D. Sinclair (New York: Oxford University Press, 1939).

33. The particular hideousness of Dante's treatment of the topos is noted by Leo Spitzer, who observes that in the single phrase "usciva inseme / parole e sangue" [there came / words and blood together (43–44)], "the two sense-data are fused together: there gushes forth a stream of 'speech-endowed blood,' of 'bleeding screams'—a hideous revelation of the hybrid" ("Speech and Language in *Inferno XIII*," in *Dante: A Collection of Critical Essays*, ed. John Freccero [Englewood Cliffs, NJ: Prentice-Hall, 1965], 81).

34. Spitzer argues that delle Vigne's mangled branch is, in effect, far more uncanny than the torn myrtle of Polydorus: ". . . this hybrid creation in Dante is

more *monstrously* hybrid than anything to be encountered among the ancients" (81). More recently, Jeremy Tambling writes that nature in Canto 13 of the *Inferno* "is harsher, more pagan, and resists metamorphosis into something more natural . . ." (*Dante and Difference: Writing in the "Commedia"* [Cambridge and New York: Cambridge University Press, 1988], 58).

35. It is worth noting here the pun on branches (or "vines") that constitutes delle Vigne's name.

36. In her excellent discussion of what she terms the "polysemousness of language" and its resulting ambiguity for allegory, Maureen Quilligan argues that "Vergil's reference to an extremely unlikely mythological event in his own poem, which he then insists Dante ought to have believed, posits the question: in what way are poetic fictions true?" (*The Language of Allegory: Defining the Genre* [Ithaca and London: Cornell University Press, 1979], 107). I would add that although Virgil would appear to have had the last word in this epistemological debate, Dante overgoes his epic predecessor in this struggle to determine who "owns" the poetic "truth" of the trees. Because delle Vigne *did* exist as a real historical figure (as chief counsellor to Frederick II of Sicily), and because delle Vigne *did* take his own life, the literary result is nothing less than an ambiguous moment of "truth," whereby "fictive" history is being used to bolster the credibility of Virgil's "historical" fiction in order to demonstrate that human beings *can* be transformed into trees. Virgil's claim to delle Vigne that Dante required a testing of one of the *Aeneid*'s more prominent *meraviglie* is noteworthy as, in effect, Dante's Virgil is implicating all poetic endeavor as unreliable and deceptive, even as he writes about "real" man-trees. Put simply, in the Wood of the Suicides, poetic "truth" resides in the freedom of the imagination to make a tree something it is not.

37. *SE* 17:244.

38. "Fiction and Its Phantoms," 544; italics Cixous's.

39. Ibid., 540.

40. As William J. Kennedy observes of the episode, ". . . Ariosto's portrayal of Astolfo's plight entails no tortured agony or painful bloodshed, partly because the circumstance is played for fun . . ." ("Ariosto's Ironic Allegory," *Modern Language Notes* 88:1 [1973]: 47).

41. All references to the *Orlando furioso* are taken from *Ludovico Ariosto: Orlando Furioso*, ed. Lanfranco Caretti (Turin: Einaudi, 1966). The English prose translation is *Ludovico Ariosto: Orlando Furioso*, trans. Guido Waldman (London: Oxford University Press, 1974).

42. I would argue that Ariosto's "return" to the uncanny is enacted not in the *Furioso*, but rather in its troubled and fragmented continuation, the *Cinque Canti*. In Book 2 (in a passage obviously influenced by Lucan), Ariosto describes a Bohemian forest that has been enchanted by Medea:

. . . era una antica
selva di tassi e di fronzuti cerri,
che mai sentito colpo d'inimica
secure non avea né d'altri ferri.

(101)

[. . . there was an ancient forest of yew trees and leafy oaks, which had never felt the blow of an unfriendly axe nor of any other blade.]

Ariosto's description carries us back, of course, to Lucan and his animated wood:

e per potervi star meglio sicura,
di spirti intorno ogn'arbor avea pieno,
che rispingean con morti e con percosse
chi d'ir nei suoi segreti ardito fosse.

(105)

[and in order to feel even more secure there, she filled every tree around with spirits, to repel with death and blows whoever was bold enough to enter its secret places.]

Like Lucan's Caesar, Charlemagne orders his soldiers to cut down the trees, but they are afraid of the enchanted wood. Again, like Caesar, Charlemagne hacks at the trees until his soldiers finally join in, and, predictably, the trees fall in heavy resistance:

Cade l'eccelso pin, cade il funebre
cipresso, cade il venenoso tasso,
cade l'olmo atto a riparar che l'ebre
viti non giaccian sempre a capo basso;
cadono, e fan cadendo le latebre
cedere agli occhi et alle gambe il passo.

(125)

[The lofty pine falls, the mournful cypress falls, the poisonous yew falls, the elm falls, fit to keep drunken vines from lying face down upon the ground; they fall and in falling open up hidden recesses to the eyes and pathways to the legs.]

It is in this episode, far more than in the Astolfo episode, that Ariosto reveals his inclination to return to an uncanny topos. (All references to the *Cinque Canti* are from *Cinque Canti*, ed. Lanfranco Caretti [Turin: Einaudi, 1977]. The English translation is from the unpublished manuscript of David Sheers.)

43. For an excellent account of this episode as Orlando's crisis of self-knowledge, see Albert Russell Ascoli, *Ariosto's Bitter Harmony: Crisis and Evasion in the Italian Renaissance* (Princeton: Princeton University Press, 1987), 322–26. As Ascoli writes, "How strange to discover that it is not the success but the *failure* of reference which we often desire . . ." (324).

44. In his late autobiographical essay, "A Disturbance of Memory on the Acropolis" (1936), Freud defines "derealization" as a particular form of denial or disavowal. It is a "momentary feeling," an attempt to convince oneself that "'*What I see here is not real*'" (*SE* 22:244; italics Freud's).

45. The poet's last name is also a direct echo of the "tassi" that will fall to the axes of Goffredo's men in Book III.76.

46. All references to Tasso's prose are taken from *Torquato Tasso: Prose*, ed. Ettore Mazzali (Milan and Naples: Riccardo Ricciardi Editore, 1959). The En-

glish translation of the *Discorsi del Poema Eroico* is *Torquato Tasso: Discourses on the Heroic Poem*, trans. Mariella Cavalchini and Irene Samuel (Oxford: Clarendon Press, 1973).

47. All references to the *Gerusalemme Liberata* are taken from *Torquato Tasso: Gerusalemme Liberata*, ed. Lanfranco Caretti (Turin: Einaudi, 1971). The English prose translation is *Torquato Tasso: Jerusalem Delivered*, trans. Ralph Nash (Detroit: Wayne State University Press, 1987).

48. For a detailed treatment of Tancredi's "murder" of Clorinda as a psychic drama of narcissism and melancholia, see my chapter on Tasso in my book *Translations of Power: Narcissism and the Unconscious in Epic History* (Ithaca: Cornell University Press, 1992).

49. "Fiction and Its Phantoms," 543.

50. *SE* 18:22. In her brilliant, ground-breaking chapter "Torquato Tasso: The Trial of Conscience," Margaret W. Ferguson has argued for the episode of Tancredi's wounding of Clorinda as reflecting a kind of intertextual *agon* between Tasso and his epic predecessor Ariosto. Ferguson sees "an analogy between his [Tasso's] authorial act of imitation and the hero's act of wounding a tree" (*Trials of Desire: Renaissance Defenses of Poetry* [New Haven and London: Yale University Press, 1983], 127). What Ferguson emphasizes is the extent to which Tasso's "anxiety of influence" is (uncannily) enacted over the bleeding tree. (Given Ariosto's pseudo-comic treatment of the bleeding tree episode, I would argue instead for Lucan as the more immediate source for Tasso's "anxiety of influence" in regard to the animate trees of epic.)

51. *SE* 17:249.

52. "Fiction and Its Phantoms," 543.

53. Ibid.

WRITING THE SPECULAR SON

JONSON, FREUD, LACAN, AND
THE (K)NOT
OF MASCULINITY

DAVID LEE MILLER

> What is there yet in a son
> To make a father dote, rave or run mad?
> *(The Spanish Tragedy* [1601]

MY SUBJECT in this essay is the peculiar anguish of an insistent dream. It is hard to define this dream, for it has no one text but insists within the symbolic order of Western culture, sustained there by the mortal fascination of many dreamers. A cultural propensity, it seizes on subjects as the means of its realization. Yet if it has no one text the dream does possess a distinct character. It is the essential dream of a culture founded by Abraham and refounded by Jesus on the sacrifice of the son's body to the Father's word. It is a father's dream about the death of his son.

My interest is not just in the dream but in its haunting power: the feelings it arouses and their spectral ability to rematerialize in responsive witnesses. A principal effect of this power is the cultural transference of masculinity. If gender is "performatively produced" then any of a culture's discourses may occasion its reproduction. The dream of the spectral son is perhaps the most resonant occasion for a distinctly homosocial masculine pathos, a pathos that works (in Lacan's favored metaphor) to tighten the "knot" of gender.[1]

Only the texts through which it passes can convey the fascination that carries the dream along a chain of dreamers. We will consider Ben Jonson's "On my First Sonne," Freud's *The Interpretation of Dreams*, and Lacan's *Four Fundamental Concepts*. All three are marked as secondary revision of patriarchy's intolerable dream thought, for the acts of writing or saying that produce these texts do so in an effort to recuperate the pathos of the dream by cinching the (k)not of masculine gender.

BEN JONSON, BORN DEAD

In the spring of 1603 Queen Elizabeth died, and James VI of Scotland traveled south to London to be crowned. He arrived in May along with the bubonic plague. Ben Jonson meanwhile had left the city. It is uncertain whether this was due to the king's progress or that of the pestilence; it was probably both. The country estate of Sir Robert Cotton, at Conington in Huntingdonshire, was a good place to be during plague time, when the mortality rate in neighborhoods like St. Giles, Cripplegate (where Jonson's family lived) could easily exceed 50 percent.[2] But Cotton's library was also an excellent place to be during the planning stages of the Jacobean succession: as David Riggs observes, Cotton (knighted by James on May 11) was an important figure in "the intellectual avant-garde of the new monarchy," and if Jonson wanted to seize opportunities for patronage opening under the new regime, there was probably no better way to position himself than by joining William Camden and others at Conington (97).

Surviving the plague was virtually a class privilege in early modern London: "Members of the lower classes," writes Riggs, "were forbidden to leave the city; they had no choice but to remain and die" (95). Joshua Scodel quotes "the official prayer for plague in 1603" as prescribing fatherly care: "the chief remedy to be expected from man is that everyone would be a magistrate to himself and his whole family."[3] This was, however, a double-edged prescription. As Riggs observes, "Any city dweller who had access to a country house could be virtually certain of escaping the disease by vacating the town. The mortality bills for the great epidemic of 1665, to cite an extreme case, list over 100,000 Londoners but do not include a single magistrate, courtier, or wealthy merchant" (93–95). In this sense Jonson was too much a magistrate to his family. In the same year, 1603, his friend John Florio published a translation of Montaigne that laid out the implicit logic of his choice:

> There are few men given unto Poesie, that would not esteeme it for a greater honour, to be the fathers of *Virgils Ænidos*, than the godliest boy in *Rome*, and that would not rather endure the losse of the one than the perishing of the other. . . . Nay, I make a great question, whether *Phidias* or any other excellent Statuary, would as highly esteeme, and dearely love the preservation, and successfull continuance of his naturall children, as he would an exquisite and match-lesse-wrought Image, that with long study, and diligent care he had perfected according unto art.[4]

Jonson had confronted the "great question" less drastically in a poem published the year before, about the time he separated from his wife. The poet depicts himself spending "halfe my nights, and all my dayes, / Here in a cell, to get a darke, pale face, / To come forth worth the ivy, or the bayes"; it is hard not to agree that "compulsive work habits" were part of what alienated Jonson from his wife, and thus from his children.[5] Yet according to Florio's Montaigne, "what we engender by the minde . . . are brought forth by a far more noble part, than the corporall, and are more our owne. We are both father and mother together in this generation" (85). In these terms, Jonson would have been sacrificing domestic fatherhood for a metaphysical paternity in which he and his writings comprised a nuclear family in one person, an unconscious parody of trinitarian theology.[6] Within the space of domestic estrangement lay a gap of literary ambition and class status that was relentlessly gendered by this ideology of procreativity. The journey to Conington first widened this gap and stressed its overdetermination, then brought home Montaigne's "great question." Sometime after arriving Jonson dreamed that his oldest son had died. The next day he awoke and found it true. Years later he reconstructs the dream for William Drummond:

> When the king came in England, at that time the pest was in London. He being in the country at S[i]r Robert Cotton's house with old Camden, he saw in a vision his eldest son, th[e]n a child and at London, appear unto him w[i]t[h] the mark of a bloody cross on his forehead, as if it had been cutted w[i]t[h] a sword; at which, amazed, he prayed unto God; and in the morning he came to Mr Camden's chamber to tell him, who persuaded him it was but an apprehension of his fantasy, at which he should not be dejected. In the meantime comes th[e]r[e] letters from his wife of the death of th[a]t boy in the plague. He appeared to him, he said, of a manly shape, and of th[a]t growth that he thinks he shall be at the resurrection.[7]

In time of plague, a red cross nailed to the door marked households under quarantine. As Riggs observes, "in Jonson's dream the red cross (the 'day residue' of Freudian dream analysis) was transposed from the door of the house in London onto the boy's forehead 'as if it had been cutted with a sword'" (95). The sword's edge leaves its mark also in the break between the last two sentences of the passage in Drummond. We cannot be certain whether Jonson or his auditor is the "author" of this effect, but the news of Benjamin's death punctuates the narrative sharply: the following sentence ("He appeared to him . . .") reverts to the apparition, then leaps forward to the narrative present with "he said" before turning back once more to close the gap with a wishful afterthought.

Benjamin was, in his father's words, "exacted" by fate on the very day he became a "boy" for his culture: his seventh birthday. Scodel writes, "In early modern England seven was considered the crucial age of transition at which children became subject to gender-specific behavior and boys left the feminine, nurturing world of their mothers, nurses, and school dames in order to enter the masculine, disciplined world of fathers and schoolmasters" (244–45). He adds, "Jonson himself probably entered Westminster School and discovered his spiritual father, Camden, at the traditional age of seven" (245). It was at Westminster too that Jonson first met Robert Cotton. Clearly, then, the trip to Conington evoked for Ben Jonson the circumstances under which the masculine world of learning, and with it social advancement, had opened to him for the first time. In Cotton's library he was returning to the scene of his nativity in manhood and letters—returning, then, to a threshold he was still trying to cross, in pursuit of a status his birth had not conferred. But he found himself resuming this transition on his *son's* seventh birthday. On the day *he* should have left it, the younger Jonson remained behind in a venue at once lower-class, feminine, and deadly. And he died.

In the dream he appears full grown. This is a comforting thought, suggesting the Resurrection. But behind the wistful closing remark to Drummond lies a dark opposite: the father's compulsion to usurp his son's transition to "manly" status, the fear that this wish might be too literally granted, and a guilty anxiety lest the son return, magnified and vengeful, for a ghostly squaring of accounts. The cross he wears is similarly a mark of contradiction: transforming the sign of the plague into a bleeding incision, almost a *stigmatum*, Jonson's dream condenses the ideas of writing, swordplay, and crucifixion. The dream does not say who wields the terrible instrument that marks the boy for sacrifice, but the implication is clear: Benjamin is the child of his father's right hand. In his apparition the dream evokes another son who died to glorify the Father. Christianity tells us Christ died for our sake and because of our sin; but it also tells us that *someone* had to die to preserve the integrity of the Father's law, which would otherwise be thrown into contradiction. Christ was crucified not only for our sins, but also in the name of the Father.

Jonson's biological father died a month before he was born. These two events, his own birth and his father's death, are strikingly condensed in Jonson's description of himself as "Posthumous born" (Riggs, 9). In 1598, as he lay under sentence of death for killing Gabriel Spencer—with a rapier—Jonson converted to Catholicism, renegotiating his relationship with the heavenly Father. He got off by pleading "benefit of clergy," escaping the hangman's noose through a loophole in the law, but his thumb was branded with the letter T ("for Tyburn," Riggs explains, "where he would have been hanged" [53]). Are the rapier and the T-shaped brand not recollected in the thought of a cross "cutted with a sword" into a grown boy's forehead? The unhappy conjunction of paternity with mortality comes back to haunt him now as though his son's death were the price of his own survival, much as his father's death had been the price of his birth, or Christ's death the price of his salvation. It is a blasphemous and unfatherly thought: that the mortal child was crucified for his father's symbolic identity.

Jonson's poignant reference to the Resurrection both repudiates and expresses this thought. The dead son's "manly shape" is at once the "growth" he never attained and the menacing form in which he will—and does—rise from the grave. The apparition in the dream embodies a terrible accusation that "the father will face again at the end of time, for the thought of Resurrection brings with it that of Judgment Day. In its unspoken indictment the dream takes on the sword's cutting force. No wonder if the stricken dreamer prays to God, or if on awakening he turns to that other "spiritual father" Camden. For what could he have said to the manly child?

The dream cuts like a sword. This is partly a retroactive pathos: the dream is more terrible because it came true. Through his death, and through the temporal detour of writing ("in the meantime comes there letters"), the preternaturally manly boy defeats the fatherly Camden. We can rationalize premonitions but not decrease their fascination: Jonson's dream gives the uncanny impression of an effect that anticipates its cause.

It can do so only if what it heralds has already happened. For Jonson in 1603, it clearly had. Benjamin's premature manhood in the dream, a variation on the literary topos of the *puer senex*, carries with it the thought that the proper sequence of things has been violated. The year before, Jonson had used this motif to commemorate Salomon Pavy, attributing the boy's untimely death to his skill at playing old men: Sal projected a dramatic illusion stronger than fate, but far from enabling a triumph over death this artistic coup only hastens it. Beneath the sad wit of the compliment lies a bitter reality. "Like many of the Chapel Children," Riggs explains, "Salomon Pavy had been kidnapped by Nathaniel Giles, the Queen's choirmaster, who forcibly abducted him into the company at the age of ten. The children and their parents had no legal redress—the boys were impressed on the authority of the Queen. . . . Sall was old before his time; his life was a performance wherein he was doomed to play a part devised by cynical adults" (91–92). In Jonson's poem death completes and, as it were, perfects the premature adulthood forced on children abducted for royal art. The Fates reenact the choirmaster's kidnapping in the name of a still higher authority, and "Heaven," like the queen, "vowes to keepe him."

The blow of fate comes to the spectral son anticipated always by its own echo. Withheld from manhood by death yet ushered into it prematurely by art, Benjamin Jonson and Salomon Pavy are temporal conundrums. Between themselves they twin the chronology inscribed in each, by which death precedes life like a script to be enacted under duress or a sword carving the text of enforced piety into the body. Both deaths echo an antecedent fantasy that drew Jonson repeatedly toward the imaginary figure of the dead child. "All his life," writes Ann Barton, "Jonson responded with what for the sixteenth and seventeenth centuries was abnormal intensity to the deaths of children, those of other people as well as his own."[8] Riggs compares him to Dickens: Jonson "could identify with lost children because he too had known misfortune at an early age" (88). A very early age, if he was "Posthumous born."

Riggs and Barton have traced the preoccupation with dead children and grieving parents that runs through Jonson's life and work during the years 1601 to 1603. Among the most striking examples are five additions to *The Spanish Tragedy* that "Barton attributes to Ben Jonson. "The author of the additions," she writes, "has only one preoccupation: fatherhood, and the difficulty of coming to terms with the death of a child. It is a most Jonsonian concern" (19). Riggs cites the closing lines of the "Apologetical Dialogue," where Jonson announces enigmatically, "There's something come into my thought, / That must, and shall be sung" (87). "Although he declines to say what it is that has 'come into my thought' at the close of the 'Apologetical Dialogue,'" Riggs observes, "he leaves a conspicuous trail of evidence, and all of it leads back to the figure of a dead child" (88–89). Riggs believes it was the death of Jonson's daughter Mary that caused "this latent empathy with the dead child" to "stir his imagination during the autumn of 1601" (88). It may well have been. But the dead child is *already* latent in the poet's mind, where it stirs more than empathy. In the epitaph for Mary, her death forces Jonson to confront the contradictions in his conception of fatherhood. Ann Lauinger remarks that Jonson's inability to mourn through empathy excludes him from the consolation imagined for Mary's mother: "Fatherhood, this poem implies, augments the father's sense of self; his creation augments his identity, and his relation to his child includes a component of personal power. Motherhood, on the other hand, depends more on empathy and submerges the mother's sense of self in the other, the child."[9] In contrast to the sense of exclusion in "On my first Daughter," Jonson enters with magnificent empathy into the unhinged grief of Kyd's Hieronimo. It is as if a sense of generically masculine bereavement preceded Mary's death, which therefore elicits emotions in Jonson for which it is neither the source nor quite the proper occasion. Kyd's filial tragedy (a popular favorite, somewhat dated by the turn of the century) offers a suggestive image for this prevenient text of masculine grief. It seems to have offered Jonson a compelling occasion for imagining bereavement. If he *was* responding to Mary's death in revising *The Spanish Tragedy*, then his response transforms her death completely, returning compulsively to the question he wrote for Hieronimo: "What is there *yet in a son* / To make a father dote, rave or run mad?"[10]

There is "yet in a son," insistent, ineradicable, the uncanny causality of a death that from the first is always happening again. Such causality cannot arise from a unique event. We may uncover some childhood experience of helplessness or isolation that brings home with a shock the fact of dependency, some seemingly random injury that registers as punitive. Yet whatever blow of circumstance delivers the existential shock of mortality, it can only *retroactively* be experienced as having done so. It comes as a shock because we were so unprepared; shock becomes trauma as we assimilate the blow, apprehending it as having been *caused*. The event is thus belatedly grasped as the occasion but not the cause of the trauma. The cause is something else, something that was already there, waiting, when the occasion arrived, a tendency or even an inevitability—fate itself—perversely given over to accident. This reversal of causality condenses the event and its subjective aftereffect into a compound imaginary form; it collapses the two moments in order to reverse them. In this sense the trauma is always, like Jonson himself, "Posthumous born."

What I am calling the "specular son" is an avatar of the trauma, a hieroglyph of uncanny causality, and a resident specter of the masculine imaginary. This specter appears to Jonson in his dream, and the opening lines of "On my First Sonne" are an impossible imaginary speech act addressed to it:

> Farewell, thou child of my right hand, and joy;
>   My sinne was too much hope of thee, lov'd boy,
> Seven yeeres tho'wert lent to me, and I thee pay,
>   Exacted by thy fate, on the just day.
> O, could I loose all father, now. For why
>   Will man lament the state he should envie?
> To have so soone scap'd worlds, and fleshes rage,
>   And, if no other miserie, yet age?
> Rest in soft peace, and, ask'd, say here doth lye
>   BEN. JONSON his best piece of *poetrie*.
> For whose sake, hence-forth, all his vowes bee such,
>   As what he loves may never like too much.
>
> (Herford & Simpson 8:41)

Commentators have described the possessive and deeply narcissistic love expressed in this epitaph.[11] But as a figure of temporal reversal the specular son undermines the distinction between self and other on which these judgments rest. The poem is marked by its yearning resistance to such obliteration: when Jonson writes "O, could I loose all father, now," the conditional verb betrays his longing to give up paternity even as it laments his inability to do so.

Scodel sees the poem as compensatory: it provides the burial monument and ritual that the child, as a plague victim, probably did not receive; it makes Jonson imaginatively present at the scene from which he was absent (so present, he excludes the mother who *was* there); and it makes him the agent of an action ("I thee pay") rather than the passive victim of an event he learns about only belatedly. To this I would add that the poem makes Jonson the *author* of Benjamin's death, and thus, reflexively, of his own. "Farewell" is the first, not the last, word of a poem in which Jonson "writes" the spectral son by inscribing himself in the form of Benjamin's absence. Lauinger's comment on the epitaph for Mary applies to this one as well: "To submit fully to the will of heaven and to resign his local fatherhood in favor of the divine paternity must have seemed to Jonson like embracing his own extinction" (226). "Embracing his own extinction" seems to me exactly what Jonson does in "On my First Sonne," with this qualification: the poem is his way not just of "embracing" but of seeking to *author* his own extinction. The impulse to master fate in this way bespeaks a wish to untie the temporal knot of the trauma by repeating its inversion of cause and effect, going back to reenact deliberately, knowingly, the blow for which one had been so unprepared—and by going back, to take possession of it, to inscribe oneself as author in the empty space of the absent cause.

Benjamin's death is not his own but his father's: it punishes the *father's* sin; it signifies *his* conditional rather than absolute tenure on fatherhood. It also turns the father back into a son, as he stands before the absolute Father humbled, reminded of the wound he was born having suffered. The poem addresses its poignant salutation to the boy, but the father's relation to his son is quickly subsumed by his stance toward God: "I thee pay," he writes—not I pay *to* you (as your due) the fatherly care you lacked; but I pay *you*, like money or a gift, to the eternal paradigm of fatherhood in recognition of His absolute claim. Cast in the second person, this sentence is as exacting as fate: a pitiless reminder that Benjamin is not a boy, but a dead boy—the child not of Jonson's marriage but of his right hand.

The closing lines of the poem lower its transaction from heaven to earth, as the son mediates now between the father and an anonymous questioner. But the child is still caught up in an exchange between others. The apostrophe is at its thinnest, the contradictory incoherence of the fictional address at its bleakest, in the sheer impossibility of the speech act imagined for his voice. It is a common error to attribute the final lines to Benjamin; they are "spoken," if at all, only by the father who tells a dead child what to say on that inconceivable occasion when it will "speak."

The formulaic tag of monumental inscription, "Here doth lye," reminds us with laconic force that death, writing, and the author-father have all in their ways preempted the phantom "voice" of the dead child. Scodel observes that Jonson's use of the "ask'd, say" formula echoes Spenser's envoi to *The Shepheardes Calender*, and therefore "emphasizes that his seeming address to his son is really a figure for his confrontation with his own written words" (253). We might add that the son's seeming address to the unnamed asker radically disfigures the topos of epitaph, and loses all father in the bargain. The commonplace "here doth lye" is wrested into local habitation by the audacious substitution of poem for child. The fictional "here" of the unerected tombstone fades retroactively before the literal space of words on a page, as the poem abandons the lost body of the dead boy to commemorate itself, to commemorate its own commemoration. The message to be conveyed is addressed, finally, neither to the child nor to the supposed questioner, but to the grieving father from whom it issues: "For whose sake, hence-forth, all his vowes bee such, / As what he loves may never like too much."

Benjamin's death is reinscribed in the epitaph as his appropriation in the name of the Father, a taking-possession in which the poet seeks to become himself the son of his writing hand.[12] Jonson was always, in a profound sense, his own first son, and this poem performs the impossible act of inscription by which he intends to take possession of his own dispossession by death. It *is*, after all, "his best piece of poetrie": Jonson knew this, and said so with stunning candor. We know it too, even as we read his boast. He would name two more sons Benjamin, but only the children of Jonson's right hand would survive. His consolation was that of Montaigne's exclusive maker: his name lived on through the "Sons of Ben"—heirs of the letter, begotten through the textual inversions by which Ben Jonson, "Posthumous born," gave birth to his own death.

FREUD: "THIS MOVING DREAM"

If Jonson's desire to write the specular son figures his resistance to death, it does so by apprehending death as the dream's uncanny priority, or what I call its *insistence*. Almost three hundred years separate Jonson's dream from Freud's, yet the parallels between them are detailed and unmistakable. They include the figures of the dead child and the guilty father—present this time to witness the death, but still unable to prevent it; the question of voice, of who speaks or falls silent; the wound to the forehead; the topos of the *puer senex*; the temporal structure of the trauma, with its inversions of causal sequence; the struggle to *write* the dream as a resistance to its insistent force; and the tendency to rewrite the female or ungendered child specifically as a *son*, which shows this resistance retying in spite of itself the insistent (k)not of masculinity.

The Interpretation of Dreams is a kind of unwritten autobiography, filled with Freud's own fantasies and marked by the reticence with which he divulges them. Often his dreams are intriguing in ways the analysis refuses to touch on. Among the most intriguing, however, is a dream reported to him by one of his patients:

> The preliminaries to this model dream were as follows. A father had been watching beside his child's sick-bed for days and nights on end. After the child had died, he went into the next room to lie down, but left the door open so that he could see from his bedroom into the room in which his child's body was laid out, with tall candles standing round it. An old man had been engaged to keep watch over it, and sat beside the body murmuring prayers. After a few hours' sleep, the father had a dream that *his child was standing beside his bed, caught him by the arm and whispered to him reproachfully, "Father, don't you see I'm burning?"* He woke up, noticed a bright glare of light from the next room, hurried into it and found that the old watchman had dropped off to sleep and that the wrappings and one of the arms of his beloved child's dead body had been burned by a lighted candle that had fallen on them.[13]

Freud uses this dream to open the seventh chapter of his study. Having set forth in detail the principles of dream-formation, he seeks in the final chapter to explain the generic qualities that make dreaming so different from waking life. He does so by elaborating a speculative model of the mental "apparatus" together with a hypothesis about how this apparatus functions differently in dreams than it does in conscious perception. To introduce the discussion he chooses a striking and enigmatic dream that nevertheless "raises no problem of interpretation and the meaning of which is obvious" (549). He needs a hook, something to catch the reader by the arm but not draw him off into a long interpretation. A dream, then, whose striking features will not be idiosyncratic but generic, since it is the generic qualities of dreaming to which he wants now to turn our attention. He needs a dream that belongs to no one in particular, a dream that is everyone's: "this model dream."

The dream of the burning child is a father's dream, but it is not Freud's. It was reported to him by a woman patient. Yet the dream was not hers either. She heard it in a lecture, and carried the dream from doctor to doctor. "Its actual source," writes Freud, "is still unknown to me." Then he adds: "Its content made an impression on the lady, and she proceeded to 're-dream' it, that is, to repeat some of its elements in a dream of her own, so that, by taking it over in this way, she might express her agreement with it on one particular point" (547). Freud says no more about this lady. We can only wonder. What sort of impression did it make on her? Which elements did she redream, and why? On what "particular point" did she not only agree but feel a need to *express* her agreement? Was the wish she expressed in any way bound up with the desire that carried her to a lecture on dream interpretation in the first place? Was that desire in turn bound up with her transference onto Freud, or with the countertransference?[14] Did she in any sense redream the dream in order to produce it for her analyst, in response to a desire she sensed or imagined in him?

"Its content made an impression on the lady." This content concerns the death of a child: it is a father's dream. Why does a woman in analysis redream a father's dream of loss in order to *express her agreement with it?* Does she do so to please the father to whom she bears the dream? The father, perhaps, *for* whom she bears it? The father of dream interpretation as such, whose writing gave birth to an institution that, even more than his children, came to bear his name?

Freud does not answer these questions. In his account the lady vanishes, her secret mission accomplished. She does so in order for Freud himself to take over the narrative, expressing his agreement with it on one particular point. The dream thus passes through a chain of dreamers. The unnamed lecturer from whom the woman heard it had already taken it over to make a point. Freud's patient does the same, and so again does Freud. All three are in agreement, for "the explanation of this moving dream is simple enough and, so my patient told me, was correctly given by the lecturer" (548). This moving dream, moving from dreamer to dreamer along a chain of corroboration, leaves us wondering finally who is dreaming whom. Is the dream dreaming its dreamers as they dream it? What "peculiar feature" makes it so mobile and so apt to elicit agreement?

For some reason Freud does not tell us; he defers the exposition the dream was supposed to introduce. Something is deeply amiss in the argumentative sequence of Chapter 7. No sooner has Freud identified the "new path" we must follow than he senses a need to be wary, "to pause and look around, to see whether in the course of our journey up to this point we have overlooked anything of importance." And indeed we have. A fearful obstacle arises, "a difficulty which we have not hitherto considered but which is nevertheless capable of cutting the ground from under all our efforts at interpreting dreams" (549). This mortal blow must be warded off. A long digression intervenes before we can resume our journey in the confidence of "having now repelled the objections that have been raised against us, or having at least indicated where our defensive weapons lie" (571).

Such is the path by which Freud approaches his model of "the mental apparatus." Now at last he can tell us the peculiar feature (peculiar, yet also generic) that "calls for explanation." The dream illustrates "the essential characteristics that differentiate dreams so strikingly from waking life": it possesses an eerie sensory intensity, the hallucinatory hyperreality so peculiar to dreams; and it represents an expected, hypothetical, or desired reality as *present*, invested with the full force of that eerie intensity. Over and above the interpretation of the dream, its intensity "calls" for explanation. Father, it asks, don't you see I'm burning?

The problem is one of sequence. Freud warns us in introducing his model of the mind that although his metaphors give an impression of spatial order, the important point is the way an excitation passes through the various systems of the apparatus "in a particular *temporal* sequence" (575). This sequence begins with sensory perception and ends in motor discharge. Between perception and action occur memory and choice: memory follows perception, sorting its contents according to their logical relations; consciousness precedes motor discharge, exercising voluntary control. But suppose that in sleep the daytime "advance" of this sequence from perception to motor discharge were blocked at the threshold of consciousness? Wishes arising from the unconscious might circumvent this by doubling back, reversing their flow, so to speak, through the grids of the memory system. As wishes moved backward through these grids, logical relations would dissolve and dream thoughts would turn into mental pictures, like a sentence rewriting itself in rebuses. Now the wish could move "forward" again as perception, evading the censorship this time by appearing not as thought but as the "raw material" of the senses.

This is how Freud derives the special quality of dreams. They know only the present tense because their regressive movement breaks down logical and chronological relations as it translates thoughts "backward" into pictures. The resulting images have a hallucinatory intensity for two reasons. First, dream thoughts arise from infantile memories that "in themselves retain a high degree of sensory vividness, and these memories work like magnets, pulling blocked dream thoughts backward through the mental apparatus. One reason, then, is regression. The second is displacement. "In most dreams," writes Freud, "it is possible to detect a central point which is marked by peculiar sensory intensity. . . . This central point is as a rule the direct representation of the wish-fulfillment . . . for, if we undo the displacements brought about by the dream-work, we find that the *psychical* intensity of the elements in the dream-thoughts has been replaced by the *sensory* intensity of the elements in the content of the actual dream" (600). But if this is correct—if the sensory intensity of the dream image corresponds to the psychical intensity of the dream thought it translates—then the generic intensity of dreams is not separate from their interpretation after all. In his discussion of the burning child Freud wanted to keep these issues separate. The work of interpretation was easy, he declared, it met with no obstacles, but it left the phenomenon of vividness unexplained. Many pages later, after strange displacements and regressions in the sequence of the argument, we learn that in fact the interpretation of a dream remains incomplete *until* it has translated sensory vividness back into psychical intensity. Father, says the dream, I'm burning *for you to see.*

What does Freud not see? He knows nothing about the original dreamer, and therefore cannot recover the infantile scene that, according to his theory, must be transferred onto the recent experience reflected in the dream, charging it with sensory intensity. But what could be the "actual source" of a dream that belongs to no one dreamer? Freud takes it over for his own purposes, yet once he has done so his account of these purposes immediately starts to behave like a dream, displacing the peculiar into the generic, then zigzagging back from the goal of the argument into an imagery of pathways, defensive weapons, and cutting away the ground.

Perhaps the "peculiar feature" about which Freud seems at once so insistent and so reticent in discussing this dream is precisely its singular combination of sensory-emotional intensity with the *absence* of a motivating memory. This absence not only serves the immediate purposes of his argument, it enables Freud, or anyone, to appropriate the dream—or be appropriated by it—on a deeper level, supplying its missing origin from their own associations and redreaming the dream to identify with its haunting question.

The first wish this dream satisfies for Freud is his wish for a dream whose interpretation should seem at once blocked and without obstacle, at once circumstantially withheld and too obvious to require comment. But perhaps it enters into a deeper train of associations. Years later, in 1919, Freud adds to the explanation of the mental apparatus a dream of his own. It is a wartime dream about news from the front concerning his son, and it arises, as Freud discreetly says, from "the envy which is felt for the young by those who have grown old, but which they believe they have completely stifled" (599). If this envy has a sexual component, it amounts to a kind of reversed, belated Oedipal wish, a father's fantasy about replacing his son in the affections of the mother-wife. Again, a problem of sequence: if Ben Jonson imagined himself usurping his son's escape from the mother-wife, Freud imagines his son replacing *him* in her affections. In his 1933 lecture on "Femininity," Freud will write that it is in her maternal identification that a woman "acquires her attractiveness to a man, whose Oedipus attachment to his mother it kindles into a passion." Then he adds: "How often it happens, however, that it is only his son who obtains what he himself has aspired to! One gets an impression that a man's love and a woman's love are a phase apart psychologically."[15]

The anxiety betrayed in this exclamation from the text of 1933 is already evident in Freud's wartime dream:

> Indistinct beginning. *I said to my wife that I had a piece of news for her, something quite special. She was alarmed and refused to listen. I assured her that on the contrary it was something that she would be very glad to hear, and began to tell her that our son's officer's mess had sent a sum of money (5000 Kronen?) . . . something about distinction . . . distribution. . . . Meanwhile I had gone with her into a small room, like a storeroom, to look for something. Suddenly I saw my son appear. He was not in uniform but in tight-fitting sports clothes (like a seal?), with a little cap. He climbed up on to a basket that was standing beside a cupboard. I called out to him: no reply. It seemed to me that his face or forehead was bandaged. He was adjusting something in his mouth, pushing something into it. And his hair was flecked with grey. I thought: "Could he be as exhausted as all that? And has he got false teeth?"* Before I could call out again I woke up, feeling no anxiety but with my heart beating rapidly. My bedside clock showed that it was two thirty. (597–98)

As in Jonson's dream, the child has aged and has been wounded in the "face or forehead." When the dream occurs, the Freuds have heard no news from the front "for over a week." In the dream Freud tries to give his wife "good news" about their son that "she, alarmed, refuses to hear. The day before, he has received "a sum of money . . . derived from an agreeable occurrence in my medical practice" (598). This day residue appears in the dream invested with an unconscious wish for news of the son's death in battle. Freud's analysis traces this wish to an infantile memory, an accident dating back to his second year: climbing "on to a stool in the store-closet to get something nice that was lying on a cupboard or table," he had fallen and been struck by the stool "behind my lower jaw; I might easily, I reflected, have knocked out all my teeth. The recollection was accompanied by an admonitory thought: 'that serves you right'; and this seemed as though it was a hostile impulse aimed at the gallant soldier" (599).

Reaching for "something nice," the child falls. It serves him right, too: he has overlooked the danger of his position, so the ground is cut out from under him, and he is struck from behind. The dream work, in linking Freud's son to Freud *as* son, in displacing the gallant soldier onto the greedy child, seems to recall and then reverse this Oedipal punishment. It is as if Freud wants to pass along to his son the arbitrary blow of fate, together with the admonitory thought "that serves you right."

This dream has curious links to *Beyond the Pleasure Principle*, which dates from the same period. Derrida notices the way Freud's account of the "fort-da" game in that text aligns the father with the daughter in the absence of the son-in-law, who also is at the front.[16] Freud's analysis of this dream locates Ernst and his soldier-father in the dream work as links in the chain binding Freud to his grown son. Significantly, Freud is linked not to the soldier-father but to the resentful son: in *Beyond* he notes that Ernst "used to take a toy, if he was angry with it, and throw it on the floor, exclaiming: 'Go to the fwont!' He had heard at that time that his absent father was 'at the front,' and was far from regretting his absence; on the contrary he made it quite clear that he had no desire to be disturbed in his sole possession of his mother."[17] The central figure in both scenes is a woman, the mother-wife or daughter-wife in whose ambiguous affections father and son imagine themselves changing places. The feminine gaze acts as a pivot on which the Oedipus complex reverses itself: the problem is one of sequence. This reversibility, in which the son's resentment may begin as his father's preemptive fantasy, is suggested by the intriguing image from Freud's wartime dream of his son as a *puer senex*, a young child whose "hair was flecked with grey." This is the image he associates with Ernst and the son-in-law, and ultimately with his own childhood accident.

In the sequence of the dream this child takes his father's place. Freud has gone with his wife into "a small room, like a storeroom, to look for something." There in the small room, where father and mother are together, the son appears. It is he who climbs up to reach the shelf—not to remove something, but to place it, perhaps to replace it, "as though he wanted to put something on the cupboard." The father, now an adult, returns to the scene of his Oedipal mishap, accompanied this time by the mother-wife whose possession he has since gained, though he may be losing her to a younger rival (how often it happens!). The son appears to have taken his place, as in the 1933 essay, obtaining what the father had aspired to, enacting the gesture of desire that triggered fate's punitive blow in the guise of an accident. The accident has already taken place, yet the gray-haired child may be trying to undo it—his gesture, like the dream itself, a belated effort (always belated) to *put back* "something nice" that is missing from the maternal cupboard.

In the dream, Freud remembers, "I called out to him: no reply." Is the failure to reply another sign of death? Or do the signs of premature aging that follow so strangely in the dream already constitute a reply of sorts? "Before I could call out again I woke up," says Freud, "feeling no anxiety but with my heart beating rapidly. My bedside clock showed that it was two thirty." After a dream so full of temporal dislocations, so preoccupied with aging, envious retrospection, castration, and premature death, the awakening glance at the bedside clock may register more than the hour. Don't you see? To whom are you calling out in this dream, your son or yourself? And what can you have been meaning to say? Is your cry a warning, or are you now the burning child who "calls" for explanation?

The dream of the burning child enters into a chain of associations lead-ing back to the cupboard and the blow to the jaw (where Freud's cancer would later strike its uncanny blow). It may be invested, then, with the father's intolerable wish to witness his son's death and take his son's place in life. Yet side by side with the wish to bequeath castration, Freud's wartime dream expresses a wish to go back and undo it. After all, if chro-nology can be reversed, if a son might die in his father's place, then per-haps it is not necessary to die at all. Perhaps a father might evade death not only by trading places with his son but by going backward (like a crab, says Hamlet) to undo its blow. Backward in time, into a realm Lacan calls that "of the *unborn*." The analogy is suggestive: the relation of repression to the unconscious, says Lacan, "is the abortionist's relation to limbo."[18] If this is so then to dream may be to reenter limbo in search of the prematurely mortal infant that is oneself, cut off by the threat of castration yet still urgent to be born.

It may be at this level that the "peculiar feature" that "draws Freud to the burning child is finally revealed. As we have seen, problems of se-quence and regression are central to the argument of Chapter 7, which seems troubled by the fear of a blow that will cut the ground away. They are at issue most obviously in Freud's insistence that, although the tempo-ral sequence of mental operations is irreducible, dreaming reverses this sequence. They are at issue again as Freud worries over his use of the telescope and "reflex apparatus" as figures for an unknown process: such reliance on visibilia in a theoretical argument is equivalent to the regres-sive phase of dream work, which translates thoughts back into visual images. Freud's analogies seek to illustrate, not dissolve, logical relations, but they cannot avoid spatializing time. He even illustrates the analogy to the reflex apparatus with a series of diagrams (576–80). Concrete images of abstract processes are frequent in the volume and indeed throughout Freud's work, but these diagrams have no counterpart anywhere else in *The Interpretation of Dreams*.

As the argument progresses, we learn that dreaming is "regressive" in more than a merely technical sense. Dreams not only reverse the sequence of mental operations involved in cognition, they do so by harking back to infantile memories. These memories are "primitive" in mode as well as content, and dreams not only reactivate the unfulfilled wishes for which the memories serve as "screens," they also resume the hallucinatory form of infantile wishing (606). This argument attains its most complex layer-ing of regressions when Freud, in his most striking anticipation of *Beyond the Pleasure Principle*, thinks backward to the evolutionary origins of the apparatus he has sketched and imagines that wishing began as the organ-ism's hallucinatory recathexis of memory traces left by a prior satisfac-tion (604–5). Motor functioning arises at all, he suggests, only because

the hallucinatory "short path of regression" does not effectively rees-
tablish the objective conditions of satisfaction: to do that we must act
upon the world.

Freud's struggles with the progressive and regressive movements of his
argument, and his preoccupation with comparable movements in the
mental apparatus, suggest that the idea of sequence, and above all the
difference between reversible and irreversible sequences,[19] carries for him
a powerful set of unconscious associations with the idea of his own death.
Especially with the idea of his death as premature, an accident that has
already happened, the childhood memory of which he displaces onto his
son in a mixed effort to evade death by passing it on and by undoing it.

The dream of the burning child offers an extraordinary subtext for the
argument to which it seems so casually, indeed so reluctantly, connected.
The dream gains much of its pathos from the situation in which it occurs,
the father keeping a sleepless vigil "for days and nights on end" at the
sickbed of his dying child. His vigilance is helpless to prevent the child's
death, and so he is forced to witness the most dreadful violation of proper
sequence, what Freud, writing to Binswanger about Sophie's death,
would later call "the monstrous fact of children dying before their parents."[20] Leaving an old man to watch over the dead body in his place, the
exhausted father retires to sleep in the next room, *leaving the door open*
to the room where the body is laid out. A few hours later he is awakened
by the dream, which harks back to his ordeal of helpless watching as the
child whispers "reproachfully: 'Father, don't you see I'm burning?' "

Let us return for a moment to Freud's hypothesis about the mental
apparatus—this, after all, is what he wants the story to lead us toward.
Among the implications of this theory, he points out, is that the censorship, so often cast in a negative role as the agency of repression, as the
warden of conventional morality—even, in Lacan, as the abortionist—
"deserves to be recognized and respected as the watchman of our mental
health" (606). Without it, unconscious fantasies would have access to the
power of movement. This is crucial. For Freud then goes on to ask, "Must
we not regard it . . . as an act of carelessness on the part of that watchman
that it relaxes its activities during the night, allows the suppressed impulses in the *Ucs.* to find expression, and makes it possible for hallucinatory regression to occur once more? I think not. For even though this
critical watchman goes to rest—and we have evidence that its slumbers
are not deep—it also shuts the door upon the power of movement" (607).
The father of the burning child goes to sleep with the door open. It is not
the censorship but the dream itself that makes him stumble on the threshold of awakening as its countercognitive flash of regression balks his return through the open door. The opening is why he wakes up: "The glare
of the light shone through the open door into the sleeping man's eyes."

This signals a failure of vigilance: the watchman has fallen asleep. And the dream, which intervenes between the father's perception of the glare and his awakening into the power of movement—this dream in *its* "zig-zag" movement—links the watchman's failure with the father's helpless vigil and the fever it could not prevent. Yet according to Freud's own theory it must also hark back further, back to some infantile memory in which the father, it may be, occupies the place now taken by his dead child. Such a memory would have been revived by the contrary wishes that must have tormented the exhausted father: the wish to be able somehow to prevent the blow that has already fallen, but also the wish to evade that blow himself by trading places with the child, by *witnessing* the child's death. Not until his vigil has ended, not until he *sees* the child die, can the weary father at last give in to sleep. *Could he be as exhausted as all that?*

For Freud, the open door is a threatening signal. The wish that lies suspended across its threshold (like an unborn child in limbo) is indeed what Lacan calls it, "the most anguishing mystery" (34). So anguishing, our very mental health would be threatened if "this moving dream" ever crossed the threshold into "the power of movement"—as indeed it might if the censorship, that *critical* watchman, ever went to sleep without closing the door.

LACAN: "THE TRUE FORMULA OF ATHEISM"

> . . . no one can say what the death of a child is, except the
> father *qua* father, that is to say, no conscious being.
> For the true formula of atheism is not *God is dead*—
> even by basing the origin of the function of the father upon his
> murder, Freud protects the father—the true formula of atheism
> is *God is unconscious*.
> (Lacan, 59)

In "This Sex Which Is Not One" Irigaray suggests that men recover the masculine body as erotic object—from which they are alienated—in the pleasure of touching their infant sons.[21] There is something irresistible in the resilience of a child's body. My son sometimes goes to sleep lying on my chest. I stroke his back lightly with my fingertips, and as sensual pleasure mingles with affection I wonder whether the burning child may not be ignited by desire. One evening as he drifted off I said, "I love you." With a trace of sleepy annoyance he murmured, "Why do you ask me that, when you already know I do?" Something in him overheard the demand spoken backward in my desire, and answered in the unconscious voice of God.

Freud puts the dream of the burning child into circulation on a grand scale. To rewrite Freud—to redream psychoanalysis, to go back and get it right, seeing what the Father missed—has been a prevailing temptation of modern letters. The problem, said Lacan, is one of sequence: by a historical accident, a blow of fate, Freud was born too soon to avail himself of structural linguistics. We must therefore read him retroactively, loyal to his discovery of the unconscious, but recognizing it both as it would have been for Freud ("structured like a language") and as it will have been for us: according to "the true formula of atheism," the voice of God.

Lacan discusses the dream of the burning child in his 1964 seminar, *The Four Fundamental Concepts of Psychoanalysis*. He too redreams it, and it was the obscure lyric intensity of his remarks on the dream that left me burning with what he calls "the most anguishing mystery, that which links a father to the corpse of his son close by, of his dead son" (34). This is a well-known mistake: Freud writes not of a son but of a child, "das Kind." Strange that a reader like Lacan, who identifies the unconscious with the letter of the text and who often reads Freud hyperliterally, should commit such an obvious blunder. On the other hand, if my reading of Freud is correct, then Lacan's mistake follows the logic of the text, completing and making explicit, as it were, an identification lurking in the dream work of Freud's argument. Unless it precedes and produces that logic. A problem of sequence: it was under the influence of Lacan's mistake that I went back to Freud. I wrote a draft on Chapter 7 of *The Interpretation of Dreams* without once noticing that Freud writes "child," not "son," and was completely out of countenance when a friend pointed out the mistake. (Father, don't you see? Apparently not.) I have no idea now whether, in my reading, Freud's text produces Lacan's mistake or Lacan's mistake produces Freud's text. Who is the father here, who the son? All of us, though, are produced by foreclosure of the ungendered and elision of the feminine: Freud, Lacan, and Miller all, like Ben Jonson, unwittingly transform a feminine or ungendered child into the specular son. In this way they (we?) repeat the compulsive founding gesture of masculinity. Whether as objects of avoidance, in Jonson, or of desire, in Freud and Lacan, female or genderless figures serve principally to confirm masculine identity.

Between introducing the dream of the burning child and returning to discuss what it reveals, Lacan substitutes a dream of his own. It too is a dream of awakening, but now the open door, the door that the dreamer leaves open and that Freud wants the censorship to close, is shut. Stealing a nap in his office one day, Lacan is awakened by a knocking. Between hearing the knock and becoming conscious of it, he has a dream. He tells this story to illustrate how the subject of consciousness, the "I" that knows "that I am there, at what time I went to sleep, and why I went to sleep" (56), is both subverted and constituted in the interval between perception and consciousness—that is, between the sensory-receptive and motor-active ends of the diagrams in Chapter 7 of *The Interpretation of Dreams*.

Lacan never bothers to report the content of his dream—only that it "manifested to me something other than this knocking." Exactly what it manifested we cannot know, but we can guess at the desire it may have expressed. Lacan's discussion of the burning child, which precedes and follows the account of his dream like knock and awakening, contains other slight inconsistencies. In his own case, he notes, "the knocking . . . is, to all appearances, what woke me." Returning a moment later to Freud's text, he declares that the dream of the burning child "is *also* made up entirely of noise" (57, my italics). For a moment he seems to confuse the two dreams, forgetting the child's appearance in the dream Freud reports, and his gesture of catching the father "by the arm." This oversight appears to express a kind of impatience with the stages of argumentation, a proleptic leaping ahead to his conclusion: a problem of sequence. Lacan wants to insist that in either instance what shakes the dreamer awake is not the external stimulus, the sound of the knock or the glare of the flame,[22] but an encounter with the "real" of the unconscious—which touches him, inexplicably, where the fire has touched his son's body: on the arm. For Lacan however the *tuché* is not touch but sound, a reproachful and beseeching whisper. He cannot wait for the dream work to substitute this sound for the visual stimulus of the glare or the unnerving hand on the arm, so he anticipates and completes this substitution in his memory of Freud's text, declaring a little too hastily that the dream is "made up *entirely* of noise." This despite his insistence in principle on "the total distinction between the scopic register and the invocatory, vocatory, vocational field" (118).

Lacan seems to be repeating the dream in that second field, handing it over from the scopic register to "the invocatory drive, which is the closest to the experience of the unconscious" (104). It is there, in relation to the unconscious traces of spoken words, that Lacan places the baffling experience he calls "tuché," the always-missed encounter with "the real." The moment of awakening, for Lacan, is the moment in which we glimpse the disappearance of this "real" as it retreats into the limbo of the unborn. In its place we grasp *only* our reflection, never ourselves: "after the awakening knock," he writes, "[I am] able to sustain myself, apparently only in a relation with my representation, which, apparently, makes of me only consciousness. A sort of involuted reflection—in my consciousness, it is only my representation that I recover possession of" (57). Consciousness for Lacan is always "Posthumous born."

The vocatory field is also the vocational field, the field of the psychoanalytic "calling." Always contemptuous of ego-psychology, Lacan identified the psychoanalytic calling with the voice of the unconscious itself, aborted by repression, wandering in the Limbo of the unborn (which Catholic theology placed between Hell and Purgatory), calling out to the Father who abides in the scopic register, urging him to *see* what he can only hear. "What we have in the discovery of psychoanalysis," writes Lacan, "is an encounter, an essential encounter—an appointment to which we are always called with a real that eludes us" (53). With a flourish of wit he transforms the analytic session as appointment, as encounter between patient and analyst, into the "missed encounter" with the unconscious, the essential and anguishing mystery around which analysis, for Lacan, is always suspended.

This is precisely the transformation Lacan's unreported dream performs: in response to a knock at the door (announcing his next appointment?) the sleeping analyst first hears the true call of his vocation, hears himself called not to consciousness but to "the real." So he dreams, zigzagging back toward a door that is already closing, toward a rendezvous with "the beauty behind the shutters" (134)—only to awaken, reluctantly it seems, to the "impatient knocking" at his office door (56). It is in terms of this scenario that he keeps misremembering details of Freud's text. In an earlier reference, we read: "As he is falling asleep, the father sees rise up before him the image of the son" (34). Freud says the father awakened "after a few hours' sleep" (547). It is Lacan whose dream awoke him from "a short nap" in response to "impatient knocking"—Lacan, then, who felt as if he were just falling asleep. Felt, perhaps, as if his falling asleep and his waking up had been unfairly *reversed*, calling him back from his rendezvous with "the real" to what may be merely a drowsy encounter with another ego. For when the ego knocks at the door of analysis, the analytic project founders: "To appeal to some healthy part of the subject thought to be there in the real . . . is to misunderstand that it is precisely this part . . . that closes the door, or the window, or the shutters, or whatever—and that the beauty with whom one wishes to speak is there, behind, only too willing to open the shutters again. . . . [I]t is to the beauty one must speak" (131). The beauty: something other than this knocking.

Freud wanted to slow down, look back, find his defensive weapons. Lacan is in a hurry. Like Alice's white rabbit forever consulting a broken watch, he is always late for a very important date. The trauma is a date for which he can never be on time, since for Lacan it is an *essentially* missed encounter, a blow that falls before we are ready and to which we therefore always respond too late. Yet he cannot resist bearing personal witness to the originary moment, composing himself, like Jonson or Freud, as the author of the trauma: "I, too, have seen with my own eyes, opened by maternal divination, the child, traumatized by the fact that I was going away despite the appeal, precociously adumbrated in his voice, and henceforth more renewed for months at a time—long after, having picked up this child—I have seen it let his head fall on my shoulder and drop off to sleep, sleep alone being capable of giving him access to the living signifier I had become since the date of the trauma" (63). This child is only asleep, not dead, but for Lacan he is nonetheless the "burning child." Lacan repeats the gesture of Jonson and Freud in making the mother-wife at once marginal to the father's recognition of the trauma and yet strangely central to it, since her divining presence hovers between father and son as the very medium of perception. Madame Lacan lingers here as a self-effacing supplement: like the holy ghost in an Oedipal trinity, she exists as an adjective modifying the noun of her mediation. Yet by this mediation she gives the father access to the originary scene. Only she can open his eyes to the trauma.

We have seen how this dream insists like a symptom within each effort to rewrite it. What gives it the power to sustain this migratory witness, disclosing itself in one dreamer after another and retying its knots of emotion in each? One answer may be that the specular son configures for the fantasy the male subject's traumatic and compulsively repeated assumption of an impossible gender identity. There may be other answers as well; there are other dreamers, including women: Freud's unnamed patient, or more recently Jane Gallop. But for Jonson, Freud, and Lacan the dream seems to repeat the lived contradiction of masculinity.

Butler argues that gender identity, or what Stoller calls the "gender core,"[23] is constituted not only by the incest taboo and the Oedipal crisis it precipitates, but prior to that by the taboo on homosexuality, which creates the heterosexual desires presumed by the Oedipal model. This prior repression of homosexuality appears in Sophocles' treatment of the Oedipus myth, which "forgets" that in earlier versions "the tragic sequence is initiated because Oedipus' father, Laius, loved a beautiful youth, Chrysippus," and so drew down upon Thebes the wrath of Hera, guardian of marriage.[24] Freud has recourse to the truncated, Sophoclean version of the story; retracing the path that leads from his 1917 essay "Mourning and Melancholia" to the account of ego formation in *The Ego and the Id* (1923), Butler suggests how the theory of gender acquisition might look if we assumed a primary taboo on homosexuality. The prohibition against desire for the same-sex parent, she argues, would differ crucially from the prohibition against desire for the parent of the opposite sex. The prohibition against heterosexual incestuous desire does not require renunciation of the desire itself, but only of its primary object; the desire may be deflected toward an exogamous object, rather than renounced. But the prohibition against homosexual incestuous desire extends its taboo over the *desire* itself and not just its primary object. Since the desire may not pursue nonincestuous alternatives through displacement, Freud's theory suggests that it may be fixed and internalized instead through the dynamics of melancholia. Thus "gender identification is a kind of melancholia in which the sex of the prohibited object is internalized as a prohibition" (63).

This argument need not assume a primary bisexuality, although it might appear to do so. It does assume that gender and sexuality as such are retroactively organized and imprinted in the body through the interplay of prohibition, identification, and incorporation. Even if prohibition begins as a twofold taboo on homosexual aims *and* objects, there is no need to imagine such desires as already existing fully articulated in the infant, consciously or otherwise. They may crystallize within a primary flux of infantile fantasy and sensation as possibilities defined in the moment of denial, desires given form and emphasis by the very act of repression that erases them from awareness.

Freud distinguishes between mourning and melancholy according to whether the object of loss is consciously recognized. If it is, then the object can be sustained internally while it is gradually relinquished, as ties of association severed by the loss are individually reviewed and dissolved in preparation for new attachments. The ego retains the imprint of the lost object, but it also mourns and moves on. If the loss is not consciously recognized, however, then identification remains fixed: ties of attachment are not available for conscious review and dissolution. Desire for the same-sex parent is unavailable for mourning because it undergoes a prior and more thorough repression than heterosexual desire. This repression fixes the "gender core" in most children by the age of three. Butler suggests that melancholy is the mechanism by which gender thus imprints itself on the body, making the body its "living signifier." Identification here takes the form of incorporation, which "*literalizes* the loss *on* the body and so appears as the facticity of the body, the means by which the body comes to bear 'sex' as its literal truth" (68).

If Butler is right, then the dream of the specular son may hark back to the melancholy incorporation of the masculine body; it may enact a return through dream and compulsive error of the unmourned, unrelinquished object of a forbidden desire. To name this originary object is impossible insofar as it has always already been transformed by the taboos through which we gain access to speech. We may imagine it as a primal erotic body, neither the child's nor the father's, since the two are not yet distinct, but an imaginary fusion whose symbolic anti-type is the *puer senex*. Repression will write the word *father* in place of this primal body, splitting it between a desexualized conscious object, the rival parent of the Oedipal scenario, and a lost erotic object that "the child's body yearns to replace as its "living signifier." The specular son insists upon this unmourned, unacknowledged loss. His forehead bears the mark of submission to the law of gender, but his burning touch is that of the primal erotic body. He asks us to "see" what Lacan says we can only hear, but beyond that he asks us to touch and be touched by something we can only dream. He asks us to substitute for the preemptive blow of fate an originary caress that could revive the dead father as bodily desire.

Without this touch the (k)not of gender will not loosen in our hands. Freud's theory suggests that if the lost object could become conscious, it would then be available to mourning: knots are loosened by recognition of the "nots," the prohibitions, that have tied them. Can we hope, then, in Jonson's phrase, to "loose all father"? The question reminds me of one more dream, the last one recorded in Freud's analysis of "Dora." In it she wanders the streets of an unfamiliar town, then enters the place where she lives to find a letter from her mother saying that Dora, having run away, can now come home. Her father is dead. After some difficulty finding her way, she is greeted at the door by a maidservant who announces that her mother and "the others" are at the cemetery. Dora, however, does not join them. She has finished mourning the father, and her self-exile is over. She sees herself climbing the stairs: "I went to my room, but not the least sadly, and began reading a big book that lay on my writing table."[25] The father's death frees Dora to come home, but instead of mourning she mounts the stairs to *her* room and opens a book. Whatever the name of the "big book" on Dora's writing table, it is the mother's "letter" and not the father's that summons her to read it. We can be fairly sure it was not *The Interpretation of Dreams*.

What text might *we* begin to read if the phantom of patriarchy were laid to rest? Unnamed perhaps because not yet read, the book Dora takes up at the end of her dream offers a tempting blank space in which to write utopia. Such a gesture would be suspect, though: the book belongs to Ida Bauer, her "best piece of poetrie." In that sense it really isn't blank—it carries the traces of a specific life history, traces according to which it should be read as the dreams of Jonson, Freud, and Lacan have been. This essay depends on the hope that, although the knots of gender are tied long before we learn to read—a problem of sequence—since their effects extend into reading we may yet engage them there. In the space where texts elicit our fantasies, we may seek to loosen the (k)nots of filial paternity. To do so we must *finish* mourning the body of patriarchy, which still makes "living signifiers" of us all.

NOTES

This essay is dedicated to John Y. Miller and to Jack Pruett Miller, for whom it was written. For help with the German text of *The Interpretation of Dreams* I am indebted to Thomas Kovach; for help with the French text of *The Four Fundamental Concepts of Psychoanalysis*, to Lynn Pruett. Thanks also to Greg Jay, Elizabeth Meese, Lynn Pruett, Harry Berger, and David Riggs for invaluable suggestions, and to Arthur Kinney for the use of his library.

1. The idea of transferential effects in reading and writing has been developed in a substantial body of criticism. I am especially indebted to Jane Gallop, *Reading Lacan* (Ithaca: Cornell University Press, 1985); Madelon Sprengnether, *The Spectral Mother: Freud, Feminism, and Psychoanalysis* (Ithaca: Cornell University Press, 1990), whose notion of the "spectral mother" prompted me to think about a "spectral son"; and the collection *In Dora's Case: Freud—Hysteria—Feminism*, ed. Charles Bernheimer and Claire Kehane (New York: Columbia University Press, 1985). On gender as "performatively produced," see Judith Butler, *Gender Trouble: Feminism and the Subversion of Identity* (New York: Routledge, 1990), p. 24. Subsequent references given parenthetically in the text. "Homosocial" is Eve Sedgwick's term in *Between Men: English Literature and Male Homosocial Desire* (New York: Columbia University Press, 1985). For the "knot" of gender, see Jacques Lacan, "The Meaning of the Phallus," in *Feminine Sexuality: Jacques Lacan and the école freudienne*, ed. Juliet Mitchell and Jacqueline Rose, trans. Jacqueline Rose (New York: Norton, Pantheon Books, 1985), p. 75: "What we are dealing with is an antinomy internal to the assumption by man (*Mensch*) of his sex: why must he take up its attributes only by means of a threat, or even in the guise of a privation?" A parenthetical *k* emphasizes the "not," the element of prohibition or privation, in this knot.

2. David Riggs, *Ben Jonson: A Life* (Cambridge: Harvard University Press, 1989), p. 95. Subsequent references given parenthetically in the text. On p. 97 Riggs estimates the actual death rate in St. Giles from July to December of 1603 to have been around 80 percent (2,400 deaths among 3,000 residents).

3. Joshua Scodel, "Genre and Occasion in Jonson's 'On My First Sonne,'" *Studies in Philology* 86 (1989): 235–36 n. 3. Subsequent references given parenthetically in the text. This essay appears revised in Scodel, *The English Poetic Epitaph: Commemoration and Conflict from Jonson to Wordsworth* (Ithaca: Cornell University Press, 1991).

4. Michel de Montaigne, *The Essayes*, trans. John Florio, 3 vols. (London: J. M. Dent, 1928), 2:88. Subsequent references given parenthetically in the text. Wesley Trimpi suggests the relevance of the essay "Of the Affection of Fathers to their Children" to a discussion of Jonson's poem in "BEN IONSON his best piece

of *poetrie*," *Classical Antiquity* 2, no. 1 (April 1983): 149–50, but argues that Jonson, "as if directly contradicting Plato's preference for children of the mind . . . firmly asserts that this child of the body is *his* 'best' piece of poetry—that is, the best thing *he* has made" (150). Scodel argues that "Jonson rejects Montaigne's crucial distinctions and categories . . . by making the identity of his child-poem dependent upon himself alone" (254–55). I argue rather that Jonson enacts Montaigne's distinctions, sacrificing the dead boy to the book in whose image he will be commemorated.

5. "Apologetical Dialogue," lines 233–35, as cited by Riggs, p. 93, commenting on Jonson's work habits.

6. David Riggs reminds me that in 1607 Jonson would inscribe a quarto of *Volpone* in just such terms "To his loving Father, & worthy Freind Mr. John Florio: The ayde of his Muses." Jonson casts himself this time as the son, but the trinitarian pattern (father, son, and Holy Muse) remains. (*Ben Jonson*, ed. C. H. Herford and Percy and Evelyn Simpson, 11 vols. (Oxford: Oxford University Press, 1925–52), 1:56 and 8:665. Subsequent references given parenthetically in the text, with the use of *j* and *v* modernized as above. Although Jonson named his first son after himself, his first daughter and second son were named Mary and Joseph; Riggs suggests that Joseph, born in 1599, was also in Jonson's mind during the revisions of *The Spanish Tragedy*, and that he probably died in the 1603 plague that killed his older brother Benjamin (54, 96–97).

7. *Conversations with Drummond*, lines 214–24, cited from *Ben Jonson*, ed. Ian Donaldson (New York: Oxford University Press, 1985), pp. 600–601.

8. Ann Barton, *Ben Jonson, Dramatist* (Cambridge: Cambridge University Press, 1984), p. 19. Subsequent references given parenthetically in the text.

9. Ann Lauinger, "'It makes the father, lesse, to rue': Resistance to Consolation in Jonson's 'On my first Daughter,'" *Studies in Philology* 86 (1989): 229.

10. Thomas Kyd, *The Spanish Tragedy*, ed. Phillip Edwards (Cambridge: The Revels Plays, Harvard University Press, 1959), p. 125 ("Third Addition," lines 9–10, emphasis added).

11. Much commentary on the poem is pious or sentimental. More detached accounts of the narcissism that sustains the poem's piety may be found in Scodel; G. W. Pigman III, *Grief and the English Renaissance Elegy* (Cambridge: Cambridge University Press, 1985), pp. 88–89; and Katharine Eisamann Maus, *Ben Jonson and the Roman Frame of Mind* (Princeton: Princeton University Press, 1984), pp. 119–23.

12. It was in 1604 that Jonson changed the spelling of his name. Riggs links this orthographic innovation with the motive of self-creation in the elegy for Benjamin: "the new spelling proclaimed his uniqueness: there were many Johnsons in Jacobean London, but only one Jonson. In a narrower sense, the change of name set him apart from his real father and his three children, all of whom had been Johnsons. The aggrieved parent who wrote 'On My First Son' had wished that he could 'loose all father, now'; the altered spelling, which appears in the first occurrence of his name after the death of his sons, reaffirmed that intention. 'Johnson' was an inherited name ('son of John') that connoted filial and paternal attachments; 'Jonson' was an invented name that implied autonomy" (114–15).

13. Sigmund Freud, *The Interpretation of Dreams*, ed. and trans. James Strachey (New York: Avon, 1971), pp. 547–48. Subsequent references given parenthetically in the text.

14. My reading is anticipated here by Gallop, p. 183, who anticipates my argument in a more general way by discussing the dream interpreter's identification with the dreamer (172) and by characterizing her own reading of Lacan as a "redreaming" (183).

15. Sigmund Freud, *New Introductory Lectures on Psychoanalysis*, trans. and ed. James Strachey (New York: Norton, 1965), p. 134.

16. Jacques Derrida, *The Post Card: From Socrates to Freud and Beyond*, trans. Alan Bass (Chicago: University of Chicago Press, 1987), pp. 311–12.

17. Sigmund Freud, *Beyond the Pleasure Principle*, trans. and ed. James Strachey (New York: Norton, 1961), p. 10.

18. Jacques Lacan, *The Four Fundamental Concepts of Psycho-Analysis*, ed. Jacques-Alain Miller, trans. Alan Sheridan (New York: Norton, 1978), p. 23. Subsequent references given parenthetically in the text.

19. My sense of the contrast between reversible and irreversible sequences in Freud's argument is indebted to the distinction between reversible and irreversible "codes" in Roland Barthes, *S/Z*, trans. Richard Miller (New York: Hill and Wang, 1974), pp. 13, 18, 30. In "On Deathwork in Freud, in the Self, in Culture," in *Psychoanalysis, Creativity, and Literature: A French-American Inquiry*, ed. Alan Roland (New York: Columbia University Press, 1978), p. 87, J. B. Pontalis observes that Freud's preoccupation with the date of his death during the period 1890–95 "indicates a desire for immortality, for nonirreversible time."

20. Quoted by Max Schur, *Freud: Living and Dying* (New York: International University Press, 1972), p. 329.

21. Luce Irigaray, *This Sex Which Is Not One*, trans. Catherine Porter with Carolyn Burke (Ithaca: Cornell University Press, 1985), p. 27: "Perhaps man and woman no longer caress each other except through that mediation between them that the child—preferably a boy—represents? Man, identified with his son, rediscovers the pleasure of maternal fondling; woman touches herself again by caressing that part of her body: her baby-penis-clitoris." I read Irigaray here as implying that "man" identifies with his son as the object of fondling even as he assumes the maternal role of *doing* the fondling: the son in this way allows the masculine imaginary to close the gap between subject and object that opens within the symbolic as a result of the masculine tendency to identify exclusively with the subject position.

22. Slavoj Žižek, *The Sublime Object of Ideology* (London: Verso, 1989), refers in discussing this dream to "the smell of smoke" (45), a detail not mentioned in Freud's text or Lacan's. The recurrent impulse to invent plausible external stimuli betrays each writer's desire to place himself at the trauma's scene of origin, bearing witness to its material truth. Žižek's larger point is consistent with my argument: the dreamer awakens, he says, because "the dream, the reality of his desire . . . is more terrifying than the so-called external reality itself. . . . He escapes into so-called reality to be able to continue to sleep, to maintain his blindness, to elude awakening into the real of his desire" (45).

23. Robert Stoller, *Presentations of Gender* (New Haven: Yale University Press, 1985), pp. 11–14.

24. Jonathan Dollimore, *Sexual Dissidence: Augustine to Wilde, Freud to Foucault* (Oxford: Clarendon, 1991), p. 204.

25. Sigmund Freud, *Dora: An Analysis of a Case of Hysteria*, ed. Philip Rieff (New York: Collier, 1963), p. 114.

LIST OF CONTRIBUTORS

Elizabeth J. Bellamy teaches English at the University of New Hampshire. She has published a number of articles in such journals as *Diacritics*, *ELH*, *SAQ*, and she is the author of *Translations of Power: Narcissism and the Unconscious in Epic History* (Cornell University Press, 1992).

Harry Berger, Jr. is Professor Emeritus of Literature and Art History at the University of California at Santa Cruz. His books include *The Allegorical Temper: Vision and Reality in Book II of the Faerie Queene*; *Imaginary Audition: Shakespeare on Stage and Page*; and *Second World and Green World: Studies in Renaissance Fiction-Making*. He is currently completing *Representing Gynephobia*, a study of *The Book of the Courtier* and *The Faerie Queene*, and is working on a study of Graphic Imperialism in early modern Europe.

Lynn Enterline is an Assistant Professor of English and Comparative Literature at Yale University. She is the author of *The Tears of Narcissus: The Language of Melancholia in Early Modern Writing* (Stanford University Press, 1995). The essay in this volume is part of a book she is currently writing entitled *Pursuing Daphne: Body and Voice in Ovid and the Renaissance Ovidian Tradition*.

Valeria Finucci is an Associate Professor of Romance Studies at Duke University. She is the author of *The Lady Vanishes: Subjectivity and Representation in Castiglione and Ariosto* (Stanford University Press, 1992) and has published articles in such journals as *Italica*, *Stanford Italian Review*, *Italian Quarterly* and *Annali d'Italianistica*. She is currently working on a book on the politics of the body in the Italian Renaissance.

Marjorie Garber is Professor of English and Director of the Center for Literary and Cultural Studies at Harvard University. Her books include *Dream in Shakespeare: From Metaphor to Metamorphosis*; *Coming of Age in Shakespeare*; *Shakespeare's Ghost Writers: Literature as Uncanny Causality*; and *Vested Interests: Cross-Dressing and Cultural Anxiety*. She is currently working on a book on bi-sexuality.

William Kerrigan is Professor of English at the University of Massachusetts at Amherst. His books include *The Sacred Complex: On the Psychogenesis of Paradise Lost*; (with Gordon Braden), *The Idea of the Renaissance*; and *Hamlet's Perfection*.

Natasha Korda is a doctoral candidate in comparative literature at The Johns Hopkins University. She has published articles on psychoanalysis and Renaissance drama, and is currently completing a dissertation on domesticity and consumer culture in the early modern period entitled *Household Stuff: Shakespeare's Domestic Economies*.

David Lee Miller, Professor of English at the University of Kentucky, is the author of *The Poem's Two Bodies: The Poetics of the 1590 "Faerie Queene,"* and of numerous essays on Spenser. His essay for this volume is part of a work in progress called *Filial Pieties: Writing the Specular Son*, on patterns of filial piety and sacrifice in Virgil, Shakespeare, Dickens, and Freud.

Juliana Schiesari is Associate Professor of French and Italian at the University of California, Davis. She is the author of *The Gendering of Melancholia: Feminism, Psychoanalysis and the Symbolics of Loss in Renaissance Literature* and co-editor of *Refiguring Woman: Perspectives on Gender and the Italian Renaissance*. Currently, she is working on a book about "femininity" and the culture of animals since the early modern period.

Regina Schwartz is Associate Professor of English and Religious Studies at Duke University. She has authored *Remembering and Repeating: On Milton's Theology and Poetics*, edited *The Book and the Text: The Bible and Literary Theory*, and just completed a book on monotheism, violence, and identy. She is currently working on a book about the Eucharist in Reformation controversy and poetry.

INDEX